Foundations

of

Programming

using

C & C++

written by

Richard J. Easton
Guy J. Hale

Indiana State University

KENDALL/HUNT PUBLISHING COMPANY
4050 Westmark Drive   Dubuque, Iowa 52002

TABLE OF CONTENTS

CHAPTER 1

Getting Started

1.1 - Introduction

The purpose of this book is to provide you with a firm foundation for programming with the C and C++ programming languages. Thus, you will not only be learning important and fundamental concepts of programming, but you will also be learning how to use C and C++.

Also, in this chapter we will introduce you to Turbo C++ 3.0, a very popular C++ compiler which is distributed by the Borland Corporation. Turbo C++ can be run under DOS, Windows 3.x, or Windows 95, and has a very simple and nice Integrated Development Environment (IDE) in which we can write and debug C/C++ programs.

All programs in this text were developed and tested using Turbo C++ 3.0. However, It should be noted that there are other C/C++ compilers available, and if so desired the reader may decide to use one of these. In this case, very few (if any) changes would be necessary for the multitude of programming examples presented in this text.

After completing this chapter, the reader should be able to:

1. understand the history and development of the C and C++ programming languages.

2. understand how to design a simple program.

3. begin to understand and use the Turbo C++ Integrated Development Environment

4. understand how to enter, edit, compile, link and run a simple C++ program.

This book illustrates each new concept with straight forward examples. We do actual programming rather than just talking about it. In order to run the examples and do the exercises you need to understand some of the conventions that are used throughout the text.

1. Occasionally an example contains line numbers, that is, a number to the left of the line. These numbers are NOT part of the program and must not be

entered. Their only purpose is so that we can refer to them in our explanations.

2. <Key> The use of angle brackets indicate the key within the brackets is to be pressed. For example, <F2> means to press the F2 function key.

1.2 - A Short History

Dennis Ritchie developed the C programming language in 1972 while working at AT&T Bell Laboratories. The C programming language was used in developing the UNIX operating system and was originally designed to run on a PDP-11 computer. The language was named C because it's predecessor was called B. The B language was developed by Ken Thompson, who was also at Bell Laboratories (Can we guess why he named the language, B?)

Because of the power of the C language, its use spread quickly beyond Bell Labs. Programmers everywhere began to use the language for all sorts of applications. However, as different versions of C compilers were developed, variations began to cause standardization problems. In response to these problems, a committee was formed in 1983 to establish a standard definition for the C programming language. This committee has established **ANSI** (American National Standards Institute) standards. Most modern C and C++ compilers adhere to this standard.

In 1980, Bjarne Straustrup, also of AT&T Bell Labs, added classes and a few other features to C resulting in a language that was known as "C with Classes". Later in 1983, several extensions were made, notably operator overloading and virtual functions, (these concepts will be discussed in detail in later chapters) resulting in the language that is now known as C++. The name C++ (C plus plus) was coined by Rick Mascitti. One of the most notable feature of C++ is the extension of what C calls **structures** into what C++ calls **classes**. Structures, classes and the resulting objects evolved into **object-oriented programming** or **OOP** for short. Structures, classes, and objects are discussed in their proper context later within this book.

Since their development, C and now C++, have unobtrusively become the languages of choice of an ever increasing number of programmers. Since object oriented programming has grown into a national trend, C++ has become the most popular of the OOP languages. All major computer vendors offer C++ on their machines. Implementations of C++ include the popular Borland's C++ compilers, Visual C++ from Microsoft, the standard-setting USL C++ from AT&T , Hewlett-Packard C++, etc.

The C and C++ programming languages are currently being used extensively in the writing of all types of software packages. This includes all kinds of systems software such as compilers and operating systems. For example, practically all of the UNIX operating

2

system was written in C.

1.3 - Why C/C++?

Today, there are numerous high level programming languages to choose from such as C, C++, Pascal, BASIC, COBOL, Modula 2, etc. There are several reasons for the success and popularity of C and C++. Among these are relative portability, power, flexibility, and efficiency.

When we say that C and C++ are relatively portable we mean that source code for programs can be moved from one computer to another and recompiled with little or no required modifications. For example, most traditional programs written using standard C/C++ can be run on other computers without unexpected results. However, many companies like Microsoft and Borland have added very nice extensions to the C/C++ languages. These extensions give the programmer increased capabilities (for example screen controls); however, these nice new extensions are not normally portable to other machines and operating systems.

One of the major strengths of the C/C++ programming languages is that they are not only high-level languages, but that they also serve as low-level languages. This means that the programmer has all of the nice upper level structures and capabilities. However, in addition the programmer has the power to interact directly with the operating system and the low level hardware of the computer itself. C and C++ can be used to write operating systems, utilities, and system applications. The C programming language has been the language of choice for many professional programmers for writing operating systems, systems applications, word processors, windows applications, etc. With the advent of C++ and its many additional benefits over C, many more programmers are switching to C++, and we can expect to see this trend continue.

The flexibility of the C and C++ languages flows from their power and portability. Microcomputers, minicomputers and mainframes use C and now C++. Many programs, as mentioned earlier, may be moved to different machines with little or no change to the code.

The syntax of the code can be a strength or weakness depending on the programmer's level of skill. Experienced programmers can pack large amounts of code and power in one or two lines. However, less experienced programmers may have difficulty following the syntax. A good example is the following block of comparatively simple code.

```
for(I=0; I < 10; I++)              or              for(I=0;i < 10; cout << I++);
    cout << I ;
```

3

Basically, this code initializes the integer variable I to a value of 0, prints the value of I, adds one to the value of I, prints the new value of I, etc., until the program reaches a final value of 10. When the value of 10 is reached, the loop is terminated and this value is not printed. The output is

    0123456789

The expression **I++** adds 1 to the value of I during each iteration of the **for** loop. This concept is explained in detail in Chapter 2. The **for** loop is discussed in detail in Chapter 3.

1.4 - Basic Program Development

As mentioned earlier, Turbo C++ 3.0 includes a very powerful IDE (Integrated Development Environment) that allows us to enter, compile, link, and run a program in a relatively smooth and simple manner.

In writing and running a program the first step is to type in the statements of the program using the built in editor. Then we choose the **menu** option to call the compiler to **compile** our file. This compilation converts our C++ program file into machine language and stores it in a file with an **.OBJ** extension. During this compilation process, syntax errors discovered by the compiler are listed. These syntax errors (frequently referred to as compile time errors) should now be fixed by the programmer..

This process would be relatively simple if compiling were the end, and we could simply run this object code (the .OBJ file). However, there is another required step called linking. Linking is necessary for several reasons. First, your program will usually make use of routines that are included in various libraries. Secondly, you may not want to compile all of the program at the same time. Larger C/C++ programs usually contain a large number of functions that are written in several files. The linking process links all of the necessary object files together in order to produce the final executable program. The executable program is stored in a file with an .EXE extension. To run the program, this **.EXE** file is loaded into memory and executed.

After the executable program (.EXE file) has been created, the original source code is needed only if we wish to make changes. If changes are made in the source code after compilation, the program must be recompiled and linked again in order for the changes to become effective. We must point out that compilation of a program will not catch logic or run-time errors. These can be caught only by testing and debugging. All of these new concepts will become clear as we proceed through the first few lessons.

1.5 - Using the Turbo C++ IDE

The Turbo C++ IDE includes a full-screen editor, the compiler, the linker, and a built in debugger. This gives us all of the very important tools that are needed in order to type in source code, compile, link, run, and debug..

We will take a quick look at how we can start Turbo C++ and use it to enter and run a simple program. We will enter and save a C++ program; then we will compile, link, and run it. In this section we will make you comfortable with the mechanics of entering and running a simple program.

Note: Normally, when Turbo C++ is installed, it is put in a subdirectory called TC on hard drive C: Then, the executable files including the compiler, TC.EXE, are put in the subdirectory called TC\BIN. If your installation was different than this, then you will need to modify the following according to your installation.

If you are using Windows, then just select the Turbo C++ icon. However, in DOS we would need to do the following:

1. Go to the DOS prompt.

    C:>

2. Use the Change Directory command to move to the Subdirectory that contains the Turbo C++ compiler.

    C:> CD TC\BIN <Ret>

3. Type TC at this DOS prompt.

    C:\TC\BIN> TC<Ret>

You should now see the following screen:

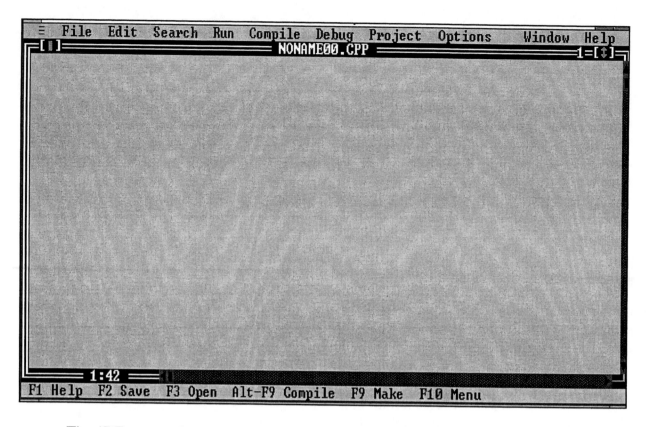

```
  ☰   File  Edit  Search  Run  Compile  Debug  Project  Options    Window  Help
 ┌─[■]══════════════════════════ NONAME00.CPP ═══════════════════════════1=[↕]─┐
 ╞                                                                             ╡
 │                                                                             │
 │                                                                             │
 │                                                                             │
 │                                                                             │
 │                                                                             │
 │                                                                             │
 │                                                                             │
 │                                                                             │
 │                                                                             │
 │                                                                             │
 │                                                                             │
 │                                                                             │
 └──── 1:42 ════◄▌──────────────────────────────────────────────────────────►─┘
  F1 Help  F2 Save  F3 Open  Alt-F9 Compile  F9 Make  F10 Menu
```

   The IDE screen is divided into three visible components: the menu bar at the top,
the window area in the middle, and the status line at the bottom.

Menu Bar

   The menu bar is used to access all of the menu commands. The menu bar includes
the options, **File, Edit, Search, Run, Compile, Debug, Project, Options, Window, and
Help.** Each of these options can be chosen in any one of three ways:

   Press the **<Alt>** key along with the boldfaced letter of the
   menu item you want to choose. For example, **<Alt><E>** would
   access the **Edit** option.

   If you have a mouse, move the mouse pointer to the item and click the left mouse
   button.

   Move the cursor to the menu bar by pressing **<F10>**. Now use the
   right and left arrow keys to move along the bar until you get to
   the choice you want and press **<Ret>**.

6

Either of these actions will display what is called a pull-down menu. It is called a pull-down menu since it appears that you have reached up and pulled it down like you would a window shade.

The pull down menus for each of the menu items are listed below along with a brief explanation of the options that we will be using to create, save, and run our first few programs. We will explain the other options later in the text as they are needed.

The File Menu

```
 File   Edit   Search
┌──────────────────────┐
│ New                  │
│ Open...          F3  │
│ Save             F2  │
│ Save as...           │
│ Save all             │
├──────────────────────┤
│ Change dir...        │
│ Print                │
│ DOS shell            │
├──────────────────────┤
│ Quit          Alt+X  │
└──────────────────────┘
```

New: This option is used when we want to write a new program (or file). It opens up a new window in which we create our program or program module.

Open: This option is used to load an existing file from a disk into an edit window. It opens a file-selection dialog box in which we can either type in the file name or choose the file name from a list of file names..

Save: This option saves the program in the active window to a floppy disk or to a hard drive. If we have not yet named the file, a Save Editor File dialog box is opened to let us rename and save it in on the drive (and in the directory) of our choice.

Save as...:   This option lets us save the file in the active window. It allows us to rename the file and specify the directory and drive.

Change dir...:   This option lets us specify which drive (and directory) we wish to make the current active drive (and directory)..

Print: This option is used to print the file that is in the current window.

DOS Shell: This option is used to exit Turbo C++ temporarily and go to a DOS shell (in order to execute one or more DOS commands). We can return to C++ by typing the word EXIT.

Quit: This is the option to exit the Turbo C++ IDE.

The Edit Menu

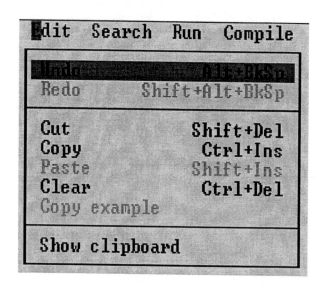

The **Edit** menu lets us cut, copy, and paste text in our files. We will discuss any of these options that we need later when we in fact need them.

The Search Menu

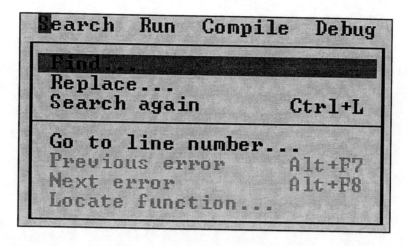

The **Search** menu lets us search for text, function declarations, and error locations in our files. Again we will discuss any of these options that we need later when we use them.

The Run Menu

The **Run** menu lets us run a program and also control execution during debugging. We will discuss all of these options later.

The Compile Menu

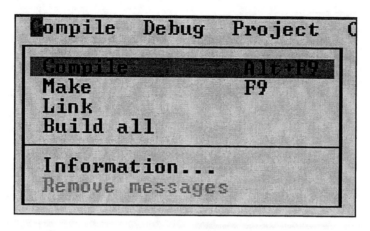

The **Compile** menu lets us compile a single file, and it also lets us compile projects which consist of several files. We will discuss the options in this menu later as we need them.

The Debug Menu

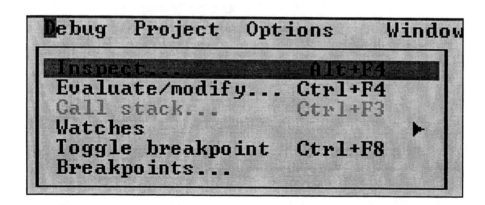

The **Debug** menu includes several options to help with debugging. We will study the use of the Debug options later.

The Project Menu

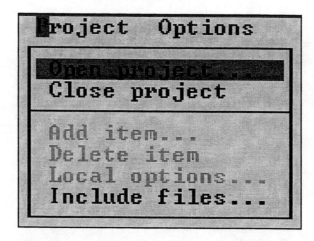

The **Project** menu includes options to allow us to work with projects. We will discuss these options later when we need them.

The Options Menu

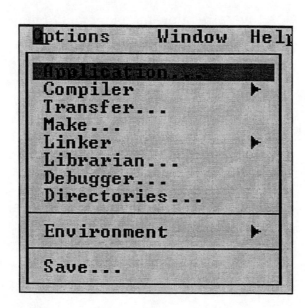

The **Options** menu contains commands that let us view and change various default settings in the Turbo C++ IDE. We will discuss some of these options later as we need them.

The Window Menu

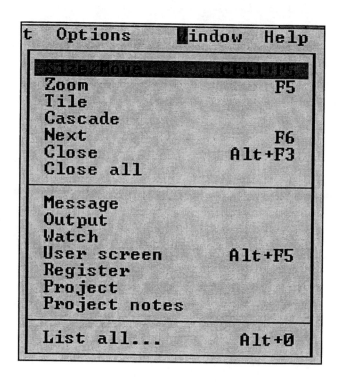

The **Window** menu contains several window management options.

Size/Move: This is used to change the size or position of the active window.

Zoom: This command is used to resize the active window.

Close: This is used to close the present active window.

Close all: This will close all of the windows that we have opened.

List: This used to get a list of all of the windows that we have opened.

The Help Menu

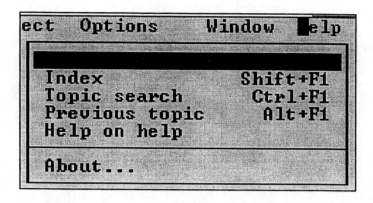

The **Help** menu is used to give us access to online help that is built into the Turbo C++ IDE.

On the right hand side of some menu options is a key combination.. This key combination gives us a fast way of performing the same action. For example, the **Run** option of the **Run** both compiles and runs the active program. This action may be performed anytime by holding down the **<Ctrl>** key and pressing the function key, **<F9>**.

Now let us look at the rest of the IDE screen.

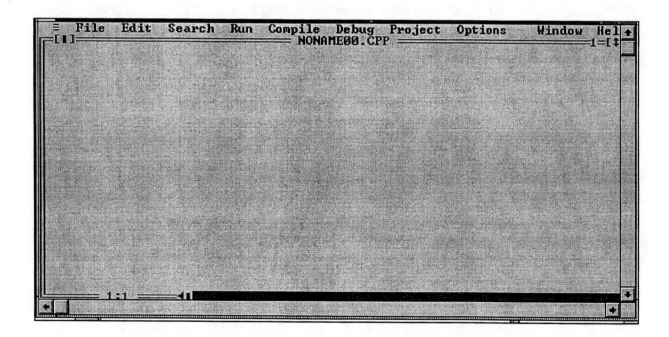

The largest part of your screen shows the Edit Window section. The menu bar is above the Edit Window section and the status bar is below. Most of your work will be done in edit windows, where you will enter and edit your files.

Next, we need to discuss the six control areas which follow:

Close box: In the upper left corner is a small box. Using a mouse to click on this box closes the current window. It may also be closed from the **Window** option of the menu bar (select the **Window** menu and then select the **Close** option).

Title bar: The title bar is located in the top center of the screen. When C++ is activated or the **New** option of the **File** menu is selected then a default name such as **NONAME00.CPP** appears here. This is the default name for the active program. At this point, you may select either **Save** or **Save as** from the **File** menu and then supply your own name for the file. The title bar will now show the new name for the file. Another option is to type in all or part of the file before you rename and save it.

Windows Number: The Turbo C++ IDE permits up to nine windows to be open at one time. In the upper right corner of the window is a number, 1 to 9, showing how many windows are currently open. It is possible to get a list of the open windows by pressing **<Alt><0>** or by selecting **Window** on the menu bar and choosing **List**. To work in a window, the window must first be made active. There are four different ways to do this.

(1)   Hold down the **<Alt>** key and type the number of the window to make active.

(2)   From the **Window** option of the menu bar select **List**. Use the up and down arrows to select the **Window** desired or choose **Next**.

(3)   Click the mouse anywhere in the desired window (which you wish to be made active).

(4)   Press the **<F6>** key repeatedly until the window you desire becomes the active window.

Zoom box: To the right of the window number is as arrow. Clicking on this arrow **Zooms** the window to its largest size. If it is at the largest size, clicking on the double arrow returns it to normal size. This may also be accomplished by selecting **Window** from the menu bar and choosing the option **Zoom**.

Scroll bars: The scroll bars are found along the right side and the bottom of the window. Clicking on these scrolls the screen within the window. The right hand scroll bar will scroll the contents of the window up and down. The bottom scroll bar scrolls right and left.

Resize box: Placing the cursor In the lower right hand corner of the window permits dragging the window to the desired size.

1.6 - A First Program

Now that you have some knowledge of the IDE we are ready to try a first program. We will begin by entering and running the following simple program.

```cpp
// prog1_1.cpp - A first program.
#include <iostream.h>
int main()
{                               // begin main program
  int I;                        // declare integer variable I
  for (I=1; i<11; I++)          // set up the for loop
    cout << I << endl;          // print current value of I
  // end for
  return 0;
}                               // end main program
```

At this point you do not need to understand every line of the program. Our immediate goal is to learn how to use the IDE to enter and run the program.   We first turn on the computer and load the Turbo C++ IDE as we have discussed earlier.   If the window with the file name **NONAME00.CPP** does not appear, then select the **File** menu and then select the **New** option. Recall that are three different ways that we can do this. One of the ways is to press the **<Alt>** and **<F>** keys, and since the **New** option is now highlighted, then simply press <Ret>.

We can now type in the program. After (or during) the typing of the program we need to save it to a hard drive or to a floppy disk. In order to save the program in a file called **PROG1_1.CPP** we can press the **<Alt><F>** keys to access the **File** option and then choose the **Save as...** option from the pull down menu. When the following prompt:

   File name:

appears, we could type **A:\PROG1_1.CPP** after the prompt

File name: A:\PROG1_1.CPP

and the file will be saved on our floppy disk on drive A:. On the other hand, If we wish to save our file in the root directory of hard drive C:, then we could enter the following:

File name: C:\PROG1_1.CPP

Note: Be sure and save your file (program) frequently and especially before you attempt to run it. Nasty things can happen such as a power problem or the locking up of your computer. There is nothing more frustrating than having to completely retype a file.

Note: The default extension is normally **.CPP**.. If we wish to force the compiler to compile the program as a **C** program rather than a **C++** program, then we should enter an extension of **.C** rather than **.CPP**. If so desired, we may change the default extension from **.CPP** to **.C** in the **Options** menu.

We are now ready to try running our program. A quick way to do this is to press the **<Alt><R>** keys to choose the **Run** option from the main menu, and then select the **Run** option by pressing the **<Ret>** key. Assuming there are no errors, the program will be compiled, linked, and then run. However, in order to see the screen containing the output, we will have to press the **<Alt><F5>** keys. We should then see the output

1
2
3
4
5
6
7
8
9
10

16

We then press any key in order to return to the screen containing the program.

If when we try to run our program, the compiler finds compiling or linking errors, then a message window is automatically opened. This message window displays a list of errors and warnings. In order to correct a compiler error or warning, we can double click on the error, and the IDE will position the cursor on the source line that caused the error. To correct the error, just press the **<Return>** key and then correct the error. Repeat this process for the remaining warnings and errors.

In addition to correcting errors, you should also attempt to remove the warnings. Since the program will run even when there are warnings, many beginning programmers tend to ignore warnings and only worry about errors. This is not a good practice, since many of the warnings catch programming mistakes just as the errors do. This leads us to a slight problem with the way we said to run our program. Suppose that we run a program by selecting **Run** from the **Run** menu. Also, suppose that there are warnings but no errors. The problem is that the compiler will not normally stop and let us look at the warnings. It will ignore the warnings and just run the program. Thus, we do not even know that warnings exist.

In order to see the warnings, we should use an alternative way of running our program First all, we select the **Compile** menu and then select either the **Make** or the **Build all** option (we will discuss the differences between **Make** and **Build all** in Chapter 4). Either of these will compile and link our program; but as yet not run it. Thus, the compiler window will still be visible so that we can check out any warnings. Then, if there are no warnings, we can run the program by selecting the **Run** menu and then the **Run** option.

When we have finished running our program, then we may either want to write a new program or exit from the Turbo C++ IDE. If we want to enter a new program we again choose the file option by pressing **<Alt><F>** and choose the **New** option from the pull down menu. If we want to exit the IDE we can choose the **Exit** option from this same menu. However, before we exit the IDE we may want to close all windows by selecting **Close all** in the **Window** menu. If we don't, the Turbo C++ IDE will try and reload all of the same files the next time that we enter it.

Using the Turbo C++ Editor

The editor in the Turbo C++ IDE allows us to use many of the editing commands and key combinations which were developed in one of the original word processors for microcomputers, **WordStar**. Following is a list of these commands and key combinations:

Frequently used edit commands

```
==================================================
```

\<Ctrl>\<s> or **\<->>**	move one character right
\<Ctrl>\<d> or **\<<->**	move one character left
\<Ctrl>\<e> or **< >**	move up one line
\<Ctrl>\<x> or **< >**	move down one line
\<Ctrl>\<a>	move left one word
\<Ctrl>\<f>	move right one word
\<Ctrl>\<r> or **\<PgUp>**	move up one screen
\<Ctrl>\<c> or **\<PgDn>**	move down one screen
\<Ctrl>\<y>	delete current line
\<Ctrl>\<q>\<y>	delete to end of line
\<Ctrl>\<q>\<s> or **\<Home>**	move to beginning of line
\<Ctrl>\<q>\<d> or **\<End>**	move to end of line
\<Ctrl>\<q>\<e>	move to top of screen
\<Ctrl>\<q>\<x>	move to bottom of screen
\<Ctrl>\<q>\<r>	move to top of file
\<Ctrl>\<q>\<c>	move to end of file
\<Ctrl>\<k>\<b>	mark beginning of block
\<Ctrl>\<k>\<k>	mark end of a block
\<Ctrl>\<k>\<v>	move a marked block
\<Ctrl>\<k>\<c>	copy a marked block
\<Ctrl>\<k>\<w>	write marked block to disk
\<Ctrl>\<k>\<r>	read file into current file
\<Ctrl>\<k>\<y>	delete marked block

```
==================================================
```

It is very comforting to know that we will not have to learn all of these commands to use the editor. In fact we can get along quite nicely by using only the arrow keys along with the **\<del>** and the backspace keys.

1.7 Summary

In this chapter we have given a brief history of the development of the C and C++ programming languages. We have also discussed the importance of C/C++ in the world today.

We then turned our attention to the development of our first C/C++ program. This included the use of the built in editor and a brief introduction to the many menus and options in the Turbo C++ Integrated Development Environment. We have just begun our journey into the world of C/C++ programming.

1.8 Questions

1.1   What is meant by a portable programming language?

1.2   How do we load the Turbo C++ IDE?

1.3   In the Turbo C++ IDE how do we save a program on our disk in drive A: with the name **PROG1_1.CPP**?

1.4   In the Turbo C++ IDE how do we compile, link, and run a DOS program?

1.5   What does **I++** do to the value of variable **I**?

1.9 Exercises

1.1   Enter and run program **PROG1_1.CPP**.

1.2   Enter and run a program that will display the counting integers 1 through 20.

1.3   Enter and run a program that will display the even integers 2 through 30. (Hint: use **I = I+2** or **I+=2**. We will discuss this later.)

1.4   Enter and run a program that will display the odd integers 1 through 25.

1.5   Enter and run a program that will display the integers from 20 down to 1. (Hint: use **I--** which will decrement **I** by 1).

CHAPTER 2

Programming Basics

2.1 - Introduction

In Chapter 1 we discussed how we can use the Turbo C++ IDE to write, compile, and run a simple C++ program. In this Chapter, we will begin our study of the various pieces of C++ programs.

We will discuss the header files that we must include with our programs in order to use various library functions. We will discuss the simple data types that are available, how we define variables to store this data, and what rules we have to obey when we define these various variables. We will discuss how we can use compiler directives to define constants and how we can also define constant variables.

Also, in this chapter we will discuss the basic C and C++ arithmetic operators and in addition some of the other operators that have been added to the C and C++ languages that are not available in other languages.   We will discuss some of the input and output capabilities that are available as carry overs from the C language and in addition the input and output capabilities that are unique to the C++ language. One of the reasons that we will study input and output in C as well as in C++ is because one of the tasks that we will face as programmers is to rewrite C programs into C++ programs.

After completing this chapter, the student should be able to

1.   understand when we have to use each of the header files **stdio.h**, **iostream.h**, and **iomanip.h** in a program.

2.   understand what simple data types are available in C and C++ programs, how we define variables for each of these types, and what variations of these data types can be defined using words such as **long**, **short**, **double**, **signed**, and **unsigned**.

3.   understand how we can define program constants using the compiler directive **#define** and also by defining variables using **const**.

4. understand how we can initialize variables as they are defined. In addition, understand the relative size of each of the data types.

5. understand how we can use the C/C++ functions, **printf()**, **scanf()** for input and output. We will see how we can format string output as well as the output of integer and real data.

6. understand how we can use the new C++ input / output stream objects, **cin** and **cout**. We will see how we use the manipulators defined in the **iomanip.h** header file to format string output as well as the output of integer and real data.

7. understand the standard arithmetic operators that are used in C and C++, as well as the increment, decrement, and the compound operators that are unique to the C and C++ languages.

8. understand how to convert input and output statements from C to C++ and simple C programs to C++ programs.

2.2 - The #include Directive and Header Files

Let us begin the section by taking a look at a new program which we will name **prog2_1.cpp**.

```
//*********************************************************************************
// prog2_1.cpp      Program to: 1. Ask the user for a name
//                               2. Print Hello followed by the name which was input.
// Written by: Eva May Hale
// Date: July 7, 1996
//*********************************************************************************
#include <iostream.h>
#include <stdio.h>
#include <conio.h>
int main( )                             /* Function main */
{
   char name[21];                       // Declare the name array
   cout << "Enter your name: ";         // Ask the user for the name
   gets(name);                          // Get the name into array, name
   cout << "Hello " << name << endl;    // Display Hello and the name
   getch();                             // Wait for a key press
   return 0;                            // Exit with OK
}
```

Let us now discuss the **prog2_1.cpp** program and what it does. The first 6 lines are comment lines. This top box of comments describes such things as the purpose of the program, the name(s) of the programmer(s), and the date. Notice that each of these lines begins with two slashes. This is the syntax for the new C++ style comment which begins with two slashes and is terminated by the physical end of the line.

The old style comment used with traditional C compilers begins with the two characters /* and ends with the two characters */. We used the old style type comment when we wrote the comment

/* Function main */

The old style comment can actually encompass more than one physical line. The comment is not terminated until the */ characters are found. A traditional C program can only include the old style comments. However, a new C++ program can use either (or both) comment styles.

Note: The programmer should be extremely careful when using the old style comments. Be sure that each comment is correctly terminated with */. Many problems can been caused by incorrectly terminated comments.

The preprocessor directive

#include <stdio.h>

does what its name implies. It includes the text from the file, **stdio.h**, into our program. Thus, the source code from the header file, **stdio.h**, is now included in our program. The reason for doing this is that the file, **stdio.h**, contains the declaration (prototype) for the input function, **gets()**. Similarly, the preprocessor directive

#include <iostream.h>

causes the text from the file, **iostream.h**, to be included in our program. It contains the declarations necessary for us to use **cout** and **endl** in our program. We will discuss this in more detail later. Finally, we needed

#include <conio.h>

since, **conio.h** contains the declaration (prototype) for the **getch()** function.

22

The single global declaration:

```
char name[21];
```

allocates memory space for a 21 character array. This space will be used to store the characters of the name that the user types in when the program runs. When a string of characters is typed in by the user, a terminator byte with a value of 0 is appended to the end of the characters. Since space is also needed for this 0 byte, the user should not type in more than 20 actual characters.

The next line:

```
int main()
```

begins the **main** function. As the name implies, in C and C++, the **main** function is the main function of the program. This is where the program begins execution. All statements that are to be included in function, **main**, are enclosed in the block enclosed by the curly braces, **{** and **}**. Also, notice that each statement in **main** ends with a semicolon. The first statement,

```
cout << "Enter your name: ";
```

will cause the string

```
Enter your name:
```

to be sent to the standard output stream, **stdout**. This is by default normally directed to the monitor.

The next statement,

```
gets(name);
```

will allow the user to type in a name from the keyboard. The string of characters which are input (until the return key is pressed) are stored in memory in the space allocated as

```
char name[21];
```

Notice that we could have a problem if the user types in more than 20 characters. (We will discuss possible solutions to this problem later.)

The next statement,

```
cout << "Hello, " << name << endl;
```

will first of all display

> Hello,

followed by the name that was entered from the keyboard and stored in **name**. Thus, if the name, **John Smith**, was typed in by the user, then the output will be

> Hello, John Smith.

The **endl** that was output at the end of the statement stands for **endline** and tells the compiler that both a carriage return, **<CR>**, and a linefeed, **<LF>**, are to be output to the screen. Thus, the cursor will now be moved to the beginning of the next line.

The statement

> getch();

is a call to the **getch()** function which will wait for the user to press any key. We use this in the previous program so that the output will remain on the screen until we press a key.

The final statement in the function, main(),

> return 0;

exits the program and sends a value of 0 back from function **main()**. The value of 0 normally means that there were no problems. We will discuss C and C++ functions in greater detail later. However, we should note that the **int** in

> int main()

means that function **main** will return an integer value. Thus, the statement,

> return 0;

is also fulfilling the obligation that function **main()** is supposed to return an integer value.

Now that you understand what the program does, you should enter the program and run it.

Now then, let us return to our discussion of the header files. As mentioned above, the **#include** directive does exactly what its name implies; it includes source code from another file into your program. Thus,

> #include <stdio.h>

causes the source code from the file **stdio.h** to be inserted into the program in place of the **#include <stdio.h>** directive. The name **stdio** stands for **standard input/output** and is a carry over from traditional C compilers. The name **iostream** stands for **input/ output stream** and belongs to the C++ language. The name **conio.h** stands for **console input/output** and declares special functions that are particularly written for input/output on IBM PC's and compatibles.

Notice that the **#include** directive is not followed by a semicolon. Also, notice that the name of the file was included between inequality signs **<>**. This indicates that the system should search for this file in the directory path(s) specified in the **Options/ Directory** path(s) for **Include** files. If we would include the file name in double quotation marks **" "**, **#include "stdio.h"**, rather than the inequality signs, then the system will first look for the file in the current active directory; then, if the file is not found there, the search will go to the **Options/Directory** path(s) for **Include** files (just as for the **<>**). Thus, if we typed,

        #include "stdio.h"

then the system will first of all search the current active directory for the file **stdio.h**. Then, if the file is not found, the system will search for the file in the path(s) specified in the **Options/Directory** path(s) for **Include** files.

The header files, **stdio.h, iostream.h,** and **conio.h** are just three of the many header files which are supplied with the compiler. We will be using many of these as we proceed through the remainder of this text. The reader is encouraged to load the file **stdio.h** into the editor and investigate the source code included in this file. However, part of the code may seem a little strange at first, until the programmer becomes more experienced with the C++ language.

Finally, it is tempting for C and C++ beginners to think that there is something magical about the header files. This is not really true. These are just source files which contain certain declarations. In fact, as you will see later, we can write our own header files. As we work through the lessons in this chapter, we will see the need to include additional header files, such as **iomanip.h**, **stdlib.h**, and **string.h**.

2.3 - Defining Program Constants

There are two ways of defining constants that are to be used in a program. The **#define** directive is often used to create a symbolic constant. For example, if we wish to define a constant **INTEREST_RATE** we can use the following compiler directive:

        #define INTEREST_RATE 0.10

Then, when the program is compiled, every reference to **INTEREST_RATE** will be replaced with 0.10. Notice that we do not use an equal sign, =, and we do not put a semicolon at the end of the **#define** directive. It is standard practice to use all caps when we define constants, however, it is not required. We illustrate the use of the **#define** directive in the following program:

```
// prog2_2.cpp Program to illustrate the use of the
//                    #define directive.
#include <iostream.h>
#include <iomanip.h>
#define INTEREST_RATE  0.10
int main()
{
  double loan_amount, int_earned, total_due;

  cout << "Enter the amount of your loan: ";
  cin >> loan_amount;

  int_earned = loan_amount * INTEREST_RATE;
  total_due = loan_amount + int_earned;

  cout.setf(ios::showpoint);
  cout.setf(ios::fixed);
  cout.precision(2);
  cout << "Interest earned = $"
       << setw(5) << int_earned << endl;
  cout << "Total  due = $" << setw(7)
       << total_due << endl;
  return 0;
}
```

When the above program is compiled, the name, **INTEREST_RATE**, will be replaced with 0.10. A sample run of the program might appear as follows:

```
Enter loan amount: 2000.00
Interest earned = $200.00
Total due = $2200.00
```

In this small program there is only one replacement for **INTEREST_RATE**. However, in larger programs, there may be several replacements. Thus, if we would decide to change the value for **INTEREST_RATE**, we would only have to change the declared value once (in the **#define** directive) rather than in each of the several locations of the value, 0.10. When the above program executes, the user is asked to enter the amount of the loan. Then, the interest earned, **int_earned**, and the total amount due, **total_due**, are calculated. Finally, the total amount due is printed to the screen. (Note: we will discuss the details of this program in more detail later in this chapter.)

A program may contain as many **#define** statements as desired. If there are several **#define** directives, the programmer may wish to place them in a separate file and then include this file in the program by using the **#include** statement.   This file is usually designated as a header file using the **.h** extension.

Program constants can also be defined as variables by using the word **const** when the variable is defined. We must assign the data at the same time. For example,

```
const float RATE = 0.10;
const float PI = 3.1416;
const int SIZE = 50;
```

all define constant variables and assign values that cannot be changed by the program. Notice that we use an assignment (**=**) and a semi-colon (**;**) when we define constant variables. The first program could be rewritten as follows:

```
//prog2_3.cpp - Program to illustrate the use of the
//                      const directive.
int main( )
{
    const float INTEREST_RATE = 0.10;
    double loan_amount,  int_earned,  total_due;

    cout << "Enter loan amount: ";
    cin >> loan_amount;
    int_earned = loan_amount * INTEREST_RATE;
    total_due = loan_amount + int_earned;
    cout.setf(ios::showpoint);
    cout.setf(ios::fixed);
    cout.precision(2);
    cout << "Interest earned = $" << setw(5)
        << int_earned << endl;
    cout << "Total due = $" << setw(8)
        << total_due << endl;
    return 0;
}
```

It is normally considered preferable to use **const** rather than the older **#define** since in a **const** declaration, we can specify the exact data type (such as **float**).

2.4 - Data Types and Variables

The **simple data types** in C++ are: character, integer, and real. For a simple data type, only one data item can be stored at each storage location that is set up for the given variable of that type. The keywords that we use for these simple data types are the following: **char, int,** and **float**. Real data is referred to as **floating point** data. The amount of memory reserved for each type may vary depending on the system and the compiler being used. There is also a simple data type, **double**, that is used for a real data type that needs more precision. The Pascal language included a fourth simple data type called Boolean. The C and C++ languages do not include this type. We will discuss how this is handled in Chapter 3.

When we are using Turbo C++, the amount of memory reserved for a normal integer variable is two bytes. **ANSI**, (American National Standards Institute) stipulates the minimum ranges for each of the basic data types as shown in Table 2.1. The Turbo C++ compiler adheres to these standards and therefore allows one byte for a character, two bytes for a normal integer, four bytes for a normal float and eight bytes for a double.

There are variations of these simple data types to aid in handling different sizes of the simple data types. To use these variations, we use the key words, **long, unsigned, double, signed and short** with **char, int, and float**. Table 2.1 gives the complete list along with the size of the storage location (in bytes) and the size of the data item that can be stored in that location.

The keyword, **void**, is used to indicate that no storage is to be set aside or that no data is to be returned. The following table describes the various declarations for the simple data types, the amount of storage that is allocated for each type, and the size of the data that can be stored for each of these types.

Table 2.1: ANSI minimal range values

Type	Bytes	Bits	Minimal Range
char	1	8	-128 to 127
unsigned char	1	8	0 to 255
signed char	1	8	-128 to 127
int	2	16	-32,768 to 32,767
unsigned int	2	16	0 to 65,535
signed int	2	16	-32,768 to 32,767
short int	2	16	-32,768 to 32,767
unsigned short int	2	16	0 to 65,535
signed short int	2	16	-32,768 to 32,767
long int	4	32	-2,147,483,648 to 2,147,483,647
signed long int	4	32	-2,147,483,648 to 2,147,483,647
unsigned long int	4	32	0 to 4,294,967,295
float	4	32	3.4e-38 to 3.4e+38 (6-7 digit precision)
double	8	64	1.7e-308 to 1.7e+308 (15 digit precision)
long double	16	128	1.7e-4932 to 1.7e+4932 (19 digit precision)
void	0	0	

It is quite easy to declare a variable. We simply follow the general form for a declaration:

type   variable-name;

For example,

```
int   number;
char   onechar;
float   monthly_pay;
```

declares the variable **number** to be of type integer and reserves two bytes in memory, the variable **onechar** to be of type character and reserves one byte of memory, and the variable **monthly_pay** to be of type real and reserves four bytes of memory.

When we define variables for use in our programs, we need to consider the following:

1.   The type of data that we will be using.

2.   The size of the data that we will be using in our program.

3.   The names that will be descriptive for these variables.

If we are dealing with numeric data that requires decimals for accuracy, then we must use **float, double,** or **long double** rather than **int**. As can be seen in **Table 2.1**, **double** will give use better accuracy than **float**, and **long double** will give use better accuracy than **double.** Thus, we normally choose the type depending on the accuracy that we need in our program.

If we are using numeric data that does not require decimals, then we should use an integer type rather than one of the data types for a real number. The types, **char, unsigned char, signed char, int, unsigned int, signed int, short int, unsigned short int, signed short int, long int, signed long int,** and **unsigned long int** are all integer types. We select the specific type depending on the integer size that we are using. For example, if we know that a variable which we will call **num** will have integer values between 0 and 40,000, then we could declare **num** to be type **unsigned int.**

        unsigned int num;

Overriding Default Types

When the statement

        num = 12;

is encountered, the literal 12 is interpreted as a signed integer. However, suppose that we may wish it to be considered as an unsigned integer. We can do this by adding either a letter **u** or a letter **U** after the digits (as follows):

        num = 12U;   or   num = 12u;

Similarly, the programmer can override the default floating point type. The statement

        amount = 1250.75;

looks as though we are assigning a float number (1250.75) to **amount**. However, Turbo C++ normally interprets floating point literals as type **double**. This is done in order to give better accuracy. if we wish to obtain maximum accuracy, then we can add the letter **L** as a suffix after the digits of the number. For example,

$$1250.75L \qquad \text{or} \qquad 1250.75l$$

will tell the compiler that the literal should be a **long double** rather than a **double.**

We can also use **L** with integers. Thus,

$$123L \qquad \text{or} \qquad 123l$$

will tell the compiler to consider the literal 123 as a **long** (integer) rather than a normal integer. In addition, we can use **unsigned** and **long** together with integers, so that

$$245UL \qquad \text{or} \qquad 245ul$$

will tell the compiler to consider the integer 245 as an **unsigned long** integer.

Integer Literals

In programming we have to be able to express integer data as decimal, as binary, as octal, or as hexadecimal. The term **decimal** means that we use ten characters to count, namely 0, 1, 2, 3, 4, 5, 6, 7, 8, 9. This is familiar since we have grown up with this notation. The number 201 in decimal is evaluated as

$$231 = 2 * 100 + 3 * 10 + 1$$

The term **binary** means that we use two characters to count, namely 0 and 1. The term **octal** means that we use eight characters to count, 0, 1, 2, 3, 4, 5, 6, 7 and the term **hexadecimal** means that we are using 16 characters to count so that we use the decimal digits and add the letters A, B, C, D, E, F. The sixteen characters are 0, 1, 2, 3, 4, 5, 6, 7, 8, 9, A, B, C, D, E, F. The C/C++ languages allow us to write integers as literals using decimal, octal, or hexadecimal notation. The hexadecimal notation is appropriate when we are considering addresses. We will have little occasion to use octal. Each of the following literals will be considered as decimal (base 10)

$$23, 0, -135$$

If we want an integer to be interpreted as **octal**, then we precede the literal integer with a zero. Thus, each of the following would be considered as octal integers.

$$023, 021, -0135$$

If we want an integer to be interpreted as a **hexadecimal**, then we precede the literal integer with the two characters, **0x** or **0X**. Thus, all of the following would be considered as hexadecimal integers.

0x23, 0X23, 0x9F

Notice the differences in the expansions for the following decimal, octal, and hexadecimal numbers:

23 (in decimal) = 2 * 10 + 3 = 23 (in decimal)

023 (in octal) = 2 * 8 + 3 = 19 (in decimal)

0x23 (in hexadecimal) = 2 * 16 + 3 = 35 (in decimal)

We can see that it makes a considerable difference when we use the same digits in the different bases (decimal, octal, and hexadecimal).

Try this: Show the expansion and give the decimal value for each of the following:

215   _____

0215   _____
                       _____

0x215   _____
                       _____

0xAB   _____
                       _____

If the reader is not familiar with the different number systems, then he/she should work through the material in Appendix A.

Variables in C and C++

The C and C++ languages are **case sensitive**. This means that the variables, **area, Area,** and **AREA** are all different variables. One adopted pattern in DOS programming is to use <u>only</u> lower case letters for all variables and <u>only</u> upper case letters for constants. However, in windows programming a mix of upper and lower case is commonly used.

A variable name can use upper and lower case characters, (**a..z, A.. Z**), digits **0..9**, and the underscore, _. The first character must be a letter or the underscore. The number of characters that can be used depends on the compiler. The old Turbo C compiler allowed 32 characters while the newer Borland Turbo C++ compiler allows any length. However, even though any number of characters is allowed, only the first 32 are significant. In this text we will only use a letter as the first character, Turbo C++ uses the underscore for special names.

Good programming practice requires that we use meaningful variable names; names that describe what the data actually represents. For example, if we want to store four integer exam scores and compute a real average, then we might choose

```
int     exam1, exam2, exam3, exam4;
float   average;
```

We would not want to use following names:

```
int     w,y,z,q;
float   r;
```

since these do not give the reader any idea of what the variable names represent. In long variable names, the underscore is frequently used to make the names easier to read. For example,

```
float   exam_average;
```

is easier to read than

```
float   examaverage;.
```

When defining a variable name, we need to be careful and not use a reserved word. A reserved word is a name which already has been declared by the compiler. Both C and C++ have numerous reserved words. Table 2.2 below includes reserved words in C++. Many of these are also reserved in C. A good programmer will always check the manuals or interact with help for an exact list of reserved words for the C/C++ compiler being used. The programmer will then make sure not to use these reserved words for any other use.

Another advisable practice is <u>not</u> to begin a user defined variable name with the underscore character. The reason for this is that C and C++ use the underscore in their libraries for a number of built-in variable and function names.

Table 2.2 C++ Reserved Words.

==

asm	_cs	extern	interrupt	register	struct
auto	default	far	_loadds	_regparam	switch
break	delete	float	long	return	template
case	do	for	near	_saveregs	this
catch	double	friend	new	_seg	typedef
cdecl	_dsh	goto	operator	short	union
char	else	huge	pascal	signed	unsigned
class	enum	if	private	sizeof	virtual
const	_es	inline	protected	_ss	void
continue	_export	int	public	static	volatile
					while

==

Try this: Which of the following are not good choices for variable names? Why?

_num1 _____

1num _____

inline _____

NUM _____

number1 _____

Initializing Variables

When we declare a variable, the compiler may or may not assign a value to that variable. For example, if we write the following:

```
int num1, num2;
char ch1;
int main()
(
    ...;
    ...;
}
```

then, since the variables are declared outside of any function, the compiler will assign values to them. Each of these variables, **num1**, **num2** and **ch** will be initialized to a value of 0. However, if we declared these same variables within the **main** function as follows:

```
int main()
{
        int num1, num2;
        char ch1;
        ...;
        ...;
}
```

then only the memory is set aside, and the variables will have the values of whatever garbage is already in memory.   Regardless of where you place your declarations, it is not good programming practice to rely on the compiler to initialize your variables. You should do the initializations yourself.

In fact, if we desire to do so, the C and C++ programming languages allow us to initialize the variables as they are defined. Thus we could initialize the variables **num1** and **num2** to zero and also initialize **ch** to the character 'A' at the same time that we declare them with the following statements:

```
int num1 = 0,
    num2 = 0;
char ch = 'A';
int main()
(
        ...;
        ...;
}
```

or

```
int main()
{
        int num1 = 0,
            num2 = 0;
        char ch = 'A';
        ...;
        ...;
}
```

Thus, it is very easy to declare a variable and initialize it at the same time. However, if so desired, we can declare the variables first and then initialize them later, as follows:

```
        int num1, num2;
        char ch;
        int main()
        (
                num1 = 0;
                num2 = 0;
                ch = 'A';
                ...;
                ...;
        }
```

or

```
        int main()
        {
                int num1, num2;
                char ch;
                num1 = 0;
                num2 = 0;
                ch = 'A';
                ...;
                ...;
        }
```

Combining Data Types

When we add an integer to a real we are mixing data types. As programmers, we must be aware of how expressions with mixed types are handled. Generally the smaller (or simpler) of the two data types is converted to the larger (or more complex). For example, if we add an integer to a float, then the integer is first of all converted to a float and then the addition is performed. For example, for the following code:

```
        int num1 = 5;
        float num2 = 6.5;
        float sum;

        sum = num1 + num2;
```

num1 will be converted from the integer value 5 to the float value of 5.0.; then the two float values will be added (5.0 + 6.5). Finally, the float result (11.5) will be assigned to **sum.**

The method of converting data types before the operation is performed is called **data promotion**. This conversion is done in order to obtain more accurate results.

36

As a second example, consider the following code:

```
float        num1 = 10.4;
double       num2 = 154.54;
double       result;

result = num1 + num2;
```

In evaluating **num1 + num2** the first step will be to promote **num1** from a **float** to a **double**. Then the sum will be found. Finally, the **double** result will be assigned to **result**.

As a third example, consider the following:

```
unsigned char    num1 = 10;
int              num2 = 300;
int              result;

result = num1 + num2;
```

In evaluating **num1 + num2** the first step will be to promote **num1** to an integer. Then the sum will be found and assigned to **result**.

Try this: What are the resulting data types for each of the following
             if we assume the following declarations:

             int num1; char ch1; float num2; double num3;

             num2 + num3   _____

             num1 + num2   _____

             num1 + num2 + num3   _____

             num1 + ch1   _____

             ch1 + num2   _____

37

Try this: Suppose we have the following declarations:

    int exam1 = 90, exam2 = 81;
    float average;

What is the value that will be assigned to **average** with the following statement

    average = (exam1 + exam2) / 2;   _____

Why do we not get the expected result of 85.5?   _____

How should this code be written?   _____

Type Casting

It is frequently advisable for us as programmers to force a type conversion from one type to another. The C and C++ compilers allow us to temporarily specify a data promotion by using what is called **type casting**. When we type cast a variable, we temporarily change the data type to the new one that we specify. There are two formats that we can use for type casting. If we wish to promote

        int exam1;

to **float**, and compile as a C++ program, then we can do this with either of the two expressions:

        (float) exam1   or   float (exam1)

However, if we compile as a C program then we can only use the first of these two forms:

        (float)exam1

If we try to use the second form, we will get a syntax error. Thus, assuming we compile as a C++ program and have the following declarations:

        int   exam1, exam2;
        float   average;

then we can compute **average** by type casting in a variety of ways. The two most obvious choices would be

        average = (float (exam1 + exam2)) / 2;

38

or

average = (exam1 + exam2)/float(2);

However,

average = float ((exam1 + exam2) / 2);

would not produce the desired result. Why? _____
_____
_____

How about the statement? Explain.

average = float (exam1 + exam2) / 2; _____
_____
_____

Try this: Assume that we have the following declarations

int num1; float num2; double num3;

use type casting to promote the appropriate variables
to guarantee the most accurate results.

num1 + num2   _____

num1 - num3   _____

num3 / num2   _____

num1 + num2 * num3   _____

The C programming language was designed as a **moderately typed** language. On the other hand, Pascal is known as a **strongly typed** language. The C++ program language is a little bit more fussy about interchanging data but is still a moderately typed language. What do we mean by all of this? The stronger the typing, the more strict the compiler is in matching and using different types. Thus, C++ is stricter than C with regard to its handling of different types. As a consequence of this, C++ is better in giving warnings and errors for problems concerning data types..

2.5 - Input & Output Using scanf() and printf().

In this section we will investigate some of the input/output capabilities in C and C++. In C++ we may still use the traditional input/output functions from C. However, C++ contains some additional capabilities for both input and output. The functions that we will discuss in this lesson are the two functions, **printf()** and **scanf()**. These were the standard general input/output functions that were available in the original C programming language. They are still available in C++. Recall, that the function declarations (prototypes) for these functions are contained in the **stdio.h** header file.

Output

One of the most popular output functions in C (and still available in C++) is **printf()**. The following program uses **printf()**:

```
#include <stdio.h>
int main()
{
  printf("Hello");
  return 0;
}
```

to output the string "Hello". The line

```
#include <stdio.h>
```

causes the compiler to include the header file, **stdio.h**, in the program when it is compiled. This file contains the necessary declarations for using the **printf()** function. (Since it is a text file, the programmer may view or print **stdio.h**). In the program

```
// prog2_4.cpp Program to illustrate the use of the
//                  function printf( ).
#include <stdio.h>
int main()
{
  int num = 4;
  printf("The value of num is %d.",  num);
  return 0;
}
```

the output will be the following:

```
The value of num is 4.
```

40

The **printf( )** function uses a **format string** followed by the variables and/or data that is to be substituted for the various format specifiers in the string.

printf(" Format String", var1, var2, ..., varK);

Some examples in addition to the above are the following:

printf("A character = %c", '$');   A character = $

printf("An integer = %d", 765);   An integer = 765

printf("A real number = %f", 23.45);   A real number = 23.45000

printf("A string = %s", "Hello, World");   A string = Hello, World

The percent character (**%**) is the special character that is used in the format string in order for the **printf()** function to tell how the data is to be printed. It is used to define the format specifiers for data. It is always followed by a formatting character that specifies the data type that is to be printed. The use of the **printf( )** function is governed by the following set of rules:

1.   The control string to be printed must be enclosing in double quotes.

2.   The variable type in the argument list must match the specified type. In the first example %c is replaced with the '$' character. In the second example %d is replace by an integer (the integer 765).

3.   The number and type of variables in the argument list must match the number and type of specifiers used.

4.   When there is a control string and an argument list they are separated by a comma and each argument is separated by a comma.

5.   The argument list may contain literals or variables.

6.   **printf()** requires **#include <stdio.h>.**

Table 2.3 contains the complete list of format specifiers for the **printf()** function.

Table 2.3: Format specifiers for printf()

Specifier	Format
Numeric	
%d	signed decimal integer
%i	signed decimal integer
%o	unsigned octal integer
%u	unsigned decimal integer
%x	unsigned hexadecimal integer displays a, b, c, d, e, f
%X	unsigned decimal integer displays A, B, C, D, E, F
%f	signed real floating point standard decimal
%e	signed real floating point scientific notation
%g	signed real floating point (%f or %e whichever is shorter)
%E	Same as %e, using E for exponent
%G	Same as %g, using E for exponent if e format is used
Character	
%c	Single character
%s	String of characters
Pointer	
%p	Address of a pointer variable Either XXXX : YYYY or YYYY
%n	Address of an integer pointer variable

In addition, the letter 'l' can be used with **%d, %i, %u, %x, %o** to specify long integer. For example, **%ld**.

Printing Headings

Suppose that we wish to center the heading **"Program #1"** on 80 columns. Since the heading is 10 characters in length and we want to center on 80 columns, we have 80 - 10 = 70 columns left so that 35 blanks must be printed before the heading.

Program #1

In order to print 35 blanks, we print one blank in a 35 place field. This is done with the statement

```
printf("%35c", ' ');
```

We then print the heading with the statement

```
printf("Program #1\n");
```

We include the newline character, **'\n'**, in order to move the cursor to the beginning of a new line after the heading has been printed. The newline character, **'\n'** causes a **carriage return** and a **linefeed** to be output to the screen. Thus, to print the heading centered on 80 columns we can use the two statements

```
printf("%35c", ' ');
printf("Program #1\n");
```

These two statements can be combined into one that will use both the character and string format specifiers.

```
printf("%35c%s\n", ' ', "Program #1");
```

Notice the difference of where the new line character,**'\n'**, has been placed. It would work just as well if we left it as part of the heading. Normally it is placed in the format string.

Try this: Give the statement that will center the heading CS 256
on 80 columns.

Suppose that we want to print the headings **"Exam1"**, **"Exam2"**, and **"Exam3"** on one line beginning in columns 20, 40, and 60.

20	40	60
Exam1	Exam2	Exam3

For the first heading, we print 19 blanks and then print the heading.

```
printf("%19c", ' ');
printf("Exam1");
```

The cursor is now in column 25 and we need to print blanks through column 39. Thus, we need to print 40 - 25 = 15 blanks. We print the 15 blanks followed by the heading with the statements

43

```
printf("%15c", ' ');
printf("Exam2");
```

The next step would be to again print 15 blanks followed by the third heading and then the newline character. This would be done with the two statements:

```
printf("%15c", ' ');
printf("Exam3\n");
```

The headings would be printed with the six statements:

```
printf("%19c", ' ');
printf("Exam1");
printf("%15c", ' ');
printf("Exam2");
printf("%15c", ' ');
printf("Exam3\n");
```

or with the single statement

```
printf("%19c%s%15c%s%15c%s\n", ' ', "Exam1", ' ', "Exam2", ' ', "Exam3");
```

Another method for printing headings in specific columns is to count the number of blanks plus the number of characters in the string and use the total number of positions as the field width for the string. Thus, in order to center the heading **"Program #1"** on 80 columns, we would add the 35 blanks to the 10 characters of the string and use the statement:

```
printf("%45s\n", "Program #1");
```

Similarly, the heading "exam1" could be printed beginning in column 20 with the statement

```
printf("%24s", "Exam1");
```

and the three headings with the statement,

```
printf("%24s%19s%19s\n","Exam1","Exam2","Exam3");
```

Try this: Give the statements that will print the two column headings

        Month   Interest

beginning in columns 10 and 30 respectively.

_____

_____

_____

_____

Blank Lines

Each time we print the newline character, '**\n'**, we send a carriage return and a line feed to the screen. If the cursor is at the beginning of a new line, then in order to print three blank lines, we can send three new line characters. Thus, we would use the statement:

```
printf("\n\n\n");
```

Integer Data

The same techniques can be used to format the output for integer data. We can use either of the format specifiers, **%d** or **%l**. Suppose that we have integer data stored with the statements

```
int  num1 = 76,  num2 = 85,  num3 = 92;
```

and we want to print the data stored at **num1, num2,** and **num3** beginning in columns 22, 42, and 62 respectively. As before, we can first print the blanks and then print the data or we can use a field of length equal to the number of blanks plus the length of the field for the data. To print the data stored at **num1** in columns 22 and 23 we would do the following:

```
printf("%21c", ' ');                    or              printf("%23d", num1);
printf("%2d",  num1);
```

In order to print the data stored at **num2** in columns 42 and 43 we need to print 18 blanks followed by the data stored in **num2**.

```
printf("%18c", ' ');                    or              printf("%20d", num2);
printf("%2d",  num2);
```

To print the data stored in **num3** in columns 62 and 63 and then print the newline character, we use the statements:

```
printf("%18c", ' ');                    or          printf("%20d\n", num3);
printf("%2d\n",  num3);
```

The data is printed in columns 22, 23 and 42, 43 and 62, 63 with either of the sets of statements:

```
printf("%21c", ' ');                    or          printf("%23d", num1);
printf("%2d", num1);                                printf("%20d", num2);
printf("%18c", ' ');                                printf("%20d\n", num3);
printf("%2d",  num2);
printf("%18c", ' ');
printf("%2d\n",  num3);
```

This can also be done with one statement.

```
printf("%21c%2d%18c%2d%18c%2d\n", ' ', num1, ' ', num2, ' ', num3);
                    or
printf("%23d%20d%20d\n", num1, num2, num3);
```

Try this: Three digit integers are stored in the variables, **num1** and **num2**.
              Write the statements to print the data in columns 30 -> 32 and
              50 -> 52.

_____
_____
_____
_____

Left Justification

It is also possible to define a field and have integer data printed left justified in that field. This is done by placing a minus sign in front of the field length and after the % sign. For example, the following statements would produce the indicated output.

```
print("%-10d% -10d% -10d\n", 76, 90, 82);
```

7 6 _ _ _ _ _ _ _ _ 9 0 _ _ _ _ _ _ _ _ 8 2 _ _ _ _ _ _ _ _

Real Data

In order to format real data we need to worry about the field size along with the number of decimal places. This is done by specifying the field size followed by the number of decimal places. The field size includes the number of digits, the decimal point, and the number of decimal places.

field_size.dec_places

If we wanted to print the real number 75.345 as it appears, in a field of 6 places with 3 decimal places (notice that we count the decimal point as part of the total field width), then we would use the format specified

```
%6.3f
```

Suppose that we have real data stored with the statements

```
float  exam1 = 79.5,  exam2 = 83.25,  exam3 = 90;
```

and we want to print each value in the format xx.xx beginning in columns, 20, 40, and 60 respectively. The field width is 5, 2 digits plus the decimal point plus the two decimal digits. Thus, we will use the format specified **%5.2f** for the numeric output. We first need to print 19 blanks and then the data stored at **exam1** with the statements

```
printf("%19c", ' ');           or           printf("%24.2f", exam1);
printf("%5.2f",  exam1);
```

Now we can print blanks in columns 25 through 39, a total of 15, and the data stored in **exam2** with the statements

```
printf("%15c", ' ');           or           printf("%20.2f", exam2);
printf("%5.2f",  exam2);
```

The next statements print blanks in columns 45 through 59 followed by the data stored at **exam3** and the newline character.

```
printf("%15c", ' ');           or           printf("%20.2f\n", exam3);
printf("%5.2f\n",  exam3);
```

The above can be done with either of the single statements:

```
printf("%19c%5.2f%15c%5.2f%15c%5.2f\n", ' ', exam1, ' ',
         exam2, ' ', exam3);
```

or

```
printf("%24.2f%20.2f%20.2f\n", exam1, exam2, exam3);
```

Try this: Interest and an amount of money are stored in the variables, **interest** and **amount**. Write the statements that will print the data in the formats xx.xx and xxxx.xx beginning in columns 20 and 50 respectively.

_____
_____
_____
_____

If we want to print an amount of money, then we will often want to print a $ in front of the data. If the data is stored in amount and is to be printed in the format

$xxxxx.xx

beginning in column 40, then we would use the following statements.

```
printf("%40c%8.2f", '$', amount);
```

Try this: Rewrite the statements in the previous, **Try this:**, so that each of the data items is preceded by a $.

_____
_____
_____
_____

Control characters

There are special **control characters** that can be used in the format string to perform special output operations, like ringing the bell, doing a backspace, etc. A list of these special control characters is given in Table 2.4.

48

Table 2.4: Control characters

Control	Result
\a	bell
\b	backspace
\f	formfeed
\n	new line (linefeed)
\r	carriage return
\t	tab
\v	vertical tab
\\	backslash
\'	single quote
\"	double quote
\?	question mark

For example, the statement

```
printf("\a");
```

would ring the bell.

Data Input

It is not enough to be able to print a message and variables to the console. You must also be able to input information. The C programming language includes the **scanf()** function as one of its main input functions, and it is still available in C++. Like **printf()**, **scanf()** requires the **stdio.h** header file. Consider the following example:

```
//prog2_6.cpp Program to illustrate the use of the
//                    function scanf( )
#include <stdio.h>
int main()
{
   int num1;
   printf("Please enter an integer\n");
   scanf("%d", &num1);
   printf("The integer entered was %d\n", num1);
   return 0;
}
```

In this example the user is requested to enter an integer. Then the function, **scanf()**,

49

accepts the integer value, **%d**, and stores it at the address of the variable **num1**. The **&** in front of a variable must be used and it tells the compiler to use the address of the variable to find the location in which to store the value. The **&** operator is called the **address of** operator.

One important fact is that **scanf()** stops reading at the first blank, tab, or <Ret>. For example in the following:

```
printf("Enter 5 integers to be summed\n");
sum = 0;
for(I=1; I <= 5; I++) {
  scanf("%I", &num);
  sum = sum + num;
} // end for
```

Since **scanf()** stops at the first blank and since the program requests 5 numbers the operator may either enter all 5 numbers on one line separating each number by a space or by entering each number on a different line by following the number with a <Ret>. The following are the examples of acceptable input:

10 45 67 98 34<Ret>   or   10<Ret>
                                         45<Ret>
                                         67<Ret>
                                         98<Ret>
                                         34<Ret>

On the first pass, 10 is read and added to **sum**, on the second pass 45 is read, and so on until all five numbers are read and added to **sum**.

However, the fact that **scanf()** stops reading at a blank causes problems with string input. For example, consider the following code:

```
char name[21];

printf("Please enter your name: ");
scanf("%s", name);
printf("Your name is %s ", name);
```

Note: When we used name in the **scanf()** function we did not use the **&** sign in front. Since name is actually the address of the first character in the array, then we are actually sending the address of the array. Thus, the **&** sign is not needed. We will discuss this in more detail in Chapter 6.

When this code is executed, we see the following:

> Please enter your name: <u>Linda Lee Easton</u>
> Your name is Linda

When the user enters

> Linda Lee Easton

the only input that **scanf()** picks up is the first name Linda. The input is terminated at the first blank. The fact that **scanf()** uses a blank as a terminator, forces us to use other functions for string input. One function that we can use is the **gets()** function that we illustrated in **prog2_1.cpp**. The above code can then be written as

```
printf("Please enter your name: ");
gets(name);
printf("Your name is %s ", name);
```

The format specifiers for **scanf()** are listed in Table 2.5 below and the function **gets( )** is defined in the **stdio.h** header file.

Table 2.5: Format specifiers for scanf( )

==

Code	Meaning

==

Integer

%d	decimal integer
%l	decimal integer
%o	octal integer
%x	hexadecimal integer
%u	unsigned decimal integer

Character

%c	single character
%s	string of characters

Real

%f	real - floating point
%e	real - floating point

Pointer

%p	Pointer - address

==

The format specifiers , when used with **scanf( )**, do not need any field width. When we are going to input a 2 digit integer we can simply use the statement

```
scanf("%d", num);
```

and not

```
scanf("%2d", num);
```

2.6 - Input and Output Using cin and cout

The C++ programming language includes additional capabilities that are used for input and for output, namely the objects, **cin** and **cout**.. In fact, many C++ programs are written using only **cin** and **cout** for input/output. The objects **cin** and **cout** are included in the new **iostream** library. This library was added to the language in an attempt to solve some of the problems with the standard I/O library functions such as **scanf( )** and **printf()**. We will compare **cin** and **cout** with **scanf( )** and **printf( )** and decide for ourselves whether the improvements were accomplished. The C++ language refers to **cin** and **cout** as **streams**. The stream object **cout** sends output to the standard output stream (as does the **printf()** function), and **cin** gets its input from the standard input stream (as does the **scanf()** function). In this section we will study how we can use **cin** and **cout** to do input and output in our programs.

As we have seen, stream output is accomplished by using **cout** with the **insertion** or **put to operator**, **<<**. For example, the statement

        cout << "Hello, World!\n";

writes the string "Hello, World!" to the screen followed by the newline (carriage return and linefeed) to the screen.

Output Manipulators

In order to format output using the **cout** stream we can use either output manipulators or member functions, whose declarations are contained in the header files, **iostream.h** and **iomanip.h** . The manipulator, **setw()**, is used to specify the width of a field. The manipulator, **setprecision()**, or the member function **precision()** can be used to specify the number of decimal places for real, floating point, output. We illustrate this with some examples:

        cout << setw(5) << 25;   _ _ _ 2 5

Integer output is right justified in the specified field.

        cout << setw(10) << "Hello";   _ _ _ _ _ H e l l o

String data is right justified in the specified field.

        cout << setw(5) << '$'; $ _ _ _ _

Character data is left justified in the specified field. This creates a problem when we are trying to print a specified number of blanks. Printing a single blank in a field of length 5 will not print 5 blanks. Try it! We can however accomplish what we want to do by printing a string of one character rather than a single character. The statement

        cout << setw(5) << "$";   _ _ _ _ $

does print the single character right justified in the field.

Formatting String Output

Let us see how we can use **cout** to center the heading **"Program #1"** on 80 columns. As was the case in the previous section, we need to print 35 blanks followed by the heading. We can print the 35 blanks with the statement

```
cout << setw(35) << " ";
```

and then print the heading with the statement

```
cout << "Program #1";
```

We can move the cursor to the beginning of the next line with the statement

```
cout << endl;
```

The newline manipulator, **endl**, is defined in the header file, **iostream.h**, and is used to output a carriage return/linefeed pair and to flush the output buffer.

As an alternative to the above, we can center the heading by right justifying it in a field width of 45 with the following:

```
cout << setw(45) << "Program #1" << endl;
```

Try this: Give the statement that will center the heading "CS 256" on 80 columns.

As we did using the **printf()** function in section 2.5, we will write the statements that will print the headings, **"Exam1"**, **"Exam2"**, and **"Exam3"** beginning in columns 20, 40, and 60 respectively. We can first print 19 blanks followed by the heading exam1 with the statements

```
cout << setw(19) << " ";          or          cout << setw(24) << "Exam1";
cout << "Exam1";
```

We then print 15 blanks followed by the heading Exam2 and 15 blanks followed by the heading Exam3 with the statements

```
cout << setw(15) << " ";    or    cout << setw(20) << "Exam2";
cout << "Exam2";                  cout << setw(20) << "Exam3";
cout << setw(15) << " ";          cout << endl;
cout << "Exam3";
cout << endl;
```

These statements can all be replaced with the single statements

```
        cout << setw(19) <<  " " << "Exam1" << setw(15) << " "
                << "Exam2" << setw(15) << " " << "Exam3" << endl;
```

                                or

```
        cout << setw(24) << "Exam1" << setw(20) << "Exam2"
                << setw(20) << "Exam3" << endl;
```

When we continue a statement on a new line we must be careful to break the statement where blanks do not affect the output. We would not want to break the statement by typing a **<Ret>** within a string .

Try this: Give the statements that will print the two column headings
             Month   Interest
    beginning in columns 10 and 30 respectively.

Blank Lines

In order to print blank lines we can use the newline character, **'\n'**, as we did with **printf()**, or we can use **endl**. In order to send a newline we can use either of the statements

```
        cout << '\n';
```

                or

```
        cout << endl;
```

Thus, we can print three blank lines, assuming that our cursor is at the beginning of a new line, with either of the statements

```
        cout << endl << endl << endl;
```

                or

```
        cout << "\n\n\n";
```

The character '\n' outputs a carriage return and a line feed; however, in addition to

55

the output of a carriage return and a line feed, **endl** also flushes the output buffer. For example, when we print the heading "Program #1" centered on 80 columns we can use the following to output the heading, move the cursor to the beginning of the next line and also flush the output buffer:

cout << setw(45) << "Program #1" << endl;

When we want to print a number of blank lines, we will normally use a string consisting of '\n' characters. For example, if we want to print six blank lines we will use the statement

cout << "\n\n\n\n\n\n";

Integer Data

Let us now look at the formatting of integer output.   For the integer data stored with the statements

int num1 = 76, num2 = 85, num3 = 92;

we can print the first data item in columns 22 and 23 with

cout << setw(21) << " " << num1;   or   cout << setw(23) << num1;

The data stored at **num2** and **num3** can be printed in columns 42, 43 and 62, 63 with the statements

cout << setw(20) << " " << num2;   or   cout << setw(22) << num2;
cout << setw(20) << " " << num3;   cout << setw(22) << num3;

We would then move the cursor to the beginning of a new line with the statement

cout << endl;

We can accomplish the above output with the single statement

cout << setw(23) << num1 << setw(22) << num2
        << setw(22) << num3 << endl;

Try this: Three digit integers are stored in the variables **num1** and **num2**. Write the statements to print the data in columns 30 -> 32 and 50 -> 52.

_____

_____

_____

_____

Real Data

In order to format real data we can use two of the **stream manipulators** that are available for use with **cout**. These are the **setw()** manipulator that we have used above and the **setprecision()** manipulator or the **precision( )** member function to specify the number of decimal places that will be printed. For example, the statement

```
printf("%5.2f", 79.26);
```

specifies a field of length 5 with 2 decimal places and would produce the following output:

```
79.26
```

This could be done using **cout**, **setw()**, and **setprecision()** as follows:

```
cout << setw(5) << setprecision(2) << 79.26;
```

If we use the member function, **precision( )**, in place of the stream manipulator, **setprecision( )**, then we would use the two statements:

```
cout.precision(2);
cout << setw(5) << 79.26;
```

Note the difference in how the member function, **precision( )**, is used with cout,

```
cout.precision(2);
```

and how the stream manipulator, **setprecision( )**, is used.

```
cout << setprecision(2);
```

Once either **setprecision()** or **precision( )** is used, the specified precision remains in affect until one of the two is used again. This is unlike the **setw()** manipulator that is used to specify a field width each time a data item is printed.

When we use **setprecision(0)** or **precision(0)**, the precision is set to the default number of decimal places, which is 5.

Suppose that we have real data stored with the statement

```
float exam1 = 79.5,  exam2 = 83.25,  exam3 = 90;
```

and we want to print this data in the format xx.xx beginning in columns 20, 40, and 60 respectively. The field is of length 5 and the precision is 2. Thus, **exam1** is printed with the statements

```
cout << setw(19) << " ";
cout << setw(5) << setprecision(2)  << exam1;
```

or

```
cout << setw(24) << setprecision(2) << exam1;
```

The data stored at **exam2** and **exam3** is then printed with the statements

```
cout << setw(15) << " ";
cout << setw(5) << exam2;
cout << setw(15) << " ";
cout << setw(5) << exam3 << endl;
```

or

```
cout << setw(20) << exam2 << setw(20) << exam3 << endl;
```

Note: The number of decimal places was set when we used **setprecision(2)** before we printed **exam1**. We do not have to use it again before we print either **exam2** or **exam3**.

This line of output could be printed with the single statement

```
cout << setw(24) << setprecision(2) << exam1
     << setw(20) << exam2 << setw(20) << exam3
     << endl;
```

Try this: Suppose that an amount of interest and an amount of money are stored in the variables, **interest** and **amount**. Write the statements that will print the data in the formats xx.xx and xxxx.xx beginning in columns 20 and 50 respectively.

_____
_____
_____
_____

Try this: Rewrite the above statements so that each of the data items is preceded by a $.

_____
_____
_____
_____

The Turbo C++ compiler does not always output real data in the format that we expect. Consider the following statements:

float exam1 = 92, exam2 = 85.3, exam3 = 85.25;

When we execute the following statement:

cout << setw(5) << setprecision(2) << exam1
    << setw(15) << setprecision(2) << exam2
    << setw(15) << setprecision(2) << exam3;

the following output occurs:

92 _ _ _ _ _ _ _ _ _ _ _ _ _ 85.3 _ _ _ _ _ _ _ _ _ _ _ 82.25

The compiler does not automatically print trailing zeros. In order to force the trailing zeros to be printed we can use either of the following statements:

cout.setf(ios::fixed);   or   cout << setiosflags(ios::fixed);

The first statement uses the <u>member function</u>, **setf( )**, and the second statement uses the <u>stream manipulator</u>, **setiosflags( )**. The use of this is illustrated with the following program.

```
//prog2_7.cpp Program to illustrate the use of the showpoint
//                    specified.
#include <iostream.h>
#include <iomanip.h>
int main( )
{
   cout << 79.0000 << endl
        << 79.9000 << endl
        << 79.9900 << endl;
   cout.setf(ios::showpoint);
   cout << 79.0000 << endl
        << 79.9000 << endl
        << 79.9900 << endl;
   return 0;
}
```

Output from this program will be the following:

```
79
79.9
79.99
79.000000
79.900000
79.990000
```

Another problem that we will encounter is when we want to print a larger floating point number in decimal format. Suppose we have the following floating point data stored at **amount** with the statement

float amount = 230000.95;

and we want to print this data in the same format. We would use the following statement:

cout << setw(9) << setprecision(2) << amount << endl;

However, the output

2.3000095e05

is not what we might expect. This is scientific notation and not the decimal notation that we want. In order to guarantee that we will get standard floating point output we can use one of the following statements in our program:

cout.setf(ios::showpoint);   or   cout << setiosflags(ios::showpoint);

60

This is illustrated in the following program.

```
//prog2_8.cpp Program to illustrate the use of the fixed
//                      format specified.
#include <iostream.h>
#include <iomanip.h>
int main( )
{
   float amount = 230000.95;
   cout << setw(9) << setprecision(2)
        << amount << endl;
   cout.setf(ios::fixed);
   cout << setw(9) << setprecision(2)
        << amount << endl;
   return 0;
}
```

Output from this program will be the following:

```
2.3e+05
230000.95
```

We can do both the **fixed** and **showpoint** with one statement using the | (or) operator. We would use either of the statements:

```
cout.setf(ios::fixed | ios::showpoint);
```
or
```
cout << setiosflags(ios::fixed | ios::showpoint);
```

When we are doing floating point output, with two decimal places, we will usually use one of the following sets of three statements.

member functions	stream manipulators
cout.setf(ios::showpoint);	cout << setiosflags(ios::showpoint);
cout.setf(ios::fixed);	cout << setiosflags(ios::fixed);
cout.precision(2);	cout << setprecision(2);

Showpoint and **fixed** are two of the several format flags that can be used with the **setf( )** member function and the **setiosflags( )** manipulator. The flags are used to get the output stream, **cout**, to print floating point data in a desired format. A list and description of the most often used format flags is given in Table 2.6.

Table 2.6: Format flags

==

Flag	Manual	Meaning
ios::showpoint	Always show the decimal point with a default of 6 decimal digits.	Do not resort to scientific notation for larger numbers
ios::showpos	Display a leading + sign when the number is positive.	
ios::fixed	Display up to 3 integer digits and 2 digits after the decimal point. For larger numeric data revert to scientific notation.	Always print the specified number of decimal places, even the trailing zeros.
ios::scientific	Use exponential notation for numeric data.	
ios::dec	Display in decimal format.	
ios::oct	Display in octal format.	
ios::hex	Display in hexadecimal format.	
ios::left	Left-justify output	
ios::right	Right-justify output	

==

The following program illustrates the use of the number system format flags.

```
//prog2_9.cpp Program to illustrate the use of the number
//              system format flags.
#include <iostream.h>
#include <iomanip.h>
int main( )
{
   cout << setiosflags(ios::dec) << 179 << endl
        << setiosflags(ios::oct) << 179 << endl
        << setiosflags(ios::hex) << 179 << endl;
   return 0;
}
```

Output from this program will be the following:

```
179
263
b3
```

In addition to using the conversion flags with the member function, **setiosflags( )**, we can also use three stream manipulators that are defined in **iostream.h**. These manipulators are **dec**, **oct**, and **hex**. The above output statement can be written using these manipulators as follows:

```
cout    << dec << 179 << endl
        << oct << 179 << endl
        << hex << 179 << endl;
```

Using these manipulators sets the conversion for all subsequent output statements until the conversion is changed by using another of the manipulators. This is not the case when we use the member function **setiosflags( )**.

Left Justification

Left justification of data can be done using the **ios::left** format flag. The statement

```
cout    << setiosflags(ios::left) << setw(10) << 76
        << setw(10) << 90
        << setw(10) << 82 << 67 << endl;
```

produces the following output

```
76_____90_____82_____67
```

We will need to use this justification in Chapter 6 when we want to print names left justified in a field of specified width.

Special Control Characters

We can ring the bell or print other special control characters using **cout** just as we did with **printf()**. The following statement would ring the bell.

```
cout << '\a';
```

Data Input

The C++ language has the stream **cin**, corresponding to **cout** for output, that is used for input, normally from the keyboard. It is easier to use than the input function **scanf()**, since it does not have to have any format specifiers. In order to input the real exam score from the keyboard and store the data at

```
float exam1;
```

we can use the statements

```
cout << "Input an exam score: ";
cin >> exam1;
```

> **Note:** The stream manipulator, **cin,** uses only the variable name, **exam1,** and does not need the address indicator, the **&** character. Remember that if we use **scanf()** to input the value for **exam1,** then we would have to use **&exam1** instead of just **exam1.**

The input stream, **cin,** uses blanks, tabs, or carriage returns to separate data on input. Thus, if we try to input a string using **cin,** we encounter the same problem that we had when we used **scanf()**. The following code:

```
char name[21];

cout << "Input your name: ";
cin >> name;
cout << "Your name is " << name << endl;
```

produces the following output

Your name is Linda

even though the input was

Input your name: <u>Linda Lee Easton</u>

We could partially solve the problem by using **gets()**, however **gets()** terminates the input only when the <Ret> is encountered and does not consider the amount of storage that has been allocated for the string. Thus, the user could type in more than the number of characters specified in the array declaration. This additional data could overwrite other data and cause disastrous results.

The member function **getline()** included with **cin** was written in order to handle this type of situation. The form of the **getline()** function is

```
cin.getline(array, length);
```

The first parameter is the array name that has been used to define the storage, and the second parameter is the <u>size</u> (in bytes) of the array. Thus, we would change the above code to the following:

```
cout << "Input your name: ";
cin.getline(name, 21);
cout << "Your name is " << name << endl;
```

The output from this code would now be the following:

```
Input your name: Linda Lee Easton
Your name is Linda Lee Easton
```

The notation that is used for this function looks different. However, it is standard notation for using the member functions of **objects**. The statement

```
cin.getline(name, 21);
```

tells the object **cin** that it is to use it's member function **getline()** to get a string of at most 20 characters and store it in the array **name.** The string is entered from the keyboard. Note that the second parameter is the size of the array and should be one more than the maximum length of the string that we want to store. (We will study objects and their member functions in detail in Chapter 11.)

We have seen how we can use some of the manipulators to format output using **cout**. The complete list of manipulators is included in the following table. Other manipulators will be explained as they are needed throughout the remainder of the text.

Table 2.7: Manipulators for cout and cin

Manipulator	cout/cin	Purpose
dec	cout/cin	decimal input/output
endl	cout	flushes output buffer and inserts CR/LF
ends	cout	inserts a null into a string
flush	cout	flushes output buffer
hex	cout/cin	hexadecimal output/input
oct	cout/cin	octal output/input
resetiosflags(long)	cout/cin	resets various format bits
setbase(int)	cout/cin	set base
setfill(int)	cout/cin	set fill character for field padding
setiosflags(long)	cout/cin	set various format bits
setprecision(int)	cout/cin	set precision floats to specified number of decimal places
setw(int)	cout/cin	sets the field width

Zero Fill

If we wish to pad with zeros rather than blanks we can place a 0 in front of the width in the **printf()** and use **setfill(0)** with **cout**. For example,

        int num = 25;

        printf("%010d", num);   or   cout << setw(10) << setfill(0) << num;

will produce the following output:

        0000000025

Printing Graphics Characters

As you may know, the standard **ASCII** character set uses only seven of the eight bits of a byte to code a character. Using seven of the eight bits gives a possible 128 characters which include the uppercase and lowercase letters, the digits from 0 to 9, punctuation characters, and control characters such as the linefeed and the backspace. When the IBM-PC came into existence, it was decided that all eight bits would be used which gives 256 possible characters. This character set is referred to as the **IBM ASCII** character set and includes graphics characters, foreign language symbols, and other special characters.

We have seen how we can print the standard ASCII characters using the function **printf( )** or the stream **cout**. Printing graphics and other nonstandard characters require a special approach. We know how to print certain special characters with a backslash escape sequence, however the graphics and nonstandard characters require the backslash followed by the number representing their character code. The number can be in either octal or hexadecimal notation. For example, the four graphics characters that represent the suits in a deck of cards have the following ASCII codes:

club	5	♣
diamond	4	♦
heart	3	♥
spade	6	♠

The program to print the name followed by the symbol, one per line using **printf( )**, would be the following:

```
// prog2_10.cpp Program to print the graphics characters
//                      for the four suits of a deck of cards.
#include <stdio.h>
int main( )
{
   printf("Clubs = \x5\n");
   printf("Diamonds = \x4\n");
   printf("Hearts = \x3\n");
   printf("Spades = \x6\n");
   return 0;
}
```

The same program using **cout** would be the following:

```
//Prog2_11.cpp Program to print the graphics characters
//                 for the four suits of a deck of cards using cout.
#include <iostream.h>
int main( )
{
   cout << "Clubs = " << "\x5" << endl
        << "Diamonds = " << "\x4" << endl
        << "Hearts = " << "\x3" << endl
        << "Spades = " << "\x6" << endl;
   return 0;
}
```

Try this: Write the program using **printf()** to output the open happy face character and the filled happy face character on the next line (in the IBM ASCII character set).

```
#include <stdio.h>
int main()
{
   printf(_____);
   printf(_____);
   return 0;
}
```

Try this: Write the same happy face program using **cout.**

```
#include <iostream.h>
int main()
{
   cout <<_____;
   return 0;
}
```

2.7 - Return Values

So far in our programs, we have been using functions such as **main()**, **printf()**, and **scanf()**. Without going into great detail concerning how to use functions you need to understand a little about function return values. If so desired we may cause a function to return some value. One possible use of this value is to determine the success or failure of the function. The general format for the three above mentioned functions is:

```
int main(void)
int printf(control-string, argument-list);
int scanf(control-string, argument-list);
```

The **int** in front of each of these functions specifies that the function is supposed to return an integer value to the code segment which called it. At the end of function **main( )** we have been including the statement

```
return 0;
```

The purpose of this statement was to return the integer value 0 when function **main( )** is completed. For function, **main( )** this value is returned to the operating system. It is common to return a value of 0 to mean that everything went OK in the program and that it terminated normally.

When using **printf()** the integer value returned is the number of characters successfully printed. We illustrate with a simple example:

```
int count;
count = printf("Hello, Jim");
printf("\n%d", count);
```

Output from this block of code was the following:

```
Hello, Jim
10
```

The 10 indicates that the entire string was printed.

The library function, **scanf()**, will return the integer number of input items that were successfully read, converted and saved in variables. A value equal to the constant **EOF** (defined in **stdio.h**) is returned if an end-of-file was encountered during the read operation. A value of 0 is returned, if no input items are read and stored.

In Chapter 4 we will write our own functions and we will learn how we can write functions that return data using the function name like we have illustrated with the above library functions.

2.8 - The C and C++ Operators

Now that you can write simple input/output programs let us look at some of the ways of manipulating data. One way of doing this is to use the standard C and C++ operators. We have already used various operators so that in this section we will summarize what we have been doing as well as discuss other operators that we will encounter throughout the sections in this text.

The Assignment Operator

If we are familiar with BASIC, then you will know that the equal sign (=) is used for both the assignment operator and to check for equality. When the Pascal programming language was developed, it used the := for assignment and the = to check for equality. The C and now the C++ programming language uses = for assignment and == to check for equality.

The assignment operator does just what it says that it will do. It assigns whatever is on the right to the variable that occurs on the left. For example:

```
int I;
I = 10;
```

assigns the value of 10 to the integer variable I. The statement:

```
I = I + 2;
```

would add the value of 2 to the current value of I, 10, and then assigns the new value, 12, to the variable I.

We will study the equality operator, ==, in Chapter 3.

The Arithmetic Operators

The C++ compiler recognizes a number of arithmetic operators that are the symbols that are used to perform multiplication, division, addition and subtraction. The most common ones are defined in Table 2.8.

Table 2.8: Arithmetic Operators

==

Operator	Action

==

Operator	Action
+	addition
-	subtraction
*	multiplication
/	real division
%	modulus division (integer remainder)

==

We use these operators to form expressions that are assigned to variables or to be printed. For example,

```
num1 = 20 - 35;
sum = exam1 + exam2 + exam3 + exam4;
average = (exam1 + exam2 + exama3 + exam4) / 4.0;
```

The statement

```
cout << 78 * 12;
```

will cause the Turbo C++ compiler to issue a warning message since we asked it to print the expression without the use of parentheses. We need to change the syntax to the following:

```
cout << (78 * 12);
```

Spaces around operators are not required. The following statements are equivalent

```
int_earned=amount*month_rate;
```

or

```
int_earned = amount * month_rate;
```

Note: We want to get in the habit of spacing around operators in statements and expressions in order to make them easier to read.

Since we use these arithmetic operators between two values, whether the values are numbers, variables, or a combination of both, then these operators are referred to as **binary operators**.

Addition operator: +

The **addition operator**, +, is used to add two values. For example:

```
int I;
I = 10 + 17;
```

Here the addition operator, +, combines the values of 10 and 17 to get 27. The 27 is then stored at the memory location labeled I. The addition operator is binary because it works on only two values at a time. In the example,

```
int j = 20;
j = j + 1;
```

the value 20 is stored at the integer storage location **j** and then the value of **j** is increased by 1 with the statement

```
j = j + 1;
```

so that the value stored at **j** is now 21.

Subtraction operator: -

The **subtraction operator**, - , does ordinary subtraction. The subtraction is performed, and then the result is assigned to the variable on the left by the assignment operator. An example of subtraction is the following:

```
int I;
I = 17 - 10;
```

The value 10 is subtracted from the value 17 and the result, 7, is stored in the memory location labeled I. Like addition, subtraction is a binary operator working on only two values at a time. Another example,

```
int I = 20;
I = I - 1;
```

The value 20 is assigned to I. Then the value 1 is subtracted from the value of 20 and the result 19 is assigned to I.

Multiplication Operator: *

Like addition and subtraction, the multiplication operator is a binary operator so that it acts on two values at a time and does ordinary multiplication . For example, the statements

```
int I;
I = 3 * 2;
```

perform the multiplication 3 * 2 and assign this product to I. The statement,

```
num = 25;
num = num * 2;
```

multiplies the value of **num** by 2, resulting in 2 * 25 = 50 and then assigns this new value to **num**. The statement

```
num_square = num * num;
```

can be used to compute the square of the value stored at **num**.

Division operator: /

The division operator is used to perform division, however, it is a little more complicated than multiplication. If division is performed using two integer values, then the result is an integer. For example, the following statements produce the indicated output:

```
cout << (20 / 4) << endl;                    5
cout << (82 / 5) << endl;                    16
cout << (84 / 11) << endl;                   7
```

If either of the values is real, (float, double, etc.), then the result is real. The following statements will produce the indicated output:

```
cout << setw(3) << setprecision(1)
     << (20 / 4.0) << endl;                  5.0

cout << setw(5) << setprecision(2)
     << (81.0  / 5) << endl;                 16.20
```

Thus, if we wish to perform division so that the result is real, then either the numerator, or the denominator, or both must be a **float, double,** etc. The following statements should compute the average:

```
int exam1 = 98, exam2 = 85, exam3 = 92;
float average;

average = (exam1 + exam2 + exam3) / 3;
cout << setw(5) << setprecision(2) << average
     << endl;
```

However, they do not produce the desired results. The value of

```
(exam1 + exam2 + exam3) / 3
```

73

is calculated as the integer value 91. Then, in order to assign this value to the float variable **average**, the 91 is converted to a float value. Thus, the output was the following:

91.00

Since each of the values on the right hand side of the statement is an integer, the result of the computation is again an integer that is then assigned to the float **average**. The computed integer value is 91. If we wish to leave the exam scores as integer variables, then we would want to use the following statement to compute the average.

average = (exam1 + exam2 + exam3) / 3.0;

or

average = (exam1 + exam2 + exam3) / float(3);

This will result in the desired result. The output will be the following:

91.67

Modulus operator: %

Whenever we do integer division, we obtain two values, the quotient and the remainder. For example, if we divide the integer 80 by the integer 11, the quotient is 7 and the remainder is 3.

$$
\begin{array}{r}
7 \\
11\overline{)80} \\
\underline{77} \\
3
\end{array}
$$

It is sometimes useful to obtain the remainder that occurs when we do integer division. For example, suppose that we know the number of months and that we want to compute the number of years and the number of remaining months. This is illustrated with the following program.

```
//prog2_12.cpp Program to illustrate the use of the
//              division operators.
#include <iostream.h>
int main( )
{
   int years, months, rem_months;
```

```
        cout << "Input the number of months: ";
        cin >> months;
        years = months / 12;
        rem_months = months % 12;
        cout <<  months << " months, is equal to "
             << years << " years and " << rem_ months
             << " months" << endl;
        return 0;
    }
```

Sample output from this program is the following:

```
            Input the number of months: 235
            235 months is equal to 19 years and 7 months
```

Try this: Finish the program that will compute the number of **hours**
and **minutes** for a given number of **minutes**.

```
        // prog2_13.cpp convert minutes to hours and minutes
        #include <iostream.h>
        #include <iomanip.h>
        int main( )
        {
          int hours, remaining, minutes;

          cout << "Enter the number of minutes: ";
          cin >> minutes;

          hours = _____
          remaining = _____

          cout << _____ << " minutes equals " << _____
               << " hours and " << _____ << " minutes " << endl;

              return 0;
        }
```

We will ask the reader to write and run this program as one of the exercises.

Operator Precedence

Computations with the operators, **+**, **-**, *****, **/**, and **%** are done in a certain order if we do not use parentheses. The operator precedence is given in Table 2.9.

Table 2.9: Operator Precedence

==

Operator	Operation
*, /, %	multiplication, division, integer remainder
+, -	addition, subtraction

==

The three multiplication and division operations are of higher priority than the two operations, addition and subtraction. When one or more operators on the same level occur in an expression, then the operations are performed from left to right. For example,

$$20 / 4 * 2$$

$$5 * 2$$

$$10$$

The same is true for + and -.

$$15 + 3 - 2$$

$$18 - 2$$

$$16$$

When an expression contains operators on different levels, all of the operations on the higher level are performed before any of the operations on the next lower level are performed.

$$20 / 4 + 8 \% 3 - 1$$
$$5 + 2 - 1$$
$$7 - 1$$
$$6$$

Try this: Show how each of the following is evaluated as we did in the above examples.

36 / * 2 % 4   _____

_____

_____

2 * 3 - 8 / 3   _____
                       _____
                       _____

15 % 11 - 3 - 4 * 5   _____
                       _____
                       _____
                       _____

> **Note:** A good programming practice is to not rely on the precedence of the operators to evaluate an expression. Use parentheses to clearly indicate the order in which an expression is to be evaluated.

For example, it is good programming practice to write the expression

>   2 * 3 - 8 / 3   as   (2 * 3) - (8 / 3)

and the expression

>   15 % 11 - 3 - 4 * 5   as   (15 % 11) - 3 - (4 * 5)

Unary operators

The **+** and **-** serve as signs or unary operators. This means that each of these operate on a single value only. The statement

>   I = -10;

stores the negative value, -10, in the memory location labeled I. The minus sign is used any time that we wish to store a negative literal. When we store a positive literal, the plus sign is optional. We can use either of the following:

>   days = 365;

>   or

>   days = +365;

We can use the unary operators with variables

increment = value * -factor;

This statement multiplies the data stored at **value** by the negative of the data stored at **factor**. The data stored at factor is not altered. If we had the declarations int value = 20; int factor = 5; then the statement would be evaluated as

increment = 20 * (-5);
            = -100;

the data stored at **value** is still 5. We can also use the unary minus operator to negate any mathematical expression. For example,

x1 = -(2*x - 3*y);

When consecutive operators are encountered in an expression then we must make sure to insert a space between them. For example,

value = amount - -expense;

It would be better to write the expression using parenthesis.

value = amount - (-expense);

We cannot write it using consecutive minus signs without a space.

value = amount -- expense;

The two minus signs, if written consecutively, would cause an entirely different result to be computed. The same would happen if we used two consecutive plus signs. We will see why this is the case in the next paragraph when we study the increment and decrement operators.

Increment and decrement operators: ++ and --

As we become more experienced as programmers, we will find that it is often necessary to increment of decrement a variable. When we **increment** a variable, we increase it's value by one and when we **decrement** a variable, we decrease it's value by one. The C and C++ languages provide an easy way to increase or decrease a variable by one. Either of the following increases the variable **x** by one.

```
        x++;

or                    (same as           x = x + 1;)

        ++x;
```

To decrease a variable by one we can use the -- operator and either of the statements

```
        x--;

or                    (same as           x = x - 1;)

        --x;
```

Depending on where it is being used, there may be a difference between preceding the variable with the operator and following the variable with the operator. In the following example, one is added to **x** after it's value has been printed.

```
        x = 4;
        cout << x++ << endl
         << x <<  endl;
```

Output was the following:

```
        4
        5
```

In the above example, x is initialized to 4. In the next statement, the value of x, 4, is printed and then the value of x is increased by 1. This value of x, 5, is then printed.

When we use the increment operator preceding the variable, then the value of the variable is increased by one before it is used. For example, the statements

```
        x = 4;
        cout << ++x << endl
            << x << endl;
```

produce the following output.

```
        5
        5
```

In this example, one is added to **x** before it is printed so that 5 is printed both times.

Try this: What is the output for each of the following:

```
x = 10;
y = ++x;
cout << x << endl;          _____
cout << y << endl;          _____
x = 10;
y = x++;
cout << x << endl;          _____
cout << y << endl;          _____
```

Compound Assignment Operators +=, -=, *=, /=, %=

When the beginning programmer first sees a statement like

```
I = I + 1;
```

it does not look quite right. Mathematically, there is no value of I for which I is equal to I + 1. However, we must remember that the statement is an assignment statement and not a statement of equality. Thus, the expression on the right is evaluated first. Then, the value is assigned to the variable on the left.

When writing programs, we frequently need to change the value of a variable by a given amount. For example,

```
num2 = num2 + 2;
```

    or

```
amount = amount + int_earned;
```

The C and C++ programming languages have added operators, called **compound assignment operators**, that can be used to accomplish the same results.. The above statements would be written using the += operator (the two symbols must be written without a space) We would write

```
num2 = num2 + 2;                        as              num2 += 2;
```

        and

amount = amount + int_earned;   as   amount += int_earned;

The other compound operators are illustrated with the following examples.

num1 = num1 - 3;   num1 -= 3;

num2 = num2 * 2;   num2 *= 2;

num3 = num3 / 5;   num3 /= 5;

num4 = num4 % 2;   num4 %= 2;

Try this: Rewrite each of the following so that they use the compound operators.

num7 = num7 - 7;   _____

rate = rate / 12;   _____

months = months % 12;   _____

Try this: Rewrite each of the following so that they use the standard arithmetic operators.

sum -= 5;   _____

minutes %= 60;   _____

interest += int_earned;   _____

power *= power;   _____

Operator Precedence Again

When we include the unary operators, the increment and decrement operators, and the compound operators in the precedence table then we have the following.

Table 2.9 Operator Precedence

===

Operator	Operation

===

unary +, -	unary
++, --	increment, decrement
*, /, %	multiplication, division
	integer remainder
+, -	addition, subtraction
+=, -=, *=, /=, %=	compound operators

===

Since the compound operators are on a precedence level lower than the math operators, we must be careful. The statement

cost = 2 * cost + labor - contribution;

is not the same as

cost *= 2 + labor - contribution;

The *= would be done after the

2 + labor - contribution

was evaluated so that the second statement is the same as the statement

cost = cost * (2 + labor - contribution);

Try this: Rewrite each of the following using standard arithmetic operators

num1 += 2 * num2;   _____

num3 *= num4 % 5;   _____

2.9 - Converting C to C++

One of the tasks that we will face as programmers is to convert programs that are written in C to programs in C++. In this section, we will begin to explore this process by reviewing how we convert input and output statements that have been written in C to statements in C++. As we have seen, the following statement prints the headings "Month", "Interest Earned", and "Amount", in columns 10, 30, and 60 respectively.

```
printf("%14s%30s%21s\n", "Month", "Interest Earned", "Amount");
```

We could use C++'s new capabilities by simply replacing **printf( )** with **cout** and using the **setw( )** function in place of the **%s** string format specifier. We would use the following statement:

```
cout << setw(14) << "Month"
     << setw(30) << "Interest Earned"
     << setw(21) << "Amount" << endl;
```

Suppose that we have data stored in the variables, **month**, **intearned**, and **amount**. The variable **month** is an integer and the other two variables are real. The data stored in these variables is printed in the following format

xx	$xx.xx	$xxxx.xx
10	30	60

with this statement in C.

```
printf("%11d%19c%5.2f%25c%7.2f\n", month, '$', intearned, '$', amount);
```

In order to use **cout**, we will make use of the format member functions, **precision( )** and **setf( )**. We will also use the specifier **fixed** to guarantee that the decimal places are printed even if they are zero and **showpoint** to guarantee that the number will be printed in decimal rather than defaulting to scientific notation. The statements that we will use are the following:

```
cout.precision(2);
cout.setf(ios::showpoint);
cout.setf(ios::fixed);
cout << setw(11) << month
     << setw(19) << "$" << setw(5) << intearned
     << setw(25) << "$" << setw(7) << amount << endl;
```

We recall that we use a string "$" rather that the single character '$' since single characters are not right justified in the specified field. We could also use the stream manipulator functions **setprecision( )** and **setiosflags( )** and use the following block of code.

```
cout << setprecision(2) << setiosflags(ios::fixed | ios :: showpoint)
     << setw(11) << month << setw(19) << "$"
     << setw(5) << intearned << setw(25) << "$"
     << amount << endl;
```

The following block of code prints messages to the user so that an amount of money, a

```
```

yearly interest rate and a number of years can be input from the keyboard.

```
printf("Input the amount to invest: );
scanf("%f", &amount);
printf("Input the yearly rate, x.x for x.x%: ");
scanf("%f", &rate);
printf("Input the number of years: ");
scanf("%d", &years);
```

This block of code is easily converted by replacing **printf( )** with **cout** and **scanf()** with **cin**. The code would be rewritten as follows:

```
cout << "Input the amount to invest: ";
cin >> amount;
cout <<"Input the yearly rate, x.x for x.x%: ";
cin >> rate;
cout << "Input the number of years: ";
cin >> years;
```

Try this: The following statement prints the headings "Exam1", "Exam2" "Exam3", and "Average" in the specified columns. Convert the statement to C++.

```
printf("%14s%15s%15s%17s\n", "Exam1", "Exam2"
        "Exam3", "Average");
```

cout << _____

_____

_____

Illustrate where the headings are printed.

_____

Try this: The following statement prints real data stored in the variables **exam1**, **exam2**, **exam3**, and **average** in the specified columns. Convert by using **cout.**.

```
printf("%13.1f%15.1%15.1%16.2\n", exam1, exam2, exam3, average);
```

84

```
cout    _____
        _____
        _____
        _____
        _____
```

Illustrate how the data is printed out and in which columns.

_____

Try this: The following block of code allows the user to input 3 exam scores from the keyboard. Convert by using **cout** and **cin**.

```
printf("Input an exam score: ");
scanf("%f", &exam1);
printf("Input a second exam score: ");
scanf("%f", &exam2);
printf("Input a third exam score: ");
scanf("%f", &exam3);

cout << _____
        _____
        _____
        _____
        _____
        _____
```

2.10 - Summary

In this very important chapter we began our investigation of some of the various parts of C and C++ programming. We discussed the use of various header files such as **stdio.h, iostream.h** and **iomanip.h**. Following this, we covered two different ways of defining constants in a program (by using **#define** and by using **const**).

We were then exposed to the simple data types in C and C++ (**int, float,** and **char**) and also the variations of these data types (using **long, short, double, signed,** and **unsigned).** After discussing the various data types, we learned how to declare and, also, initialize variables of these simple data types.

Then, came a study of some of the very important input/output capabilities in C and C++. This included the use of the traditional C functions: **printf(),** for output and **scanf()** for input. Next, we investigated the new **cout** and **cin** output and input objects which are now available in C++. We discussed how to format output using **printf()** and the various output format specifiers, **%d, %f, %c,** and **%s.** We discussed how to center headings and how to print column headings beginning in specific columns. We also discussed how we can print integer data in a specified number of columns and real data with a specified number of decimal places.

We learned how to use the standard arithmetic operators that are available in both C and C++. Finally, we looked at some of the special operators: the increment, decrement, and compound operators.

We discussed how we can convert input and output statements that have been written in C to C++.

2.11 - Questions

2.1   What characters can we use to define a variable in a C++ program?

2.2   What characters can be used to begin a variable name?

2.3   How many characters can we use in a variable name and how many are significant?

2.4   What is the **#include** directive used for? Give an example.

2.5   What is the **#define** directive used for? Give an example.

2.6   What is a simple data type?

2.7   What are the simple data types in C/C++?

2.8   How are the simple data types declared?

2.9   What extensions can be added to the simple data type declarations?

2.10   What is the difference between an **int** variable and an **unsigned int** variable?

2.11   Which header file contains the definitions for the **printf( )** and **scanf( )** functions?

2.12   Which header file contains the definitions for the stream operators **cin** and **cout**?

2.13 Which header file contains the definitions for the stream manipulators **setprecision( )** and **setw( )**?

2.14 What are the two ways that we can send a CR and a LF to the screen using **cout**?

2.15 How many bytes are set aside for variables of each of the following data types?

  a. char b. integer c. float d. double

2.16 When we are dealing with **int** data, what is the maximum value that we can use? What about **long int**?

2.17 What is meant by a reserved word in a programming language?

2.18 How do we tell the C++ programming language that the number 23 is to be considered as each of the following:

  a. decimal b. octal c. hexadecimal

2.19 What is the assignment operator in C++? What operator is used for equality?

2.20 What do we mean when we talk about the standard ASCII character set? What characters are printable in this set?

2.21 What do we mean when we talk about the IBM ASCII character set? What characters are printable in this set?

2.22 How do we print the diamond character using **printf( )**?

2.23 How do we print the diamond character using **cout**?

2.24 What are the three different statements that we can use to add 1 to the variable I?

2.12 - Exercises

2.1 Give the statements needed to define **int_num1** as an integer variable, **num2** as a **float** variable, **num2** as a **double** variable, and **ch** as a character variable.

2.2 Give statements to define integer variables **num1** and **num2** and initialize them to zero.

2.3 Give the statement to define **PI** as the real constant 3.14. Use the **define** directive.

2.4 Give the C++ statement to define **PI** as a real constant 3.14.

2.5 If **ch** is a character variable, **num1** is integer, **num2** is real, and **num3** is **double**, what is the data type of each of the following:

a. ch + num1   b. ch + num2   c. ch + num3
d. num1 + num2   f. num1 + num3   g. num2 + num3

2.6 Give the statement to print the integer data stored in **num** in a 10 place field preceded by zero's. Use **printf( )**.

2.7 Give the statement to print the integer data stored in **num** in a 10 place field preceded by zero's, using **cout**.

2.8 Give the statement to print the integer data stored in **num** in a 10 place field preceded by *'s, using **printf( )**.

2.9 Give the statement to print the integer data stored in **num** in a 10 place field preceded by *'s, using **cout**.

2.10 Give the statements to print a prompt message to the screen and input an age. Use **printf( )** and **scanf( )**.

2.11 Give the statements to print a prompt message to the screen and then input your hourly wage. Use **printf( )** and **scanf( )**.

2.12 Give the statements to print a prompt message to the screen and then input your first name. Use **printf( )** and **scanf( )**.

2.13 Give the statements to print a prompt message to the screen and then input your entire name. Use **printf()** and **gets( )**.

2.14 Same as 2.10 only use **cin** and **cout**.

2.15 Same as 2.11 only use **cin** and **cout**.

2.16 Same as 2.12 only use **cin** and **cout**.

2.17 Same as 2.13 only use **cout** and **cin.getline( )**.

2.18 Give the statement using **printf( )** to print the heading **Indiana State University** centered on 80 columns.

2.19 Give the statement using **printf( )** to print the heading **Program #1** centered on 80 columns.

2.20 Give the statement using **cout** to print the heading **Indiana State University** centered on 80 columns.

2.21 Give the statement using **cout** to print the heading **Program #1** centered on 80 columns.

2.22 Give the statements that will print the headings **Exam1**, **Exam2**, **Exam3**, and **Exam4** beginning in columns 10, 25, 40, and 55 respectively. Use **printf( )**.

2.23 Give the statements to print the headings from 2.22 in the same columns using **cout**.

2.24 Give the statement to print three blank lines using **printf( )**.

2.25 Give the statement to print three blank lines using **cout**.

2.26 Give the statements to ring the bell using **printf( )** and **cout**.

2.27 A real variable **num** has data stored. Give the statement using **printf( )** to print the data in the format xxx.xx beginning in column 25.

2.28 Do exercise 2.27 using **cout**.

2.29 The variables **exam1, exam2, exam3**, and **exam4** have data that is to be printed in the format xx.xx beginning in columns 10, 25, 40, and 55 respectively. Give the statements using **printf( )** that will produce this output.

2.30 Do exercise 2.29 using **cout**.

2.31 An employee works for Indiana State University and is paid $6.50 per hour for the first 40 hours per week and time-and-a-half for every hour over 40 hours. Write a program that will allow the user to input the number of hours worked per week and will compute and print out the weekly salary.

2.32   Write each of the following as C++ statements.

a. The area of a circle is equal to PI times the radius squared.

b. $y = \dfrac{x - 1}{x + 2}$

c. $y = \dfrac{x^2 - 2x + 1}{x + 5}$

d. r = 1/r1 + 1/r2

2.33   Write a program that will allow the user to input the radius of a circle from the keyboard and compute and print out the circumference and the area of the circle. Declare **PI** as the constant 3.14159 and use the formulas Area = PI * R^2 and Cir = 2*PI*R.

2.34   Write a program that will compute and print out the first five powers of a positive integer that is input from the keyboard. If the user inputs 3, then the output would be
   3 raised to the first power is 3
   3 raised to the second power is 9
   3 raised to the third power is 27

2.35   Write a program that will allow the user to input any two positive integers. The program should compute and print out the quotient and the remainder when the first is divided by the second. The output would be
   Input an integer: 35
   Input a divisor: 4
   The quotient = 8
   The remainder = 3

2.36   Write a program that will allow the user to input a number of minutes. The program will compute and print out the number of hours and remaining minutes.

2.37   Write a program that will allow the user to input a number of seconds. The program will compute and print out the number of hours, minutes, and remaining seconds.

CHAPTER 3

Program Control Structures

3.1 Introduction

In the first two chapters, the programs involved mainly sequential processing. That is, program statements were performed in order, one after the other, until the end of the program. Frequently, it is useful to repeat a block of code for a desired number of times or until a condition is met. Most languages have **programming structures** that allow programs to repeat a block of statements. These structures are also called **control structures** and include the **for loop**, the **while ... do**, and the **do ... while**. We will refer to these structures as **loops**. It is also useful to be able to execute one block if a given condition is true. This can be done with the **if** structure. If we wish to execute one of two blocks of code based on a given condition, then we can use the **if ... else** structure, and the condition is evaluated to determine which block of code to execute. Each of these structures is introduced in this chapter. In order to use these structures, we must understand the use of the logical and relational operators that are used to set up test conditions for these programming structures.

After completing this chapter, the student should be able to

1. use the relational operators to set up logical expressions as test conditions.

2. use the relational operators to combine logical expressions.

3. use the **for loop** to execute a block of code a given number of times.

4. use the **while ... do** and **do ... while** loops to execute a block of code until a given condition is met.

5. use the **if...then...else** structure to execute one block of code or another based on a given condition.

6. use the **break** and **continue** statements to alter normal processing of the loops.

7. understand how to use the **conditional operator, ?,** to write a short version of an **if ... else** statement.

8.   understand how to use the **switch - case** structure to simplify code involving nested **if...then...else** statements.

3.2 - Relational Operators

Relational operators permit the comparison of two values or expressions. They are used to form expressions that can be evaluated as either true or false. These are the expressions that are used as test conditions for the **for loop**, the **while...do**, the **do...while**, and the **if...then...else** structures. Expressions that can be evaluated as true or false are called **logical** or **boolean expressions**. The relational operators are listed in Table 3.1.

Table 3.1 Relational operators

Operator	Meaning	Example
<	less than	num < 2
>	greater than	cost > 100.00
==	equal to	age == 50
<=	less than or equal to	size <= 6.0
>=	greater than or equal to	temp >= 72
!=	not equal to	age != 25

Notice that equality in C++ is done using the operator **==** while assignment is done with the operator **=**. This is an important distinction and may be easily confused by the beginning programmer. BASIC uses the operator, **=,** for both equality and assignment, while Pascal uses the operator, **=,** for equality and the operator, **:=,** for assignment. In addition, Pascal uses the operator, **<>,** for not equal while C++ uses the operator **!=.**

It is important to note that C++ does <u>not</u> support a boolean data type; integer variables are used instead. The relational operators compare two values or expressions and return a value of either 1 or 0. Like all C++ expressions, relational expressions are evaluated to yield a numerical result. In the case of relational expressions, the value of the expression can only yield an integer value of 1 or 0. A condition that the C++ compiler would consider as true evaluates to an integer value of 1, and a false condition evaluates to an integer value of 0. However, if C++ encounters an expression that evaluates to some other value, it will consider a 0 value as false and any non-zero value as true. We illustrate these two ideas with two examples.

```cpp
// program 3_1.cpp - Program to print values for true and false
#include <iostream.h>
int main()
{
   int true, false;
   true = (10 > 2);
   false = (10 < 2);
   cout << "true = " << true << ", false = "
        << false << endl;
   return 0;
}
```

Output from this program was the following.

true = 1, false = 0

This shows that C++ evaluates a false expression as 0 and a true expression as 1.

In C++, the value of a relational expression is not as important as the way the expression is used in a program and the way that C++ interprets this expression. In the examples that follow you will see that C++ interprets a zero value as false and any non-zero value as true. Without spending time on the workings of the **while loop** we can illustrate this with the following program. The while loop is discussed in detail in section 3.6

```cpp
// prog3_2  - Program to test values for true and false
#include <iostream.h>
int main()
{
   int I = 2;
   while (I)            // while I != 0
   {
      cout << I << endl;
      I--;
   } // end while
   return 0;
}
```

While the value of the variable I is not 0, the value for I is printed and I is decremented by 1. When the value of I reaches 0, the loop ends. The first time through the loop I = 2 so that this value is printed and I is decremented by 1 with the statement I--;. The **while(I)** is tested again with the value of I being 1. This value is printed, I is decremented by 1 and the **while** condition is again tested only this time the value of I is 0. Since the value of I is zero, the condition is false and the loop is exited. The following is the output from this program.

In C and in C++ it is common practice to define constant variables **TRUE** and **FALSE** using the **#define** directive or the **const** variable declaration. As you know from chapter 2, caps are commonly used to define constants since this increases the readability of the program code. The constants can be defined with either of the sets of statements

```
#define FALSE 0                    or          const int FALSE = 0;
#define TRUE  !FALSE                            const int TRUE = !FALSE;
```

3.3 - Logical Operators

The C++ language recognizes three logical operators. The symbol **&&** is used for the **AND** operator, the symbol **||** is used for the **OR** operator, and the symbol **!** is used for the **NOT** operator. These operators are used to combine logical expressions to form an expression that is again a logical expression. Logical expressions that involve one or more logical operators are called **compound logical expressions**.

The following truth tables show how these logical operators are evaluated. In each table, **p** and **q** represent logical expressions having a value of 1 for true and 0 for false.

Table 3.2 logical operator truth tables
================================
&& - AND
========================

p	q	p && q
1	1	1
1	0	0
0	1	0
0	0	0
========================

|| - OR

p	q	p || q
1	1	1
1	0	1
0	1	1
0	0	0

! - NOT

p	!p
1	0
0	1

We can see that **p && q** is true only if both p and q are true, while **p || q** is true if either p or q is true.

Given the above tables it is possible to use statements and establish conditions that involve **compound logical expressions**. Suppose that we want an expression that is true if **cost** is greater than 1000.00 and **number** is less than or equal to 95. You would write the expression as

(cost > 1000.00) && (number <= 95)

or as

cost > 1000.00 && number <= 95

Try this: Write an expression to determine whether **age** is between 21 and 63.

In C++, the parentheses are not really required. However, they will improve the readability of the code. In some languages, such as Pascal, the parentheses are required.

If we want an expression that is true if either **cost** is greater than 1000.00 or **number** is less than or equal to 95, then we would use the following expression.

(cost > 1000.00) || (number <= 95)

Try this: Write an expression to determine whether **age** is less than 21 or greater than 63.

Suppose that we have the following declarations

    int num1 = 10, num2 = 2, num3 = 5;

then, each of the following expressions is valid.

    num1 <= num2
    (num1 / num2) > num3
    ((num1 * num2) == num3) && ((num1 - num3) > num2)

They would be evaluated as follows:

    num1 <= num2   num1 / num2 > num3
    10 <= 2   10 / 2   >   5
    false   5 > 5
                       false

    (num1 * num2 == num3) && (num1 - num3 > num2)
    (20 == 5) && (5 > 2)
    false && true
    false

Try this: State why each of the following is not a valid expression and write the correct version.

    num1 =< num2   _____
                                _____

    num2 !== num1   _____
                                _____

    (num3 > num2) & (num1 > 5) _____
                                _____

    Before we use the relational and logical operators, we need to take another look at the precedence table that includes the new operators that we have just introduced. This table combines the arithmetic operators with the relational and logical operators and shows their precedence in high to low order.

Table 3.3 Operator precedence

Operator			Associativity
*	/	%	L - R
+	-		L - R
< >	<=	>=	L - R
==	!=		L - R
&&			L - R
||			L - R

The way that precedence has been established in C++ allows us to write logical expressions as we did above, for example

num1 / num2 > num3

If we write the third example without the use of parentheses, we should be able to see that this will yield the same value. It is not as easy to evaluate and we certainly do not want to have to refer to the table every time that we write a logical expression.

num1 * num2 == num3 && num1 - num3 > num2

> **Note:** We will always use parentheses in order to make each expression clearly indicate the order in which the expression is to be evaluated.

We would normally write the previous expression as follows:

((num1 * num2) == num3) && ((num1 - num3) > num2))

When the C++ compiler evaluates a compound logical expression like

(X <= 5) && (Y >= 7)

it uses what is called a **short-circuit evaluation**. This means that only enough of the expression is evaluated to determine whether the expression is true or false and then the evaluation stops. Given the expression (A && B), if A is false, then the entire expression is false regardless of the true or false value of B. Similarly, given the expression (A || B), if A is true, then the entire expression is true regardless of the value of B. In both cases the C++ compiler would not evaluate the expression B.

Expressions and Statements

Up to this point we have been using expressions and statements but have not defined them nor looked at the difference between them. An **expression** is any valid combination of constants, operators, and variables. Every expression results in a value. Some examples of expressions are as follows.

```
10 + 15
I * (a1 + b * 2)/15
p = 5 + 3
a++
```

As we have seen, expressions can be combined using the relational and/or logical operators to form **logical expressions**. These expressions return a value of true or false.

```
(10 + 15) || (a * b)
(a + b) && (c + d)
```

Each expression has a value, but expressions do not cause action in a program. An action is caused by a statement. A **statement** is an order for a program to do something. A statement must end with a semicolon. If we consider the following

```
I = 10
I = 10;
```

then the first I = 10 is an expression and may not stand alone while I = 10; is a statement and assigns the value of 10 to the variable I.

3.4 - The For Loop

The **for loop** is one of the programming structures that we can use to execute a block of code a given number of times. The following is the general form of the **for loop**.

```
for (initialization; condition; update expression) {
    statement1;
    statement2;
    statement3;
        .
        .
} // end for
```

In Chapter 1, we considered the following simple program that will print the integers 0 --> 9, one per line.

```cpp
// prog3_3.cpp
#include <iostream.h>
int main()
{
    int I;
    for(I = 0; I < 10; I++)
        cout << I << endl;
    // end for
    return 0;
}
```

In this example, the **for loop** allows us to initialize the variable I to 0, **(I = 0)**, test the condition **(I < 10)**, and then increment the value of I, **(I++)**, each time through the loop. The parentheses following the keyword **for** contain what is called the "for loop expression". The loop expression is divided into three separate expressions separated by semicolons. The three expressions are called the "initialize expression", **I = 0**, the "test expression", **I < 10**, and the "update expression", **I++**. Lets follow the execution of the loop, as it is described with the following figure.

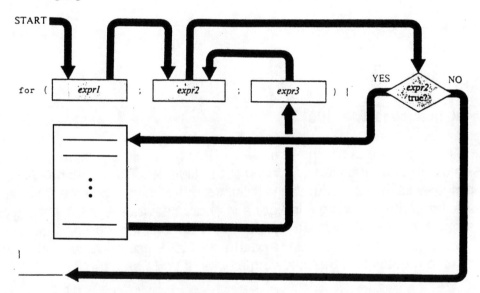

First, the initialization expression is executed and the integer variable I is set to 0. Then, the test condition is examined; that is, the value of I is compared to 10. If the value of I is less than 10, then the body of the loop is executed. In this example, the value of I is printed followed by a carriage return and a line feed. After the body of the loop has been executed, the update expression, **I++**, is executed, increasing the value of I by 1. The test condition is again checked and the process continues. This process continues until the test condition is false. In this example, until I is equal to or greater than 10.

If the **for loop** has more than one statement in the body of the loop, then these statements must be enclosed by using the braces, **{** and **}**. If the braces are not used, then the loop is terminated with the semicolon at the end of a single statement. We illustrate this with another example. This example computes and prints out the first 20 positive integers and their squares.

```cpp
// prog3_4.cpp Program to print out the first 20
//  positive integers and their squares
#include <iostream.h>
int main()
{
   int num, numsq;
   for (num = 1; num <= 20; num++)
   {
     numsq = num * num;
     cout << "num = " << num;
     cout << " num squared = " << numsq << endl;
   } // end for
   return 0;
}
```

Output from this program is the following.

```
num = 1 num squared = 1
num = 2 num squared = 4
               .
.num = 20 num squared = 400
```

The next example prints out the standard ASCII printable characters one per line. The printable characters are the blank, ' ', through the tilde, '~'. The blank has ASCII code 32 and the tilde has ASCII code 126. We will illustrate the flexibility of the C++ language by using a character variable with both integer and character values. In C++, the type **char** is treated as a one byte integer. We do not need any special function or code to convert between the ASCII code for the character and the character itself. We will ask the reader to write programs to test each of the following blocks of code as exercises.

```cpp
char ch;                              char ch;
for(ch = 32; ch <= 126; ch++)         for(ch = ' '; ch <= '~'; ch++)
   cout << ch << endl;                   cout << ch << endl;
// end for                            // end for
```

Each of the above generates the same output. However, since a variable of type **char** is treated as a one byte integer, we must be careful. If we were to write the following block of code,

```cpp
char ch;
for(ch = 32; ch <= 127; ch++)
```

```
        cout << ch << endl;
    // end for
```

the output would not be what we might expect. When **ch** is set to the value of 127, and **ch** is 8-bits, we have 127 = 01111111 binary. When this value is incremented, we get 10000000 which is considered to be a negative integer. Thus, the value of **ch** is less than 127 and we have an infinite loop. Anytime that the high-bit is set (1), then the integer value becomes a negative integer value. In order to avoid this problem we can use **unsigned char** rather than **char**. This allows us to use all 8-bits and use integer values of 0 through 255 as values for our variable. The following block of code would yield the desired results.

```
        unsigned char ch;
        for (ch = 32; ch <= 127; ch++)
            cout << ch << endl;
        // end for
```

Study these two different blocks of code to make sure that you understand exactly what each is doing.

In order to illustrate a common programming error that occurs using the **for loop**, consider the following program. What will be the output?

Fix it:
```
    // prog3_5.cpp
    #include <iostream.h>
    int main()
    {
        int num2, I;
        for(I = 1; I <= 10; I++);
        {
            num2 = 2 * I;
            cout << num2 << endl;
        } // end for
        return 0;
    }
```

_____

_____

_____

_____

_____

We would first expect the output to consist of a list of the first 10 multiples of 2, one per line. However, the only thing that is output to the screen is the following.

    22

The semicolon, ;, at the end of the loop expression causes the body of the loop to consist of no statements. Therefore, what we intended as the body of the loop is only executed one time. Since the value of **I** is 11 when the test expression is false, we get the one value of 22 output to the screen.

There is another feature of C++ that we can illustrate with the above example. In C++ you can wait to define the type of the variable until it is first used. We can define the variable **I** to be of type **int** in the initialization portion of the **for loop**. Thus, the loop statement could be written as

```
for (int I = 1; I <= 10; I++)
```

The complete program could then be written as follows.

```
// prog3_6.cpp
#include <iostream.h>
int main()
{
  int num2;
  for (int I = 1; I <= 10; I++)
  {
    num2 = 2*I;
    cout << num2 << endl;
  } // end for
  return 0;
}
```

Try this: Write the block of code, using a for-loop, to compute and print the first 15 multiples of 3, one per line.

```
for (_____
{

    _____
    _____
} // end for
```

We now consider a more complicated example. We want to write a Savings Account Program that will do the following. It will allow the user to input an amount of money, an interest rate, and a number of years. It will compute the monthly interest rate and the number of months. The program should print out a table showing the month, the amount of interest earned during that month, and the new amount in the account at the end of each month assuming that the interest is compounded monthly. The program should print out a main heading centered on 80 columns with appropriate column headings and formatted output. It should then print a summary showing amount, interest rate, years, and final amount. An outline for this program would be the following:

Input Data
   amount, intrate, years

Compute monthly interest rate and number of months
   mrate, months

Save amount for summary
   oldamount

Print Headings
   Main heading
   Column headings
        Month,   Interest,   Amount

Print Table & Compute the Final Amount
   For I = 1 to months
        Compute Interest Earned
        Compute new amount in account
        Print month, intearned, and amount
   End-For

Print Summary
   oldamount
   intrate
   years
   amount in account

If the heading for the program is "Second National Bank", then since the string is 20 characters long, it can be centered with the statement

        cout << setw(50) << "Second National Bank" << endl;

As we have seen, this statement prints 30 blanks followed by the heading. The statement to print the column headings "Month", "Interest", and "Amount" beginning in columns 10, 35, and 65 respectively, would be the following:

        cout << setw(14) << "Month"
              << setw(28) << "Interest"
              << setw(29) << "Amount" << endl;

In order to print the values of **month**, **intearned,** and **amount** in the formats, xx, $xx.xx, and $xxxx.xx beginning in columns 12, 35, and 65 respectively we can use the statement

```
cout << setw(13) << month
        << setw(23) << "$" << setw(5) <<  intearned
        << setw(24) << "$" << setw(8) <<  amount
        << endl;
```

We are assuming that we have set the precision at 2. As we discussed in Chapter 2, in order to guarantee that we will have the desired output format when we use **cout**, we have to use two statements to set the output flags for this output stream. The first statement is

cout.setf(ios::fixed);

that is used to guarantee that trailing zeros will be printed. The second statement is

cout.setf(ios::showpoint);

that is used so that the output will always be in decimal format and will not default to scientific notation when the value gets large. In addition, since we are printing monetary values, we will want two decimal places so that we will want to use a third statement

cout.precision(2);

The statements that will compute the monthly interest rate and the number of months are the following:

```
mrate = rate / 12;
months = years * 12;
```

We are assuming that the user will input 0.05 for 5%. We will make this instruction part of the message that we print to the screen.

The statements to print the summary would be the following:

```
cout << "Amount = $" << setw(8) << oldamount << endl;
cout << "Years = " << years << endl;
cout << "Interest rate = " << setw(4) << rate * 100
        << '%' << endl;
cout << "Final amount =  $" << setw(8)  << amount << endl;
```

The complete program is the following.

```
// prog3_7.cpp - Savings Account Program
// Program to print a table showing the month, the interest earned, and the
// new amount at the end of each month. The amount, the number of years,
```

```cpp
// and the yearly interest rate are to be input by the user.
#include <iostream.h>
#include <iomanip.h>
#include <conio.h>
int main()
{
    int years, months;
    float rate, mrate, amount, oldamount, intearned;
// Input the data
    clrscr( );
    cout << "Input the amount of money: ";
    cin >> amount;
    cout << "Input the number of years: ";
    cin >> years;
    cout << "Input the interest rate, 0.05 for 5% : ";
    cin >> rate;
// Compute monthly rate,  number of months, and save amount
    mrate = rate / 12;
    months = years * 12;
    oldamount = amount;
// Print headings
    clrscr();
    cout << setw(50) << "Second National Bank" << endl;
    cout << endl << endl;
    cout << setw(15) << "Month"
            << setw(28) << "Interest"
            << setw(29) << "Amount" << endl;
// Compute interest earned, new amount & print out the table
    cout.setf(ios::fixed);                  // print trailing zeros
    cout.setf(ios::showpoint);              // print in decimal
    cout.precision(2);                      // print two decimal places
    for( int I = 1; I <= months; I++) {
        intearned = amount * mrate;
        amount = amount + intearned;        // or amount += intearned
        cout << setw(13) << I                // I is current month
            << setw(23) << "$"
            << setw(5) << intearned
            << setw(24) << "$"
            << setw(8) << amount
            << endl;
    } // end for
// Print Summary
    cout << endl << endl;
    cout << "Amount =  $" << setw(8) << oldamount << endl;
    cout << "Years = " << years << endl;
```

```
        cout << "Interest rate =  " << setw( 4) << rate * 100
            << '%' << endl;
        cout << "Final amount = $" << setw(8) << amount << endl;
        return 0;
    }
```

Output from a run of this program with **amount** = 1000.00, **years** = 1, and **rate** = 0.05 was the following.

Second National Bank

Month	Interest	Amount
1	$ 4.17	$ 1004.17
2	$ 4.18	$ 1008.35
3	$ 4.20	$ 1012.55
4	$ 4.22	$ 1016.77
5	$ 4.24	$ 1021.01
6	$ 4.25	$ 1025.26
7	$ 4.27	$ 1029.53
8	$ 4.29	$ 1033.82
9	$ 4.31	$ 1038.13
10	$ 4.33	$ 1042.46
11	$ 4.34	$ 1046.80
12	$ 4.36	$ 1051.16

Amount = $ 1000.00
Years = 1
Interest rate = 5.00%
Final amount = $ 1051.16

Variations With The For Loop:

Not all parts of the **for loop** are required. Any of the three parts, the initialization, the condition, or the update expression can be omitted. However, the semicolons must always be present.

> **Note:** We are showing these variations that can be used with the for-loop only to illustrate the power and flexibility of the C++ language. We may see some code written this way. However, we will <u>not</u> use any of these variations. Straight forward coding is definitely the easiest to follow.

In the following program the update expression is left blank.

```cpp
// prog3_8.cpp Program to illustrate the for loop with no update
//                expression.
#include <iostream.h>
int main()
{
  int num5, n;
  for (n = 1; n <= 5; )
  {
    num5 = 5 * n;
    cout << num5 << endl;
    n++;
  } // end for
}
```

In this example, **n** is set to 1 and is incremented inside of the for loop rather than in the loop expression. The output from this program was the following:

```
5
10
15
20
25
```

The initialize expression can also be placed before the **for loop** as in the following example.

```cpp
n = 1;
for ( ; n <= 5; n++)
{
  num5 = 5 * n;
  cout << num5 << endl;
}
```

In addition, both statements can be removed from the loop expression.

```cpp
n = 1;
for ( ; n <= 5; )
{
  num5 = 5 * n;
  cout << num5 << endl;
  n++;
}
```

If the test expression is omitted from the loop expression, then there is no way for the loop to be terminated. In the following example there is no condition. It is always evaluated as true. Thus, the following code is an infinite (never-ending) loop.

```
for(;;)
    cout << "How do I get out of here?\n";
```

The **initialize** and/or the **update** expression can consist of more than one statement. This is illustrated with the next two examples.

```
// prog3_9.cpp
#include <iostream.h>
#include <iomanip.h>
int main()
{
    int num, square, cube;
    for( num = 1,  cout << "Integer" << setw(11) << "Square" << setw(7)
        << " Cube" << endl; num <= 15; num++)
    {
        square = num * num;
        cube = square * num;
        cout << setw(4) << num
             << setw(11) << square
             << setw(9) << cube << endl;
    } // end for
    return 0;
}
```

In this **for loop**, the initialize expression consists of two statements separated by a comma. We cannot use a semicolon, since this would terminate the initialize expression. Both statements are executed and then the test expression is evaluated. The output from this program was the following:

Integer	Square	Cube
1	1	1
2	4	8
3	9	27
.	.	.
.	.	.
15	225	3375

Note that the comma <u>must</u> be used to separate the statements when more than one statement is used in either the initialize expression or in the update expression of the loop. We illustrate this idea with one more example.

A hotel has a special family rate for up to 10 family members. The first person pays $50 and each additional family member pays $10. The program prints out a table of charges.

```
// prog3_10.cpp
#include <iostream.h>
#include <iomanip.h>
int main()
{
  int guest, cost;
  cout << "Guests  Cost" << endl;
  for(guest = 1, cost = 50; guest < 11; guest++, cost += 10)
    cout << setw(5) <<  guest << setw(6) << cost << endl;
  // end for
  return 0;
}
```

This **for loop** is more complicated because two variables are initialized; **guest** is set to 1 and **cost** is set to 50. Since the number of guests is less than 11 the **cout** stream is performed. The variable **guest** is incremented by 1 and 10 is added to the **cost**. The second time through the loop, **guest** has a value of 2 while **cost** has a value of 60. The loop continues until **guest** reaches 11. The output is the following:

Guests	Cost
1	50
2	60
3	70
4	80
5	90
6	100
7	110
8	120
9	130
10	140

There are limitations, however. We cannot use two statements in the **initialize** expression if one of them includes a type declaration. The C++ compiler will not accept

```
for (int I = 1, cout << "Hello\n"; I <= 15; I++);
```

It would flag the **cout** statement. If we remove the **int** declaration for **I**, then it compiles successfully.

3.5 - The while...do Structure

The **while...do** is another programming structure that is available in most programming languages. It is used anytime that we want to execute a block of code based on the outcome of a logical expression. The expression is checked before the block of code is executed. In the C++ programming language, this structure consists of the single keyword, **while**. The logical expression that is to be evaluated follows the **while**. Next comes the body of the loop that is to be performed only if the logical expression is true. The general format of the **while** structure is the following.

```
while( condition ) {
    statement1;
    statement2;
    statement3;
        .
        .
        .
} // end while
```

The begin - end braces, **{ }**, are necessary if there is more than one statement to be executed. Without these braces, the compiler assumes that a single statement will be executed. A while loop consisting of a single statement can be coded as

```
while (condition)
    statement;
// end while
```

When a **while loop** is executed, the condition is tested. If the condition is true, then the statements between the begin - end braces will be executed. After the last statement is executed, control comes back to the top, and the condition is tested again. If the condition is false, the statements will be skipped, and control is passed to the statement after the end of the **while loop**. The execution of a **while loop** is illustrated with the following figure.

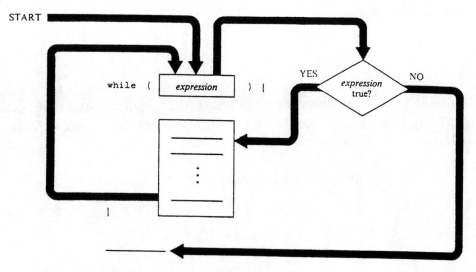

START

while (*expression*) {

YES   *expression* true?   NO

}

The while statement.

We illustrate the use of the **while loop** by rewriting some of the same examples that we used with the **for loop**. In the first example, we use a **while loop** to compute and print out the first 20 positive integers and their squares.

```cpp
// prog3_11.cpp
#include <iostream.h>
int main()
{
  int num, numsq;
  num = 1;
  while(num <= 20) {
    numsq = num * num;
    cout << "num = " << num
         << "  num squared = " << numsq
         << endl;
    num++;
  } // end while
  return 0;
}
```

The output from this program will be the same as it was from **prog3_4** when we used the **for loop**. In the above program, the integer **num** is set to 1, and we use the condition, **num <= 20**, as the test condition for the loop. The condition is checked, and if it evaluates to true, the body of the loop is executed. The last statement in the loop increments the value of **num** by 1. At the end of the body of the loop, control goes back to the top, and the condition is again evaluated. The process continues until the condition evaluates to false. When the condition becomes false, the body of the loop will be skipped, and the first statement following the end of the **while loop** is executed. In the above example, it is the statement

        return 0;

We consider another example. Each of the following blocks of code will output the standard printable ASCII characters one per line. We explained these examples when we did the same thing using the **for loop**. We will ask the reader to write the programs to test each of these blocks of code as exercises.

```
unsigned char ch;            unsigned char ch;

ch = ' ';                    ch = 32;
while (ch <= '~') {          while (ch <= 126) {
   cout << ch << endl;          cout << ch << endl;
   ch++;                        ch++;
} // end while              } // end while
```

We consider another simple example using a **while loop**. This program computes and prints out the multiples of 7 that are less than 200, one per line.

```
// prog3_12.cpp
// This program computes and prints multiples of 7
// that are less than 200, one per line.
#include <iostream.h>
int main()
{
  int num7 = 7;
  while (num7 < 200) {
    cout << num7 << endl;
    num7 += 7;
  } // end while
  return 0;
}
```

The output from this program was the following.

        7
        14
        21
        .
        .
        .
        196

Try this: Write a while-loop that will compute and print out the
odd, positive integers less than 50, one per line.

```
oddnum = ____;
while ( _____ ) {
  cout << _____;
  oddnum _____;
} // end while
```

Before we move on we want to rewrite the above program in order to illustrate the flexibility of the **for ... loop** in C++. The second expression of the for loop allows it to be used so that it acts like a while loop. We rewrite the above program to illustrate what we mean.

```
// prog3_13.cpp Program to compute and print out the multiples of
//                 7 less than 200, using a for ... loop
#include <iostream.h>
#include <iomanip.h>
int main()
{
  for (int num7 = 7; num7 < 200; num7 += 7)
    cout << num7 << endl;
  // end for
  return 0;
}
```

The output from this program would be exactly the same as from **prog3_12.cpp**.

We now want to consider a second version of our Savings Account Program. This time we would like the user to be able to input an amount of money, a yearly interest rate, and a final amount of money that he/she would like to end up with at the end of an investment period. The program is to compute and print out a table showing the month, the interest earned, and the amount in the account at the end of each month. The loop should end when the amount reaches the desired final amount. The program should count the number of months and print out a summary that shows the initial amount, the interest rate, the final amount, and how long that it took to reach the desired final amount in years and months.

In addition, we illustrate the use of another screen control function that is contained in the **conio** library. This function is

gotoxy(col, row);

and is used to move the cursor to the specified column, (x position), and row, (y position) on the screen. The home position on the screen is the upper left position and has coordinates, (1,1). The statement

gotoxy(1,1);

moves the cursor home. This function is very handy for formatting screen output. In order to use this function and also the **clrscr()** function we must include the **conio.h** header file. The statement

gotoxy(10, 5);

would position the cursor at column 10 row 5 so that we could print any heading or message that we wish at that position with a **cout** statement. We will illustrate the use of this function when we write the block of code for the input of the data.

An outline for this second Savings Account Program is the following:

Input the data
        amount, intrate, famount

Compute monthly interest rate
        mrate

Save amount
        oldamount

Print headings
        main heading
        column headings
                Month, Interest, Amount

Print table and compute number of months
        set month to 0
        while (amount < famount)
            Compute intearned
            Compute amount
            Increment month
            Print month, intearned, amount
        end-while

Compute years, remaining months
        years, rmonths

Print summary
        Print oldamount
        Print famount
        Print intrate
        Print years
        Print rmonths

The code to input the data will first generate the following screen:

```
        10                              50

5       Amount                          Final Amount
6       $*****.**                       $*****.**


                        25
20                      Interest Rate - 0.055 for 5.5%
                              *.***
```

The cursor would then be moved to the indicated positions for the user to type the appropriate data. The code to generate the screen and input the data would be the following:

```
gotoxy(10, 5);
cout << "Amount";
gotoxy(10, 6);
cout << "$*****.**";
gotoxy(50, 5);
cout << "Final Amount:";
gotoxy(50, 6);
cout << "$*****.**";
gotoxy(25, 20);
cout << "Interest Rate - 0.055 for 5.5%";
gotoxy(32, 21);
cout << "*.***";
// Input the data
gotoxy(11, 6);
cin >> amount;
gotoxy(51, 6);
cin >> famount;
gotoxy(32, 21);
cin >> intrate;
```

The code to compute the number of years and the remaining months after the program has counted the number of months is written using the integer division operators that calculate the quotient and remainder.

```
years = months / 12;
rmonths = months % 12;
```

We can now write the program since the rest of the code is similar to the first Savings Account Program. We will use a while loop instead of the for loop since we want the loop to continue until the amount in the account reaches the desired final amount.

```cpp
//prog3_14.cpp Program to calculate the period of time needed to
//               accumulate a specified amount of money given an
//               initial amount and a yearly interest rate. The interest
//               is compounded monthly.
#include <iostream.h>
#include <iomanip.h>
#include <conio.h>
int main()
{
    int years, months, rmonths;
    float amount, famount, intearned,
         rate, mrate, oamount;
// Generate Data Input Screen
    clrscr( );
    gotoxy(10, 5);
    cout << "Amount";
    gotoxy(10, 6);
    cout << "$*****.**";
    gotoxy(50, 5);
    cout << "Final Amount:";
    gotoxy(50, 6);
    cout << "$*****.**";
    gotoxy(25, 20);
    cout << "Interest Rate - 0.055 for 5.5%";
    gotoxy(32, 21);
    cout << "*.***";
// Input the data
    gotoxy(11, 6);
    cin >> amount;
    gotoxy(51, 6);
    cin >> famount;
    gotoxy(32, 21);
    cin >> rate;
    // Compute monthly interest rate & Save amount
    mrate = rate / 12;
    oamount = amount;
```

```cpp
// Print headings
   clrscr( );
   cout << setw(50) << "Second National Bank" << endl;
   cout << endl << endl;
   cout << setw(14) << "Month" << setw(28) << "Interest"
        << setw(29) << "Amount" << endl;
// Print table and compute number of months
   cout.setf(ios::fixed);
   cout.setf(ios::showpoint);
   cout.precision(2);
   months = 0;
   while ( amount < famount ) {
      months++;
      intearned = amount * mrate;
      amount += intearned;
      cout << setw(13) << months << setw(23) << "$"
           << setw(5) << intearned  << setw(24) << "$"
           << setw(8) << amount << endl;
   } // end while
// Compute years and remaining months
   years = months / 12;
   rmonths = months % 12;
// Print summary
   cout << endl << endl;
   cout << "Amount =  $" << setw(8) << oamount << endl;
   cout << "Final amount = $" << setw(8) << famount << endl;
   cout << "Interest rate = " <<  setw( 4) <<  rate * 100
        << "%" << endl;
   cout << "Years = " << years << endl;
   cout << "Months = " << rmonths << endl;
   return 0;
}
```

Output from this program with **amount** = 1000.00, **famount** = 1200.00, and **rate** = 0.05 was the following:

Second National Bank

Month	Interest	Amount
1	$ 4.17	$ 1004.17
2	$ 4.18	$ 1008.35
3	$ 4.20	$ 1012.55
.	.	.
.		.
.		
44	$ 4.98	$ 1200.76

Amount = $ 1000.00
Final amount = $ 1200.00
Interest rate = 5.00%
Years = 3
Months = 8

3.6 - The do...while Structure

The **do...while** structure or loop, is closely related to the **while loop**. It has the following general form.

```
do {
  statement 1;
  statement 2;
      .
      .
      .
} while (condition);
```

In this case the **do...while** loop keywords **do** and **while** are separated by the statements to be performed which must be enclosed in begin - end braces. The condition is tested at the end of the loop. Since the test occurs at the end of the loop, the loop is always performed at least once.

We can trace the execution of a do while loop with the following figure.

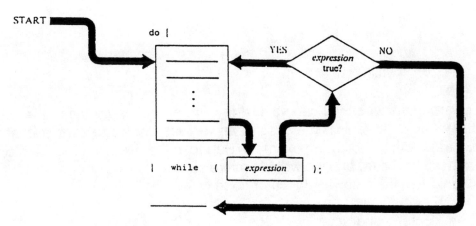

START

do {

YES · · · NO

expression true?

| while (expression);

The do while statement.

We illustrate the use of the **do ... while** structure with the example to compute and print out the multiples of 7 that are less than 200.

```cpp
// prog3_15.cpp Program to print the multiples of 7 that are less
//                   than 200, one per line using a do - while.
#include <iostream.h>
int main()
{
int num7 = 7;
  do {
    cout << num7 << endl;
    num7 += 7;
  } while (num7 < 200);
  return 0;
}
```

Note: When we use a while loop, the condition is tested first. We use this programming structure when we may not want the code executed even once. When we use a do while, the condition is tested after the block of code is executed. We use this structure when we want the code executed at least one time.

The code to print out the printable ASCII characters one per line can also be written using the **do ... while**.

```
ch = ' ';
do {
    cout << ch << endl;
    ch++;
} while (ch <= '~');
```

There are times when we can save a few lines of code by using the **do ... while** instead of the **while ... do**. This is the case when we want the code executed at least one time. We illustrate with the following example. Suppose that we want the user to input one character from the keyboard and we want to make sure that it is a 'y' or a 'Y'. Using a while ... loop we would use the following block of code

```
cout << " Enter a character, 'y' or 'Y': ";
ch = getche();
while ((ch != 'y') && (ch != 'Y'))
{
    cout << "invalid character, enter 'y' or 'Y': ";
    ch = getche();
} // end while
```

We see that when we use a **while loop**, the message to the user and the input of the character has to be coded twice. Using a **do ... while** we would have the following.

```
do {
    cout << "Enter a character, 'y' or 'Y': ";
    ch = getche();
} while ((ch != 'y') && (ch != 'Y'));
```

In this case, we simply have to code the input statement one time. In this example we have used one of the many functions that are available for character input. The function

getche( )

allows us to input a character without having to type a return after we type the character. The 'e' at the end of **getche( )** means to echo the character we type to the screen. The function **getch( )** will not echo the character typed. When we use either **scanf( )** or **cin**, we have to type <u>both</u> the character and the return. We will discuss the collection of character input functions in Chapter 5.

Any code that can be written using a **while ... do** can also be written using a **do ...**

120

while and conversely. The choice depends on the problem being considered and the style preferred by the programmer. We consider one more example.

The next block of code writes a menu to the screen and waits for a choice to be input by the user.

```
unsigned char choice;
do {
  clrscr();
  gotoxy(28,10);
  cout << " Database Maintenance Menu\n";
  gotoxy(28,11);
  cout << "     1.  Add new records\n";
  gotoxy(28,12);
  cout << "     2.  Change existing records\n";
  gotoxy(28,13);
  cout << "     3.  Delete records\n";
  gotoxy(28,14);
  cout << "     4.  Stop\n"
  gotoxy(28,15);
  cout << " Enter your choice: ";
  cin >> choice;
//     Code to execute appropriate choice
//     would go here.
} while( (choice < '1') || (choice > '4') );
```

The menu is always written at least once. If the user enters an invalid choice the menu is rewritten until a valid choice is entered. We will ask the reader to write and test this program as one of the exercises.

We consider one more example which will be a revision of the above menu code. In this example we use the function **getch()** to input the user's character. If it is invalid, we ring the bell and do not let the user out of the **do while** until a valid character is pressed. In the improved version, since **getch()** does not echo the character to the screen, we do not have to repeat the code to clear the screen and print the menu.

```
unsigned char choice;
clrscr();
gotoxy(28,10);
cout << "Database Maintenance Menu" << endl;
cout << setw(30) << ' ' << "1. Add new records." << endl;
cout << setw(30) << ' ' << "2. Change existing record." << endl;
cout << setw(30) << ' ' << "3. Delete records." << endl;
cout << setw(30) << ' ' << "4. Stop." << endl;
```

```
do {
   choice = getch();
   if ((choice < '1') || (choice > '4'))
     putch(7);
   else {
//        Code to execute appropriate choice
//        would go here.
   } // end if
} while (choice != '4');
```

Try this: Write a block of code, using a do while, to compute and print out
the odd, positive integers less than 50, one per line.

```
oddnum = _____
do  {

        _____
        _____
        _____
} while ( _____ );
```

3.7 - The if ... else Structure

The **if... else structure** has two forms. It allows us to execute a block of code if a
logical expression is evaluated as true; and skip this block of code if the expression is
false. It can also be used to execute one block of code if a logical expression is true and
another block of block of code if the expression is false. It is not a looping structure. The
general forms for this structure are the following.

```
if ( condition ) {        or        if (condition) {
    statement1;                         statement1;
    statement2;                         statement2;
        .                                   .
        .                                   .
        .                               } else {
} // end if                             statementa;
                                        statementb;
                                            .
                                            .
                                        } // end if
```

As is the case with all of the other programming structures, if more than one
statement is be executed, then these statements must be placed within the begin-end
braces. Execution of an if - else statement can be traced using the following figure.

122

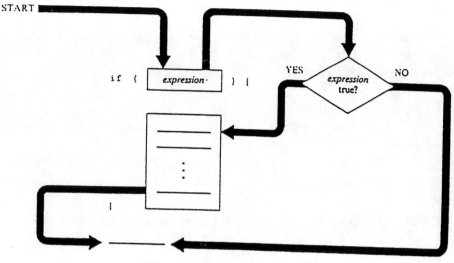

The if statement.

An example of a simple if statement is the following:

```
cout << "Enter the student's score" << endl;
cin >> score;
if(score > 95)
    cout << "The student deserves an A" << endl;
// end if
```

In this case, the user is prompted for a score. If the entered **score** is greater than 95, then the message, "The student deserves an A", is printed. Since their are no braces, the block of code to be executed consists of simply the one **cout** statement.

This next example asks the user to input an integer less than 10 and checks to see if the number entered is 7.

```
cout << "Input an integer under 10: ";
cin >> num;
if (num == 7)
    cout << "I thought that it would be 7!" << endl;
// end if
cout << "Thanks for entering " << num << endl;
```

Two sets of output from this code was the following:

```
Input an integer under 10: 7
I thought that it would be 7!
```

Input an integer under 10: <u>3</u>
Thanks for entering 3

The next example checks to see if a person earned more than $500.00. If so, the tax is 5% of this amount; otherwise, the tax is $0.00.

```
tax = 0;
if (income > 500.00)
   tax = 0.05 * income;
// end if
cout << "You owe $" << setwidth(5) << setprecision(2)
   << tax << endl;
```

Fix it: The block of code illustrates a common programming error.

```
if (hours = 40)                 if (_____
   pay = 12.25 * 40;               pay = _____
// end if                        // end if
```

In the above example, the C++ compiler simply <u>assigns</u> the value of 40 to hours and evaluates this non-zero value as true. For the first block of code, the statement

```
pay = 12.25 * 40;
```

is always executed.

Adding the **else** to an **if statement** permits a choice between two blocks of code to be executed. If the condition tests to true, then the first block of statements is performed. If the condition tests to false, the second block of statements is performed. An example is the following:

```
if(score > 69)
   cout << "You pass" << endl;
else {
   cout << "Sorry, you fail" << endl;
   cout << "You must study harder" << endl;
} // end if
```

The condition, **score > 69**, is evaluated. If the value returned is true, the first message is printed. There is only one statement to be performed; therefore, the begin-end braces are omitted. If this statement is executed, then the **else** block of statements is skipped. If the condition is evaluated as false, the code following the else statement is performed. Since there are two statements to be performed, they must be enclosed within the curly braces.

This next example computes the income tax owed. The tax is 2% of the first $25,000.00 and 2.5% of the income over this amount.

```
if (income <= 25000.00)
   tax = 0.02 * income;
else
   tax = 0.025 * (income - 25000.00) + 500.0;
// end if
```

Note that the $500.00 is 2% of $25,000.00.

The following program will allow the user to input a temperature in either Fahrenheit or Celsius along with a letter 'f' or 'c' to indicate which temperature was input. The program will compute and output the corresponding temperature.

```
// prog3_16.cpp
#include <iostream.h>
#include <iomanip.h>
#include <conio.h>
int main( )
{
   char ch;
   float temp, celsius, faren;
   clrscr();
   cout << "Enter a temperature in celsius, or fahrenheit: ";
   cin >> temp;
   cout << "Enter 'c' for celsius or 'f' for fahrenheit: ";
   ch = getche();
   cout << endl;
   if (ch == 'f' || ch == 'F') {
      celsius = (5.0 / 9.0) * (temp - 32);
      cout << "temperature " << setw(6) << setprecision(2)
           << temp << " degrees fahrenheit = " << endl
           << setw(6) << celsius << " degrees celsius " << endl;
   } else {
      faren = (9.0 / 5.0) * temp + 32;
      cout << " temperature " << setw(6) << setprecision(2)
           << temp << " degrees celsius = " << endl
           << setw(6) << faren << " degrees fahrenheit" << endl;
   } // end if
   return 0;
}
```

We can expand our coding to allow several possible choices by using nested **if...else statements**. For example, we would have

```
if( condition ) {
        .
    statement(s);
        .
} else if( condition ) {
        .
    statement(s);
        .
} else {
        .
    statement(s);
        .
} // end else
```

In this case, each condition is tested until a true value is returned. When a true value is returned, that block of code is performed, and the rest of the blocks are skipped. If a true condition is not met, the final **else** block is performed. Note that the last block is simply an **else** with no condition. This is referred to as the default statement and is perform only if none of the others return a value of true. A specific example is the following:

```
if(score >= 90)
        cout << "The student deserves an A" << endl;
else if(score >= 80)
        cout << "The student deserves a B" << endl;
else if(score >= 70)
        cout << "The student deserves a C" << endl;
else if(score >= 60)
        cout << "The student deserves a D" << endl;
else
        cout << "The student deserves a F" << endl;
```

In this example, the student's **score** is compared, in turn, to each value that determines the grade to be given. As soon as a true value is returned, the grade is printed, and the program branches to the end of the if statements. If no true value is returned, the final sentence, "The student deserves a F", is printed.

3.8 - The break & continue Statements

Whenever a **break statement** is encountered within a loop, the loop is terminated and the program continues with the next statement following the loop. We illustrate this with an example. As we discussed, the function **getche()** returns one character from the keyboard echoes it to the screen. We will discuss the function again in Chapter 7.

126

```
                    for(;;)
                    {
                        cout << "Input any character: " << endl;
                        ch = getche();
                        if((ch == 'X') || (ch == 'x'))
                            break;
                        // end if
                    } // end for
                    cout << "Goodbye" << endl;
```

In the above block of code, a **for loop** with no condition is used. This loop will always be evaluated as true and continue forever unless a method is established to exit the loop. This is accomplished in the **if statement**. If the character entered is either an uppercase or lower case **x,** the **break** statement exits the loop and the program prints "Goodbye".

We can use the **break** statement to exit any loop, **while ... do**, **do...while**, and the **for loop**. The **break** statement is also used with the **switch statement** that will be discussed in section 3.11. Another example is the following.

```
                    count = 0;
                    cout << "You get 10 chances to guess a number\n";
                    cout << "between 1 and 100";
                    while (count < 10) {
                        cout << "Input a number: ";
                        cin << number;
                        if (number < 76)
                            cout << "too small\n";
                        else if (number > 76)
                            cout << "too large\n";
                        else {
                            cout << "You are correct!!!\n";
                            break;
                        } // end if
                        count++;
                    } // end while
                    // break jumps to here
```

The Continue Statement

Unlike the **break statement**, the **continue statement** does not terminate the loop, but simply returns control to the top of the loop. When a **continue** statement is called from within a loop, the remainder of the loop is skipped, and the program returns to the control part of the loop, checks the condition and continues, or terminates depending on the results of the condition comparison. We illustrate this with an example.

```
for(x=0; x < 100; x++)
{
  if( x % 2 != 0)
    continue;
      // end if
  cout << x << endl;
} // end for
```

In the above **for loop** the number **x** is divided by 2, and the remainder compared to 0 (**x % 2 != 0**). If there is no remainder, then the number, **x**, is an even number, so that the number is printed. If there is a remainder, then **x** is odd, the **cout** stream is skipped, and control is returned to the **for statement**. We illustrate with one more example.

```
// prog3_17.cpp  Computes and prints out the average of  10 exam scores
// input from the keyboard. It  checks and ignores invalid exam scores.
#include <iostream.h>
#include <iomanip.h>
int main()
{
  int count;
  float score, total, average;
  total = 0;
  count = 0;
  while (count < 10) {
    cout << "Input an exam score: ";
    cin >> score;
    if ((score < 0) || (score > 100))
      continue;
    total += score;
    count++;
  } // end while
  average = total / count;
  cout << "Average = " << setw(5) << setprecision(2)
     << average << endl;
  return 0;
}
```

This program only accepts scores that are in the range, **0 <= score <= 100**, and continues until 10 such scores are input by the user. Each time that an invalid score is entered, the **continue** statement is executed returning control back to the beginning of the **while loop**. The **score** is not added to **total** and **count** is not incremented.

3.9 - The Conditional Operator, ?

The C++ language allows a special short hand form for the **if...else** statement. This is done using the operator, **?**, which is referred to as the **conditional operator**. This is best illustrated with an example.

```
a = (x < 0) ? -x : x;
```

This statement is read as "if **x** is less than 0 set the value of **a** to -x, else set the value of **a** to **x**." This statement is exactly the same as

```
if(x < 0)
   a = -x;
else
   a = x;
```

The **conditional** operator is not as easy to read as the **if...else** statement but requires less coding. We consider another example. Suppose that we want to rewrite the following block of code using the **conditional** operator.

```
if (num > 70)
   grade = 'P';
else
   grade = 'N';
```

This would be coded as follows:

```
grade = (num > 70) ? 'P' : 'N';
```

Now, suppose that we wish to rewrite the following using an **if ... else**.

```
max = (num1 > num2) ? num1 : num2;
```

This can be done as follows:

```
if (num1 > num2)
   max = num1;
else
   max = num2;
```

Try this: Rewrite the following block of code using the conditional operator ?.

```
if (income <= 25000.00)
    tax = income * 0.02;
else
    tax = 0.025 * (income - 25000.00) + 500;
```

```
tax = ( _____ )
      ? _____
      ? _____ ;
```

Try this: Rewrite the following block of code using an if - else.

```
message = ( score > 69 ) ? "You passed " : "You failed ";
```

```
if ( _____ )
    message = _____ ;
else
    message = _____ ;
```

3.10 - The Switch Statement

Nested **if...else** statements can become fairly complicated and tricky to code. In order to simplify this type of code, the C++ programming language has a structure called the **switch statement**. The **switch statement** accepts either an integer or character type of variable and permits different blocks of code to be executed depending on the values of the variable. The variable that is used is called the **switch variable**. The structure of the **switch** statement is as follows.

```
switch ( op )
{
    case value1 :      // executed if op = value1
        statement1;
        statement2;
                .
        break;          // exit to end of switch
    case value2 :      // executed if op = value2
        statement1;
        statement2;
                .
```

```
        break;              // exit to end of switch
          .
          .
      default :              // executed if no other case applies
          statement1;
          statement2;
          .

    } // end switch
```

Note that the **break;** statement at the end of each block, transfers control to the end of the **switch** statement. Without the **break** statement in each **case** block, the execution would "fall through", executing all remaining statements.

We illustrate the use of this structure with a program to compute a letter grade for an exam score that is in the range 0 --> 100. In order to compute a value to use in the **switch** structure, we divide the exam by 10 to obtain an integer in the range 0, 1, ..., 10.

```cpp
// prog3_18.cpp Program to illustrate the use of the switch structure
#include <iostream.h>
#include <iomanip.h>
int main()
{
  int exam, examnum;
  char grade;
  for (int i = 1; i <= 3; i++) {
    cout << "Input an exam score: ";
    cin >> exam;
    examnum = exam / 10;
    switch (examnum) {
      case 10:
      case  9: grade = 'A';
            break;
      case  8: grade = 'B';
            break;
      case  7: grade = 'C';
            break;
      case  6: grade = 'D';
            break;
      default : grade = 'F';
    } // end switch
    cout << "Exam = " << exam << endl;
    cout << " Grade = " << grade << endl;
```

```
        } // end for
        return 0;
}
```

Output from a run of this program was the following:

```
Input an exam score: 76
Exam = 76
Grade = C
Input an exam score: 92
Exam = 92
Grade = A
Input an exam score: 45
Exam = 45
Grade = F
```

The next example again uses the **switch** statement to compute interest earned on a given amount input from the keyboard by the user. The user is to choose a given interest rate from a menu. This program illustrates the use of the function **getch()** to input a choice from the keyboard without echoing it to the screen.

```
// prog3_19.cpp  Program to illustrate the use of the switch statement.
//
#include <iostream.h>
#include <iomanip.h>
#include <conio.h>
#define FALSE 0
#define TRUE !FALSE
int main()
{
    unsigned char ch;
    float principle, interest;
    int okchar;
do {
    clrscr();
    cout << "Enter the loan amount: ";
    cin >> principle;
    cout << endl << "Choose an Interest rate: " << endl;
    cout << " a.  5% interest" << endl;
    cout << " b.  8% interest" << endl;
    cout << " c. 10% interest" << endl;
    cout << " d. 15% interest" << endl;
    cout << "Enter the letter of your choice: ";
    okchar = TRUE;
    do {
```

```
          ch = getch();
          switch(ch) {
            case 'A':
            case 'a': interest = (principle * .05);
                   break;
            case 'B':
            case 'b': interest = (principle * .08);
                   break;
            case 'C':
            case 'c': interest = (principle * .10);
                   break;
            case 'D':
            case 'd': interest = (principle * .15);
                   break;
            default:  putch(7);
                   okchar = FALSE;
          } // end switch
        } while (!okchar);
        cout << endl << endl;
        cout.setf(ios::fixed);
        cout.setf(ios::showpoint);
        cout.precision(2);
        cout << "principle = $" << setw(6) << principle << endl;
        cout << "Interest = $" << setw(6) << interest << endl;
        cout << "Total = $" << setw(6) <<  principle + interest << endl;
        cout << "Do you wish another problem? ";
        do {
          ch = getch();
        } while ((ch != 'Y') && (ch != 'y') && (ch != 'N') && (ch != 'n'));
      } while ((ch == 'Y') || (ch == 'y'));
      return 0;
      }
```

In this program the user is asked to input the principle of a loan and is given a menu of possible interest rates. The user enters a letter to choose one of the rates. The **switch** statement accepts the input, using the function **getch()** so that the character is not printed at the screen. A single character is stored in the variable **ch**. The fact that the character is not echoed to the screen keeps us from having to clear the screen and print the menu again. The value in **ch** is then compared to the various values used in the various **case** statements. Note that each **case** statement allows for either the upper or lower case letter. If a correct selection is entered, the interest rate is calculated. The **break** statement then breaks out of the **switch** statement, but not out of the **do while** loop. If an invalid character is entered, the bell is sounded, and the program waits for the user to input another character. This is handled by the **default** in the **switch** statement. When a valid choice is entered, the **interest** is computed. The **interest**, **principle**, and the new **total** are output to the screen. The user is then asked if he/she wants to do another problem, and a **do while** is used to trap the input until a valid, 'Y','y', 'N', or 'n' is entered as a choice. If an 'N' or 'n' is entered, then the outside **do while** is exited and the **return 0** statement ending the program is executed.

3.11 Summary

In this chapter, we have studied the programming control structures that are available in C++. These are the structures that are needed in order for us to write structured programs. We have studied the **for - loop**, the **while - do**, and the **do - while** structures that allow us to repeat a given block of code zero, one, or more times, based on the condition of certain variables. We have studied the use of the **relational operators** , (==) equal, (<) less than, (>) greater than, (<=) less than or equal, (>=), greater than or equal, and (!=) not equal to. These can be used to form logical (boolean) expressions. We studied the use of the three **logical operators**, (!) NOT, (&&) AND, and (||) OR that we used to combine logical expressions to control the execution of the programming structures. We have illustrated the use of these structures in a variety of programs, and we will continue to see their use throughout the rest of this text.

We studied the **if - else** programming structure which allows us to execute one block of code or another based on the value of a boolean expression. This structure is the major decision making structure in C++. We studied the simple **if**, the **if - else**, and nested **if - else** programming structures in programming examples. We also studied the use of the **switch - case** structure that can be used to simplify the coding of nested **if - else** statements. We saw how the **break** statement was used in the **switch - case** statement to cause the immediate exit from the structure. In addition we illustrated how to use the **break** statement in other blocks of code. We studied the use of the **continue** statement which was used to return control to the beginning of a loop. We also illustrated how we can use the **conditional operator, ?**, to write a short hand version of an **if ... else** block of code.

3.12 Questions

3.1 What are the relational operators? How are they coded in C++?

3.2 What is a logical or boolean expression?

3.3 What are the boolean operators? How are they coded in C++?

3.4 What are the three programming structures for repeating a block of code?

3.5 Which of the three programming structures is used
  a. if we want to repeat a block of code a given number of times.
  b. if we want to check to see if we want to execute a block of code at the beginning, and continue to execute the code as long as the expression that we check is true.
  c. if we want to execute a block of code and then check to see if we want to execute it again.

3.6 What is the programming structure that allows us to choose between two different blocks of code?

3.7 What is the difference between a **while .. do** structure and a **do .. while** structure?

3.8 What is the difference between a **for** structure and a **while .. do** structure?

3.9 What are the three expressions that control the execution of a **for loop**?

3.10 What separates the three expressions of the **for loop**?

3.11 How does a **for loop** operate?

3.12 When can the first condition of the **for loop** be omitted? Give an example.

3.13 When can the third condition of the **for loop** be omitted? Give an example.

3.14 Can the second condition of the **for loop** be omitted? Why or why not.

3.15 Explain what the **return** statement is used for. Give an example.

3.16 Explain what the **continue** is used for. Give an example.

3.17 When do we use an if structure? Give an example.

3.18 When do we use an if - else structure? Give an example.

3.19 What is the conditional operator used for? Give an example.

3.13 Exercises

3.1 Suppose that we have integer variables, num1, num2, and num3 defined and initialized with the statements:
    int num1 = 10;

```
        int num2 = 20;
        int num3 = 15;
```

Evaluate each of the following expressions:

a. num1 > num2

b. num1 !> num3

c. (num1 + num3) > (num2 + num1)

d. !(num1 > num2)

e. (num1 <= num2) && (num3 > num2)

f. (num1 < num2) || (num2 < num3)

g. (num1 < num2) && (num1 > num3)

h. (num2 < num3) && (num3 <= num2)

i. (num1 >= num2) || (num2 < num3)

j. (num1 < num3) || !(num1 > num2)

k. !(num3 > num2) && !(num3 < num1)

l. (num1) || (!num2)

3.2 Write logical expressions that will check each of the following:
   a. age is over 21.
   b. age is between 21 and 65.
   c. age is not between 21 and 65.
   d. pay is between 10.00 and 20.00
   e. pay is less than 20.00.
   f. pay is greater than 25.50.

3.3 Write the block of code that will compute and print out the first 20 positive multiples of 3.

3.4 Write the block of code that will compute and print out the positive multiples of 7 that are less than 500.

3.5 Write the block of code from 3.2 using a **for loop** , without first counting the number of multiples

3.6 Write a program that will use a for loop to print a table of ten integers, their squares, and their cubes.

3.7 Write a program that contains a loop that will request two integers from the user and print the two integers and their product to the screen. The program should continue until the user enters a value of zero for the first integer.

3.8 Write a program that requests the principle of a loan. The program will then calculates the compound interest at a rate of 5%, compounded monthly. Assuming nothing is paid on the principle print a table that shows the month, the monthly interest, and the new principle for a period of 5 years.

3.9 Write a program that will request an employees name and the hours worked for the week. Print the name, the hours worked the regular pay, gross pay, taxes, and net pay in the following format:

Name: Regular hours: Overtime hours:
Regular Pay: Overtime Pay:

Taxes: Net Pay:

Use the following information for your calculations:

Pay per hour for the first 40 hours = $20.00
Over 40 hours use time and a half
Tax rate: 30%

3.10 Write a program that will ask the user to input one positive integer from the keyboard. The program will compute and print out the partial sums, 1, 1+2, 1+2+3, ..., 1+2+3+...+n.

311 Write a program that will ask the user to input one positive integer from the keyboard. The program is to compute and print out the first n terms of the Fibonacci sequence. The first few terms of the sequence are the following:

    1, 1, 2, 3, 5, 8, 13, 21, ...

Note, that each term is the sum of the preceding two terms of the sequence.

3.12 Write the if - else statement equivalent to each of the following:

    a. min = ((num1 > num2) ? num2 : num1;

    b. tax = (amount > 1000.00) ? 0.15 * amount : 0.10 * amount;

3.13 Rewrite each of the following using the conditional operator.

    a. if (hours > 40)
        amount = 30 * (hours - 40) + 20 * 40
     else
        amount = 20 * 40;

    b. if (num > 100)
        x = num - 100;
     else
        x = 100 - num;

CHAPTER 4

Subprograms in C++

4.1 - Introduction

When beginning to work on a new program we should <u>not</u> just sit down at the computer and start typing in the program. Instead we begin by thinking about the overall goal of the program and then the main things that the program must do to accomplish this goal. In other words, just as an architect designs a house before he starts to build it, we need to carefully design our program before we start coding it.

We start by thinking of the main objective of the program. Then we break this main objective down into tasks. We may then want to break these tasks into smaller subtasks. Then, when we code the program, we can write each of these small tasks and subtasks as a separate module of code. This process is called modular programming or structured programming.

The C++ languages strongly encourage us to use modular programming by allowing us to write each module as a separate C++ function. Thus, a well written program in C++ becomes a collection of separate functions which are then compiled and linked together.

In this text we have already used many functions that are included in the C++ language library files. For example, we have previously used **printf()**, **scanf()**, and **gets()**. These are just three of the many C++ functions that we may use from the library files that are supplied to us when we buy a C++ compiler.

In addition to using these built in functions in our programs, we will also write our own functions to do certain tasks that we want performed. It is actually quite easy to write our own functions. Each function is just a collection of statements to which we give a special name. For example, the name for the built in function **gets()**, stands for **getstring**. When we write our own functions we should use meaningful names for the functions.

As stated above, using functions allows us to break a program down into meaningful units. Dividing a program into modules is one of the major features of structured programming. It also makes editing and debugging much easier, and usually reduces total program size. Also, if we put the code for different functions in different files, then we may reuse these functions in other programs. For example, the built in function, **gets()**, can be used in all kinds of programs. We can do the same with functions that we write.

After completing this chapter the student should be able to

1.   understand the concept of modular design.

2.   understand how to code a function in C++.

3.   understand the use of function prototypes (declarations),
     how they can be coded, and when they should be used.

4.   understand how to pass constant data and data by value to a function.

5.   understand how to return data using the function name.

6.   understand how to return data by passing variables by reference.

7.   understand the concept of a programming project in Turbo C++.

8.   understand how to write multi-file programs, how to compile the different
     modules to create the **.OBJ** files, and how to link these .OBJ files together
     to create the **.EXE** program.

9.   understand how to document each of the functions that we choose to write
     for a given program.

4.2 - Modular Design and the Use of Functions

As discussed in the Introduction (4.1), we design a program by breaking a program
down into tasks. We then code each of these tasks as one or more separate functions.
This approach normally leads to a relatively short **main()** function. Instead of doing all of
the detailed programming steps in **main(),** we call the various functions to perform these
details. Thus, function **main()** may resemble a traffic controller, in that its job is just to
control the calling of other functions.

> **Note:** A rule of thumb is that the amount of code used for a function should not
> exceed one page.

Let us once again consider the Savings Account program that we wrote in Chapter
3. Recall that the program allows the user to input an amount of money, a yearly interest

rate, and a number of years. The program then outputs a table showing the month, the interest earned, and the amount of money at the end of each month, assuming that the interest is compounded monthly. It also prints a summary after the table. For this program we use the following outline:

Get the data from the user.

Compute months and monthly interest rate.

Print the headings.

Print the table showing the month, the interest earned, and the amount in the account at the end of each month.

Print the summary of results.

We want to write this program so that it calls a separate function to accomplish each of the steps in the outline. The main program will then consist of a series of function calls. The code for function **main()** is the following:

```
int main()
{
    getdata();
    compute();
    printheadings();
    printtable();
    summary();
    return 0;
}
```

In addition to the above, we will have to add the statements to include the necessary header files, define the variables that will be needed to store the data, write each of the above functions, and show where we need to code these functions in order for them to be used by the main program. We will write each of these functions in the following sections as we explain how functions are written and how data is passed back and forth between the calling program and the functions.

Note: Functions in C++ cannot be coded inside of the calling program. Nesting of functions is not permitted. However, any C++ function can call any other C++ function.

4.3 - Functions With No Parameters

We first consider functions that do not use any parameters. These functions are to receive no data from the calling program and will not return any data to the calling program. The first example is the **printheadings()** function from the savings account program. The purpose of this function is to print a main heading centered on 80 columns and then to print column headings beginning in columns 10, 35, and 60.

```
// printheadings() Function to print headings on the screen.
void printheadings(void)
{
    cout << setw(50) << "Second National Bank" << endl;
    cout << endl << endl;
    cout << setw(14) << "Month"
         << setw(28) << "Interest"
         << setw(23) << "Amount" << endl;
    return;
} // end printheadings()
```

In the function heading line:

```
        void printheadings(void)
```

the void in front is the return type of the function. Our function will not return a value as the function name. Thus, we use **void** to indicate that no function value will be returned. The **void** inside of the parentheses indicates that there are no arguments (or parameters) for the function. We will discuss this in detail a little later in this chapter. Be patient.

Note: The **return** statement is not really necessary. The programmer may wish to include the **return** at the end of the function just to indicate that this is where we are exiting the function. It is possible to exit a function in more than one place depending on certain events occurring in the function. Thus, it is possible to have more than one **return** statement in the same function.

The **printheadings()** function can be tested with the following simple program.

```
//prog4_1.cpp Program to test the function printheadings( )
#include <iostream.h>
#include <iomanip.h>
void  printheadings( void );          // function prototype
int main()
```

```
    {
       printheadings( );
       return 0;
    } // end - main()
    // printheadings() Function to print headings on the screen.
    void printheadings(void)
    {
       cout << setw(50) << "Second National Bank" << endl;
       cout << endl << endl;
       cout << setw(14) << "Month"
              << setw(28) << "Interest"
              << setw(23) << "Amount" << endl;
       return;
    } // end printheadings()
```

The main program and the function can be coded in the same file called **prog4_1.cpp**. We have placed the coding for function **printheadings()** after the code for function **main()**. However, we could have reversed this order. As it is, since the compiler will see the function call before it sees the function code, we need to include a statement, called the **function prototype**:

```
            void printheadings(void)
```

This prototype is similar to the declaration for a variable (like **int num;**), except that the prototype is a declaration for a function. This tells the compiler the interface for the function; that is, it tells the compiler the name for the function, the return type (in this case, void), and the argument types (in this case, void).

Now, let us turn our attention to writing the function **print3()** . This function will compute and print out the first 25 multiples of 3.

```
    // print3()  Function to compute and print out the first
    //           25 multiples of 3.
    void print3( void )
    {
       int num3;
       for (int I = 1; I <= 25; I++)
       {
          num3 = 3*I;
          cout << num3 << endl;
       } // end for
       return;
    } // end print3
```

142

Again the two uses of **void** are used to inform the C++ compiler that the function is not returning any data using the function name and also that it will not receive or pass any data using parameters. The following program can be used to test the function **print3()**:

```
// prog4_2.cpp Program to test the function print3()
//
#include <iostream.h>
int main()
{
   void print3( void );          // function prototype

   print3();                     // function call
   return 0;
}
// Function definition
// print3() Function to compute and print the first
//          5 multiples of 3 to the screen.
void print3( void )
{
   int num3;
   for (int I = 1; I <= 5; I++)
   {
      num3 = 3 * I;
      cout << num3 << endl;
   } // end for
   return;
} // end print3()
```

In the above program we have again coded the function, **print3()**, after the **main()** program where it is called. As before, we must tell the C++ compiler that when it sees the function call, that the actual writing of the code for the function is after the code for the main program. Again, this is done by using the function prototype statement. However, this time we have placed the statement inside of the main program.

```
void print3( void );
```

> **Note:** When the function is actually coded after a call is made to the function (such as when the function is called from function **main()**, then we must include a function prototype statement before the call is made to the function.

If we place the function prototype statement before the main program, then the function can be called by any other function coded in the file. If the function prototype is placed in the main program, before the variables are defined, then the function can only be called by the main program.

This is the same idea as when we discussed global and local variables. Variables defined before the **main()** are global and can be accessed anywhere in the file. Variables defined inside of the main program are local variables and can only be accessed within that function.

Note: Many programmers place the function prototypes before the **main()** function and then code the remaining functions after the **main()** function. This is the style that we will adopt.

The program to test the function **print3()** with the function prototype placed before the **main( )** is the following:

```
//prog4_3.cpp Program to test the function print3().
//
#include <iostream.h>
void print3( void );          // function prototype
int main()
{
   print3();                  // function call
   return 0;
}
//print3()
void print3( void )
{
   int num3;
   for(int I = 1; I <= 5; I++)
   {
      num3 = 3*I;
      cout << num3 << endl;
   } // end for
   return;
} // end print3()
```

There is one other way that functions can be coded in the same file with the main program. The function can be coded before the main program and eliminate the need for the function prototype. This is illustrated as follows:

```
// prog4_4.cpp Program to illustrate the use of functions
//
#include <iostream.h>
void print3( void )
{
  int num3;
  for (int I = 1; I <= 5; I++)
  {
    num3 = 3 * I;
    cout << num3 << endl;
  } // end for
  return;
} // end print3()
int main()
{
  print3();
  return 0;
}
```

Output from all three programs was the following:

```
3
6
9
12
15
```

Note: It is recommended by the developers of the ANSII C Standards that we include function prototype statements for every function. We will follow these recommendations.

4.4 - Functions with Pass by Value Parameters

In this section, we will illustrate how we pass data to a function by using what are called **pass by value** parameters. When we write a function, we must decide what data (if any) that the function needs to be furnished by the calling program. For example, suppose that we want to rewrite the function, **print3( ),** so that it will print out five multiples of a specified integer. The integer is to be furnished by the calling program. We then decide that we will call the function which we will name **print5mult()** as follows:

```
int number;

number = 10;
print5mult(number);
```

The variable **number** is called an **argument** (it can also be called an **actual argument**) in the function call:

```
print5mult(number);
```

Instead of involving the variable, **number,** we could have made the function call simpler by just writing the call as:

```
print5mult(10);
```

Now, let us take a look at how we might write the function, **print5mult()**.

```
// print5mult()  Function to compute and print out the first
//                5 multiples of num, one per line.
void print5mult(int num)
{
   int mult;
   for (int I = 1; I <= 5; I++)
   {
     mult = num * I;
     cout << mult << endl;
   } // end for
   return;
} // end print5mult()
```

When we write the function, we must decide upon a variable name which will receive the data value that we sent (the value 10). The variable name that we chose was **num**. This is of type integer. The function beginning line,

```
void print5mult(int num)
```

lists **int num** as the type and variable which will receive the value that the calling function sends to the function. The variable **num** is called a **formal argument** (or **parameter**). Thus, an **argument** (in the calling function) sends a value to the function's **formal argument** (or **parameter**). In our example, the variable **number** (or 10) was the **argument**, and variable **num** (in function **print5mult()**) is the **formal argument** (or **parameter**). Since we are sending the value of 10 as input to the function, we may think of **num** as being an **input parameter** to our function.

146

The keyword **void** tells the compiler that no information is to be returned using the function name.

When the C language was first developed, the function statement was done differently. For example, the type declaration for the parameter in function **print5mult()** would be done as follows:.

```
void print5mult(num)
int num;
```

That style is now considered obsolete. However, you should be aware of it in case you run across an older C program.

> **Note:** When the ANSII standards for the C programming language were developed, the new style inline declarations like we used with
> **void print5mult(int num)**
> was added to the language. The C++ programming language adopted these inline declarations. The old style declarations are now considered obsolete.

If we are asked to modify or rewrite existing C programs, we will want to change any old style declarations for parameters that we may find

```
void print5mult( num)
int num;
```

to the new style inline declarations.

```
void print5mult( int num )
```

The first program that we will write to test this function is a program in which we pass a **constant value** to the function.

```
// prog4_5.ccp Program to test the function print5mult(),
//          by passing a constant value.
#include <iostream.h>
void print5mult(int);        // function prototype
int main()
{
   print5mult(10);           // function call to print out multiples
   return 0;
}
```

```
// print5mult() Function to compute and print out the first
//                    5 multiples of num, one per line.
void print5mult(int num)
{
   int mult;
   for(int I = 1; I <= 5; I++)
   {
      mult = num * I;
      cout << mult << endl;
   } // end for
   return;
} // end print5mult()
```

Output from a run of this program was the following:

```
10
20
30
40
50
```

The function prototype can be done with either of the statements:

```
void print5mult( int num);
```

or

```
void print5mult(int);
```

In the prototype, it is not necessary to specify the variable name, only the type. We will use both styles throughout the text.

In the next program we will pass data to function **print5mult()** by using a **variable** in the calling program.

```
// prog4_6.cpp Program to test the function print5mult(),
//          by passing data by value.
#include <iostream.h>
void print5mult(int num);   // function prototype
int main()
{
   int number;
```

```
        cout << "Input a positive integer: ";
        cin >> number;
        print5mult(number);
        return 0;
} // end main
// print5mult() Function to compute and print out the first
            5 multiples of the integer num, one per line.
void print5mult(int num)
{
    .           // Code goes here
    .
} // end print5mult()
```

Output from a test run of this program was the following:

```
        Input a positive integer: 2
        2
        4
        6
        8
        10
```

We will write one more version of this function so that it will print out multiples of a given integer. Both the integer and the number of multiples are to be furnished by the calling program. We will let the reader write a program to test this function as one of the exercises.

```
    // printn() Function to print out a given number of
    //         multiples of a given integer.
    //
    void printn(int num, int n)
    {
      int num1;
      for(int I = 1; I <= n; I++)
      {
        num1 = num * I;
        cout << num1 << endl;
      } // end for
      return;
    } // end printn()
```

If the variables in the main program are **number** and **times**, defined with the statement int number, times;

then storage is set aside in memory, and the variable names reference the data at these storage locations. The data is input by the user and stored at these locations. If this data were, 2 and 5, then we would have the following in memory:

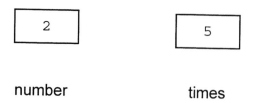

number   times

When the function is called, memory space is allocated for each of the two parameters, **num** and **n**. The addresses for **num** and **n** are different than those for **number** and **times**. The data stored for **number** and **times** is copied to the memory locations for **num** and **n**.

num   n

Using the data stored at **num** and **n**, the multiples are computed and printed to the screen. When the function is exited, the locations for **num** and **n** are destroyed. The process of sending a copy of a data value to the function is called **pass by copy** or **pass by value**.

We are now ready to code another of the functions from our Savings Account program. We will code the function, **printtable()**, which will print a table showing the month, the interest earned, and the amount of money in the account at the end of each month. The three input parameters for this function are the initial amount of money in the account, the monthly interest rate, and the number of months. The function would be coded as follows:

```
// printtable() - Function to print the table showing the month, the
//                interest earned, and the amount in the account at the
//                end of each month. Interest compounded monthly.
void printtable(float amount2, float mrate2, int mths2)
{
  float int_earned;
  cout.setf(ios::showpoint);      // print trailing zeros
  cout.setf(ios::fixed);          // print in decimal notation
  cout.precision(2);              // print 2 decimal places
  for(int I = 1; I <= mths2; I++) {
    int_earned = amount2 * mrate2;
```

```
            amount2 += int_earned;
            cout << setw(7) << I << setw(27) << "$"
                << setw(5)  << int_earned
                << setw(20) << "$"
                << setw(8)  << amount2
                << endl;
       } // end-for
       return;
    } // end - printtable()
```

The program to test this function will have to send the amount of money, the number of months, and the monthly interest rate. This can be done simply by assigning values to the appropriate variables and then sending them as arguments to the function.

```
//prog4_7.cpp Program to test the function
//                printtable( )
#include <iostream.h>
#include <iomanip.h>
#include <conio.h>
void printtable(float, float, int );
int main()
{
   float amount, mrate;
   int months;
   amount = 1000.00;
   months = 24;
   mrate = 0.055 / 12;
   clrscr();
   printtable(amount, mrate, months);
   return 0;
}
void printtable(float amount2, float mrate2, int mths2)
{

       // Code goes here
}
```

Memory Allocation for Input Parameters:

We will now discuss how the memory is allocated for variables by the C++ language so that the data can be passed to the function from the calling program. When the main program is executed, it first sets up storage locations for each of the variables, **amount**,

mrate, and **months**.

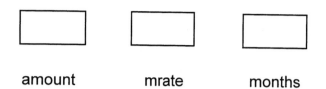

amount   mrate   months

Data is then stored at each of these locations when the three assignment statements are executed.

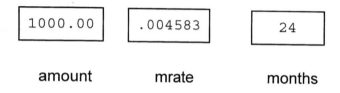

amount   mrate   months

When the function, **printtable()**, is called, storage is set up for each of the parameter variables, and the data is copied to these three new storage locations.

amount2   mrate2   mths2

The code for the function is then executed using the data stored at these locations. The table is printed, and when the return in the function is executed, these three variables and their storage locations are no longer in existence. This is a very simple process that we need to understand if we are to understand the difference between **passing data by value** and **passing data by reference**. We will discuss passing **data by reference** in section 4.6.

4.5 - Returning Data Using the Function Name

In this section, we will show how we can write functions that will compute a single value and pass the computed value back to the calling program using the function name. The first example will be a function that will compute and return the average of two real numbers. The function will compute the average and return this value to the calling program using the function name. For this function, we have two input parameters, **num1** and **num2**.

Recall that when we write our main program, **main()**, we had it return the integer value zero. In order to do this, we placed **int** before **main()**

        int main()

and placed a zero following the **return** statement at the end of the main program.

        return 0;

We will use these same ideas a function that will compute and return the average of two real numbers. We will call this function **find_aver()** which is written as follows:

```
float  find_aver(float num1, float num2)
(
    float aver;
    aver = (num1 + num2) / 2;
    return (aver);
}
```

The type declaration, **float**, is placed before the function name to indicate that a value of that type is to be returned as the function name. The average of the two integer values stored at **num1** and **num2** is computed and assigned to the local variable, **aver**. The final statement places this value after the **return** so that it is passed back to the calling program. In the **main()** function, we could define a variable **average**, of type **float**, and call the function with the statement

        average = find_aver(value1, value2);

A program that can be used to test this function is the following:

```
// prog4_8.cpp Program to test the function find_aver()
#include <iostream.h>
#include <iomanip.h>
float find_aver(float, float);          // function prototype
int main()
{
    float value1, value2;
    float average;
    cout << "Enter a number: ";
    cin >> value1;
    cout << "Enter another number: ";
    cin >> value2;
    average = find_aver(value1, value2);
```

```
    cout.setf(ios::fixed);
    cout.setf(ios::showpoint);
    cout.precision(2);
    cout << "The average of " << setw(5) << value1
         << " and " << setw(5) << value2 << " is "
         << setw(5) << average << endl;
    return 0;
}
// find_aver() Function to compute and return the average of
//              two real numbers.
float find_aver(float num1, float num2)
{
    float aver;
    aver = (num1 + num2) /2;
    return (aver);
} // end find_aver()
```

The identifiers, **value1** and **value2**, are called **local variables** for the function main. When the function **find_aver()** is called, the data values stored at **value1** and **value2** are copied to the memory set aside for the parameters **num1** and **num2** in the function. The average of the two real numbers stored at **num1** and **num2** is computed and returned using the function name. Then the value is assigned to the variable **average.** Thus, in the statement

        average = find_aver(value1,value2);

the result is returned as a value for

        find_aver(value1,value2);

Output from a test run of this program produced the following results:

        Enter a number: 25.6
        Enter another number: 76.3
        The average of 25.60 and 76.30 is 50.95

For the above function, two real numbers are to be furnished by the calling program and the real average is to be computed and returned using the function name.

For the next example, we will write a function that will compute and return the largest of two real numbers. Since the function is to compute the largest of two real numbers, it will have two input parameters of type float. The computed largest of these two real numbers will be of type float and will be returned using the function name.

154

The function is fairly easy to code and is written as follows:

```
// largest() - Function to compute and return the largest of
//          two real numbers.
float largest( float num1, float num2)
{
   float big;
   if (num1 < num2)
     big = num2;
   else
     big = num1;
   // end if
   return(big);
} // end largest
```

We will ask the reader to write a program to test this function as one of the exercises.

If we consider the functions that we are to write for the Savings Account program, we will probably conclude that there aren't any that return a single value. However, we could write two functions, one to compute the monthly interest rate and the other to compute the number of months. These two functions would replace the single function **compute()**. The following is the function to compute the monthly interest rate:

```
float m_rate(float int_rate1)
{
  float mon_rate;
  mon_rate = int_rate1 / 12;
  return (mon_rate);
}
```

We ask the reader to finish the code for the function to compute the number of months below. As exercises, we will ask the reader to code programs to test each of these functions, and in addition we will ask the reader to write a version of the Savings Account program that uses these two functions.

Try this: Write the function to compute the number of months.

```
_____comp_months(_____
{

    _____

    _____

    _____

    _____

    _____
} // end comp_months()
```

4.6 - Returning Data by Using Pass by Reference Parameters

Another way that the C++ language returns data to a calling function is by **passing a variable by reference** (this is new in C++ and will <u>not</u> work with C). What this means is that instead of sending a copy of the value of a variable, we send the address of the variable. The way that we tell the compiler that we want to pass the address is to simply include an **&** after the type declaration and before the variable parameter. We illustrate this idea by rewriting the function **find_avg()** so that it returns the average using a parameter rather than by using the function name. The function would be coded as follows:

```
// find_avg()   Function to compute and return the average of two
//          real numbers.
void find_avg(float num1, float num2, float &avg)
{
   avg = (num1 + num2) /2;
   return;
} // end find_avg
```

Note that the output parameter is the parameter **avg** and the code to tell the compiler to pass the address to the function rather than create a new storage location is:

```
        float &avg
```

The **&** operator is called the **address of operator** and can go either after the float or before the variable

```
        float  &avg                or                float&  avg
```

The **&** tells the C++ compiler that the address of the variable is to be passed. Thus, the address is sent rather than a copy of the data value. Since the function now knows the address of the original variable, we are able in the called function (if so desired) to change the value stored for this original variable. In essence, we may then think of the function as sending output back to the calling function (into this original variable). Therefore, we may then think of this parameter as being an output parameter (output from the function back to the calling function). A program to call and test this function follows:

```cpp
// prog4_9.cpp Program to test the function find_avg()
#include <iostream.h>
#include <iomanip.h>
int main()
{
  void find_avg(float num1, float num2, float  &avg);
  float value1, value2, average;
  cout << "Input a real number: ";
  cin >> value1;
  cout << "Input another real number: ";
  cin >> value2;
  find_avg(value1, value2, average);
  cout.setf(ios::fixed);
  cout.setf(ios::showpoint);
  cout.precision(2);
  cout << "The average of " << setw(6)  << value1
       << " and " << setw(6) << value2 << " is "
       << setw(6) << average << endl:
  return 0;
}
void  find_avg(float num1, float num2, float  &avg)
{
  avg = (num1 + num2) / 2;
  return;
}
```

Memory Allocation for Pass by Reference Parameters:

When we run this program the main program first sets up storage locations for the variables **average**, **value1**, and **value2**.

average	value1	value2

Data is input from the keyboard and stored at **value1** and **value2**.

	34.5	78.9
average	value1	value2

When the function, **find_avg()** is called, copies of the variables, **value1** and **value2** are sent to the parameters, **num1** and **num2**. However, since **avg** is a pass by reference parameter, then it will be given the address of the argument, **average.**

	34.5	78.9
average avg	num1	num2

The code from the function **find_avg()** is then executed using these memory locations. When the average is computed with the statement

avg = (num1 + num2) /2;

The result is stored at **avg** which is also the same as **average**. Thus the result is automatically known to the calling program. Output from a run of this program follows:

Input a real number: <u>34.5</u>
Input another real number: <u>78.9</u>
The average of 34.5 and 78.9 is 56.85

Try This: Rewrite the function **largest()**, from the previous section, so that it returns the largest of two real numbers using a parameter rather than by using the function name.

```cpp
// largest() Function to compute and return the largest of
//           two real numbers using the function name.
void largest(float num1, _____
{
    if _____
       _____
    else
       _____
       _____
}
```

The program to test this function can be almost the same as **prog4_8.cpp**. We will ask the reader to write this program as one of the exercises.

The next example is the function **get_data()** from the Savings Account program. This function is to get the amount of money, the number of years, and the monthly interest rate from the user. The data is to be entered from the keyboard. The function is to return these values to the main program. Thus, the function would not have any input parameters but would have 3 output parameters, the amount, the number of years, and the interest rate. The function prototype is the following:

```cpp
void getdata(float  &amt1, int  &years1, float  &rate1);
```

The function can be coded as follows:

```cpp
// getdata() Function to ask the user to input an amount,
//           a number of years, and an interest rate. These
//           values are to be returned to the calling program.
void getdata(float& amt1, int& years1, float& rate1)
{
    cout << "Input the amount in the account: ";
    cin >> amt1;
    cout << "Input the number of years: ";
    cin >> years1;
    cout << "Input the interest rate, 0.05 for 5% : ";
    cin >> rate1;
    return;
} // end getdata()
```

We will ask the reader to write a program to test this function as one of the exercises.

In order to print the table the program has to compute the number of months from the number of years that is input by the user. It also has to compute the monthly interest rate from the yearly interest rate. In section 4.4, we wrote two functions, **m_rate( )** to compute the monthly rate, and **comp_months( )** to compute the number of months. Now we want to write a function called **compute()** that will compute and return both of these values. This function will have two input parameters, the number of years and the yearly interest rate. It will have two output parameters, the number of months and the monthly interest rate. The function prototype will then be as follows:

```
void compute(int years2, float rate2, int  &months2, float  &mrate2);
```

We can now code the function.

```
// compute ()  Function to compute and return the number of months
//           and the monthly interest rate, given a number of years
//           and the yearly rate.
void compute(int years2, float rate2, int  &months2, float  &mrate2)
{
   months2 = 12 * years2;
   mrate2 = rate2 / 12;
   return;
} // end compute()
```

In section 4.4, we wrote the function to print the table, **printtable()**. However, if we consider what this function does as it prints out the various lines in the table, it is also computing the new amount of money that we have in the savings account. Since we want to print this final amount in the summary, we will want to pass this amount back to the calling program. We can now easily modify **printtable()** so that this amount will be passed back to the calling program. We simply have to make **amount2** an output parameter by changing the function prototype as follows:

```
void printtable(float &amount2, int mnths2, float mrate2)
```

We have one additional function that we have to write in order to complete the Savings Account program, and that is the function to print the summary, **summary()**. This function will need only input parameters: the amount invested, the interest rate, the number of years, and the final amount. The function prototype will be the following:

```
void summary(float amount3, int years3, float intrate3, float famount);
```

We will ask the reader to write this function as one of the exercises. We can now code the

160

Savings Account program.

```cpp
// prog4_10.cpp - Savings Account Program
#include <iostream.h>
#include <iomanip.h>
#include <conio.h>
// Function prototypes
void printheadings( void );
void getdata(float amount2, int years2, float intrate2);
void compute(int years3,  float intrate3, int &mnths3; float &mrate3);
void printtable(float &amount4, int mnths4, float mrate4);
void summary(float amount5, int years5, float intrate5, float famount5);
int main()
{
    float amount, intrate, mrate, famount, old_amount;
    int months, years;
    clrscr( );
    getdata(amount, years, intrate);
    compute(years, intrate, months, mrate);
    clrscr( );
    printheadings( );
    old_amount = amount;
    printtable(amount, months, mrate);
    summary(old_amount, years, intrate, amount);
    return 0;
}
//
//   Functions go here
//
```

We conclude this section with one more example from Chapter 3. In **prog3_12.cpp**, we were given the amount of money, the amount that we wanted to end up with, and the interest rate. The program was to compute and print out the number of years and the number of months needed for us to accumulate the given final amount. We will write a function to compute and return the number of years and the number of months. The input parameters will be the amount, the final amount, and the rate. The output parameters will be the number of years and the number of months.

The function is written as follows:

```cpp
//savings()   Function to compute the number of years and months
//            needed to have famount in an account starting with
//            amount and earning rate percent compounded monthly.
```

```
void savings(float amount1, float rate1, float famount1, int& years1, int& months1)
{
    float intearned;
    float mrate1 = rate1 / 12;
    months1 = 0;
    while (amount1 < famount1)
    {
        intearned = amount1 * mrate1;
        amount1 += intearned;
        months1++;
        return;
    } // end while
    years1 = months1 / 12;
    months1 = months1 % 12;
}// end savings()
```

We will ask the reader to write a program to test this function as one of the exercises.

4.7 - Function Documentation

One very important part of writing a function is the function documentation. There are various styles that programmers use; however, the information given by the documentation is essentially the same for all styles. The documentation for each function should include the following information:

1. The name of the function and a brief description of what the function does.

2. What information that it needs from the calling program. This would be a list of input parameters.

3. What information is passed back to the calling program. This is a list of the output parameters.

4. Does the function return any information back using the function name?

5. Does the function call any other functions.

We will illustrate how this is done by writing documentation for some of the functions that we have written in the preceding sections. The first is the **printheadings()** function.

162

```
//*******************************************************************
//* printheadings() - Function to print the main heading
//*                   and column headings.
//* Input Parameters:      None.
//* Output Parameters:     None.
//* Returns:               Nothing.
//* Calls:                 Nothing.
//*********************************************************************
```

The second function is the function **getdata()**.

```
//***************************************************************************
//* getdata() - Function to get the amount, the interest
//*             rate, and the number of years as it is
//*             entered by the user from the keyboard.
//* Input Parameters:      None.
//* Output Parameters:     float amount - Initial amount of
//*                                       money to invest.
//*                        float intrate - Yearly interest rate.
//*                        int years - Number of years that the
//*                                    money is to be invested.
//* Returns:               Nothing.
//* Calls:                 Nothing.
//***************************************************************************
```

Earlier, the function **printtable()** was modified so that it returned the amount of money in the account at the end of the investment period.

Try This: Write the documentation for the function **printtable( )**.

```
//*****************************************************************************
//* printtable() - _____
//*                _____
//*                _____
//* Input Parameters:     _____
//*                       _____
//*                       _____
//*                       _____
//* Output Parameters:    _____
//*                       _____
//* Returns:              _____
//* Calls:                _____
//*****************************************************************************
```

163

We will ask the reader to write the documentation for the other functions from the Savings Account program as exercises.

4.8 - Storage Classes

In this section we will take a closer look at the variables that are used in a program. These will include the variables that are defined in the main program and those defined in all of the functions that are called by the main program. We will discuss the following two questions:

1) When a variable is defined in a program or one of the functions in this program, what functions can access this variable? This is called the **visibility** of a variable.

2) Once a variable is defined, how long does the variable stay in existence? This is called the **lifetime** of the variable.

In the C++ language, these two questions are answered by what are called **storage classes**. There are three storage classes, **automatic**, **external**, and **static**. The first of these classes is the most widely used class.

Automatic Variables

All of the variables that are defined inside functions, including inside **main()**, are called **automatic** variables. There is a keyword **auto** that we could use to emphasize that a variable is automatic. We could define an automatic variable, **num1**, with the statement

```
auto int num1;
```

However, this would have exactly the same effect as using the statement

```
int num1;
```

Thus, automatic is the default storage class. The following two versions of the function, **funct1()**, define automatic variables, **num1** and **rnum1**. There is really no reason for us to use the keyword **auto**. We will always use the second version of the function **funct1()**.

```
void funct1(void)                      void funct1(void)
{                                      {
  auto int num1;                         int num1;
  auto float rnum1;                      float rnum1;
  return;                                return;
} // end funct1()                      } // end funct1()
```

An automatic variable is not created until the function is called and the statement in the function defining the variable is executed. In the above example, the variables, **num1** and **rnum1** do not exist until the function **funct1()** is called. When the function is called, memory is allocated for each of the variables. When the function exits and execution returns to the calling function, the memory that was allocated for the variables is released to be used elsewhere in the program. Thus, the variables are lost.

Note: The term automatic is used for these variables because they are automatically created when the function is called and lost when control is returned to the calling program.

The **lifetime** of a variable is the period of time between when it is created and when it is destroyed. The lifetime of an automatic variable coincides with the time period of execution for the function in which it is defined. One of the reasons that variables have limited lifetimes is to conserve memory.

The **visibility** of a variable describes where a variable can be used in a program. The term **scope** is also used to describe visibility. Automatic variables are only visible in the function where they are defined. Any attempt to reference a variable in a function where it is not visible will lead to an error message, unknown variable, being issued by the C++ compiler. Limiting the visibility of variables is another important idea from structured programming. It guarantees that variables in one function are safe from accidental alteration by other functions. As we will see later, limiting visibility is also an important aspect of object-oriented programming.

From the above discussion, we can see that for automatic variables, **lifetime** and **visibility** coincide. These variables only exist while the function is executing and are only visible inside of this function. For other storage classes, we will see that lifetime and visibility do not coincide.

One other important feature of automatic variables is that they are not automatically initialized by the compiler. We discussed this idea in Chapter 2 and we will illustrate it again in the next example. If we want an automatic variable to be initialized, then we must do it explicitly when we define the variable by using a statement like

```
int num1 = 0;
```

If we do not initialize an automatic variable, then it will have the value of what ever garbage is in the memory.

External Variables

While automatic variables are those that are defined inside of functions, **external variables** are defined outside of any function. External variables are also known as **global variables**. When a variable is external, it can be accessed by any function that is coded in the same file and follows the variable's definition. We illustrate this idea with an example. The **main()** program and two other functions, **getnum()** and **writenum()**, use the external variable, **num**. This example also illustrates how an **external** variable is initialized.

```cpp
//prog4_11.cpp Program to illustrate external variables.
#include <iostream.h>
#include <iomanip.h>
int num;                        // external variable
int main()
{
  void getnum(void);          //function prototypes
  void writenum(void);
  cout << "Value of num = " << num << endl;
  getnum();
  writenum();
  cout << "From main() " << endl;
  cout << "The number = " << num << endl;
  return 0;
} // end main()
void getnum(void)
{
 cout << "Input an integer: ";
 cin >> num;
 return;
} // end getnum()
void writenum(void)
{
  cout << "From writenum() " << endl;
  cout << "The number = " << num << endl;
  return;
} // end writenum()
```

Output from a sample run of this program was the following:

```
Value of num = 0
Input an integer: 35
From writenum()
The number = 35
From main()
The number = 35
```

In the above program, the **global** (**external**) integer variable, **num**, was defined at the beginning of the file. It was defined before the functions **main()**, **getnum()**, and **writenum()**. In this case all three functions have access to this external variable; therefore, the visibility of **num** was the entire file. The **lifetime** of the variable **num** is the entire program.

Some programmers use external variables when these variables need to be accessible by more than one function. You must be careful in the use of external variables since the wrong functions may access them. We prefer to use parameters rather than external variables in order to guarantee that this does not happen.

External variables are initialized by the C++ compiler. As we saw in the previous example **prog4_10.cpp**, these variables are initialized to 0, if the defining statement does not include initialization to another value. External variables are initialized when the file containing their definitions is first loaded and compiled. If it is initialized with the defining statement

```
int num = 1;
```

then it is initialized to this value. If it is not initialized

```
int num;
```

then it is initialized to 0. Each of these is done when the file is loaded and compiled.

Static Variables

There are two types of static variables, **static automatic** and **static external**. We will consider static automatic variables in this section and discuss static external variables in the next section when we discuss multi-file programs.

A **static automatic** variable is defined inside a function with a statement like

```
        static int num;
```

This variable has the visibility of an automatic variable, but the lifetime of an external variable. It is used when a function is to be called more than one time, and the function needs to remember a value from a previous call. We will illustrate this idea with the following example.

```cpp
// prog4_12.cpp Program to illustrate the use of
//              static automatic variables.
#include <iostream.h>
#include <iomanip.h>
int main()
{
   float compute_aver(float, float);    // function prototype
   float miles, gallons, aver;
   do {
     cout << "Enter number of miles: ";
     cin >> miles;
     cout << "Enter number of gallons: ";
     cin >> gallons;
     aver = compute_aver(miles, gallons);
     cout << "Your new miles per gallon is "
          << setw(5) << setprecision(2) << aver << endl;
   } while ( miles != 0.0);
   return 0;
}
float compute_aver(float mls, float gls)
{
   static float tmiles = 0;            // Only initialized once per program
   static float tgallons = 0;
   tmiles += mls;
   tgallons += gls;
   return (tmiles / tgallons);
} // end compute_aver()
```

Output from a sample run of this program was the following:

```
        Enter number of miles: 325
        Enter number of gallons: 10.6
        Your new miles per gallon is 30.6        // tmiles = 325, tgallons = 10.6
        Enter number of miles: 250
        Enter number of gallons: 9.8
        Your new miles per gallon is 28.19       // tmiles = 575, tgallons = 20.4
```

Enter number of miles: 0
Enter number of gallons: 0
Your new miles per gallon is 28.19

You will need to trace through the steps of the program carefully. When the function, **compute_aver()** is called the first time, the value of 325 is computed and assigned to **tmiles**, and the value of 10.6 is computed and assigned to **tgallons**. When the function is called the second time, these variables retain these values that are used to compute the new values of 575 for **tmiles** and 20.4 for **tgallons**. The reason that these values are retained is that the variables were defined as **static**.

Note: Automatic variables are allocated memory from the stack while external and static automatic variables are allocated memory from the data segment.

The following table summarizes what we have discussed in this section concerning the three classes, automatic, external, and static automatic.

Storage Type	Visibility	Lifetime	Initialized	Purpose
Automatic	function	function	No	Used by a single function
External	file	program	Yes	Used by a single function but retains value from one call to the next.
Static Auto	function	program	Yes	Used by several functions

4.9 - Multi-file Programs

Up to this point in the text, our programs have been written so that the final program included the main function and all of the other functions in a single file. In developing larger programs, this is certainly not good programming practice.

In writing well structured and modular programs, we do not want to write all of our code in one file. First of all, editing a long program can be very difficult. Also, recompiling a long program after each minor change takes considerable computer time. Good programming design calls for structuring and the separation of functions. The utilization of newer programming methods and philosophies such as abstraction and object oriented programming stresses the importance of modular programming. Developing multi-file programs also allows separate compilation of the files.

How can we develop multi-file programs and do separate compilations in C++? First of all, the exact commands to do the separate compilations and then the linking will vary with different compilers and operating systems. So, let us assume that we are using Turbo C++.

We will start with the following example for a simple main program (and file):

```
// prog4_13.cpp Program to illustrate the use of separate files.
#include <iostream.h>
#include <iomanip.h>
extern int sq(int);
int main()
{
    int num1, square;
    num1 = 10;
    square = sq(num1);
    cout << "The square of " << num1 << " is " << square << endl;
    getch();
    return 0;
}
```

The declaration,

        extern int sq(int);

tells the compiler that the function **sq()** is defined in another file. This replaces the function prototype statement that we used when the function was in the same file but was coded after the calling program.

Note: In Turbo C++, it is not really necessary that we use the word, **extern;** however it is necessary with some of the other C++ compilers.

Assume that we type this program and save it in a file named **prog4_13.cpp**. Now, let us code the function, **sq()**, and save it in a second file called **dosq.cpp** as follows:

```
//*********************************************************
//* sq - function to find the square of an integer number
//*      and return the result as an integer.
//*********************************************************
int sq(int num)
{
  return (num * num);
} // end sq()
```

This simple function computes and returns the square of **num**. Now, how do we compile and link these separate files?

Projects in Turbo C++

In Turbo C++ we first select **"Open Project"** from the **"project" menu** and then enter a project file name with a **.prj** extension.

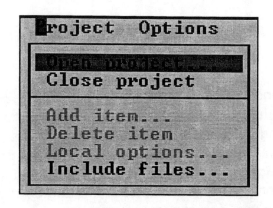

For example we could type **prog4_13.prj**. We then select the option to **Add Items** and select from the displayed directory the names of our two files **prog4_13.cpp** and **dosq.cpp**. After we have added our files we can press the **<Esc>** key and return to the main menu and select **Make** (or **Build all**) from the **Compile** menu. This will compile all of our files creating the corresponding .OBJ files. It then puts all of the .OBJ files together along with the necessary libraries, and links them all together creating the **.EXE** file. We can now run the program as usual selecting the **Run** option from the menu.

If we make any changes to any of the files, select **Make** from the **Compile** menu. This will recompile only those files that need to be recompiled and then link the files. Then, run as usual.

In order to run the program, we can select **Run** from the **Run** menu; we could debug the program with the **<F7>** and **<F8>** keys; or we could run the **prog4_12.exe** file from the operating system. The nice aspects of multiple windows in the IDE become especially apparent if we choose to debug the program by using the **<F7>** and **<F8>** keys. For example, if we continuously press the **<F7>** key to execute one statement at a time, then the IDE will load and display the correct file and statement even through we jump back and forth among several files. This makes debugging of multi-file programs very easy.

In general, we can create all of the source files first, and then call **Make** to compile and link all of the files at once; or we can create one file at a time and then compile it (but not link) and then finally call **Make** to do the linking.

We now know how to create and run a project consisting of several files in Turbo C++. At this point, you should try creating and running a project to make sure you understand the process.

In order to illustrate this concept one more time, we will redo **prog4_9.cpp** so that the procedures **getdata()**, **compute()**, **printheadings()**, **printtable()** and **summary()** are all in separate files as is the main program. We will call these files, **prog4_13.cpp**, **getdata.cpp**, **compute.cpp**, **ptheads.cpp**, **ptable.cpp** and **summary.cpp**. Recall that the functions, **getdata()**, **printheadings()**, and **printtable()** all used the input and/or output classes **cin** and **cout**. The function **get_data()** uses the **cin** and **cout** so that we must include the header file, **iostream.h**. The function **printtable()** uses **cout**, **setw()** and **setprecision()** so that we must include both of the header files, **iostream.h** and **iomanip.h**, while the functions **printheadings()** and **summary()** use **cout** and **setw()** so that we must also include both header files, **iostream.h** and **iomanip.h**.

Note: Since each of these functions is compiled separately by the C++ compiler, then each file must include all header files needed by that particular file.

We would have to add the following **#include** statements for each of the functions. We omit the documentation in order to save space.

getdata.cpp

```cpp
#include <iostream.h>
void getdata(float  &amt1, int  &years1, float  &rate1)
{
    .
    .
    .
} // end getdata()
```

compute.cpp

```cpp
void compute(float rate2, int years2, float  &mrate2, int &months2);
{
    .
    .
    .
} // end compute()
```

pthead.cpp

```cpp
#include <iostream.h>
#include <iomanip.h>
void printheadings( void )
{
    .
} // end printheadings()
```

ptable.cpp

```cpp
#include <iostream.h>
#include <iomanip.h>
void printtable(float &amt3, int months3, float mrate3)
{
    .
} // end printtable()
```

summary.cpp

```cpp
#include <iostream.h>
#include <iomanip.h>
void summary(float amt4, int years4, float oamt, float irate4)
{
    .
} // end summary()
```

The main program does not use any functions or classes, it simply calls each of the functions in order. Therefore, we do <u>not</u> need to include any header files in this file.

```
//* prog4_14.cpp - Savings Account Program using functions
//*                 in separate files.
    extern void getdata(float  &amt1, int  &years1, float  &rate1);
    extern void compute(float rate2, int years2, float  &mrate2, int  &months2);
    extern void printheadings(void);
    extern void printtable(float &amt3, int months3, float mrate3);
    extern void summary(float amount4, int years4, float intrate4, float famount4);
int main()
{
    float amount, intrate, mrate, old_amount;
    int years, months;
    getdata(amount, years, intrate);
    compute(intrate, years, mrate, months);
    printheadings();
    old_amount = amount;
    printtable(amount, months, mrate);
    summary(old_amount, years, intrate, amount);
    return 0;
} // end main
```

Assuming that we are in Turbo C++, we select **Open Project** from the project menu and name our project file, **prog14.prj**. Next, we select **Add Items** and select the following file names from the displayed directory:

> prog4_14.cpp
> getdata.cpp
> compute.cpp
> pthead.cpp
> ptable.cpp
> summary.cpp

The order in which the files are added to the project is not important.

After we have created our project file we can select **Make** from the **Compile** menu. This compiles each of the functions separately, creating the **.OBJ** files. It then links the .OBJ files together to create the final program **prog4_14.exe**. We can then run this program by choosing the **Run** option from the main menu. We encourage the reader to either create each of the separate functions or to use the provided data disk. Work through the above steps to create and run the final program. Make sure that you understand each of the steps and how the functions had to be modified and why.

Global Variables:

In these first examples, we did not attempt to share any global variables. Remember that any variable which is defined at the top of a file (and outside of any function) is visible to all functions within that file. As discussed earlier, this type of variable is called an **external** or **global variable** and is accessible by all of the functions in the file. This external variable is also visible (or accessible) to other files when we link the files in a project. Suppose, for example, that we want more than one file to have access to the character buffer, **charbuff**. We will not talk about arrays until Chapter 6, but the reader should be able to understand the idea behind the example.

```
// prog4_15.cpp Program to illustrate the use of external
//              variables.
#include <iostream.h>
char charbuff[81];
extern void getname(void);
int main(void)
{
    getname();
    cout << "Hello, " << charbuff;
    return 0;
}
```

This main program in the first file defines charbuff as an array of **char** elements. It then calls the function **getname()**, which we will write in the second file, to ask for the user's name and store it in the global buffer, **charbuff**. Upon return, the **main( )** function prints "Hello" and the name the user typed. The second file will be the following:

```
//**************************************************************************
// getname() - Function to get a name typed by the user. It stores
//             the name in an array defined in the main program.
// Input Parameters : None.
// Output Parameters: None.
// Returns : Nothing.
// Calls: Nothing.
//***********************************************************/
#include <iostream.h>
extern char charbuff[];
void getname(void)
{
    cout << "Please type in your first name: ";
    cin >> charbuff;
    return;
} // end getname()
```

In this second file, we declare the global variable **charbuff** with the statement

extern char charbuff[];

Again, the **extern** indicates that the variable is actually defined in another file. It is important to note that local variables are not external variables; therefore, local variables are not visible to other files. We also have to include the header file, **iostream.h**, since **cout** and **cin** are used in this function that is coded in a separate file.

As with the first example, we can use the **"Project"** menu to create a project file and insert the names of the two files. We then have the option of either compiling each file separately and then calling **"Make"** in the **"Compile"** menu to do the linking; or we could just simply call **"Make"** in the **"Compile"** menu to do both the compilations and the linking.

In more complex programs with several files, the programmer might wish to create a header file (with a .h extension) and include in this file the common **extern** declarations. For example, suppose we put these **extern** declarations in a file called **"proj2.h"**. Then, in each file that needs to use these declarations, we put the following **#include** statement at the top:

#include <proj2.h>

4.10 - Default Arguments & Function Overloading in C++

The C++ language has two capabilities that most languages, even C, do not have. The first of these is the ability to create **default argument lists**. When we specify a default argument list, then we can write functions that will assume certain values, even if we do not pass any data using these arguments.

Default argument values are listed in the function prototype and are automatically transmitted to the called function when the corresponding arguments are omitted from the function call. For example,

void printvalues(int num1, int num2 = 25, float num3 = 75.50);

provides default values for the last two arguments, **num1** and **num2**. If any of these arguments are omitted when the function is called, then the C++ compiler will supply these default values. Sample function calls would be the following:

printvalues(10, 20, 30.5);
printvalues(10, 20);
printvalues(10);

176

The function printvalues( ) is written as follows:

```
void printvalues(int num1, int num2, float num3)
{
    cout << num1 << endl
        << num2 << endl
        << setprecision(2) << num3 << endl;
    return;
}
```

A program to illustrate the above is the following:

```
//prog4_16.cpp Program to illustrate the use of default arguments
#include <iostream.h>
#include <iomanip.h>
void printvalues(int num1, int num2 = 25, float num3 = 75.50);
int main( )
{
    printvalues(10, 20, 30.5);
    printvalues(10, 20);
    printvalues(10);
    return 0;
}
void printvalues(int num1, int num2, float num3)
{
    cout << num1 << endl
        << num2 << endl
        << setprecision(2) << num3 << endl;
    return;
}
```

Output from this program was the following:

```
10                      // first call
20
30.50
10                      // second call
20
75.5                    // default value
10                      // third call
25                      // default value
75.5                    // default value
```

Function Overloading:

In the previous sections we discussed the following three functions:

print3(void) function that prints 5 multiples of 3.

print5mult(int) function to print 5 multiples of an integer.

printn(int, int) function to print n multiples of some integer.

All of these functions perform similar tasks but have three different names. This means we have three names to remember and three places to look for the functions. The C++ language allows us to use one function name for these three different functions. This is an example of what is called **function overloading** in C++. The function name that we will use for each of the above functions is **printmult()**. The following program illustrates how we can code and use this function.

```cpp
// prog4_17.cpp Program to illustrate function overloading.
//
#include <iostream.h>
int main()
{
   void printmult();
   void printmult( int);
   void printmult(int, int);
   printmult();
   printmult(4);
   printmult(2, 6);
   return 0;
}
// printmult() Function to print 5 multiples of 3
void printmult()
{
   for(int i = 1; i <= 5; i++)
     cout << 3*i << endl;
   // end for
   return;
} // end printmult()
// printmult( int ) Function to print 5 multiples of a
//              given integer.
void printmult(int num)
{
```

```
        for(int i = 1; i <= 5; i++)
          cout << num * i << endl;
        // end for
        return;
    } // end printmult( int)
    // printmult(int, int) Function to print out a given number of
    //                     multiples of a given integer.
    void printmult(int num, int n)
    {
        for(int i = 1; i <= n; i++)
          cout << num * i << endl;
        // end for
        return;
    } // end printmult(int, int)
```

This program contains three functions all with the same name. There are three declarations, three calls, and three function definitions. The way that the C++ compiler keeps track of which function call refers to which definition is by using the number of arguments and their types. The declaration

```
        void printmult();
```

uses no arguments, so that it is completely different from the declaration

```
        void printmult( int );
```

that uses one argument. They are both different from the declaration

```
        void printmult(int, int);
```

that uses two arguments. Similarly, the three function calls

```
        printmult();
        printmult(4);
        printmult(2, 6);
```

would all be different, referring to the corresponding function definition having the same number and types of arguments.

Output from the program follows:

```
        3
        6
        9
        12
```

```
15
4
8
12
16
20
2
4
6
8
10
12
```

In the above example, we illustrated how the C++ compiler can distinguish between functions with the same name but with a different number of arguments. The C++ compiler can also distinguish between functions with the same name and the same number of arguments as long as the arguments have different types. We illustrate this idea with the following program. This program uses a modification of the function **printmult()** that was used in the previous example. This function has two versions, one to print out a specified number of multiples of an integer and the second to print out a specified number of copies of a given character.

```cpp
// prog4_18.cpp Program to illustrate a different kind of
//              function overloading.
#include <iostream.h>
int main()
{
  void printmult(int, int);
  void printmult(char, int);
  printmult(5, 7);
  printmult('*', 7);
  return 0;
} // end main
void printmult(int num, int n)
{
  for(int i = 1; i <= n; i++)
    cout << num * i << endl;
  // end for
    return;
} // end printmult(int, int)
void printmult(char ch, int n)
{
  for(int i = 1; i <= n; i++)
    cout << ch;
  // end for
```

```
        cout << endl;
        return;
    } // end printmult(char, int)
```

This program contains two functions with the same name and with the same number of arguments. There are two declarations, two calls, and two function definitions. This time the C++ compiler keeps track of which function is being used by looking at the types of the arguments. The declaration

```
        void printmult(int, int);
```

has two integer arguments so that it is completely different from the declaration

```
        void printmult(char, int);
```

that has one character argument and one integer argument. The two function calls

```
        printmult(5, 7);
        printmult('*',7);
```

would both be different, referring to the corresponding function definition having the arguments of exactly the same types. Output from this program follows:

```
        5
        10
        15
        20
        25
        30
        35
        *******
```

The C++ compiler is able to distinguish between the different functions with the same name through a process called name mangling. When C++ compiles a function it renames the function so that the new name begins with the name you gave the function; but, then, C++ adds letters to the end of the name. The letters are added according to the types of the parameters. Thus, different parameter lists will result in different mangled names. In this way, the function names appear to be the same to the programmer, but they are all different to the C++ compiler.

4.11 - Summary

Functions provide a way to help organize programs, to reduce program size, and to develop programs using modular design. Using functions allows us to give a block of code a name so that it can be executed more than one time in a program without having to write the block of code more than one time.

In this chapter you have learned how to use functions in C++. We will continue to expand on what we have learned in the chapters that follow. You have learned how to write a function, where a function can be placed in a program, when you have to include a function prototype, and where and how to write a function prototype. You have learned what it means to pass data by value and how to pass data by reference. You know how to write a function so that it can return data using the function name.

You have learned how to document each of your functions so that any programmer that uses one of these functions can see exactly what any function that does the calling has to furnish in order to use it. This is one of the most important aspects in good programming and is often lacking.

You have learned what is meant by modular design. You have learned how to write multi-file programs by creating projects in the Turbo C++ IDE.

You have studied the three storage classes, automatic, external, and static. You know how these are used in C++ and how variables of these classes are initialized by C++. You know what is meant by the lifetime of a variable. You know what is meant by a local variable and also what is the lifetime of a local variable.

You have learned that an overloaded function is actually a collection of different functions that all have the same name. You have learned how to write such a collection and how which function is to be called depends on the type and number of arguments supplied in the call.

After we have discussed pointers in Chapter 7, we will show how functions are written in C and how we can convert these functions to C++.

In Chapter 11 we will see how functions and collections of data are organized in C++ to form objects.

4.12 - Questions

4.1   In using modular programming (or structured programming), how should we design and then code our programs?

4.2   What is a function in C++?

4.3   What are the advantages of using functions?

4.4   What is meant by a function call?

4.5   Explain the difference between an **argument** and a **formal argument** (or **parameter**).

4.6   What are the three major components of a function?

4.7   What are the main parts of a function prototype?

4.8   What does it mean when we say that we are passing **data by value**?

4.9   What does it mean when we say that we are passing **data by reference**?

4.10   What is the difference between a function declaration and a function definition?

4.11   When must we use a function prototype?

4.12   Suppose that a function **sub1()** calls a function **sub2()** in a C++ program. Does the order of the functions make any difference in the program? Explain.

4.13   What is the return type of a function that does not return anything?

4.14   Explain what is meant by overloaded functions.

4.15   Write declarations for two overloaded functions, **funct1()** and **funct2()**. They both are to return a value of type **float**. The first is to take a parameter of type **int** and the second is to take two parameters of type **int**.

4.16   What is meant by the storage class of a variable?

4.17   What is an **automatic** variable? Give an example.

4.18   What is an **external** variable? Give an example.

4.19   What is a **static** variable? Give an example.

4.20   Explain how each of the data types, **int, float**, and **char** are initialized by C++ for each of the three storage classes, **automatic, external**, and **static**.

4.21   Explain how to create a **Project** in Turbo C++.

4.22   Why is it so important that we include documentation for each function that we write?

4.13 - Exercises

4.1   Write a function that will print the message, "Hello, World!", centered on the screen. The screen has 80 columns and 25 rows.

4.2   Write a function that will compute the smallest of two real numbers and return the smallest using the function name. We will send the two real numbers to the function as parameters.

4.3   Write a function that will compute and print out the circumference and area of a circle for a given radius. We will send the radius of the circle to the function.

4.4   Write the function **summary()** from section 4.5.

4.5   Write a program to test the function **largest()** from section 4.4

4.6   Write the documentation for the function **compute()** from section 4.5.

4.7   Write the documentation for the function **savings()** from section 4.5.

4.8   Write a program to test the function **savings()**.

4.9   Write a function that will prompt the user to input an amount, an interest rate, and a final amount from the keyboard. These values are to be returned to the calling program.

4.10   Write a function that will use the data from exercise 4.9 and compute the number of months that it will take for the amount to earn enough interest so that we will end up with at least the final amount in an account. Assume that the interest is compounded monthly.

4.11   Write a program that will use the functions from exercises 4.9 and 4.10 and print a summary to the screen. The summary should be something like the following:
Amount = $xxxxx.xx
Final Amount = $yyyyy.yy
Interest Rate = z.z%
Years = dd
Months = mm

4.12   Write a function that has one **char** and two **int** arguments. The first argument specifies the character, the second argument specifies the number of times that it is to be printed on one line and the third argument specifies the number on times that this is to be done.

4.13   Write a program to test the function from exercise 4.12.

4.14   Write a function that will print a given character on a given position on the screen. The character, the row, and the column are to be the arguments.

4.15   Write a program to test the function from exercise 4.14.

4.16   Create and run the project, **prog4_13.**

CHAPTER 5

Some Library Functions in C++

5.1 - Introduction

One of the nice things about the C++, and for that matter, most other high level programming languages, is that they provide access to a large collection of previously written and tested functions and other program components, ready to be used and reused in our programs. In the C++ programming language, these functions are included in **libraries**. Then, when the program is compiled, the appropriate library functions are linked together with our code to produce the final .exe file. In order to use these library functions from the appropriate libraries, we must be sure and include appropriate header files.

After finishing this chapter, the reader should be able to

1.   understand what the header files are in Turbo C++.

2.   understand what many of the library functions in Turbo C++ are and how we can use them in our programs.

5.2 - Turbo C++ Libraries & Header Files

Borland's Turbo C++ programming language comes equipped with over 450 functions and macros that we can call within our C++ programs. These routines can perform a variety of tasks including low- and high level I/O, string manipulation, file access, memory allocation, process control, data conversion, mathematical calculations, and much more. These functions and macros, called **library routines**, are all explained in detail in the Turbo C++ Library Reference Manual.

The Turbo C++ routines are contained in the library files, **Cx.LIB**, **CPx.LIB**, **MATHx.LIB**, and **GRAPHICS.LIB**. The x, stands for the particular memory model that was chosen in the Turbo C++ options before the program is compiled.. Each model, except the tiny model has its own library file and math file, containing versions of the routines written for that particular model. The tiny model has the same library and math files as the small model.

In order to use any of the library functions, we must include the appropriate header file that includes the prototype for that function. All of the library routines are declared with prototypes in one or more of the header files.

We have used a number of the library functions that are included with the C++ programming language. Some of these functions are included as part of the old C programming language and others are included as part of the new C++ programming language. In this chapter, we will indicate what functions are available for our use in the programs that we will write and in addition what header file that we have to include with our program in order to be able to use the functions. Some of the functions that we have already introduced are the **printf( )** and **scanf( )** functions that are defined in the **stdio.h** header file, the **clrscr( )** and **gotoxy( )** functions that are defined in the **stdio.h** header file, and the **cout** and **cin** streams that are defined in the **iostream.h** header file.

Header files, also called **include files**, provide function prototype declarations for library functions. Data types and symbolic constants used with the library functions are also defined in the header files, along with global variables defined by Turbo C++ and by the library functions.

The following table is a summary of the header files that are available in Turbo C++ along with a brief description of what each header file contains. We refer the reader to the reference manual, for the particular version of C++ that you are using, in order to see how the library routines compare.. You will find that many of the libraries are the same, however, you may find that your particular version may differ somewhat from Borland's Turbo C++. The header files for the libraries are contained in the directory

C:\TC\INCLUDE

and in the directory

C:\TC\INCLUDE\SYS

```
===============================================================
Header File        Description
===============================================================
```
TC\INCLUDE directory

assert.h   Provides facilities for adding assertions about the expected
                  behavior of a program and for generating diagnostics if
                  these assertions fail.

alloc.h   Provides memory management function (allocation, deallocation,
                  etc.).

bcd.h   Declares the C++ class bcd and the overloaded operators for

	bcd and bcd math functions. (C++ only)
bios.h	Declares various functions used in calling IBM-PC ROM BIOS routines.
complex.h	Declares the C++ complex math functions. (C++ only)
conio.h	Contains functions for controlling output to the screen. For example clrscr( ) and gotoxy( ).
ctype.h	Contains functions for case conversion and for testing characters. For example, checking for uppercase or lowercase, or for special characters, or for blanks.
dir.h	Contains structures, macros, and functions for working with directories and path names.
dos.h	Contains functions and various constants that we can use to interact with DOS and to make specific 8086 calls.
errno.h	Defines constant mnemonics for the error codes.
fcntl.h	Defines symbolic constants used in connection with the library routine open( ).
float.h	Contains definitions of various type float and double limits for your computer system. For example, the maximum integer n such that 10^n is representable on our computer.
fstream.h	Contains functions for input and output to files. For example, fopen( ) and fclose( ).
generic.h	Contains macros for generic class declarations.
graphics.h	Contains the prototypes for the graphics functions.
io.h	Contains structures and declarations for the low-level input/output routines.
iomanip.h	Contains the C++ streams input/output stream manipulators that are used for formatting output. For example setw( ) and setprecision( ).
iostream.h	Contains the C++ streams input/output routines (cin and cout) and the operations (such as << and >>).
limits.h	Contains definitions of various type integer and character limits for our computer system, environmental parameters, and compile-time limitations.
locale.h	Contains functions that provide country and language specific information.
math.h	Contains mathematical functions such as square root, trigonometric, logarithmic, and exponential functions. It also contains the mathematical constant definitions that are used with these functions.
mem.h	Declares the memory-manipulation functions. Some of these declarations are also in string.h.
process.h	Contains structures and declarations for the spawn... and exec... functions.
setjmp.h	Defines a type jmp_buf used by the longjmp and setjmp

	functions and declares the routines longjmp and setjmp.
share.h	Defines parameters used in functions that make use of file-sharing.
signal.h	Defines constants and declarations for use by the signal and raise functions.
stdarg.h	Defines macros used for reading the argument list in functions declared to accept a variable number of arguments such as vprintf, vscanf, etc.
stddef.h	Defines several common data types and macros.
stdio.h	Defines types and macros needed for the standard I/O package defined in Kernighan and Ritchie and extended under UNIX System V. Defines the standard I/O predefined streams stdin, stdout, stdprn, and stderr, and declares stream level I/O routines.
stdiostr.h	Declares the C++ (version 2.0) stream classes for use with stdio FILE structures.
stdlib.h	Contains prototypes of functions for number conversion (atoi), for memory allocation (free), for sorting (qsort), for searching (bsearch), for random number generation (rand, srand), and for program termination (exit).
stream.h	Declares the C++ (version 1.2) streams and input/output routines.
string.h	Contains prototypes for functions for string manipulation. Included are functions for comparing, concatenating, and copying strings. It contains prototypes for functions for testing strings for the presence of specific characters or substrings. It also contains prototypes for functions used for memory management.
strstrea.h	Declares the C++ stream classes for use with byte arrays in memory.
time.h	Contains functions for manipulating the date and time.
values.h	Defines important constants, including machine dependencies provided for UNIX System V compatibility.

TC\INCLUDE\SYS directory

stat.h	Defines symbolic constants used for opening and creating files.
timeb.h	Declares the function ftime( ) and the structure timeb that ftime( ) returns.
types.h	Declares the time_t used with time functions.

```
========================================================================
```

5.3 - The stdio.h Header File

So far in this text, we have used a number of the functions that are prototyped in the **stdio.h** header file. The stdio.h header file is available in both C and C++. We described the use of **scanf( )** and **printf( )** in detail in section 2.7 and the use of the functions **gets( )** and **puts( )** in section 2.5. The file access functions will be discussed in Chapter 10.

The following is a complete list of the functions available from the prototypes in **stdio.h**.

```
========================================================================
```

clearerr( )	fclose( )	fcloseall( )	fdopen( )
feof( )	ferror( )	fflush	fgetc( )
fgetchar( )	fgetpos( )	fgets( )	fileno( )
flushall( )	fopen( )	fprintf( )	fputc( )
fputchar( )	fputs( )	fread( )	freopen( )
fscanf( )	fseek( )	fsetpos( )	ftell( )
fwrite( )	getc( )	getchar( )	gets( )
getw( )	perror( )	printf( )	putc( )
putchar( )	puts( )	putw( )	remove( )
rename( )	rewind( )	scanf( )	setbuf( )
setvbuf( )	sprintf( )	sscanf( )	_strerror( )
strerror( )	tmpfile( )	tmpnam( )	ungetc( )
ungetch( )	vfprintf( )	vfscan( )	vprintf( )
vscanf( )	vsprintf( )		

```
========================================================================
```

The following gives a description of some of the functions that we are most apt to use.

getc()   Function to get one character from the input stream. We need to type the character followed by a <ret>. Function prototype
int getc(FILE *stream);

getchar()   Macro to get one character from stdin. It can be defined with the statement
#define getchar getc(stdin)

The function prototype
int getchar(void);

putc()   Function to output one character to a stream.
int putc(int c, FILE *stream);

putchar()   Function to output one character to stdout.
int putchar(int c);

ungetc()   Function to push a character back into the input stream.
int ungetc(int c, FILE *stream);

The following simple programs illustrate the use of these functions.

```cpp
// prog5_1.cpp Program to illustrate getc( ) and putc( ).
#include <stdio.h>
#include <iostream.h>
int main()
{
  char ch;
  cout << "Input one character: "
  ch = getc(stdin);
  cout << endl << "The character was ";
  putc(ch, stout);
  cout << endl;
  return 0;
}
```

```cpp
// prog5_2.cpp Program to illustrate puts( )
//                 and gets( ).
#include <stdio.h>
int main()
{
  char name[80];
  puts("Input your name: ");
  gets(name);
  puts("Hello ");
  puts(name);
  return 0;
}
```

5.4 - The conio.h Header File

We have used some of the functions that are declared with the header file **conio.h** such as **clrscr( )** and **gotoxy( )**. The following is a complete list of the functions that are declared with this header file.

```
==============================================================
input and output routines
cgets( )            cprintf( )          cputs( )            cscanf( )
getch( )            getche( )           getpass( )          kbhit( )
putch( )            setcursortype( )    ungetch( )
text window display routines
clreol( )           clrscr( )           delline( )          gettext( )
gettextinfo( )      gotoxy( )           highvideo( )        insline( )
lowvideo( )         movetext( )         normvideo( )        puttext( )
setcursortype( )    textattr( )         textbackground( )   textcolor( )
textmode( )         wherex( )           wherey( )           window( )
==============================================================
```

The following gives a description of some of the routines that we are most likely to be using.

clrscr()   Function to clear the current text window and move the cursor to upper left corner.
            void clrscr(void);

window()   Function to define a text window on the screen.
            void window(int left, int top, int right, int bottom);

delline()   Function to delete the line containing the cursor. It moves all lines below it up one line. This is done inside of the current text window.
            void delline(void);

clreol()   Function to clear all characters from the cursor position to the end of the line in the current text window.
            void clreol(void);

insline()   Function to insert a blank line in the current text window at the cursor position. All lines below the new line are moved down one line.
            void insline(void);

gotoxy()   Function to position the cursor on the screen inside of the current text window.
void gotoxy(int col, int row);

cprintf()   Function to write formatted output to the screen. Works like printf(), however, does not translate '\n' into carriage-return/linefeed character pairs, '\r''\n'. Works with the current text window.

getch()   Function to get one character from the keyboard, does not echo to screen. We do not have to type the character followed by the <ret>.
int getch(void);

putch()   Function to output a character to the current text window. It does <u>not</u> translate the linefeed character, '\n', to carriage-return/linefeed pairs, '\r''\n'.
int putch(int ch);

getche()   Function to read a single character from the keyboard and echoes it to the current text window. This function is unique to DOS.
int getche(void);

We illustrate the use of some of these functions with the following program.

```
// prog5_3.cpp Program to illustrate the use of cprintf( ),
//                        insline( ), and getch( ).
#include <conio.h>
int main()
{
  clrscr();
  cprintf("Insert a blank line between lines 3 and 4 \r\n");
  cprintf("This is line 2\r\n");
  cprintf("This is line3\r\n");
  cprintf("This is line 4\r\n");
  cprintf("Press any key to continue: ");
  gotoxy(1,3);
  getch();
  insline();
  getch();
  return 0;
}
```

5.5 - The math.h & complex.h Header Files

The following is a complete list of the functions that are declared with these two header files.

```
=============================================
math.h
abs( )          acos( )          asin( )          atan( )
atan2( )        atof( )          cabs( )          cell( )
cos( )          cosh( )          div( )           exp( )
fabs( )         floor( )         fmod( )          frexp( )
hypot( )        idexp( )         idiv( )          log( )
log10( )        _matherr( )      matherr( )       modf( )
poly( )         pow10( )         sin( )           sinh( )
sqrt( )         tan( )           tanh( )
complex.h
abs( )          acos( )          arg( )           asin( )
atan( )         atan2( )         complex( )       conj( )
cos( )          cosh( )          imag( )          log( )
log10( )        norm( )          polar( )         pow( )
real( )         sin( )           sinh( )          sqrt( )
tan( )          tanh( )
=============================================
```

The following are descriptions of the functions that we are most likely to be using.

abs( )   Function to return the absolute value of an integer x.
               int abs(int x);

cos()   Function to return the cosine of the angle x, assumed to be
               given in radians.
               double cos(double x);

sin()   Function to return the sine of the angle x, assumed to be
               given in radians.
               double sin(double x);

tan()   Function to return the tangent of the angle x, assumed to be
               given in radians.
               double tan(double x);

exp()   Function to return the real number e raised to the power x.
               double exp(double x);

194

fabs( )	Function to return the absolute value of the given real number. double fabs(double x);
log()	Function to return the logarithm to the base e of the given positive x. double log(double x);
log10( )	Function to return the logarithm to the base 10 of the given positive x. double log10(double x);
sqrt()	Function to return the square root of the given non-negative x. double sqrt(double x);
pow( )	Function to return the number x raised to the y power when it is defined. double pow(double x, double y);
pow10( )	Function to return 10 raised to the integer p power. double pow10(int p);
ceil( )	Function to compute the smallest integer greater than or equal to x. double ceil(double x);
floor( )	Function to compute the largest integer less than or equal to x. double floor(double x);

===

Defined Constants	Value
M_E	2.71828182845904523536
M_LOG2E	1.44269504088896340736
M_LOG10E	0.434294481903251827651
M_LN2	0.693147180559945309417
M_LN10	2.30258509299404568402
M_PI	3.14159265358979323846
M_PI_2	1.57079632679489661923
M_PI_4	0.785398163397448309616
M_1_PI	0.318309886183790671538
M_2_PI	0.636619772367581343076
M_1_SQRTPI	0.564189583547756286948
M_2_SQRTPI	1.12837916709551257390
M_SQRT2	1.41421356237309504880

M_SQRT_2   0.707106781186547524401
==

The following program illustrates the use of some of the above functions.

```
//prog5_5.cpp Program to illustrate the use of the functions
//                  pow( ), sqrt( ), fabs( ), ceil( ), and floor( ).
#include <iostream.h>
#include <math.h>
int main( )
{
   cout << pow(2,11) << endl
        << pow(3.0, 4.0) << endl
        << sqrt(121.0) << endl
        << fabs(-1.5)  << endl
        << ceil(2.1)  << endl
        << floor(2.9)  << endl;
   return 0;
}
```

Output from this program was the following:

```
4048
81.0
11.0
1.5
3.0
2.0
```

We must be careful of how we use these functions in an expression since functions have higher priority than operators. For example, the following expression is evaluated in the indicated order.

```
3 - sqrt(16.0) + 3*pow(2,4)
3 - 4.0 + 3*16
  - 1.0 + 48
      47.0
```

In addition, we must be careful of the range of values for a particular function. The statement

```
cout << pow(3, 1024) << endl;
```

would produce the following error message.

```
pow: OVERFLOW error
       1.797693e+308
floating point error: Overflow
Abnormal program termination.
```

Similarly, the following statement would also produce an error.

```
cout << ceil(1.7e1000)  << endl;
```

Try this: What is wrong with each of the following:

pow(3) _____

ceil(2.0, 3.0) _____

floor(3,5) _____

5.6 - The dos.h & bios.h Header Files

The functions that are declared in the **dos.h** header file are used for DOS operating system calls as will as for 8086 specific calls. The functions that are declared in the **bios.h** header files are used in calling IBM-PC ROM BIOS routines. The following is a list of the functions that are declared.

```
=============================================================
dos.h - interface routines, DOS and  8086
absread( )        abswrite( )        bdos( )            bdosptr( )
country( )        ctrlbrk( )         disable( )         dosexterr( )
enable( )         freemem( )         geninterrupt( )    getcbrk( )
getdfree( )       getdta( )          getfat( )          getfatd( )
getpsp( )         getvect( )         getverify( )       harderr( )
hardresume( )     hardretn( )        inport( )          int86( )
int86x( )         intdos( )          intdosx( )         intr( )
keep( )           outport( )         outportb( )        parsfnm( )
peek( )           peekb( )           poke( )            pokeb( )
randbrd( )        randbwr( )         segread( )         setcbrk( )
setdta( )         setverify( )       sleep( )           unlink( )
memory routines
```

allocmem( )   setblock( )

sound routines
delay( )   nosound( )   sound( )
time and date routines
dostounix( )   getdate( )   gettime( )   setdate( )
settime( )   unixtodos( )
bios.h - ROM BIOS routines
bloscom( )   closdisk( )   blosdisk( )   bloskey( )
blosmemory( )   blosprint( )   blostime( )
===

The following is a description of some of the above routines.

> **delay()**   Function to delay the execution of the next statement in
> a program a given number of milliseconds.
> void delay(unsigned int milliseconds);

> **sound()**   Function to produce a tone of the given number of hz.
> void sound(unsigned int frequency);

> **nosound()**   Function to turn off the tone being produced by a call to sound().
> void nosound(void);

> **sleep()**   Function to suspend the execution of a program for a given number
> of seconds.
> void sleep(unsigned int seconds);

A program to illustrate the use of some of these functions is the following. It produces a 540 hz tone for a period of 400 milliseconds.

```
// prog5_6.cpp Program to illustrate the use of the functions
//                 sound( ), delay( ), and nosound( ).
#include <dos.h>
int main()
{
  sound(540);
  delay(400);
  nosound();
  return 0;
}
```

The next program illustrates the use of one of the functions that can be used to get the time from the operating system. This function uses a structure, **time**, that is defined in the header file **dos.h**. Structures are discussed in Chapter 9.

```
//prog5_7.cpp Program to illustrate the use of the function
//              gettime( ).
#include <stdio.h>
#include <dos.h>
int main( )
{
  struct time  curtime;
  gettime(&curtime);
  printf("Current time = %d : %d : %d\n",
       curtime.ti_hour, curtime._ti_min,
        curtime.ti_sec);
  return 0;
}
```

Output from this program was the following:

```
8 : 20 : 43
```

```
//prog5_8.cpp Program to illustrate the use of the function
//              int86( ).
#include <iostream.h>
#include <dos.h>
#define DOSTIME 0x2c
int main( )
{
  union REGS  xr, yr;
  xr.h.ah = DOSTIME;
  int86(0x21, &xr, &yr);
  cout << "Current time is "
     << yr.h.ch << " : "
     << yr.h.cl << " : "
     << yr.h.dh << endl;
  return 0;
}
```

Output from this program was the following:

```
Current time is  8 : 40 : 12
```

The data type **union** is also discussed in Chapter 9.

```
// prog5_9.cpp Program to illustrate the use of the function
//                absread( ).
#include <iostream.h>
#include <dos.h>
int main( )
{
    int start, okay, drive, sector;
    char ch;
    char sectorbuf[512];
    cout << "Insert your disk in drive A: " << endl
        << "Press any key to continue: "
    cin.getch( );
    sector = 0;                        // boot sector
    drive = 0;                         // drive A
    okay = absread(0, 1, sector, sectorbuf);
    if ( okay != 0) {
      cout << "Cannot read drive A" << endl;
      exit(0);
    } // end if
    cout << "Company name and DOS version"
        << endl << endl;
    start = 0;
    for( int i = 0; i <= 7; i++ ) {
      ch = sectorbuf[start + i];
      cout << ch;
    } // end for
    cout << endl;
    return 0;
}
```

5.7 - The stdlib.h Header File

The **stdlib.h** header file contains the declarations for functions that are used for conversion, functions that are used for sorting and searching, and others. The following table lists the functions that are declared in this header file.

===
Conversion routines

atof( )	atol( )	ecvt( )	fcvt( )
gcvt( )	ltoa( )	strtod( )	strtol( )

strtoul( )   ultoa( )

Math routines

abs( )	labs( )	_lrotl( )	_lrotr( )
rand( )	random( )	randomize( )	_rorl( )
_rotr( )	srand( )		

Memory routines

calloc( )	coreleft( )	free( )	malloc( )
realloc( )			

Standard routines

abort( )	atexit( )	bsearch( )	_exit( )
exit( )	free( )	getenv( )	lfind( )
lsearch( )	putenv( )	qsort( )	swab( )
system( )			

==

The following is a description of some of the above functions.

rand()   Function to return a random integer generated in the range of 0 to RAND_MAX = 2^{15} - 1.
int rand(void);

randomize() Function to initialize the random number generator with a random value. We should also include the header file time.h when we use this function.
void randomize(void);

srand()   Function to initialize the random number generator using a given integer seed.
void srand(unsigned int seed);

random()   Function to return a random integer between 0 and a given num - 1.
int random(int num);

The following programs illustrate the use of some of these functions.

```
// prog5_10.cpp  Program to generate 10 random numbers
//               between 0 and 99.
#include <stdlib.h>
#include <time.h>
#include <iostream.h>
int main()
{
   randomize();
   cout << "Ten random integers between 0 and 99."
```

```
           << endl << endl;

      for (int i = 1; i <= 10; i++)
         cout << rand() % 100 << endl;
      // end for
      return 0;
   }
```

We will ask the reader to run this program as one of the exercises. The next program uses the function **srand( )** and the function **time( )** so that each run will generate a different set of numbers. We will ask the reader to run this program as one of the exercises.

```
// prog5_11.cpp Program to generate 5 random numbers
//                  between 0 and 99 so that each run will produce
//                  a different set of numbers.
#include <time.h>
#include <stdlib.h>
#include <iostream.h>
int main()
{
   time_t  t;
   srand( (unsigned) time(&t));
   cout << "Five random integers between 0 and 99.")
         << endl << endl;
   for (int i = 1; i <= 5; i++)
         cout << random(100) << endl;
   // end for
   return 0;
}
```

5.8 - The graphics.h Header File

The **graphics.h** header file contains the declarations for over a hundred graphics routines. These routines make the task of creating a graphics based program much easier. The following is a list of the functions that are defined in this header file.

==

arc( )	bar( )	bar3d( )	circle( )
cleardevice( )	clearviewport( )	closegraph( )	detectgraph( )
drawpoly( )	ellipse( )	fillellipse( )	fillpoly( )
floodfill( )	getarccoords( )	getaspectratio( )	getbkcolor( )

202

getcolor( )	getdefaultpallette( )	getdrivername( )	getfillpattern( )
getfillsettings( )	getgraphmode( )	getimage( )	getlinesettings( )
getmaxcolor( )	getmaxmode( )	getmaxx( )	getmaxy( )
getmodename( )	getmoderange( )	getpalette( )	getpalettesize( )
getpixel( )	gettextsettings( )	getviewsettings( )	getx( )
gety( )	graphdefaults( )	grapherrormsg( )	_graphfreemem( )
_graphgetmem( )	graphresult( )	imagesize( )	initgraph( )
installuserdriver( )	installuserfont( )	line( )	linerel( )
lineto( )	moverel( )	moveto( )	outtextxy( )
pieslice( )	putimage( )	putpixel( )	rectangle( )
registerbgdriver( )	registerbgifont( )	restorecrtmode( )	sector( )
setactivepage( )	setallpalette( )	setaspectratio( )	setbkcolor( )
setcolor( )	setcursortype( )	setfillpattern( )	setfillstyle( )
setgraphbufsize( )	setgraphmode( )	setlinestyle( )	setpalette( )
settextjustify( )	settextstyle( )	setusercharsize( )	setviewport( )
setvisualpage( )	setwritemode( )	textheight( )	textwidth( )

==

5.9 - The string.h & ctype.h Header File

The **string.h** header file declares functions that can be used to manipulate strings. It also contains the declarations for some memory-management routines. The header file **ctype.h** contains information used for character classification along with declarations for some character and string conversions macros, such as **toascii( )** and **toupper( )**. A list of the functions and macros that are declared with these header files is the following:

==

string.h String handling functions

stpcpy( )	strcat( )	strchr( )	strcmp( )
strcoll( )	strcpy( )	strcspn( )	strdup( )
strerror( )	stricmp( )	strcmpl( )	strlen( )
strlwr( )	strncat( )	strncmp( )	strncmpl( )
strncpy( )	strnicmp( )	strnset( )	strpbrk( )
strrchr( )	strrev( )	strset( )	strspn( )
strstr( )	strtok( )	strupr( )	strxfrm( )

memory routines

memccpy( )	memchr( )	memcmp( )	memcpy( )
memlcmp( )	memmove( )	memset( )	movedata( )
movmem( )			

other
_strerror( )

```
================================================================
```
ctype.h Character routines

isainum( )	isalpha( )	isascii( )	iscntrl( )
isdigit( )	isgraph( )	islover( )	isprint( )
ispunct( )	isspace( )	isupper( )	isxdigit( )

string routines

toascii( )	_tolower( )	tolower( )	_toupper( )
toupper( )			

```
================================================================
```

The functions that are declared in **string.h** will be discussed in Chapter 8. We describe some of the other functions from the above table and illustrate their use in some simple programs.

isascii( )   Macro that classifies the ASCII coded integer values. It returns the value 0 for false and a nonzero value for true (The ascii code for the given character).
int isascii(int c);

isalpha( )   Macro that classifies the ASCII coded integer value. It is defined only when isascii( ) is true. It returns 0 for false and a nonzero value for true (ch is a letter A to Z or a to z).
int isalpha(int c);

toupper( )   Function to convert a lowercase character a to z to its uppercase counterpart A to Z .

The following program illustrates the use of two of these functions.

```
//prog5.13.cpp  Program to illustrate the use of the functions
//                    toupper( ) and strlen( ).
#include <string.h>
#include <ctype.h>
#include <iostream.h>
int main( )
{
  int length;
  char string[ ] = "Indiana State University";
  length = strlen(string);
  for( int i = 0; i < length; i++) {
     string[i] = toupper(string[i]);
  } // end for
```

```
        cout << string << endl;
        return 0;
    }
```

Output from this program was the following:

    INDIANA STATE UNIVERSITY

5.10 - The iostream.h, iomanip.h, & fstream.h Header Files

These header files contain the basic stream routines for input and output. They also contain the declarations for the manipulators that are used to format input and output. The iostream library has two parallel classes, **streambuf** and **ios**. Classes will be discussed in Chapter 11. We discussed the use of the input stream **cin** and output stream **cout** in Chapter 2. We also discussed the manipulators **setw( )** and **setprecision( )** to format numeric and string output. We discussed how we used the **ios** stream to make sure that the real output was printed in decimal with the specified number of decimal places. The complete set of format state flags enumerated in the class **ios** are given in the following table:

```
=================================================
```

format state flags	description
```
=================================================
```
skipws	Skip white space on input
left	left-adjust output
right	right-adjust output
internal	pad after sign or base indicator
dec	decimal conversion
oct	octal conversion
hex	hexadecimal conversion
showbase	show base indicator on output
showpoint	show decimal point on output
uppercase	use uppercase for hex output
showpos	show '+' with positive integers
scientific	use 1.2345E2 notation for real output
fixed	use decimal notation for real output
unitbuf	flush all streams after insertion
stdio	flush stdout, stderr after insertion
```
=================================================
```

The set of output manipulators is given in the following table:

Manipulator	Syntax	Description
dec	cout << dec cin >> dec	Set decimal conversion base format flag.
hex	cout << hex cin >> hex	Set the hexadecimal conversion base format flag.
oct	cout << oct cin >> oct	Set the octal conversion base format flag.
ws	cin >> ws	Extract whitespace characters.
endl	cout << endl	Insert new line and flush stream.
ends	cout << ends	Insert terminal null in string.
flush	cout << flush	Flush an output stream.
setbase(int)	cout << setbase(n)	Set conversion base format to base n, 0, 8, 10, or 16. Zero means default.
resetiosflags(long)	cin >> resetiosflags(l) cout >> resetiosflags(l)	Clear the format bits in cin or cout specified by the argument l.
setiosflags(long)	cin >> setiosflags(l) cout << setiosflags(l)	Set the format bits in cin or cout specified by the argument l.
setfill(int)	cin >> setfill(n) cout << setfill(n)	Set the fill character to n.
setprecision(int)	cin >> setprecision(n) cout << setprecision(n)	Set the floating-point precision to n digits.
setw(int)	cin >> setw(n) cout << setw(n)	Set the field width to n.

The code

```
int i = 47;
cout << dec << i << " "
    << oct << i << " "
    << hex << i << endl;
```

produces the following output

```
47 57 2f
```

The code

```
        int num = 23;
        cout.fill('*');
        cout.width(6);
        cout << num << endl;
```

produces the following output

```
    ****23
```

If we have the statements

```
        int num1 = 25;
        int num2 = -98;
```

then the code

```
        cout.width(4);
        cout << num1;
        cout.width(6);
        cout << num2;
```

is equivalent to the single statement

```
        cout << setw(4) << num1 << setw(6) << num2;
```

Output from either of the above is

```
    __25___-98
```

5.11 - The dir.h, io.h, fcntl.h, & stat.h Header Files

The **dir.h** header file contains declarations for the structures, macros, and functions that can be use for working with directories and path names for the MS-DOS operating system. The **io.h** header file contains the declarations for the structures and functions that can be used for low-level input/output. The **fcntl.h** header file contains the declarations for constants used in connection with the library function **open( )**. The header file **stat.h** also contains the declarations for symbolic constants used for opening and creating files. The table containing the functions and symbolic constants that are declared in these four header files is the following:

```
==================================================================
```
dir.h

chdir( )	findfirst( )	findnext( )	fnmerge( )
fnsplit( )	getcurdir( )	getcwd( )	getdisk( )
mkdir( )	mktemp( )	rmdir( )	searchpath( )
setdisk( )			

```
==================================================================
```
io.h

access( )	_chmod( )	chmod( )	chsize( )
_close( )	close( )	_creat( )	creat( )
creatnew( )	creattemp( )	dup( )	dup2( )
eof( )	filelength( )	getftime( )	loctl( )
isatty( )	lock( )	lseek( )	_open( )
open( )	_read( )	read( )	setftime( )
setmode( )	sopen( )	tell( )	unlock( )
vsscanf( )	_write( )		

```
==================================================================
```
fcntl.h

O_RDONLY	Open for reading only.
O_WRONLY	Open for writing only.
O_RDWR	Open for reading and writing.
O_NDELAY	Used for UNIX compatibility.
O_APPEND	Sets the file pointer to the end of the file prior to each write.
O_CREAT	If file exists, nothing happens. If file does not exist, the file is created.
OTRUNC	If file exists, its length is truncated to 0.
O_EXCL	Used only with O_CREAT, if file already exists, then error is returned.
O_BINARY	Open in binary mode.
O_TEXT	Open in text mode.

```
==================================================================
```
sys\stat.h

S_WRITE	Permission to write.
S_IREAD	Permission to read.
S_IREAD|S_WRITE	Permission to read or write.

```
==================================================================
```

The following is a description of some of the above functions.

chdir( )   Causes the directory specified by path to become the current working directory. Returns a value of 0 if successful and a value of -1 otherwise. The global variable errno is set to
ENOENT   Path or file name not found
int chdir(const char *path);

getcurdir( )   Gets current directory for the specified drive. Returns 0 on success or -1 in the event of an error.
int getcurdir(int drive, char *directory);

mkdir( )   Creates a directory. Returns a value of 0 if the new directory was created. A return value of -1 indicates an error, and the global variable errno is set to one of the following values
EACCES   Permission denied.
ENOVENT   No such file or directory.

The following program illustrates the use of two of these functions.

```
//prog5_15.cpp Program to illustrate the use of the
//              functions getcurdir( ) and  chdir( ).
#include <stdio.h>
#include <stdlib.h>
#include <dir.h>
int main( )
{
  char olddir[MAXDIR];
  char newdir[MAXDIR];
  if (getcurdir(0, olddir)) {
    perror("getcurdir( )");
    exit(1);
} // end for
cout << "Current directory is: "
    << olddir << endl;
  if(chdir("\\")) {
    perror("chdir( )");
    exit(1);
  } // end if
  if (getcurdir(0, newdir)) {
    perror("getchrdir( )");
    exit(1);
  } // end if
  cout << "Current directory is now: "
```

```
                    << newdir << endl;
        return 0;
    }
```

We will ask the reader to run this program as one of the exercises. The following is a description of some of the functions declared in the **io.h** header file.

filelength( ) Returns the size of the file in bytes. If an error occurs, then
                 it returns -1 and the global variable errno is set to
                 EBADF   Bad file number.
                 Unique to DOS.
                 long filelength(int handle);

open( )   Opens a file for reading or writing. File specified by path.
                 The open mode is determined by the value of access.

The following is a program to illustrate the use of these functions and one of the constants defined in **fcntl.h**.

```
//prog5_16.cpp Program to illustrate the use of the functions
//                  open( ) and filelength( ).
#include <iostream.h>
#include <io.h>
#include <fcntl.h>
int main( )
{
    int handle;
    long filesize;
    handle = open("a:\prog5_15.cpp",  O_TEXT);
    filesize = filelength(handle);
    cout << "The size of the file prog5_15.cpp = "
            << filesize << endl;
    return 0;
}
```

We wil ask the reader to run this program as one of the exercises.

5.12 - The other header files

        The following table gives the functions that are declared with the remaining header files.

```
========================================================
```
process.h

abort( )	execl( )	execle( )	execlp( )
execlpe( )	execv( )	execve( )	execvp( )
execvpe( )	_exit( )	exit( )	getpid( )
raise( )	signal( )	spawnl( )	spawnle( )
spawnlp( )	spawnlpe( )	spawnv( )	spawnve( )
spawnvp( )	spawnvpe( )		

```
========================================================
```
time.h

asctime( )	ctime( )	difftime( )	gmtime( )
localtime( )	mktime( )	stime( )	strftime( )
time( )	tzset( )		

```
========================================================
```
mem.h

memccpy( )	memchr( )	memcmp( )	memcpy( )
memicmp( )	memmove( )	memset( )	movedata( )
movmem( )	setmem( )		

All but the last of these functions are declared in string.h.
```
========================================================
```
bcd.h

bcd( )	real( )

```
========================================================
```
timeb.h

ftime( )

Contains the declaration of the structure, timeb, used with ftime( )
```
========================================================
```
types.h

Contains the definitions of the types used with time.
```
========================================================
```
values.h

```
========================================================
```
signal.h

raise( )	signal( )

```
========================================================
```
setjmp.h

longjmp( )	setjmp( )

```
========================================================
```
generic.h

```
========================================================
```

Here is another program to illustrate the use of the **time( )** function.

```
//prog5_17.cpp Program to illustrate the time( ) function.
#include <time.h>
#include <iostream.h>
#include <dos.h>
int main( )
{
   time_t  t;
   t = time(NULL);
   cout << "The number of seconds since January 1, 1970 is "
        << t << endl;
   return 0;
}
```

We will ask the reader to run this program as one of the exercises. The next program illustrates the use of one of the functions declared in the header file **bcd.h**.

```
//prog5_18.cpp Program to illustrate the use of the function
//                    bcd( )
#include <iostream.h>
#include <bcd.h>
int main( )
{
   double money = 10000.00;
   bcd num;
   num = bcd(money / 3, 2);
   cout << "One third = $"
        << num << endl;
   return 0;
}
```

Output from this program was the following:

   One third = $3333.33

5.13 - Summary

In this chapter we have attempted to introduce the reader to some of the functions that are available in the various Turbo C++ libraries. Different C++ languages have different libraries so if using a different compiler, the programmer will need to check the documentation for that particular compiler. The reader will probably want to refer back to

212

this chapter as we work through the rest of the text.

5.14 - Questions

5.1 What is a library?

5.2 What is a header file?

5.3 What header file do we need to use in order to use the functions clrscr( ) and gotoxy( )?

5.4 What header file do we need to use in order to use the input and output streams cin and cout?

5.5 What header file do we need to use in order to use the format manipulators setw( ) and setprecision( )?

5.6 What header file do we need to use in order to use the functions abs( ), ceil( ), and floor( )?

5.7 What directories are the header files in on your computer system?

5.8 What statement do we use in our program so that it has access to the declarations in iostream.h?

5.9 What is another name for a header file?

5.15 - Exercises

5.1 What is the output from each of the following:

a. floor(3.2)   b. ceil(3.2)   c. floor(-19.7)
d. ceil(-19.3)   e. pow(3,2)   f. abs(-32)
g. abs(73)

5.2 Write a program that will compute and print the cosine, sine, and tangent of 47.5 degrees.

5.3 Run **prog5_10.cpp** at least twice and check it's output.

5.4 Run **prog5_11.cpp** and chek it's output. Make sure that you understand why the output from this program is different for each run and that was not the case for **prog5_10.cpp**.

5.5 Run **prog5_15.cpp** and check it's output.

5.6 Run **prog5_17.cpp** and check it's output.

CHAPTER 6

Arrays in C++

6.1 - Introduction

When we are writing a computer program, there are times when we want to be able to group together data items of a given type. Most computer languages have a data structure for doing this, as does C++. This data structure is the **array**. An **array** is a data structure that is used to store several data items of the same type under one name. The data can be of a simple data type, like **int** or **float**, or it can be of a more complex user-defined type like a **structure** or **object**. In this chapter, we will study arrays of simple data types; arrays of integers, arrays of real numbers, and an introduction to arrays of characters.

In this chapter, we will simply introduce arrays of characters and strings; but in Chapter 8, we will study strings in detail.

After completing this chapter, the student should be able to

1.   define an array to store a given number of data items of types **int**, **float**, and **char**.

2.   store data in an array by using input from the keyboard.

3.   display the values stored in an array on the screen.

4.   store values in an array by using array initialization.

5.   use arrays as parameters to a function.

6.   use advance referencing of array elements.

7.   define and use higher dimensional arrays in programs and functions.

8.   search an array for a particular data item.

9.   sort an array using a selection sort technique.

10. understand parallel arrays and how they are used in applications.

6.2 - The Array Data Structure.

A **data structure** is used to store more than one data item and can be referenced by one name. An **array** is a data structure where the data items must all be of the same data type. In Chapter 9 we will study data structures where the data can be of different data types. This data structure is called a **structure**.

If we have a program where we want to store 5 real pay rates, using simple variables, we would define 5 different variables with the statement

float pay1, pay2, pay3, pay4, pay5;

However, by using an array we can define one variable to hold all 5 pay rates. The array is defined with the statement

float payrates[5];

In order to define an array we need to do three things:

```
1. Specify the data type.
2. Choose a name for the array.
3. Specify the size of the array.
```

We can define an array for any data type. If we want to define two arrays, one to store six integer ages and one to store seven character letter grades, then we would use the statements

int ages[6];
char grades[7];

Traditionally, for microcomputers, an integer storage location is normally 2 bytes; so each of the 6 corresponding storage locations would require 2 bytes and would be referenced with the identifiers

ages[0], ages[1], ages[2], ages[3], ages[4], and ages[5]

Note: In C and C++ the array indices begin with 0 and not 1. The above indices for ages[] are 0,1,2,3,4,5 and not 1,2,3,4,5,6.

In some languages, for example Pascal, the indices of an array begin with 1.

For the array, **pay rates[]**, the 5 array elements would be referenced with **payrates[0]**, ..., **payrates[4]** and the 7 elements of the array **grades[]**, with **grades[0]**, ..., **grades[6]**.

The index for an array element can be any expression that evaluates to an integer. Each of the following would reference an array element as long as **k** has an appropriate integer value.

```
grades[k - 1]
ages[k + 2]
payrates[2*k + 1]
```

In addition, array elements can be used in statements and expressions just like any other variable. The following statements are all legal statements in C++.

```
grades[1] = 'A';
ages[4] = 39;
ages[3] = ages[4] - 10;
ages[5] = 2*ages[3] + ages[4] - 1;
```

Try this: Write the statements that will define two arrays, one to hold 8 real exam scores and the other to hold 8 letter grades.

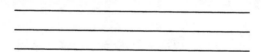

We will now illustrate how to use data stored in arrays. In the first example, we will write the block of code to find the sum of the five real data items stored in the array **pay rates**.

```
float total = 0;
for(int I = 0; I <= 4; I++)
    total += payrates[i];
// end for
```

If we did not use an array and had the five different variables, then the total would be calculated with the statement

```
total = pay1 + pay2 + pay3 + pay4 + pay5;
```

If we had to find the sum of 1000 pay rates, we can see that the for loop is a much more efficient way of finding the total, and that this can only be used if we have the data stored in an array.

In the next example, we will write a block of code to find the largest age stored in the array, **ages**. We begin by setting **largest** to the first age, **ages[0]**. We then look at each of the remaining ages, **ages[1]**, **ages[2]**, ... , **ages[5]**, and if we find a larger age, then we assign that value to **largest**.

```
largest = ages[0];
for (int I = 1; I <= 5; I++)
    if (ages[i] > largest)
        largest = ages[i];
    // end if
// end for
```

Try this: Write the block of code to find the average of the pay rates stored in the array **pay rates[ ]**.

_____
_____
_____
_____
_____

When an array is defined, the address of the first storage location is assigned to the array name. For example, the declaration for **ages** defines six integer storage locations referenced with the six integer identifiers **ages[0]**, ..., **ages[5]**. The address of the first storage location, **ages[0]**, can be referenced with either of the two identifiers, **ages** or **&ages[0]**. The addresses of the other five locations are referenced by **&ages[1]**, ..., **&ages[5]**. We will illustrate this idea by having the user input the ages from the keyboard and store them in the array. We will first input the data using **cin**, and then rewrite the code using **scanf()**. When we use **scanf()**, in the second block of code, we will <u>have</u> to use the addresses of the individual array elements.

```
for (int I = 0; I <= 5; I++)
{
    cout << "Input an integer age: ";
    cin >> ages[i];
} // end for
```

When we use **scanf()**, we would need the following:

218

```
                for (int I= 0; I<=5; I++)
                {
                  printf("Input an integer age: ");
                  scanf("%d", &ages[i]);
                } // end for
```

The next example is the block of code to print the integer ages to the screen, one per line.

```
                for (int I = 0; I <= 5; I++)
                  cout << "Age " << I << " = " << ages[i] << endl;
                // end for
```

Our final example in this section will be a program to allow the user to input 8 golf scores from the keyboard. The program is to store the data in an array, then compute and print out the average of these 8 scores.

```
            // prog6_1.cpp Program to compute and print out the average
            //                 of 8 golf scores entered by the user from the
            //                 keyboard.
            //
            #include <iostream.h>
            #include <iomanip.h>
            const int SIZE = 8;
            int main()
            {
              int gscores[SIZE];
              float average;
              float total;
            // Input the data
              cout << "Enter 8 golf scores" << endl;
              for (int I = 0; I < SIZE; I++) {
                cout << "Enter a golf score: ";
                cin >> gscores[i];
              } // end for
            // Compute the average
              total = 0;
              for (I = 0; I < SIZE; I++)
                total += ( float ) gscores[i];
              // end for
              average = total / SIZE;
            // Output the results
              cout << endl;
```

```
    cout << "Your golf average for " << SIZE;
    cout << " rounds = ";
    cout.setf(ios::fixed);
    cout.setf(ios::showpoint);
    cout.precision(2);
    cout << setw(5) << average << endl;
    return 0;
}
```

Output from a sample run of this program was the following:

```
    Enter 8 golf scores
    Enter a golf score: 85
    Enter a golf score: 92
    Enter a golf score: 83
    Enter a golf score: 95
    Enter a golf score: 102
    Enter a golf score: 78
    Enter a golf score: 83
    Enter a golf score: 94

    Your golf average for 8 rounds = 89.00
```

6.3 - Array Initialization

Arrays that are declared inside a function are called **automatic** or **local arrays** while those defined outside of a function are called **external arrays** for that function. Arrays that are defined outside of all functions are called **global arrays**. As we recall from section 4.3, a variable can be declared as **static**. When a variable, or array, is declared as **static**, it remains in existence for the life of the program. It can however, only be used in the function where it is defined. This makes it behave like a **global** array. In C++, all arrays can be initialized when they are defined.

Any **external** numeric or **static** local numeric array, that is not initialized by the program, is automatically initialized to 0. That is, all of the elements of the array are set to 0. However, local automatic arrays contain whatever garbage that is left in memory. Consider the following example.

```
    // Prog6_2.ccp  Program to test default array initialization.
    #include <iostream.h>
    #include <iomanip.h>
```

220

```
int nums1[2];
int main()
{
  int nums2[2];
  static int nums3[2];
  cout << setw(5) << nums1[0] << setw(5)
    << nums2[0] << setw(5) << nums3[0] << endl;
  cout << setw(5) << nums1[1] << setw(5)
    << nums2[1] << setw(5) << nums3[1] << endl;
  return 0;
}
```

Output from this program was the following:

```
    0    0    0
  04   01   90
```

As we have just discussed, one of the new features of C++ is that <u>any</u> array can be initialized when it is defined. Thus, we can initialize the array **ages** when we define it with one statement. For example:

int ages[6] = {25, 34, 76, 19, 53, 44};

This statement sets up 6 integer storage locations in memory and stores the 6 specified integers in the corresponding elements of the array. We would have the following:

| ages | 25 | 34 | 76 | 19 | 53 | 44 |

We can also initialize part of the array. For example, the following statement would assign data to the first two elements of the array **ages**.

int ages[6] = {25, 34};

When we initialize only part of an array, we must be careful to include the size of the array in the declaration. For example, the following statement would only define an array with storage for two integers rather than having storage for six integers as we had intended.

int ages[] = {25, 34};

Character arrays have an added feature in that they can be initialized by using either individual characters or by using strings. Thus, the array **grades** could be defined and data stored in the array with either of the statements:

char grades[7] = {'A', 'B', 'C', 'C', 'B', 'A', 'F'};

char grades[8] = "ABCCBAF";

In C++, any sequence of characters enclosed in double quotes is called a **string**. An additional byte containing the value 0 is attached to the end of every string and this byte is used to mark the end of the string. Thus, when we choose to initialize a character array using a string, then we must include an additional storage location for the 0x00 byte terminator. This byte is denoted by '\0'.

When an array is initialized as it is declared, the size of the array may be omitted. The size will automatically be defined by the number of data items stored. In the above examples we could have used the following statements:

int ages[] = {25, 34, 76, 19, 53, 44};

char grades[] = {'A', 'B', 'C', 'C', 'B', 'A', 'F'};

char grades[] = "ABCCBAF";

Once again, the 2nd statement defines 7 storage locations while the 3rd statement defines 8 storage locations (the first 7 for the 7 character letter grades and the 8th for the 0x00 byte to indicate the end of the string).

The next example illustrates the use of array initialization. We will write a program to compute the number of the day of the year, given the month and the day of that month.

```
// prog6_3.cpp Program to illustrate the use of array initialization. It
//              computes and prints out the number of the day of the year,
//              given a month and day input by the user. It does not work
//              for a leap year.
//
#include <iostream.h>
#include <iomanip.h>
int main()
{
  int days_of_month[] = {31, 28, 31, 30, 31, 30, 31, 31,
                          30, 31, 30, 31};
  int month, day, number_days;
```

```
      cout << "Enter a month (1-->12): ";
      cin >> month;
      cout << "Enter a day of that month, (1-->31): ";
      cin >> day;
      number_days = day;
      for(int I = 0; I < month - 1; I++)
        number_days += days_of_month[i];
      // end for
      cout << "The number of the day of the year is = " << number_days << endl;
      return 0;
   }
```

A sample run from this program was the following:

> Enter a month (1-->12): <u>6</u>
> Enter a day of that month, (1-->31): <u>7</u>
> The number of the day of the year is = 158

6.4 - Copying Arrays and the sizeof() Function

One of the very useful functions that is included in the C++ programming language is the **sizeof( )** function that can be used to compute the number of bytes of storage reserved for any variable. For example, if we had the following variables defined:

```
      char onechar;
      int num;
      float rnum;
      int gscores[8];
```

then we can use the **sizeof()** function, along with **cout**, to print out the number of bytes reserved for each of the variables. The next program illustrates the use of the **sizeof( )** function.

```
      //prog6_4.cpp Program to illustrate the use of the
      //                    sizeof( ) function.
      #include <iostream.h>
      #include <iomanip.h>
      int main( )
      {
        char onechar;
        int num;
```

```
    float rnum;
    double dnum;
    int gscores[8];
    cout << "One character = " << sizeof(onechar) << " byte" << endl;
    cout << "One integer = " << sizeof(num) << " bytes" << endl;
    cout << "One real = " << sizeof(rnum) << " bytes" << endl;
    cout << "One double real = " << sizeof(dnum) << " bytes" << endl;
    cout << "The array of integers = " << sizeof(gscores) << " bytes" << endl;
    return 0;
}
```

Output from this program was the following:

```
One character = 1 byte
One integer = 2 bytes
One real = 4 bytes
One double real = 8 bytes
The array of integers = 16 bytes
```

The **sizeof()** function even returns the number of bytes reserved for the entire array.

We cannot assign the data stored in an array to another array directly as we can when using simple variables. If we had the following arrays defined

```
int exams1[] = {93, 86, 87};

int exams2[3];
```

and we tried to assign the data stored in **exams1[ ]** to **exams2[ ]** with the statement

```
exams2 = exams1;
```

then this would be flagged by the compiler as an illegal statement. We can, however, copy the data one element at a time. For example, using a for loop we would have the following block of code:

```
for(I = 0; I <=2; I++)
    exams2[i] = exams1[i];
```

In order to copy arrays of characters we can use another of the functions that is supplied with the C++ programming language. This function is **strcpy( )**. For example, suppose that we define a string as follows:

char university[] = "Indiana State University";

The **string** of characters **Indiana State University** will be stored in memory at the character array address, **university**. In addition to the string of characters, a **null** byte terminator (a byte with a value of 0x00) will be stored as the last byte on the end (immediately after the characters).

Suppose, also that we declared a second character array defined with the statement

char college[25];

Now, we can copy the data stored at **university[ ]** to the array **college[ ]**, including the string terminator, **'\0'**, with the single statement

strcpy(college, university);

It is very important to remember that this function assumes that the null terminator is at the end of the **university** array. This null byte terminates the copy of the characters from one array to the other.

In section 6.5 we will write a function that will perform the same function for integer arrays as **strcpy( )** does for strings. Since we do not have any terminator for numeric arrays, the function will need to know the size of the array.

6.5 - Arrays and Functions

In this section we will discuss arrays as parameters for functions. When an array is passed to a function, the address of the array is the only item that is actually passed. This address is the address of the first storage location reserved for the array. We will illustrate this with some examples from section 4.1. In the first example we will write a function that will compute and return the average of the data stored in the array **pay rates**. We will also pass the number of data items stored as a parameter. We would need the following parameters.

payrates1[]   aver1
count1

The function would be coded as follows:

```
//***********************************************************
// find_av() - Function to compute the average of a collection
//             of real numbers stored in an array.
// Input Parameters: payrates1[] - an array of real numbers.
//                   count1      - the integer number of items
//                                 in the array.
// Output Parameters: None.
// Returns: average of the data in the array.
//
// Calls: Nothing.
//***********************************************************
float find_av(float payrates1[], int count1)
{
  float aver;
  float sum = 0;
  for(int I = 0; I < count1; I++)
    sum += payrates1[i];
  // end for
  aver = sum / count1;
  return(aver);
} // end find_av()
```

We can use the following program to test the function **find_av( )**.

```
// prog6_5.cpp Program to test the function find_av()
//
#include <iostream.h>
#include <iomanip.h>
float find_av(float payrates1[], int count1);
int main()
{
  float pay rates[] = {25.50, 30.75, 15.60, 20.35};
  float average;
  int count = 4;
  average = find_av(pay rates, count);
  cout << "The average of the " << count << " pay rates = $";
  cout << setw(5) << setprecision(2) << average << endl;
  return 0;
}
#include <a:\findav.cpp>
```

Output from a run of this program was the following:

The average of the 4 pay rates = $23.05

The above example again illustrates one of the strengths of C++. As we have illustrated, when we write the function **find_av( )** and declare the array **payrates1[ ]** as a parameter, we do not have to specify the size of the array. The reason for this is that the C++ compiler is content to consider **pay rates[ ]** as the starting address of the array, and it doesn't really care where it ends. When the function is called in the main program, the address of the array is passed to the function and the computations are performed using the stored data. The function prototype could also have been written as follows:

float find_av(float [], int);

The square brackets, **[]**, following the type declaration **float** tell the C++ compiler that the parameter is an array (of type float).

The next example will be a function that will compute and return the largest age in an array of integer ages. We will pass the array and the number of data items stored in the array as a parameter.

The function can be coded as follows.

```
//*****************************************************************
// find_big()  Function to compute the largest integer stored in
//             an array.
// Input Parameters: ages1[] - array of integers.
//                   count1 - number of integers stored in ages1[].
// Output Parameters: Nothing.
// Returns: largest integer in the array.
// Calls: Nothing.
//*****************************************************************
int find_big(int ages1[], int count1)
{
  int big1 = ages1[0];
  for (int I = 1; I < count1; I++)
   if (ages[i] > big1)
     big1 = ages[i];
   // end if
  // end for
  return(big1);
} // end find_big()
```

The program to test the function **find_big( )** would be almost the same as the program in the previous example; so, we will include the writing of the program as one of the exercises.

Using an array as a parameter is similar to using a **reference** parameter as we discussed in Chapter 4. When an array is used as a parameter, the array is not duplicated in memory. Instead, the address of the array is sent; and the original array defined by the calling program is used by the function. This method certainly preserves memory. Arrays can be very large and duplicating the entire array could be time-consuming and a waste of memory. We illustrate this idea with an example. This function **get_ages()** will allow the user to input eight integer ages from the keyboard. and since we pass the address of the array as a parameter, we know where to store the data. Then, when we return to the calling program, it can use the data that we stored in the array.

```
//*************************************************************
// get_ages() Function to get 8 integer ages input from
//               the keyboard and store them in an array.
// Input parameters: None
// Output parameters: Array of integer ages.
// Returns: Nothing.
// Calls: Nothing.
//*************************************************************
void get_ages( int ages1[ ])
{
  for (int I = 0; I < 8; I++)
  {
    cout << "Input an age: ";
    cin >> ages1[i];
  } // end for
} // end get_ages()
```

The corresponding function, **print_ages()**, to display the ages on the screen, one per line can use the code from section 6.2. The function is coded as follows:

```
//*************************************************************
// print_ages() Function to display the ages on the
//               screen, one per line.
// Input parameters: Array of integer ages.
// Output parameters: None.
```

```
// Returns: Nothing.
// Calls: Nothing
//*********************************************************
void print_ages(int ages2[ ])
{
  for (int I = 0; I < 8; I++)
    cout << "Age " << I << " = " << ages2[i] << endl;
  // end for
} // end print_ages()
```

The program to test these two functions is the following:

```
// prog6_6.cpp Program to test the two functions
//              get_ages() and print_ages().
//
#include <iostream.h>
// Function prototypes
void get_ages(int []);
void print_ages(int []);
int main()
{
  int ages[8];
  get_ages(ages);
  print_ages(ages);
  return 0;
}
#include <a:\getages.cpp>
#include <a:\ptages.cpp>
```

Output from this program was the following:

```
Input an age: 32
Input an age: 45
Input an age: 43
Input an age: 56
Age 0 = 32
Age 1 = 45
Age 2 = 43
Age 3 = 56
```

We will now write a function that will copy the contents of one integer array to another integer array. The function will have to have the array containing the data and the size of the array as input parameters and the array to which the data is to be copied as an output parameter. However, as we have just discussed, arrays are always passed by reference and therefore are always output parameters.

array1[ ]
size

array2[ ]

```
void copy_int_array(int array1[ ], int array2[ ], int size)
{
  for(int I = 0; I <= size - 1; I++)
    array2[i] = array1[i];
  return;
}
```

We will ask the reader to write a program to test this function as one of the exercises.

We can also write our own version of the **strcpy( )** function, now that we have a good understanding of how strings are stored. We simply have to copy the characters stored in the first string to the second array until we have copied the string terminator, **'\0'**. The appropriate programming structure would be the **do while** and not the **for** loop since we do not know how many characters have to be copied. We will call our function **stringcopy()**. The parameters for this function would simply be the two arrays. We will write part of the function and ask the reader to fill in the remaining steps.

Try this: Write the block of code for the function **stringcopy( )**.

```
void stringcopy(char st2[], char st1[])
{
  do {

    _____
    _____
    _____
    _____
  } while ( _____ )
  return;
}
```

We will ask the reader to write a program to test this function as one of the exercises.

6.6 - Higher-Dimensional Arrays

A **two-dimensional array** can be viewed as a collection of data arranged into rows and columns. For example, the collection of integers

230

```
34  25  78  34
10  59  78  20
99  45  53  45
```

is a two-dimensional array of integers consisting of three rows and four columns. In order to define an array to store this collection of data, we would need to define an array that has three rows and four columns. This is done with the following statement:

int nums[3][4];

This would define a collection of 3 * 4 = 12 integer storage locations that are referenced by the integer identifiers:

nums[0][0], nums[0][1], nums[0][2], nums[0][3]
nums[1][0], nums[1][1], nums[1][2], nums[1][3]
nums[2][0], nums[2][1], nums[2][2], nums[2][3]

Note: We cannot define the two-dimensional array with the statement

int nums[3,4];

This syntax is legal in some languages, but not in C++.

The first index references the row and the second index references the column. As in the case of one dimensional arrays, the row index and the column index begin at 0 instead of at 1 and end at 2 and 3, respectively, since we have 3 rows and 4 columns. Each element in the above two-dimensional array of integers is located by specifying its row and column.

	Col_0	Col_1	Col_2	Col_3
Row_0	34	25	78	34
Row_1	10	59	78	20
Row_2	99	45	53	45

Just as we did with one-dimensional arrays, <u>any</u> two dimensional array can be initialized when it is declared. We can initialize the array **nums** with the above collection of integer data using the following statement.

```
int nums[3][4] =      { {34, 25, 78, 34},
                        {10, 59, 78, 20},
                        {99, 45, 53, 45} };
```

We can find the sum of the data items contained in the second row of **nums** with the following block of code.

```
int sum = 0;
for(int j = 0; j <= 3; j++)
   sum += nums[1][j];
// end for
```

Note that the second row is referenced with the first index being fixed at 1. The four data items in that row are referenced with the index taking on the values 0, 1, 2, and 3.

We could find the largest element in the third column with the following block of code. Here the third column is referenced by fixing the second index at 2.

```
int largest = nums[0][2];
for(int I = 1; I <= 2; I++)
   if (largest < nums[i][2])
      largest = nums[i][2];
   // end if
// end for
```

Multi-dimensional arrays are stored in what is known as **row-column order**. This means that the first row is stored in order, followed by the second row in order, etc. Thus we could initialize the array **nums** without grouping it into rows as long as we list the data in row-column order. The initialization can be done with the following statement.

```
int nums[3][4] = {34, 25, 78, 34, 10, 59, 78, 20, 99, 45, 53, 45};
```

We will illustrate the use of two dimensional arrays with some examples. The first example will be to write a function that will compute and return the average of all of the data items contained in a two dimensional array.

```
//***********************************************************************
// find_avg() - Function to compute the average of a collection of
//              real numbers contained in a two dimensional array.
// Input Parameters: nums1[][] a two dimensional array of
//                             integers.
// Output Parameters: None.
// Returns: Average of the integers in nums1[][].
```

```
// Calls - Nothing.
//*************************************************************************
float find_avg(int nums1[3][4])
{
  int sum = 0;
  float aver;
  for(int I = 0; I <= 2; I++)
    for(int j = 0; j <= 3; j++)
      sum += nums1[i][j];
    // end for
  // end for
  aver = sum / 12.0;
  return  aver;
} // end find_avg()
```

The function **find_avg( )** could be tested with the following program.

```
//prog6_7.cpp Program to test the function find_avg()
#include <iostream.h>
#include <iomanip.h>
float find_avg(int nums1[3][4]);
int main()
{
  int nums[3][4] = { {34, 25, 78, 34},
                     {10, 59, 78, 20},
                     {99, 45, 53, 45} };
  float average;
  average = find_avg(nums);
  cout.setf(ios::showpoint);
  cout.setf(ios::fixed);
  cout.precision(2);
  cout << "The average = " << setw(6)
       << average << endl;
  return 0;
}
#include <a:\find2avg.cpp>
```

Output from this program was the following:

```
        The average = 48.33
```

The function prototype could also be given with the statement float find_avg(int nums[ ][4]);

or simply

float find_avg(int [ ][4]);

The reason that the statement does not need the first dimension, the number of rows, is that it is considered as an array of arrays. It does not need to know the number of arrays, but simply the size of the arrays that make up the array. That is, the C++ compiler needs to know the number of elements in each row, but, it does not need to know the number of rows. For the above example, the compiler needs to know that the array **nums** is made up of integer arrays of length four. The length of each row is four.

In the next example, we will write a function to compute the average of the data in each row and return an array containing these averages.

```
//***********************************************************************
// find_rowavg() - Function to compute the averages of each
//                         of the 3 arrays of 4 integers.
// Input Parameters -  nums1[][] - Two dimensional array of
//                                     integers.
// Output Parameters -  row_avgs1[] - Array of real averages.
// Returns: Nothing.
// Calls - Nothing.
//***********************************************************************
void find_rowavg(int nums1[ ][4], float row_avgs1[ ])
{
  int sum;
  for (int I = 0; I <= 2; I++)
  {
    sum = 0;
    for(int j = 0; j <= 3; j++)
     sum += nums1[i][j];
    // end for
    row_avgs1[i] = sum / 4.0;              // Convert to float
  } // end for
  return;
} // end find_rowavg()
```

The program to test this function is the following:

```
// prog6_8.cpp Program to test find_rowavg()
#include <iostream.h>
```

```cpp
#include <iomanip.h>
void find_rowavg(int [ ][4], float [ ]);
int main()
{
  int nums[][4] = {12,13,25,32,54,32,65,45,26,38,86,23};
  float averages[3];
  find_rowavg(nums, averages);
  cout.setf(ios::showpoint);
  cout.setf(ios::fixed);
  cout.precision(2);
  for (int I = 0; I < 3; I++)
    cout << setw(6)  << averages[i] << endl;
  // end for
  return 0;
}
#include <a:\frowavg.cpp>
```

Output from this program was the following:

```
20.50
49.00
43.25
```

When we are declaring a two-dimensional array as a parameter to a function, we do not have to specify the number of rows. We do however, have to specify the number of columns, i.e. the number of elements in each row. In the first example we could have declared **nums1[ ][ ]** as a parameter with the statements

```cpp
float find_avg(int nums1[ ][4])
```

In order to see why we do not have to specify the number or rows, but we do have to specify the number of columns, let us again consider how the data is stored in memory. Starting with the element **nums[0][0]**, the data is stored linearly, one row after another. The data is stored in the order

```
nums[0][0], nums[0][1], nums[0][2], nums[0][3], nums[1][0], nums[1][1], ->
nums[1][2], nums[1][3], nums[2][0], nums[2][1], nums[2][2], nums[2][3]
```

In order for the computer to determine the position of a given element in memory, it calculates the position by adding the appropriate offset to the beginning address of the array. In order to compute the offset, it must know the size of each storage location, the row index, the column index, and also the column size. The offset is calculated with the following formula.

$$\text{offset} = (\text{row index})*(\text{number of bytes in a row}) +$$
$$(\text{column index})*(\text{bytes per storage location})$$

The "number of bytes in a row" is calculated with the formula

$$(\text{number of bytes in a row}) = (\text{column size}) * (\text{bytes per storage location})$$

Note that <u>column size</u> is the number of elements in each row. In the formula for offset, the expression, **(row index) * (number of bytes in a row)**, gets us to the appropriate row. The expression **(column index) * (bytes per storage location)** gets us to the element of the row. Consider the array, **nums** (3 rows and 4 columns), and consider the array element **nums[2][3]**. This is the 4th element in the 3rd row. In order to compute the number of bytes needed to find the position of this element, we would have the following:

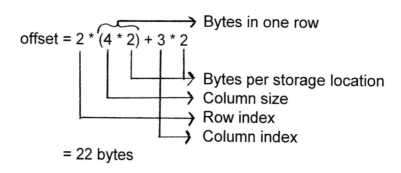

= 22 bytes

As we can see, column size, i.e. the length of each row, is necessary in order for the computer to compute the number of positions needed to find the beginning of the next row.

Everything that we have said about two-dimensional arrays can be generalized to three-dimensional arrays, four-dimensional arrays, and so on. We can declare a three dimensional array, **data**, of integers with the statement

```
int data[4][3][2];
```

We can visualize this array **data[ ][ ][ ]** in two ways. The first way would be as 4 two-dimensional arrays (each with 3 rows and 2 columns) stacked on top of each other. This will work for 3 dimensional arrays, but will not work for 4 dimensional arrays or higher. The second way to view higher dimensional arrays, is as an arrays of arrays. In the example above, it is simply viewed as an array of 4, two-dimensional arrays. This idea can easily be extended to higher dimensions.

As an example, we can declare and initialize the array **data**, thinking of it as a 4 dimensional array of two dimensional arrays, each with 2 rows and 3 columns. We would use either of the following statements:

```
int data[4][3][2] = { { {15,3}, {-2,5}, {90,32} },    // 1st array
                      { {23, 0}, {7, -2}, {67, 54} },  // 2nd array
                      { {6,-9}, {23, 10}, {0,-15} },   // 3rd array
                      { {76, 5}, {3,0}, {22,1} } };    // 4th array
```

or

```
int data[ ][3][2] = {15, 3, -2, 5, 90, 32, 23, 0, 7, -2, 67, 54,
                     6, -9, 23, 10, 0, -15, 76, 5, 3, 0, 22, 1};
```

6.7 - Advanced Referencing of Array Elements

The C++ programming language allow for a much different method of referencing elements of an array. If we have an array defined with the following statement

```
int exams[5];
```

then the standard way of referencing the five array elements is by using subscripts. The array elements are referenced with the variables

exams[0], exams[1], exams[2], exams[3], and exams[4]

In C++ the array name is actually a variable containing the address of the first byte of memory that has been reserved for the array storage. In addition, we are allowed to do arithmetic with this address so that we can reference the array elements by adding the appropriate integer value to the array name. For example, the five array elements can also be referenced with the identifiers

(exams + 0)[0], (exams + 1)[0], (exams + 2)[0], (exams + 3)[0], and (exams + 4)[0]

This notation is sometimes referred to as **advanced array notation** and is a notation that we must become familiar with if we are going to be able to master the use of **pointer variables** (that we will study in detail in the next section). The only thing that we want to do in this section is to introduce the reader to this notation and see how it can be used in referencing arrays. When we write a program using arrays, we will use the standard notation.

The code to find the sum of the data stored in the array, **exams[ ]**, using normal array notation is the following:

```
sum = 0;
for(int I = 0; I <= 4; I++)
   sum = sum + exams[i];
// end for
```

This same code written in advanced array notation is written as follows:

```
sum = 0;
for (int I = 0; I <= 4, I++)
   sum = sum + (exams + I)[0];
// end for
```

Try this: Write the following block of code so that it uses advanced array notation.

```
largest = exams[0];
for(int I = 1; I <= 4; I++)
if (exams[i] > largest)
   largest = exams[i];
// end if
// end for
```

      _____
      _____
      _____
      _____
      _____
      _____

The next example is the function **find_av( )**, from section 6.5 written using the advanced array notation.

```
float find_av(float nums1[ ], int count1)
{
  float aver;
  float sum = 0;
  for(int I = 0; I < count1; I++)
    sum += (nums1 + I)[0];
  // end for
  aver = sum / count1;
  return (aver);
}
```

We will ask the reader to write a program to test this function as one of the exercises.

Try this: Write the following block of code so that it uses standard array notation.

```
float sum = 0;                    _____
for(int I = 0; I < count; I++)    _____
    sum += (nums + I)[0];         _____
// end for                        _____
```

6.8 - Searching an Array

In this section, we will discuss how we can search an array for a particular data item. We must decide what we will do if the data item is found as well as what to do if it is not found. We will write a function that will search an array of integers along with a program to test this function. The technique that we will use to write the function will be a simple linear search. Suppose that we have the following array defined with the given data stored in the array.

```
int ages[] = {32, 19, 16, 48, 56, 21, 41, 31, 89, 16};
```

and that we want to search the array for the specific age,

```
int age = 21;
```

We can see that the above array, **ages[]**, does contain this data item and moreover, it is stored in the 6th position in the array, **ages[5]**. We will want the search algorithm to find the data item and return the index, **5**, of the array element which contains the data item. What happens if the data item is not found? In this case, we would want to return a value that could not possibly be the index of an element of the array. We will choose to return the value of -1.

The search process is fairly simple; we can use the following algorithm.

```
Set index to -1.
for I = 0 to count - 1
  if age = ages[i] then
    index = I
  end-if
end-for
```

This algorithm will return **index** equal to 5 if **age** is equal to 21 and **index** equal to -1 if **age** is equal to 15.

What happens in the case that the data item appears more than once in the array? If **age** is 16, then **index** is set to 2 the first time that a match is found and then set to 9 when a match is found again. The above algorithm would return the index of the last array element containing the data for which we are searching. This might be acceptable but, we would probably want to return either the first index or all of the indices of the array elements containing the data. We will modify our algorithm so that the first index is returned. We will consider the problem of returning all of the indices as one of the exercises. The modification of the algorithm is a nice example of how we can use the

break;

statement to exit a loop. We discussed the use of this statement in Chapter 3. The new algorithm would be the following:

```
Set index to -1.
for I = 0 to count - 1
  if age = ages[i] then
    index = I.
    break.
  end-if
end-for
```

We can now easily write a function that will search an array for a given data item and will return the index of the first element containing the item, if it is found, and -1 if the item is not found. We will return the index using the function name. We will ask the reader to write the documentation for this function as one of the exercises. We will also ask the reader to modify the function so that it returns the index as an output parameter at the end of this section. We will write a program to test this modified function as one of the exercises.

```
// search( ) Function to search an array for a given element
// Input parameters: array1[ ] - given array
//                   size1 - number of elements in the array
//                   Item1 - element that we are looking for
// Output parameters: None
// Returns: index of the array element containing item1, if
//          found or -1 if not found
// Calls: Nothing
    int search(int array1[ ], int size1, int item1)
    {
      int index = -1;
```

```
        for(int I = 0; I <= size1 - 1; I++) {
          if (item1 == array1[i]) {
            index = I;
            break;
          } // end if
        } // end for
        return index;
      }
```

   We will use the following program to test the function **search( )**. The program will
call the function three times; once for a data item that appears only once, once for a data
item that appears twice, and once for a data item that does not appear in the array. The
three data items will be input from the keyboard.

```
//prog6_9.cpp program to test the search( ) function
#include <iostream.h>
int search(int array1[ ], int size1, int item1);
int main( )
{
  int ages[ ] = {32, 19, 16, 48, 56, 21, 41, 31, 89, 16};
  int size = 10;
  int item, index;
  for(int I = 1; I <= 3; I++) {
    cout << "Input an integer data item: ";
    cin >> item;
    index = search(ages, size, item);
    if(index == -1)
      cout << "Item = " << item << " not found."
           << endl;
    else
      cout << "Item found!" << endl
           << "Item = " << item << endl
           << "Index = " << index << endl;
    // end if
  } // end for
  return 0;
}
#include <a:\search.cpp>
```

Output from a run of this program was the following:

Input an integer data item: <u>56</u>
Item found!
Item = 56
Index = 4
Input an integer data item: <u>16</u>
Item found!
Item = 16
Index = 2
Input an integer data item: <u>73</u>
Item = 73 not found.

Try this: Rewrite the function **search( )** so that it returns the index as an output parameter.

```
void search(_____)
{
  int index = -1;
  for(_____
   if (_____) {

      _____
      _____

  } // end if
  } // end for

      _____
}
```

Try this: Write the documentation for the new version of the function **search( )**.

_____
_____
_____
_____
_____
_____
_____

We will ask the reader to write a program to test this version of the function **search()** as one of the exercises.

6.9 - Sorting an Array

The concept of sorting data is also a very important topic in Computer Science. In this section, we will introduce the reader to sorting by developing a very simple version of the **selection sort**. This not a very efficient technique; however, for small collections of data, it will work fine. The reader will study sorting in detail in a second course, CS2 or Data Structures, whichever course is the next course in your Computer Science curriculum.

The sorting technique that we will discuss in this section is referred to as a **selection sort**. There are several variations of this technique; however, we will only discuss one. We will be sorting a list of integer data into ascending order. This means that after the data is sorted, each data item in the array will be greater than or equal to each of the data items in the array preceding it. This can be simply stated as follows:

If I > j, then array1[i] >= array1[j]

The basic idea of this selection sort algorithm is to find the smallest element in the array and move it to the first position, then find the next smallest element and move it to the second position, and continue this process until the next to the last position is filled. When the correct element is in the next to the last position, the sort is finished because the last element, which is the only one left, must be in the correct position. We will look at a specific example of this selection sort before we write the algorithm. Suppose that we have the following:

A[0]	:	5
A[1]	:	13
A[2]	:	-2
A[3]	:	10
A[4]	:	2

In order to get the smallest element in the first position, we compare what is stored at **A[0]** with each of the other elements, **A[1], A[2], A[3],** and **A[4]** and each time we find a smaller value we switch the two data items. We will refer to this as pass number 1. It takes 4 comparisons to complete this pass. For pass number 1, we will set **I** equal to 0 and let **j** range over the values, 1,2,3, and 4. The following illustrates pass number 1.

Pass No: 1 I = 0

	Comparison 1 j = 1	Comparison 2 j = 2	Comparison 3 j = 3	Comparison 4 j = 4	
Sorted					
A[0]	5	5	-2	-2	-2
Unsorted					
A[1]	13	13	13	13	13
A[2]	-2	-2	5	5	5
A[3]	10	10	10	10	10
A[4]	2	2	2	2	2

We now have the smallest element in the first position, and we are ready for pass no. 2. We compare the data stored at **A[1]** with what is stored at **A[2], A[3]**, and **A[4]**, and each time we find a smaller value we switch the two data items. For this pass we will set **I** equal to 1 and let **j** range over the indices 2, 3, and 4. The second pass is illustrated with the following figure.

Pass No: 2 I = 1

	Comparison 1 j = 2	Comparison 2 j = 3	Comparison 3 j = 4	
Sorted				
A[0]	-2	-2	-2	-2
A[1]	13	5	5	2
Unsorted				
A[2]	5	13	13	13
A[3]	10	10	10	10
A[4]	2	2	2	5

The third pass would set **I** equal to 2 and let **j** range over the indices 3 and 4. The last pass would set **I** = 3 and **j** would range over the single index 4. These two passes are illustrated with the following two figures:

Pass No. 3 : I = 2.

	Comparison 1 j = 3	Comparison 2 j = 4	
Sorted			
A[0]	-2	-2	-2
A[1]	2	2	2
A[2]	13	10	5
Unsorted			
A[3]	10	13	13
A[4]	5	5	10

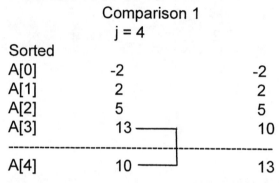

Pass No. 4 : I = 3.

	Comparison 1 j = 4	
Sorted		
A[0]	-2	-2
A[1]	2	2
A[2]	5	5
A[3]	13	10
A[4]	10	13

The process just illustrated can be described as follows:

    1. Make four passes through the array: I = 0, 1, 2, 3
    2. For pass no. 1, I = 0, do four comparisons, j = 1,2,3,4
    3. For pass no. 2, I = 1, do three comparisons, j = 2,3,4.
    4. For pass no. 3, I = 2, do two comparisons, j = 3,4.
    5. For pass no. 4, I = 3, do one comparison, j = 4.

The number of passes will be controlled with the for loop

       for(I = 0; I <= 3; I++)

while each sequence of comparisons can be controlled by a nested for loop where **j** ranges over the values from **I + 1** to 4.

       for(j = I + 1; j <= 4; j++)

    We can see that the number of passes is one less than the size of the array. We can now write the algorithm for this selection sort.

```
for I = 0 to size - 2
    for j = I + 1 to size - 1
        if (A[i] > A[j]) then
            Switch A[i] and A[j]
        end if
    end for j
end for I
```

In order to switch the data stored at **A[i]** and **A[j]** we must use three statements. We must have a temporary storage to save one of the data items so that it won't be lost when we move one element of the array to the other. We would need the following three statements:

```
temp = A[i];
A[i] = A[j];
A[j] = temp;
```

We can now write the function

```
// selsort( ) - Function to sort an array of integers in
//                 increasing order.
// Input parameters: nums1[ ], the array to be sorted
//                        count1, the size of the array
// Output parameters: nums1[ ], the sorted array
// Returns: Nothing
// Calls: Nothing
void selsort(int nums1[ ], int count1)
{
  int temp;
  for(int I = 0; I <= count1 - 2; I++)
    for(int j = I + 1; j <= count1 - 1; j++)
      if (nums1[i] > nums1[j]) {
        temp = nums1[i];
        nums1[i] = nums1[j];
        nums1[j] = temp;
      } // end if
    // end for j
  // end for I
  return;
}
```

We can test this function with the following program

```
// prog6_10.cpp Program to test the selsort( ) function.
#include <iostream.h>
void selsort(int nums1[ ], int count1);
int main( )
{
   int nums[ ] = {10, 8, 3, 5, 7, 2, 1, 6, 9, 4};
   int count = 10;
   selsort(nums, count);
   cout << "Sorted Array" << endl;
   for(int I = 0; I <= 9; I++) {
     cout << nums[i] << endl;
   } // end for
   return 0;
}
#include <a:\selsort.cpp>
```

Output from this program was as expected.

6.10 - Parallel Arrays

In most programming applications, we have to keep track of several different data items for each element used in the application. If the program deals with the employees of a company, then among other items it might want to keep track of are the name, social security number, and the pay rate for each of the employees. If a program deals with the grades for students in a particular class, the program might want to keep track of the student names, the exam scores, the averages of the exams, and the final grades for each of the students.

When the array is the data structure that is used in the program, then different arrays have to be used since the data is of different types. The name could be a string of 20 characters, the social security number a string of 11 characters, and the pay rate an array of real numbers. In the grade book program, the name could be a string of 20 characters, the exam grades would be an array of four exam grades for each student, the averages would be an array of reals, and the grades an array of characters.

If we assume that we have at most 100 employees, we would define the following arrays for the employee program:

```
const int SIZE = 100;
char names[SIZE][21];
char ssnums[SIZE][12];
float payrates[SIZE];
```

The arrays, **names[ ][ ]**, **ssnums[ ][ ]**, and **pay rates[ ]** are called <u>parallel arrays</u> because the information on the 50th employee would be contained in the three array elements

```
names[49], ssnums[49], and payrates[49]
```

If our class had at most 25 students, then we would want to define the following arrays for our grade book program:

```
const int SIZE = 25;
char names[SIZE][21];
char exams[SIZE][4];
float averages[SIZE];
char grades[SIZE];
```

The information on the 10th student in the class would be contained in the array elements

```
names[9], exams[9], averages[9], and grades[9]
```

from the parallel arrays, **names[ ][ ]**, **exams[ ][ ]**, **averages[ ]**, and **grades[ ]**.

This next example will illustrate the use of the last collection of parallel arrays to generate a final grade report for a class of students enrolled in CS 256. We will write this program using external functions in order to review this idea that was discussed in Chapter 4. We will write the program to test the function, **compgrades( )**, and we will ask the reader to write programs to test the functions **getdata( )**, **compavgs( )**, and **ptreport( )**. The program to get the data from the keyboard would be the following. We will omit the documentation and ask the reader to supply it for each of the functions as exercises.

```
#include <iostream.h>
#include <iomanip.h>
#include <conio.h>
void getdata(char names1[][21], float exams1[][4], int &count1, int MAX1)
{
  char ans, ret;
  count1 = 0;
```

```
do {
  clrscr( );
  // Generate input screen
  gotoxy(20, 5);
  cout << "Input student name: ";
  gotoxy(20, 6);
  cout << "xxxxxxxxxxxxxxxxxxxx";
  gotoxy(2, 15);
  cout << "Input 1st exam: ";
  gotoxy(8, 15);
  cout << "xx.x";
  gotoxy(25, 15);
  cout << "Input 2rd exam: ";
  gotoxy(31, 15);
  cout << "xx.x";
  gotoxy(45, 15);
  cout << "Input 3rd exam: ";
  gotoxy(51, 15);
  cout << "xx.x";
  gotoxy(62, 15);
  cout << "Input 4th exam: ";
  gotoxy(68, 15);
  cout << "xx.x";
  // Input data
  gotoxy(20, 6);
  cin.getline(names1[count1], 21);
  gotoxy(8,15);
  cin >> exams1[count1][0];
  gotoxy(31, 15);
  cin >> exams1[count1][1];
  gotoxy(51, 15);
  cin >> exams1[count1][2];
  gotoxy(62, 15);
  cin >> exams1[count1][3];
  count1++;
  gotoxy(10, 20);
  cout << "Another student? Y or N: ";
  cin >> ans
  cin.get(ret);                           // Remove <ret> from buffer
} while (((ans == 'Y') || (ans == 'y')) && (count1 < MAX1));
return;
}
```

Recall that anytime that we input data from the keyboard, we enter a **<Ret>** at the end of the data input. When we input numeric data, the **<Ret>** is skipped, so that the statement

        cin >> ans;

skips past the **<Ret>** to get the characters that were typed for the numeric data from the keyboard. However, when we return to the top of the loop and we are going to input a name from the keyboard, we cannot leave the **<Ret>** in the input buffer. If we did, the

        cin.getline(names1[count1], 21)

would see this **<Ret>** and simply store a null string. Thus, we must follow the

        cin >> ans;

with

        cin.get(ret);

The function to compute the array of averages from the array of exam scores is the following:

```
void compavgs(float exams2[ ][4], float avgs2[ ], int count2)
{
  float sum;
  for(int I = 0; I < count2; I++) {
    sum = 0;
    for(int j = 0; j <=3; j++)
      sum += exams2[i][j];
    // end for j
    avgs2[i] = sum / 4;
  } // end for I
  return;
}
```

A program to test the function **compavgs( )** is the following:

```
// prog6_11.cpp Program to test the function compavgs( ).
#include <iostream.h>
#include <iomanip.h>
#include <conio.h>
```

```
int main( )
extrn compavgs(float exams2[ ][4], float avgs4[ ], int count4);
{
  float exams[2][4] = {{79.5, 83.6, 92.5, 84.6},
                       {83.5, 89.6, 95.4, 96.7}};
  float averages[2];
  int count = 2;
  compavgs(exams, averages, count);
  for(int I = 0; I < count; I++)
    cout << "Average " << I + 1 << " = " << averages[i] << endl;
  // end for
  return 0;
}
```

Output from this program was the following:

```
        Average 1 = 85.05
        Average 2 = 91.3
```

The function to compute the array of final grades from the array of exam averages is the following:

```
void compgrades(float avgs3[ ], char grades3[ ], int count3)
{
  int intav;
  for(int I = 0; I < count3; I++) {
    intav = (int)avgs3[i];            // Compute integer average
    switch( intav)
    {
      case 90: case 91: case 92: case 93: case 94: case 95:
      case 96: case 97: case 98: case 99: case 100:     grades3[i] = 'A';
                                                        break;

      case 80: case 81: case 82: case 83: case 84:
      case 85: case 86: case 87: case 88: case 89:      grades3[i] = 'B';
                                                        break;

      case 70: case 71: case 72: case 73: case 74:
      case 75: case 76: case 77: case 78: case 79:      grades3[i] = 'C';
                                                        break;

      case 60: case 61: case 62: case 63: case 64:
      case 65: case 66: case 67: case 68: case 69:      grades3[i] = 'D';
                                                        break;

      default:                                          grades3[i] = 'F';
    } // end switch
```

```
  } // end for
  return;
}
```

The function to print the final report for the class is written as follows:

```
#include <iostream.h>
#include <iomanip.h>
#include <conio.h>
void printdata(char names4[ ][21], float exams4[ ][4], float avgs4[ ]
              char grades4[ ], int count4)
{
  clrscr( );
  cout << setw(37) << "CS 256" << endl;
  cout << setw(35) << "Grade Roll" << endl << endl << endl;
  cout << setw(6) << "Name" << setw(25) << "Exam1" << setw(7)
       << "Exam2" << setw(7) << "Exam3" << setw(7) << "Exam4"
       << setw(9) << "Averages" << setw(8) << "Grades" << endl << endl;
  cout.setf(ios::fixed | ios::showpoint);
  cout.precision(2);
  for(int I = 0; I < count4; I++) {
    cout << setw(22) << setiosflags(ios::left) << names4[i]
         << setiosflags(ios::right) << setw(4) << exams4[i][0]
         << setw(8) << exams4[i][1] << setw(8) << exams4[i][2]
         << setw(8) << exams4[i][3] << setw(10) << avgs4[i]
         << setw(7) << grades4[i] << endl;
  } // end for
  return;
}
```

We can now write the program.

```
//prog6_12.cpp Program to illustrate the use of parallel arrays
//
extrn void getdata(char names1[ ][21], float exams1[ ][4], int &count1);
extrn void compavgs(float exams2[ ][4], float avgs2[ ], int count2);
extrn void compgrades(float avgs3[ ], char grades3[ ], int count3);
extrn void ptreport(char names4[ ][21], float exams4[ ][4], float avgs4[ ],
                    char grades4[ ], int count4);
int main( )
{
```

```
      const int MAX = 30;
      char names[MAX][21];
      float exams[MAX][4];
      float averages[MAX];
      char grades[MAX];
      int count;
      getdata(names, exams, count);
      compavgs(exams, averages, count);
      compgrades(averages, grades, count);
      ptreport(names, exams, averages, grades, count);
      return 0;
}
```

We create a project file, **prog6_12.prj**, with the following files included:

```
a:\prog6_12.cpp
a:\getdata.cpp
a:\compavgs.cpp
a:\compgrds.cpp
a:\ptreport.cpp
```

We choose, **Make** and then **Compile** and if we have <u>no</u> errors, we can **Run** the program.

Output from this program was the following:

CS 256
Grade Roll

Name	Exam1	Exam2	Exam3	Exam4	Average	Grade
Bell, David	86.2	93.5	88.2	90.3	89.55	B
Bell, Marti	93.2	86.9	79.6	94.5	88.55	B
Morgie, Dave	90.3	87.5	86.8	96.2	90.20	A
Morgie, Rogene	67.4	73.5	73.1	68.4	70.60	C
Frye, Jennie	63.4	76.4	75.2	70.1	71.28	B

6.11 Summary

In this chapter we have discussed how arrays are handled in C++. We discussed how to define arrays to store the simple data types, integer, float, and character. We discussed how we can input data from the keyboard and store the data in an array and how to display data that is stored in an array to the screen. We showed how data can be stored in an array with array initialization. We also showed how we can use arrays as parameters for functions.

We discussed arrays of characters and strings. We pointed out the differences between these two arrays. We showed how we can use the function **strcpy( )**, to copy one string to another array.

We discussed how we can define and use higher dimensional arrays in our programs and functions.

We discussed advanced array notation in order to illustrate the flexibility of the C++ programming language. We will discuss this notation again in Chapter 7 when we discuss how to use pointer variables.

We discussed how we can search an array for a particular element. The technique that we used was a simple linear search where the index of the array element was returned if the data item was found in the array and -1 was returned if the data item was not found.

We introduced a very simple and straight forward sorting technique for sorting arrays called a selection sort. The topic of sorting is one that has been given a considerable amount of time and effort in computer science and will probably be discussed in detail in your second programming course, either Data Structures or CS2. The selection sort is not a very efficient method of sorting large arrays; however, it works just fine for small arrays.

We discussed how parallel arrays are used in programming applications and illustrated how some of the functions that we had written in previous sections could be used in these applications.

6.12 Questions

6.1   What is a simple data type?

6.2   What are the simple data types in C++?

254

6.3   What is a data structure?

6.4   What is an array?

6.5   What are the three things that we need to specify in a statement
        to define an array?

6.6   Why is an array always an output parameter when it is used to pass
        data between a function and a calling program?

6.7   How does an array reference each storage location?

6.8   How does an array reference the first storage location?

6.9   How does an array of three characters differ from a string of three
        characters?

6.10   How can we find the number of bytes reserved for one array element?

6.11   How can we find the number of bytes reserved for the entire array?

6.12   How much memory is allocated for each of the following, assume that
        we are on a PC using Turbo C++?

        a. char ch;   e. char name[20];   l. char vowels[ ] = {'a', 'e',
        b. int num1;   f. int nums[10];   'I', 'o', 'u'};
        c. float rnum1;   g. float rnums[5];   j. char state[] = "Indiana";
        d. double rnum2;   h. double dnums[5];

6.13   What do we mean by parallel arrays?

6.13 - Exercises

6.1   Give the statements that can be used to define each of the following:
        a. An array to store 25 integers.
        b. An array to store 30 real numbers.
        c. An array to store 50 characters.

6.2   Write a function that will compute and return the smallest element in an array of
        integers. The array should hold at most **MAX** elements and should contain **count**
        integer data items.

6.3   Write a program that will test the function from exercise 6.2.

6.4   Give the statements that can be used to define each of the following:
a. An integer array with three rows and five columns.
b. A real array with four elements where each element is an array of five reals.
c. A real array with six rows and seven columns.
d. An array with six elements where each element is an array of three integers.

6.5   Write a function that will accept a two dimensional array of integers. The array should have five rows and three columns. The function should also accept an integer and should compute and return the array where every element of the first array is multiplied by the given integer.

6.6   Write a function that will accept two arrays, each array will have three rows and four columns. The function should compute and return the array that is the sum of the first two arrays.

6.7   Write a function that will accept two arrays, the first array will have three rows and four columns and the second array will have four rows and three columns. The function should compute and return the product of the two arrays using standard matrix multiplication. The product will have three rows and three columns.

6.8   Write a function that will sort an array of real data.

6.9   Write a program to test the function from exercise 6.8

6.10   Write a program to test the function **find_av( )**, from section 6.7.

6.11   Write a program to test the function **search( )**, from section 6.8.

6.12   Write a program to test the function **getdata( )** from section 6.11.

6.13   Write a program to test the function **compgrades( )** from section 6.11.

6.14   Write a program to test the function **ptreport( )** from section 6.11.

6.15   Write a function **getdata( )** for the employee program from section 6.11.

6.16   Write a function **ptreport( )** for the data from the employee program in section 6.11.

6.17   Write a function to sort the data from the employee program by pay rate. Call the function **payratesort( )**.

256

6.18 Write a program to test the function **find_av( )**, written using advanced array notation, from section 6.7.

6.19 Write the documentation for the function **getdata( )** from section 6.11.

6.20 Write the documentation for the function **compavgs( )** from section 6.11.

6.21 Write the documentation for the function **compgrades( )** from section 6.11.

6.22 Write the documentation for the function **ptreport( )** from section 6.11.

CHAPTER 7

Pointers in C++

7.1 - Introduction

Pointers seem to be one of the most perplexing concepts for beginning programmers. However, pointers are nothing more than variables that can be used to store addresses. Pointers are a very powerful part of the C++ programming language, and when you have mastered the use of pointers, you are well on the way to becoming a C++ programmer. In this chapter, we will introduce the reader to pointers and show how they can be used to program in C++. We will discuss pointers to simple data types, i.e. to integer, **int**, to real, **float**, and to character, **char**. We will also introduce the general purpose pointer of type **void**. We will show how pointer variables and arrays are closely related.

Pointers are used by C++ programmers to do all or any of the following:

* to directly access memory in the system.

* to pass parameters to functions when these parameters are used to return values to the calling program.

* to pass arrays to functions.

* to access array elements.

* to create dynamic data structures like linked lists and trees.

Pointers are used more often in C and C++ than in other languages (such as BASIC, Cobol, or even Pascal). Some of what we will discuss in this chapter can be done without using pointers. For example, we have discussed arrays without the use of pointers and we have discussed returning data from functions by passing variables by reference. However, even though we can do a lot of programming in C++ without the use of pointers, we will see that with their use we can obtain much more from the language. In addition, one of the jobs that we will face as programmers is to update and modify existing programs; many of which will be written in C using pointers. We will be asked to upgrade these to C++ programs. In order to be able to do this it is critical that we understand how pointers are used in C programs. We will also see that understanding pointers gives us a much better understanding of the relationship between variables, addresses, memory, arrays, and functions.

After completing this chapter the student should be able to

1.   understand what is meant by a pointer variable.

2.   understand how to define pointer variables for the simple
        data types.

3.   understand how to allocate memory from the system
        using pointer variables.

4.   understand how pointers can be used to return data
        from a function.

5.   understand how pointers can be used to pass arrays to
        functions.

6.   understand how pointers can be used to access the
        elements of a one-dimensional array.

7.   understand how pointers can be used to access the
        elements of higher dimensional arrays.

8.   understand how we can write programs that use pointers
        to functions.

9.   understand how we can convert functions that are written in
        C using pointers, to functions in C++.

We will study pointers to structures in Chapter 9.

7.2 - Variables and Addresses

As we know, memory in our microcomputer is made up of a large collection of storage locations called **bytes** and each byte is made up of eight 0's or 1's, called **bits**. Each of these locations in memory is assigned an address. An address is composed of two parts: a segment number and an offset number. Each segment is 0XFFFF (or 65,535) bytes in length. However, a new segment begins every 16 bytes in memory. Thus, the segments overlap. For each segment, the offset tells us how far we have gone into the segment.

For example, consider the 1st byte in memory (absolute byte 0). Its address is simply

             segment: 0x0000
             offset: 0x0000

The address of the 4th byte in memory is

             segment: 0x0000
             offset: 0x0003

The address of the 16th byte in memory is

             segment: 0x0000
             offset:`   0x000f

The address of the 17th byte in memory is

             segment: 0x0000
             offset: 0x0010

                  or

             segment: 0x0001
             offset: 0x0000

The address of the 18th byte in memory is

             segment: 0x0000
             offset: 0x0011

                  or

             segment: 0x0001
             offset: 0x0001

The address of the 33rd byte in memory is

             segment: 0x0000
             offset: 0x0020

                  or

260

```
        segment:     0x0001
        offset:      0x0010

             or

        segment:     0x0002
        offset:      0x0000
```

The absolute memory address can be determined by multiplying the segment by 16 (adding a hex digit of 0) and then adding the offset. For example, for the 33rd byte

```
        0x00000
    +   0x  0020
        0x00020
```

             or

```
        0x00010
    +   0x  0010
        0x00020
```

             or

```
        0x00020
    +   0x  0000
        0x00020
```

In Turbo C++, when we specify that a pointer's value is to be printed, the result will normally be given as a segment and offset. We will see how this works shortly.

When we load the operating system, it occupies a portion of memory. When we load a program, it occupies another portion of memory. Every variable that is used in our program is associated with an address of a particular block of memory that is set aside by the compiler. If our program used the variables

```
        char ch;
        int num;
        float rnum;
```

then the following figure illustrates how this might look in memory.

System Memory

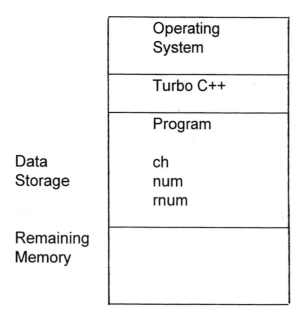

If we have the variable, **num**, defined and data stored with the statement:

        int num = 56;

then we can use the **address of** operator, **&**, to print out the address of any variable that is defined in a program. We can print out the data and the address of where the data is stored with the statements:

            cout << num << endl;
            cout << &num << endl;

We illustrate this idea with the following program:

```
// prog7_1.cpp Program to illustrate finding addresses for variables
#include <iostream.h>
int main()
{
   int num1 = 50;
   int num2 = 54;
   float rnum1 = 125.50;
   float rnum2 = 100.00;
   cout << &num1 << "   address of num1" << endl
        << &num2 << "   address of num2" << endl
        << &rnum1 << "   address of rnum1" << endl
```

```
        << &rnum2 << "    address of rnum2" << endl;
    return 0;
}
```

This simple program defines four variables, two of type **int** and two of type **float**. It assigns each of these variables values and prints out the addresses of where the data is stored in memory. These addresses will depend on many factors, the type of computer, the operating system and which version, other programs currently in memory, etc. For these reasons, you probably won't get the same output from the program as we did. Here is the output from this program on our microcomputer.

0x8f20fff4	address of num1
0x8f20fff2	address of num2
0x8f20ffee	address of rnum1
0x8f20ffea	address of rnum2

The address 0x8f20fff4 output by Turbo C++ means the following:

segment:	0x8f20
offset:	0xfff4

Similarly, the address 0x8f20fff2 means:

segment:	0x8f20
offset:	0xfff2

Remember, that the address of the variable is not the same as the data assigned to the variable. For variables of type **int** and **float**, the insertion operator, **<<**, interprets the address in hexadecimal notation, and that is what is indicated by the **0x** in front of the address. The data is stored in memory and the address that is assigned to the variable is the address of the first byte of the memory that is allocated for storage.

Note: If you are not familiar with hexadecimal notation, then you should take timeout and work through the material and examples in Appendix A.

For our above example, we can summarize as follows:

variable	address	number of bytes	data stored
num1	0x8f20fff4	2	50
num2	0x8f20fff2	2	54
rnum1	0x8f20ffee	4	125.50
rnum2	0x8f20ffea	4	100.00

It is not critical that you understand the actual method that is used by the operating system for addressing memory, but rather that you understand what is being illustrated by the program. Note, that the addresses are decreasing. Recall that in section 4.6, we discussed the fact that automatic variables are allocated memory from the system stack. This illustrates this idea since the system stack grows downward in memory.

If we define the variables as global or as external to the program, then the addresses would be increasing and have different values. We will ask the reader to write and run a program to illustrate this idea as one of the exercises. We recall that we can also use **printf()** to output data in hexadecimal using the **%x** format specifier. If we were to rewrite **prog7_1.cpp** using **printf()** in place of **cout**, we would use the following statements:

```
printf("%x\n", &num1);
printf("%x\n", &num2);
printf("%x\n", &rnum1);
printf("%x\n", &rnum2);
```

These statements do not display the leading, **0x**. We will ask the reader to rewrite **prog7_1.cpp** using **printf()** as one of the exercises.

In order to print out the data stored, rather than the addresses, we know that we would simply change the **cout** statements to the following:

```
cout << num1 << endl
     << num2 << endl
     << rnum1 << endl
     << rnum2 << endl;
```

We would most likely want to format the output for **rnum1** and **rnum2**. It is critical that we understand that the variables **num1**, **num2**, **rnum1**, and **rnum2** reference the data stored while the variables **&num1**, **&num2**, **&rnum1**, and **&rnum2** reference the addresses of where the data is stored.

We have used the operator, **&**, in two different ways. We have used it as the

264

address of operator in the above example and as the **reference** operator in Chapter 4. We must understand these differences even through they are closely related. In addition, we used **&&** as the **logical and** operator. This is an example of what is referred to as **operator overloading**.

There is one interesting fact about the **cout** stream. When we defined a character variable and tried to display the address using the following statements:

> char ch = 'A';
>
> cout << &ch << endl;

the output is the following:

> A

and not the address of the character storage location.

Try this: Define a real variable called **rnum** and assign it a value. Write the statements that will print the data stored and also print the address of where the data is stored.

> cout << _____
>   << _____

Do the same thing, only use printf( ).

> printf(_____

7.3 - Pointer Variables

The variables that we have used in the first five chapters have stored the simple data types: **float, int**, and **char**. The idea behind a **pointer variable** is very simple; it is a variable where we can store an address. In the previous section, we saw that the variables **&num1**, **&num2**, **&rnum1**, and **&rnum2** all reference addresses of memory that have been allocated for storage. These are, however, <u>constant</u> addresses. The memory allocated with the statements:

> int num1;
> int num2;

```
        float rnum1;
        float rnum2;
```

is fixed by the compiler and cannot be changed by the program. Thus, no other address can be referenced by any of the variables, **&num1**, **&num2**, **&rnum1**, and **&rnum2**. We cannot assign any other address to any of the variables. However, we can certainly assign the data to be stored at these locations with statements like

```
        num1 = 50;
        rnum1 = 125.00;
```

However, if we try to assign a different address with a statement like

```
    &num1 = 0x8f20ffe2;      or      &num1 = &num2;
```

then in effect we would be trying to allocate new memory to the variable **num1**, and the compiler will not allow the program to do this. Memory is allocated for the global variables at the beginning of the program and released at the end. For local variables (within a function) memory is allocated on the stack each time the function is called. When the function terminates, the memory is released for other uses. Furthermore, these variables cannot be allocated any other memory by a statement in the program. They have been assigned fixed addresses.

A **pointer variable** is a variable that stores an address and, moreover, can be assigned different addresses by the program. The only stipulation is that these addresses must reference a block of memory that is set aside for the appropriate data type. Thus, when we define a pointer variable, we must also tell the C++ compiler the data type that is to be stored in memory at the address that is to be assigned to the pointer variable. When an address has been assigned and memory allocated, then we say that the pointer **points to** that memory location. We can have pointers to any data type; however, in this chapter, we will only study pointers to the simple data types, integers, reals, and characters.

We now consider how we define pointer variables and assign addresses of blocks of memory to these pointers. Suppose that we want to define pointer variables **chptr**, **intptr**, and **fltptr**, each of which points to a simple data type. In C, this is done with the statements:

```
        char *chptr;
        int *intptr;
        float *fltptr;
```

As in the case with any variable, the names **chptr**, **intptr**, and **fltptr**, are our choices. The

266

preceding, *****, operator makes each of the variables a pointer variable. The ***** operator in this context can be thought of as meaning **"points to"**. When we use the statement

```
int *intptr;
```

this means that **intptr** is a pointer to **int** so that any address assigned to the variable **intptr**, should be associated with an integer storage location by the C++ compiler. One of the ways that this can be done is illustrated with the following program:

```
//prog7_2.cpp Program to illustrate one use of a pointer variable.
//
#include <iostream.h>
int main()
{
   int num = 50;
   int *intptr;
   intptr = &num;              // Store the address of an integer location
   cout << num << endl
        << *intptr << endl
        << &num << endl
        << intptr << endl;
   return 0;
}
```

Although this is a very simple program, it is critical that we understand exactly what is happening at each step. The statement

```
int num = 50;
```

defines an integer variable, **num**, allocates it two bytes of memory (on a microcomputer), and the address of that block of memory is assigned as a <u>constant</u> to the variable **&num**. The statement

```
int *intptr;
```

defines a pointer variable, **intptr**, and tells the C++ compiler that it must point to data of type **int**. This means that the only addresses that <u>should</u> be assigned to **intptr** are addresses of integer storage locations. The statement

```
intptr = &num;
```

assigns one such address to **intptr**. The variable, ***intptr**, references the data at the memory location whose address is referenced by **intptr**. Output from **prog7_2.cpp** was the following:

```
50
50
0x8f54fff4
0x8f54fff4
```

It does not matter where we put the *, operator in the declaration for our pointer variable. We can use either of the statements

int *intptr;   int * intptr;   or   int* intptr;

It is common to use the first form even though the third form helps to emphasize that the asterisk is part of the variable type (pointer to int) and not part of the variable name itself.

Memory Allocation

The other way that we can allocate a block of memory and assign the address of the block to a pointer variable is to use memory allocation functions that are available in C++. In order to allocate memory for an integer storage location, and store the address of this location in the defined pointer variable **intptr**, we can use either of the following statements:

intptr = new int;

   or

intptr = (int *)malloc(sizeof(int));

The first statement is new and unique to C++, while the second statement is a carryover from C. The second statement makes use of the two functions **sizeof( )** and **malloc( )** both are standard C++ functions. The function **sizeof( )** returns the size (number of bytes) of the storage location for the specified data type. In the above case, this would be 2 for integer data on microcomputers. The function **malloc( )** sets aside this amount of memory and returns the address of the memory location. The address is **cast** as the address of an integer storage location with the syntax **(int *)**, and is then assigned to the pointer variable **intptr**. We could have used the statement

intptr = (int *)malloc(2);

since we know the size of the integer storage location; however, using the function, **sizeof()**, will return the correct integer size independent of the computer system. We illustrate the storage that is set aside and the pointer variable with the following figure.

address		storage for integer data
intptr		*intptr

The functions **sizeof( )** and **malloc( )** are defined in the header file **stdlib.h**. Even though, it may appear that the statement

        int num1;

is equivalent to the two statements

        int *intptr;
        intptr = new int;

we want to summarize the important differences one more time. The statement

        int num1;

defines an integer variable **num1**, and allocates memory for the storage of an integer data item. We can reference the address of this memory location with the identifier **&num1**. However, the address that is assigned to **&num1** cannot be changed since the C++ compiler has allocated a fixed block of memory to **num1**. A fixed address has been assigned to **&num1**. The statement

        int *intptr;

allocates memory for the address of an integer storage location. No address has been assigned to **intptr**. The statement

        intptr = new int;

allocates memory for an integer data item and assigns the address of this memory location to **intptr**. The address assigned to **intptr** can, however, be changed by statements in the program. Thus, **intptr**, is a variable that can be assigned different addresses. Using the above declarations:

```
int num1;
int *intptr;
```

and the statement

```
intptr = new int;
```

we have the following in memory:

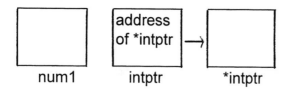

num1   intptr   *intptr

Suppose we now do the following in a program:

```
num1 = 5;
*intptr = num1;
```

Both storage locations would have the integer value 5 stored as data.

num1   intptr   *intptr

If the program now executes the statement:

```
intptr = &num1;
```

then we only have access to the one storage location since **intptr** references the same address as **&num1**.

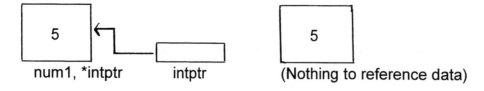

num1, *intptr   intptr   (Nothing to reference data)

   We cannot access the second storage location since we no longer have a variable referencing it's address.

270

Try this: Define a pointer variable of type float. Allocate memory for storage using **new** and assign the address to the pointer variable. Assign the value 0.75 as data.

_____

_____

_____

Do the same thing only this time use the functions **malloc( )** and **sizeof( )**.

_____

_____

_____

Every variable has three pieces of information associated with it.

1) the address of where the data item is stored
2) the size of the storage location
3) the data stored at that location

For the declarations

    int num1;
    int *intptr;

and the statements

    intptr = new int;
    num1 = 5;
    *intptr = 10;

we have the following:

data item stored	Address of the storage location	Size of the storage location
num1	&num1	sizeof(num1)
*intptr	intptr	sizeof(*intptr)

We illustrate this with the following program:

```
// prog7_3.cpp Program to illustrate the use of pointers.
//
#include <iostream.h>
int main()
{
    int num1;
    int *intptr;
    num 1 = 5;
    intptr = new int;
    *intptr = 10;
    cout << "Value stored at num1 = " << num1 << endl;
    cout << "Address of num1 = " << &num1 << endl;
    cout << "Bytes of storage allocated for num1 = " << sizeof(num1) << endl;
    cout << "Value stored at *intptr = " << *intptr << endl;
    cout << "Address stored at intptr = " << intptr << endl;
    cout << "Bytes of storage allocated for *intptr = " << sizeof(*intptr) << endl;
    return 0;
}
```

The output from this program was the following:

```
Value stored at num1 = 5
Address of num1 = 0x8f3efff4
Bytes of storage allocated for num1 = 2
Value stored at *intptr = 10
Address stored at intptr = 0x8f3e0e6a
Bytes of storage allocated for *intptr = 2
```

When we define the pointer variable, **intptr**, with the statement

        int *intptr;

the operator, *, is called an **indirection** or **dereferencing** operator.

   Using pointers requires the computer to do a double look-up. When the program wants to access the data stored at ***intptr**, it must first look at **intptr** for the address of ***intptr**, and then look at that address for the data.

   We consider the declarations that we have previously made:

        int num1, *intptr;

and describe what happens with each of the following statements.

a) num1 = 5;
b) *intptr = 25;
c) intptr = new int;
d) intptr = (int *)malloc(sizeof(int));
e) *intptr = 25;
f) &num1 = intptr;
g) intptr = &num1;

num1 = 5;	The integer 5 is stored at the integer storage location referenced by **num1**. The address of this location is referenced by **&num1**;
*intptr = 25;	This would cause an error, since no memory has been allocated for integer storage.
intptr = new int;	This allocates memory for integer storage and assigns the address to intptr.

intptr = (int *)malloc(sizeof(int));

	This is the statement, using the functions **malloc( )** and **sizeof( )**, that does exactly the same thing as the previous statement.
*intptr = 25;	Since memory has been set aside when the previous statement is executed, we can now store the integer 25 at this location.
&num1 = intptr;	This statement is illegal since the operator, **&num1** is assigned a fixed address that cannot be changed.
intptr = &num1;	The address of the storage location referenced by **num1** is now also referenced by **intptr**. Therefore, the location is now referenced by two names, **num1** and ***intptr**.

The **unary** operators, * and **&**, have equal precedence with each other and with other unary operators. They have higher precedence than binary operators.

Table 7.1:   Precedence Table

```
==================================
*, &, +, -                 unary operators
++, --                     increment, decrement
*, /, %                    multiplication, division
+, -                       addition, subtraction
+=, -=, *=, /=, %=         compound operators
==================================
```

We consider another example to illustrate this precedence. Suppose that we have the following declaration and statement:

    char *chptr;

    chptr = new char;

Furthermore, let's assume that the address of the storage location is 100. We would have the following:

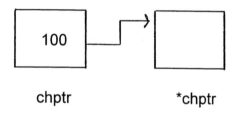

        chptr   *chptr

Describe what happens with each of the following statements.

        a) *chptr = 'A';
        b) *chptr++; or (*chptr)++
        c) *(chptr++) = 'B';

a) *chptr = 'A';   Stores the character , 'A', at the memory
                          location with address 100. The data stored
                          is represented by **chptr**.

b) *chptr++;   Increments what is stored at **chptr** by 1. Thus,
                          since the data stored is 'A', it is incremented by 1
                          and becomes 'B'. Same as (*chptr)++.

c) *(chptr++) = 'B';   Adding 1 to **chptr** adds the size of one storage
                          location to the address. Since **chptr** is a pointer
                          to char, it adds one and the address becomes 101.
                          The character 'B' is then stored at this location.

Pointers of Type void

Before we see how pointers have been used in programs, we need to discuss a general purpose pointer that is used in C++. Ordinarily, when a pointer variable is defined, it is a pointer to a specific data type. When an address is assigned to a pointer variable, the address must be the address of a storage location of the same data type. If we have the following variables defined:

```
int num;
float rnum;
int *nptr;
```

then the statement

```
nptr = &num;
```

is legal while the statement

```
nptr = &rnum;
```

is not and would generate the following compiler error message:

```
Error  Cannot convert 'float *'  to 'int *'
```

The C++ programming language include a general-purpose pointer that is an exception to the above rule. This pointer can be assigned the address of <u>any</u> data type. The general-purpose pointer is a pointer to **void** and is defined with the statement

```
void *gptr;
```

Using the general-purpose pointer variable, **gptr**, the statements

```
gptr = &num;
```

and

```
gptr = &rnum;
```

are both legal.

Pointers of type **void** have certain specialized uses, such as passing data to functions that operate independently of the data type being passed and functions that are to be called using pointers. Functions that utilize pointers of type **void** are discussed in section 7.7 when we discuss pointers to functions.

7.4 - Pointers & Arrays

Now that we understand the use of pointers for the basic data types, let us turn our attention to how pointers relate to arrays. Pointers have a direct relationship to arrays since an array name is also a pointer to the first element of an array. If we have defined an array, with four integer data items, using the statement

int nums[ ] = {10, 20, 30, 40};

then we can reference the elements of the array using standard array notation, advanced array notation, and using pointer notation. This is illustrated with the following:

nums[]	Array Notation	Advanced Array Notation	Pointer Notation
10	nums[0]	(nums + 0)[0]	*(nums + 0)
20	nums[1]	(nums + 1)[0]	*(nums + 1)
30	nums[2]	(nums + 2)[0]	*(nums + 2)
40	nums[3]	(nums + 3)[0]	*(nums + 3)

Using **standard array notation**, we can print the data one per line as follows:

```
for(int I = 0; I <= 3; I++)
    cout << nums[i] << endl;
```

Using **advanced array notation**, we would have the following:

```
for(int I = 0; I <= 3; I++)
    cout << (nums + I)[0] << endl;
```

Try this: Write the code, using **pointer notation**, to print the data one per line.

```
for(int I = 0; I <= 3; I++)
    cout <<_____;
```

If we have in addition to the array, **nums[ ]**, a pointer variable defined with the statement

```
int *numptr;
```

then we can assign the address of the array, **nums[ ]**, to **numptr** with either of the statements

```
numptr = nums;            or            numptr = &nums[0];
```

Once the address of the array has been assigned to **numptr**, we say that **numptr points to nums[ ]**. Moreover, we can access the data in the array using **numptr** just as we did using **nums**. Each of the following would print the data stored in the array **nums[]**, one per line.

```
for(int I = 0; I <= 3; I++)
  cout << numptr[i] << endl;

for(int I = 0; I <= 3; I++)
  cout << (numptr + I)[0] << endl;

for(int I = 0; I <= 3; I++)
  cout << *(numptr + I) << endl;
```

In addition, when we use the pointer variable, **numptr**, there is one additional way that we can print the data, one per line.

```
for(int I = 0; I <= 3; I++) {
  cout << *intptr << endl;
  intptr++;
} // end for
```

Since a pointer variable can be assigned different addresses, the statement

```
intptr++;
```

assigns the address of the next array element to **intptr**. It is important that we understand that we cannot do this with the array **nums[ ]**. The C++ compiler would not accept the code

```
for(int I = 0; I <= 3; I++) {
  cout << *nums << endl;
  nums++;
} // end for
```

The compiler would flag the statement

```
nums++;
```

since we are trying to assign the array **nums[ ]** a new address. The address that is assigned to the array when it is defined with the statement

```
int nums[ ] = {10, 20, 30, 40};
```

is a constant and cannot be changed.

We will not be using advanced array notation through the rest of this chapter. We will be using only array notation and pointer notation. We will need to understand both notations and be able to translate from one to the other. The following block of code finds the largest element of the array **nums[ ]**.

```
big = nums[0];
for(int I = 1; I <= 3; I++)
  if (nums[i] > big)
    big = nums[i];
  // end if
// end for
```

Try this: Rewrite the above block of code using pointer notation.

```
big = _____
for(_____
  if _____
    _____
  // end if
// end for
```

We illustrate the relationship between arrays and pointer variables with another example.

```
// prog7_4.cpp Program to illustrate the use of pointers to access
//              array elements.
#include <stdio.h>
#include <iostream.h>
#include <iomanip.h>
int main()
{
  char chars[3], *chptr;
  int nums[3], *intptr;
  float reals[3], *fltptr;
```

```
// Assign array addresses to pointer variables.
chptr = chars;
intptr = nums;
fltptr = reals;
// Print out addresses of the arrays.
cout << setw(25) << "chptr" << setw(11) << "intptr"
     << setw(11) << "fltptr" << endl;
for (int I = 0; I < 3; I++) {
  cout << "pointers + " << I << setw(10) << (chptr + I)
       << setw(10) << (intptr + I) << setw(10) << (fltptr + I)
       << endl;
} // end for
return 0;
}
```

Output from this program was the following:

	chptr	intptr	fltptr
pointers + 0 :	65470	65474	65482
pointers + 1 :	65471	65476	65486
pointers + 2 :	65472	65478	65490

Note that when a program adds 1 to the **char** pointer, **chptr**, the address increases by 1. When a program adds 1 to the **int** pointer, **intptr**, the address increases by 2. Finally, when a program adds 1 to the **float** pointer, **fltptr**, the address increases by 4. As we can see, the C++ compiler adds the size of one storage location (for the specified data type) when the program adds 1 to the pointer variable. We recall that on microcomputers that

sizeof(char) = 1
sizeof(int) = 2
sizeof(float) = 4

For arrays, adding 1 to the pointer variable, increases the address, to the address of the next element of the array. Thus, after defining an array **nums**, an int pointer, **intptr**, with the declaration

int nums[3], *intptr;

and assigning the address of the array to the pointer with the statement

intptr = nums;

we would have the following equalities:

Addresses
```
============================
intptr     == nums     == &nums[0]
intptr + 1 == nums + 1 == &nums[1]
intptr + 2 == nums + 2 == &nums[2]
============================
```

Values
```
================================
*intptr       == *nums       == nums[0]
*(intptr + 1) == *(nums + 1) == nums[1]
*(intptr + 2) == *(nums + 2) == nums[2]
================================
```

We must use ***(intptr + 1)** rather than ***intptr + 1**, since * has precedence over **+**. Using ***intptr + 1** would mean **(*intptr) + 1**, and we would be adding 1 to the integer value stored in memory rather than increasing the address to the address of the next integer storage location. As we have seen, we can also use the pointer variable, **intptr**, in array notation. Thus, we would have:

```
intptr[0] == nums[0]
intptr[1] == nums[1]
intptr[2] == nums[2]
```

As we can see, C++ allows us a lot of flexibility in notation when we are using arrays and pointers in a program. When we write programs and functions, we can use either notation, arrays or pointers. We must clearly understand how to use these notations and be able to translate from one to the other.

Try this: Suppose that we again have the array **nums[ ]** defined with the following statement

```
int nums[ ] = {10, 20, 30, 40};
```

and the pointer variable defined and assigned the address of **nums[ ]** with the statement

```
int *numsptr = nums;
```

Complete each of the blocks of code to print the data one per line.

```
for(int I = 0; I <= 3; I++)
    cout << _____ << endl;        // standard notation
// end for                               // using nums


for(int I = 0; I <= 3; I++) {
    cout << _____ << endl;        // pointer notation
    _____          // using numsptr
} // end for
```

Explain why the following code would produce an error.

```
for(int I = 0; I <= 3; I++){
    cout << *nums << endl;
    nums++;
} // end for
```
_____
_____
_____
_____

Try this: Rewrite the following block of code using array notation.

```
sum = 0;
for (int I = 0; I <= 3; I++)
    sum = sum + *(nums + I);
// end for
average = sum / 4.0;
```
_____
_____
_____
_____
_____

Consider the following function that will accept the address of an array of integers and the number of values stored as input parameters. It computes and returns the average of the integer values stored in the array. We will omit the documentation to save space.

```
void find1_avg(int nums[], int count, float &avg)
{
    int sum = 0;
    for (int I = 0; I < count; I++)
        sum = += nums[i];
    // end for
    avg = (float sum) / count;
    return;
} // end find_avg()
```

The following is a pointer version of this function.

```
void find2_avg(int *nums, int count, float &avg)
{
  int sum = 0;
  for(int I = 0; I < count; I++) {
    sum += *nums;
    nums++;
  } // end for
  avg = (float sum) / count;
  return;
} // end find_avg()
```

Note, that we have to cast **sum** as **float** since otherwise the computation of

sum / count

would result in an integer (since **sum** and **count** are variables of type **int**). We could also use the statement

avg = (sum * 1.0) / count;

We can test these functions with the following programs.

```
// prog7_5.cpp Program to test the array version of the
//             function to find the average of data in an
//             array; the function find1_avg().
#include <iostream.h>
#include <iomanip.h>
void find1_avg(int nums[], int count, float &avg);
int main()
{
  float average;
  int values[ ] = {25, 36, 34};
  find1_avg(values, 3, average);
  cout.setf(ios::showpoint);
  cout.setf(ios::fixed);
  cout.precision(2);
  cout << "Average = " << setw(4)
      << average << endl;
  return 0;
}
#include <a:\find1avg.cpp>
```

The program to test the pointer version of the function would be the following:

```
// prog7_6.cpp Program to the pointer version of the function
//                find2_avg()
#include <iostream.h>
#include <iomanip.h>
void find_avg(int *nums, int count, float& avg);
int main()
{
  float average;
  int values[] = {25, 36, 34};
  find2_avg(values, 3, average);
  cout.setf(ios::showpoint);
  cout.setf(ios::fixed);
  cout.precision(2);
  cout << "Average = " << setw(4)
       << *average << endl;
  return 0;
}
#include <a:\find2avg.cpp>
```

Output from each of these programs was the following:

Average = 31.67

As we can see from the main program, the array **values[ ]** has three elements. Note, however, in either of the functions, **find1_avg( )** or **find2_avg( )**, we have not said anything explicitly about the size of the array **nums[ ]**. The reason for this, is that the parameter declaration

int nums[];

in the function parameter list, tells the function that it is to pass the address of the array and the parameter

int count

tells the function how many elements are in the array. When we call the function **find1_avg()**, we do it with the statement

find1_avg(values, 3, average);

The array name **values**, as we recall, references the address of the first element of the array. Thus, the function call passes the address of the array, to the function **find1_avg()**. This means that the argument, **values**, in the call to the function, **find1_avg()**, can be replaced with a pointer variable, so that we are able to write the function using pointer notation, as follows:

```
void find2_avg(int *nums, int count, float &avg)
```

The following two declarations may be used interchangeably when they are used as parameters in a function.

```
int nums[];
int *nums;
```

When the function is called with the statement

```
find2_avg(values, 3, average);
```

nums references the address of the array **values**. Thus, when we use **nums[2]** in a statement, this is the same as using ***(nums + 2)**. Since **nums** references the address of the first element of the array **values**, then **nums + 2** references the address of **values[2]**. This makes ***(nums + 2)** the same as **nums[2]**, which is the same as **values[2]**. Anytime that we use an array name as a function parameter, we pass the address of the array. The function then uses this address to make changes to the array that is passed from the calling program. We need to point out another important fact. The function does *not* know the size of the array, only the address of the first element and the size of each array element. If the function needs to know the size of the array, or rather how many data items are be stored in the array, then we have to pass this number as an integer parameter.

We consider another example where we write a function that will ask the user to input a set of exam scores from the keyboard. It should store the real exam scores in an array whose address is sent to the function. When the data is entered and stored, it is stored in the array whose address was passed to the function. We will have the array and the size of the array as input parameters, and the array as an output parameter for the function. Again we omit the documentation to save space.

```
void get_data(float scores[], int size)
{
  for (int I = 0; I < size; I++) {
    cout << "Input an exam score: ";
    cin >> scores[i];
  } // end for
  return;
} // end get_data()
```

The pointer version of this same function would be the following:

```
                    void get_data( float *scores, int size)
                    {
                      for (int I = 0; I < size; I++) {
                      cout << "Input an exam score: ";
                      cin >> *(scores + I);
                      } // end for
                      return;
                    } // end get_data()
```

Note, that we could replace statement

```
            cin >> *(scores + I);
```

with the statement

```
        cin >> *(scores++);
```

A program to test this function follows:

```
        // prog7_7.cpp Program to test the function get_data().
        //
        #include <iostream.h>
        #include <iomanip.h>
        void get_data(float scores[], int size);
        int main()
        {
          float exams[5];
          get_data(exams, 5);
          cout.setf(ios::showpoint);
          cout.setf(ios::fixed);
          cout.precision(2);
          for(int I = 0; I < 5; I++)
            cout << "Exam " << I+1 << " = "
                  << setw(5) << exams[i]) << endl;
          return 0;
        } // end main
        #include <a:\getdata.cpp>
```

Output from this program follows:

285

Input an exam score: <u>75.6</u>
Input an exam score: <u>93.7</u>
Input an exam score: <u>83.5</u>
Input an exam score: <u>78</u>
Input an exam score: <u>86</u>
Exam 1 = 75.60
Exam 2 = 93.70
Exam 3 = 83.50
Exam 4 = 78.00
Exam 5 = 86.00

It doesn't matter which version of the function we use in the program, the function prototype statement

    void get_data(float *scores, int size);

and the function call

    get_data(exams, 5);

can remain exactly the same. We do not have to change either statement. We need to emphasize that we need to make sure that memory for the array has been allocated. This is done in the main program with the statement:

    float exams[5];

7.5 - Output Parameters Using Pointers

In section 4.5 we saw how we could return data from a function by passing variables by reference. This is new to C++, and could not be done in C. In order to return data from a function, in C, the function had to use pointers as parameters. In this way, the calling program passes the address of a storage location that is defined in the calling program. This is similar to what is done when we pass variables by reference. The difference is in the use of the pointer variables. We can best illustrate this idea with an example. We consider **find_avg( )** from section 4.5. This function computes the average of two integer numbers and returns this value through a variable that is passed by reference. We rewrite the function.

```
void find_avg(int n1, int n2, float &avg)
{
  avg = (n1 + n2) / 2.0;
} // end find_avg()
```

As we recall from Chapter 4, the declaration of **avg** with

```
float &avg
```

tells the C++ compiler that the address of the variable **average**, defined in the calling program, is to be passed when the function is called with the statement:

```
find_avg(num1, num2, average);
```

Now that we have discussed pointers, we can illustrate how this has to be done in the ANSII versions of C. The only way that addresses can be passed using C, is by using pointers.

In order to pass an address with a pointer variable, we define **avg** as a pointer variable in the function statement as follows:

```
void find_avg(int n1, int n2, float *avg)
```

Now in order to compute the value to pass back to the calling program, we use the following statement:

```
*avg = (n1 + n2) / 2.0;
```

When the function is called it must be given the address of the variable, **average**, with the statement:

```
find_avg(num1, num2, &average);
```

The complete code for the function is the following:

```
void find_avg(int n1, int n2, float *avg)
{
  *avg = (n1 + n2) / 2.0;
  return;
} // end find_avg()
```

The program to test this function is the following:

```
// prog7_8.cpp Program to illustrate the use of pointers
//              as parameters.
#include <iostream.h>
#include <iomanip.h>
void find_avg(int n1, int n2, float *avg);
int main()
{
  float average;
  float num1, num2;
  cout << "Input an integer: ";
  cin >> num1;
  cout << "Input another integer: ";
  cin >> num2;
  find_avg(num1, num2, &average);
  cout.setf(ios::fixed);
  cout.setf(ios::showpoint);
  cout.precision(2);
  cout << "Average = "
       << setw(5) <<  average << endl;
  return 0;
} // end main
#include <a:\findavg.cpp>
```

It is important that we note the differences in how the function is called in the main program and how the average is computed in the function. We will illustrate this concept with another example by writing a pointer version of a function that will compute and return the average of **count1** real numbers stored in an array **nums1[ ]**. The average is to be returned using an output parameter called **average1** and the array will be passed using a pointer variable, **numptr1**. We would have the following parameters.

$\searrow$ *numptr1
        count1   average1 $\nearrow$

```
void array_avg(float *numptr1, int size1, float *average1)
{
  float sum = 0;
  for(int I = 0; I < size1; I++) {
    sum += *numptr1;
    numptr1++;
  } // end for
  *average1 = sum / size1;
  return;
} // end find_avg()
```

We can test this function with the following program.

```cpp
//prog7_9.cpp Program to test the function array_avg()
//
#include <iostream.h>
#include <iomanip.h>
void array_avg(float *numptr1, int size1, float *average1);
int main()
{
  float nums[] = {76.5, 67.8, 98.4, 87.2, 69.2};
  float average;
  int size = 5;
  array_avg(nums, size, &average);
  cout.setf(ios::fixed);
  cout.setf(ios::showpoint);
  cout.precision(2);
  cout << "The average = " << setw(5) <<  average << endl;
  return 0;
} // end main
#include <a:\arrayavg.cpp>
```

The output from this program was the following.

The average = 79.82

Try this: Rewrite the function **compute( )** from section 4.6
using pointer notation. It computes the number of
months and the monthly rate from the number of
years and the yearly rate.

```cpp
void compute(_____

{

    _____

    _____

    return;
}
```

Try this: Now write a program to test this version of the function **compute( )**.

```cpp
//prog7_10.cpp  Program to test the pointer version of compute( ).
#include <iostream.h>
#include <iomanip.h>
void compute(_____
                        _____);

int main( )
{
    int years = _____;
    float rate = _____;
    int months;
    float mrate;
    compute(_____
    cout.setf(_____
    cout.setf(_____
    cout. _____
    cout << "Months = " << _____
    cout << "Monthly rate = " << _____
    return;
}
#include <a:\compute2.cpp>
```

We will illustrate output parameters using pointers with one more example. We will write a function that will exchange the values of two integer variables.

```cpp
void exchange(int *num1, *num2)
{
    int temp;
    temp = *num1;
    *num1 = *num2;
    *num2 = temp;
    return;
} // end exchange()
```

We can test this function with the following program.

```
// prog7_11.cpp Program to test the function exchange()
#include <iostream.h>
void exchange(int *num1, int *num2);

int main()
{
  int value1 = 10;
  int value2 = 20;
  cout << "value1 = " << value1 << endl;
  cout << "value2 = " << value2 << endl;
  exchange(&value1, &value2);
  cout << "After a call to exchange() :" << endl;
  cout << "value1 = " << value1 << endl;
  cout << "value2 = " << value << endl;
  return 0;
}
#include <a:\exchange.cpp>
```

Output from this program was the following.

```
value1 = 10
value2 = 20
After a call to exchange() :
value1 = 20
value2 = 10
```

As we know, the C++ language allows us to write the function **exchange()** in another way. This is a review of what we discussed in section 4.5. We include this version of the function **exchange()** so that the reader can compare the two different versions. It is critical that we understand each version and the differences between the two.

```
void exchange(int &num1, int &num2)
{
  int temp;
  temp = num1;
  num1 = num2;
  num2 = temp;
  return;
} // end exchange()
```

Try this: The following is the C version, of a function to input two exam scores from the keyboard. Write the C++ version of this function.

```
void getexams(float *ex1, *ex2)          void getexams(_____
{                                        {
  printf("Input first exam score: ");      cout << _____
  scanf("%f", ex1);                        cin >> _____
  printf("Input second exam score: ");     _____
  scanf("%f", ex2);                        _____
  return;                                  return;
}                                        }
```

Explain why we use the statement

        scanf("%f", ex1);   rather than   scanf("%f", &ex1);

_____

_____

7.6 - Pointers & Multi-Dimensional Arrays

In this section we want to study how pointers relate to multi-dimensional arrays. Suppose that we have the following declaration for a two dimensional array of integers.

        int nums[2][3];

Recall from Chapter 6, that we can view this array as a rectangular array consisting of 2 rows and 3 columns, or as a 2-dimensional array, of arrays containing three integers. We chose the latter, since it extends to higher dimensions. The next three tree diagrams show how we can reference all of these different components, using array notation, first level dereferencing, and finally using second level dereferencing.

Using **array notation**:

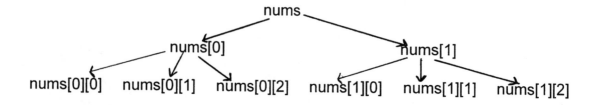

Using **first level dereferencing**:

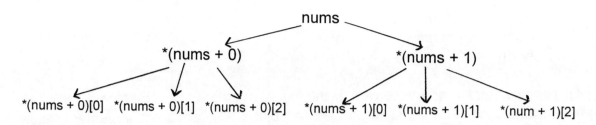

Using **second level dereferencing**:

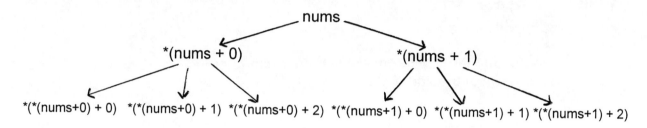

Since **nums** is the name of the array, it references the address of the first integer storage location of the two dimensional array or the address of the first array of three integers. The first array element of **nums** is **nums[0]** so that **nums[0]** references the address of it's first integer which is also the first integer of **nums**. This is **nums[0][0]**. This makes **nums** reference the same address as **nums[0]**. Therefore, what is the difference between the identifiers, **nums** and the identifier **nums[0]**? They both reference the address of **nums[0][0]**. The difference is rather subtle. There is storage set aside for **nums** while **nums[0]** is simply notation that is used by the C++ compiler. However, from the programmers viewpoint, **nums**, **nums[0]**, and **&nums[0][0]** all reference the same address. This is illustrated with the following program.

```
// prog7_12.cpp Program to illustrate addresses of two
//              dimensional arrays.
//
#include <iostream.h>
int main()
{
  int nums[3][2];
  cout << "Address of nums = " << nums << endl;
  cout << "Address of nums[0] = " << nums[0] << endl;
  cout << "Address of nums[0][0] = " << &nums[0][0] << endl;
  return 0;
}
```

The output from this program follows:

Address of nums = 0x8f54ffea
Address of nums[0] = 0x8f54ffea
Address of nums[0][0] = 0x8f54ffea

This shows that the addresses are all the same. In order to see what the differences are we need to see what happens when we use pointer arithmetic and increment these pointers.

Try this: Given the array
int nums[3][4];

Write the three different ways that we can reference the 3rd element of the 2nd array.

_____   _____   _____

Consider the following program:

```
// prog7_13.cpp Program to illustrate pointer arithmetic for
//                   higher dimensional arrays.
#include <iostream.h>
int main()
{
  int nums[3][2];
  cout << "nums = " << nums << " nums + 1 = " << nums + 1 << endl;
  cout << "nums[0] = " << nums[0] << " nums[0] + 1 =  "
      << nums[0] + 1 << endl;
  cout << "&nums[0][0] = " << &nums[0][0] << " &nums[0][0] + 1 = "
      << &nums[0][0] + 1 << endl;
  return 0;
}
```

The output from this program was the following.

nums = 0x8f58ffea   nums + 1 = 0x8f58fff0
nums[0] = 0x8f58ffea   nums[0] + 1 = 0x8f58ffec
&nums[0][0] = 0x8f58ffea   &nums[0][0] + 1 = 0x8f58ffec

We can see that incrementing **nums[0]** and **&nums[0][0]** is the same since they both reference the address of the same integer storage location. Both addresses are incremented by two, the size of an integer storage location. However, incrementing **nums** adds 6 to the address of the first array of three integers, which gives the address of the second array of three integers. This would be the same address as the address of **nums[1]** and **&nums[1][0]**.

As we can see from the previous tree diagrams, using the indirection operator, *, ***nums = *(nums + 0)** would reference the first element of **nums**, that is the array **nums[0]**. Furthermore, ***(nums + 1)** references the second element of **nums**, that is the array **nums[1]**. The elements of the array **nums[0]** can now be referenced by the variables

(*(nums + 0))[0], (*(nums + 0))[1], (*(nums + 0))[2]

while the elements of the array **nums[1]** can be referenced by the variables

(*(nums + 1))[0], (*(nums + 1))[1], and (*(nums + 1))[2]

In addition, using the indirection operator one more time, we have ****nums = *(*(nums + 0) + 0)** referencing the first element of the array, referenced by ***nums**, that is the element **nums[0][0]**. Furthermore, we have ***(*(nums + 0) + 1)** referencing the second element of **nums[0]**, **nums[0][1]**, and ***(*(nums + 0) + 2)** referencing the third element of **nums[0]**, **nums[0][2]**. We can summarize with the following table.

Elements of nums	Elements of nums[0]	Elements of nums[1]
nums[0] *(nums + 0)	nums[0][0] (*(nums + 0))[0] *(*(nums+0) + 0)	nums[1][0] (*(nums + 1))[0] *(*(nums+1) + 0)
nums[1] *(nums + 1)	nums[0][1] (*(nums + 0))[1] *(*(nums + 0) + 1)	nums[1][1] (*(nums + 1))[1] *(*(nums+1) + 1)
	nums[0][2] (*(nums + 0))[2] *(*(nums + 0) + 2)	nums[1][2] (*(nums + 1))[2] *(*nums + 1) + 2)

Study this carefully, so that you will understand the different array and pointer notations that can be used to reference the arrays, the addresses of the arrays, and the elements of the arrays. The next three programs show how we can print out the data stored in the array using each of the three different notations.

```cpp
//prog7_15.cpp Program to print out the data in the two dimensional
//              array nums[ ][ ] using array notation.
#include <iostream.h>
int main( )
{
   int nums[2][3] = {{10, 20, 30},
                     {40, 50, 60}};
   for(int I = 0; I < 2; I++)
     for(int j = 0; j < 3; j++)
       cout << nums[i][j] << endl;
     // end for
   // end for
   return 0;
}
```

```cpp
//prog7_16.cpp Program to print out the data in the two dimensional
//              array nums[ ][ ] using first level dereferencing.
#include <iostream.h>
int main( )
{
   int nums[2][3] = {{10, 20, 30}, {40, 50, 60}};
   for(int I = 0; I < 2; I++)
     for(int j = 0; j < 3; j++)
        cout << (*(nums + I))[j] << endl;
     // end for
   // end for
   return 0;
}
```

```cpp
//prog7_17.cpp Program to print out the data in the two dimensional
//              array nums[ ][ ] using second level dereferencing.
#include <iostream.h>
int main( )
{
   int nums[2][3] = {{10, 20, 30}, {40, 50, 60}};

   for(int I = 0; I < 2; I++)
     for(int j = 0; j < 3; j++)
        cout << *(*(nums + I) + j) << endl;
     // end for
   // end for
   return 0;
}
```

The output from each of these programs was the following:

```
10
20
30
40
50
60
```

Now suppose that we want to define a pointer compatible with **nums[ ][ ]**. That is, a pointer to a two dimensional array of integers. It would be a pointer to an array of two arrays of three integers each. We would use the following declaration.

```
int (*nptr)[3];
```

The parentheses around ***nptr** are necessary since [3] has precedence over *. If we tried to use the declaration

```
int *nptr[3];
```

we would have defined an array of pointers. It would be an array of three pointers to data of type integer. The 3 is necessary in the declaration since the number of elements in the arrays that are pointed to, must be specified. The declaration

```
int (*nptr)[3];
```

gives us a pointer, **nptr**, that is compatible with **nums**. If we have the declarations

```
int nums[2][3];
int (*nptr)[3];
```

we can store the address of **nums** at **nptr** with the statement

```
nptr = nums;
```

When we increment **nptr** with the statement

```
nptr++;
```

nptr would now have the address of the second array of two integers, **nums[1]**. Note, that we cannot use the statement

```
nums++;
```

since **nums** has been assigned a fixed address by the C++ compiler, and this address cannot be changed. We will illustrate these ideas with an example.

Recall the function **compavgs( )**, from section 6.11 that will accept an array of exam scores for a class of students. Each student takes four exams. The function is to compute the exam average for each student, store it in an array and pass the data back to the calling program. Note that when we pass the array, **exams[ ][ ]** as a parameter we need to specify the second dimension with the statement

```
int exams1[ ][4]

void compavgs(int exams1[][4], int size1, float avgs1[])
{
  int sum;
  for (int I = 0; I < size1; I++) {
    sum = 0;
    for (int j = 0; j < 4; j++)
      sum += exams1[i][j];
    // end for
    avgs1[i] = sum / 4.0;
  } // end for
  return;
} // end compavgs()
```

A pointer version of this function is the following.

```
void compavgs(int (*nptr)[4], int size1, float *avgptr)
{
  int sum;
  for (int I = 0; I < size1; I++) {
    sum = 0;
    for(int j = 0; j < 4; j++)
      sum += (*(nptr + I))[j];          // or   sum += *(*(nptr + I) + j);
    // end for
    *avgptr = sum / 4.0;
    avgptr++;
  } // end for
  return;
} // end compavgs()
```

We need to analyze statement 1).

```
sum += (*(nptr + I))[j];
```

Recall that the declaration

    int (*nptr)[4];

defines **nptr** as a pointer to an array of arrays of 4 integers each. Thus

*(nptr + 0), *(nptr + 1), *(nptr + 2), ..., *(nptr + (size1 - 1))

would point to the successive arrays of 4 integers. Therefore, the elements of the first array would be accessed with the identifiers

(*(nptr + 0))[0], (*(nptr + 0))[1], (*(nptr + 0))[2], (*(nptr + 0))[3]

The elements in the second array would be referenced with the identifiers:

(*(nptr + 1))[0], (*(nptr + 1))[1], (*(nptr + 1))[2], (*(nptr + 1))[3]

In general,

(*(nptr + I))[j]

will represent the (j + 1)st element of the (I + 1)st array.

The program to test the pointer version of **compavgs()** is the following:

```
//prog7_18.cpp Program to test the pointer version of
//                     program compavgs( ).
#include <iostream.h>
#include <iomanip.h>
void compavgs(int (*nptr)[4], int size1, float *avgptr);
int main( )
{
    int exams[ ][4] = {{75, 82, 93, 78},
                       {92, 97, 85, 91},
                       {72, 78, 83, 68}};
    float averages[3];
    compavgs(exams, 3, averages);
    cout.setf(ios::fixed);
    cout.setf(ios::showpoint);
    cout.precision(2);
    for(int I = 0; I < 3; I++)
       cout << "Student " << I + 1 << " has exam average = "
            << setw(5) << averages[i] << endl;
```

```
    // end for
    return 0;
}
#include <a:\cmpavgs.cpp>
```

Output from this program was the following:

```
        Student 1 has exam average = 82.00
        Student 2 has exam average = 91.25
        Student 3 has exam average = 75.25
```

7.7 - Pointers to Functions

One common use of pointers to functions is in writing programs where functions are called based on a choice selected by the user from a menu. The program prompts the user to select an option from a menu (say 0, 1, or 2) and each option is then to call a specific function. This method that uses pointers to the functions that are to be called, and stores these pointers in an array of pointers. The choice that is entered by the user is then used as a subscript in the array and the corresponding pointer is used to call the function. We illustrate this idea with a simple example.

```
//prog7_19.cpp Program to illustrate pointers to functions.
#include <iostream.h>
void sub1(int);
void sub2(int);
void sub3(int);
int main( )
{
    void (*fptr[3])(int) = {sub1, sub2, sub3};
    int choice;
    cout << "Enter your choice, 0, 1, or 2 " << endl
        << "Enter 3 to exit: ";
    cin >> choice;
    while ((choice >=0) && (choice < 3)) {
        (*fptr[choice])(choice);
        cout << "Enter your choice, 0, 1, or 2 " << endl
            << "Enter 3 to exit: ";
        cin >> choice;
    } // end while
    cout << "You entered 3 to exit! " << endl;
    return 0;
}
```

```
    void sub1(int ch1)
    {
      cout << "Your choice was " << ch1
           << " sub1( ) was called. " << endl << endl;
      return;
    } // end sub1( )
    void sub2(int ch2)
    {
      cout << "Your choice was " << ch2
           << " sub2( ) was called. " << endl << endl;
      return;
    } // end sub2( )
    void sub3(int ch3)
    {
      cout << "Your choice was " << ch3
           << " sub3( ) was called. " << endl << endl;
      return;
    } // end sub3( )
```

Output from this program was the following:

```
        Enter your choice, 0, 1, or 2
        Enter 3 to exit: 0
        Your choice was 0 sub1( ) was called.

        Enter your choice, 0, 1, or 2
        Enter 3 to exit: 1
        Your choice was 1 sub2( ) was called.

        Enter your choice, 0, 1, or 2
        Enter 3 to exit: 2
        Your choice was 2 sub3( ) was called.

        Enter your choice, 0, 1, or 2
        Enter 3 to exit: 3
        You entered 3 to exit!
```

7.8 - Converting C to C++

In this section we will continue our discussion of converting programs that have been written in C to programs in C++. As we have seen, the C and C++ programming languages use pointers extensively. They are used when data is to be returned and when arrays are to be passed to functions. Pointer variables are used to pass variables by reference and to pass arrays; i.e. anytime that an address is to be passed for a variable from the calling function or program. In section 7.5 we considered the following function.

```
void find_avg(int n1, int n2, float *avg)
{
  *avg = (n1 + n2) / 2.0;
  return;
} // end find_avg
```

This function was the C version of the following C++ function that was also written in section 7.5.

```
void find_avg(int n1, int n2, float &avg)
{
  avg = (n1 + n2) / 2.0;
  return;
} // end find_avg
```

As we can see, the C program uses the pointer variable parameter, **avg**

```
float *avg
```

and it is replaced in the C++ function with the parameter, **avg**

```
float &avg
```

that is passed by reference. In addition, the code that uses the pointer variable, **avg**

```
*avg = (n1 + n2) / 2.0;
```

is replaced with the code that used the float variable, **avg**

```
avg = (n1 + n2) / 2.0;
```

Try this: Write the C++ version of the following function.

```
void findlarge(float num1, float num2, float *large)
{
  if (num1 > num2)
    *large = num1;
  else
    *large = num2;
```

302

```
         // end if
         return;
      }

      void findlarge(_____
      {

         _____
         _____
         _____
         _____
         _____
         _____

      }
```

As we illustrated in section 7.5, pointers are used to write functions that pass data using arrays. The following function finds the average of count real numbers stored in an array.

```
      void array_avg(float *nums, int count, float *avg)
      {
        float sum = 0;
        for(int I = 0; I < count; I++) {
          sum += *nums;
          nums++;
        ) // end for
        *avg = sum / count;
        return;
      } // end array_avg
```

In order to convert this function to a function in C++, we would want to use an array in place of the pointer variable parameter

        float *nums

and replace the pointer variable

        float *avg

with the parameter using the reference operator

        float &avg

The code would also be rewritten so that it used array notation rather than pointer notation.

```
    for(int I = 0; I < count; I++)
      sum += nums[i];
    // end for
    avg = sum / count;
```

The C++ version of the function would be the following:

```
void array_avg(float nums[ ], int count, float &avg)
{
  float sum = 0;
  for(int I = 0; I < count; I++)
    sum += nums[i];
  // end for
  avg = sum / count;
  return;
} // end array_avg
```

Try this: Write the C++ version of the following function.

```
void arraylarge(float *nums, int count, float *large)
{
  *large = *nums;
  nums++;
  for(int I = 1; I <= count - 1; I++) {
    if (*nums > *large)
      *large = *nums;
    // end if
    nums++;
  } // end for
  return;
} // end arraylarge
```

void arraylarge(_____

{

  _____

  _____

  _____

  _____

  _____

  _____

  _____

  _____

}
```
```

7.9 - Summary

In this chapter, we discussed the very important concept of defining and using pointer variables in C++. We learned how to define pointer variables to the simple data types, character, integer, and real (float). We can now define a variable and a pointer variable to any of these types and understand how we can assign the address of the variable to the pointer variable. We say that the pointer variable now <u>points</u> <u>to</u> the corresponding variable. We understand that the address assigned to a variable is constant and cannot be changed by a program; however, pointer variables can be assigned different addresses. We also saw how we can allocate a block of memory to a pointer variable using the **new** operator available in C++, and also using the functions **malloc( )** and **sizeof( )** that are available in ANSII C and therefore also in C++.

We should now know how pointer variables and arrays are related. We saw how an array name is also a pointer variable that has been assigned an address as a constant. We now know how we can assign the address of an array to a pointer variable and increment the pointer variable to move through the array. We can also use pointers to pass arrays to functions. We discussed how functions written in C used pointer variables as parameters to pass addresses. This is how output parameters are used in these C functions. This is how variables are passed by reference. We discussed how these functions are used in a calling program or function.

We discussed how pointers relate to higher dimensional arrays. We illustrated pointers to two-dimensional arrays and how first and second level dereferencing can be used to access the data in an array. We illustrated how pointer variables can be used to pass two dimensional arrays as parameters to functions and how the code for a function can be written using pointer notation.

We illustrated how we can use pointers to functions. We showed how we can use an array of pointers, where the elements of the array are pointers to the functions that are to be called in the program. This technique is useful when the program allows the user to choose which function is to be called by selecting the appropriate option from a menu.

We discussed how we can convert functions that have been written in C to functions in C++. These functions used pointers to pass data by reference and to pass the address of arrays.

7.10 Questions

7.1 How much memory is allocated on your computer for each of the following data types?

      a. character
      b. integer
      c. real

      d. long integer
      e. double precision real

7.2 What is a pointer variable?

7.3 What information does the compiler need to define a pointer variable?

7.4 How are pointer variables and arrays related?

7.5 What are the differences between a pointer variable and an array?

7.6 What is the "address of" operator"?

7.7 What is the "dereferencing operator"?

7.8 What is meant by "operator overloading"? Give two examples.

7.9 Given the declaration **int num**; how do we print the address of **num** using **printf( )**.

7.10 How do we print the address of **num** using **cout**?

7.11 What are the two ways that we can allocate memory to a integer pointer variable **intptr**?

7.12 How can we allocate memory to **intptr** using the declared variable **int num** ?

7.13 How are pointers and arrays related?

7.14 Given the array and an integer pointer variable defined by the following statements
      int nums[3];
      int *numptr;
what are the two different statements that we can use to make **numptr** point to **nums**?

7.15 What header file contains the declaration for **new**?

7.16 What header file contains the declaration for **malloc( )**?

7.17   What header file contains the declaration for **sizeof( )**?

7.18   Given the statements
            int num = 50;
            int *numptr;
            numptr = #
        what does each of the following do?
        a. *(numptr++);
        b. *numptr++;

7.11 Exercises

7.1   How do we define pointer variables for each of the following data types?
        a. character   d. long integer
        b. integer   e. double precision real
        c. real   f. array of integers

7.2   Given the integer variable and an integer pointer variable defined with the statements
            int num = 10;
            int *numptr;
        write the statement that will make **numptr** point to **num**.

7.3   Using the statements from 2. write statements using **cout** that will print the data stored and the address of the storage location using the integer variable **num**. Give the statements that will print out the data stored and the address using the pointer variable **numptr**.

7.4   Do the same thing that you did in Exercise 7.3. only use the function **printf( )**.

7.5   Given the array that is defined and assigned data with the following statement, write the block of code that will print out the data stored one per line. Use standard array notation.

            int nums[ ] = {100, 200, 300, 400, 500, 600};

7.6   Write the block of code that will print the data stored in the above array, **nums**, one per line, using advanced array notation.

7.7   Write the block of code that will print the data stored in the above array, **nums**, one per line, using pointer notation.

7.8   How do we define a pointer variable, **numsptr**, and make it point to the array **nums**?

7.9   Rewrite the function **getdata()** from section 4.5 using pointers.

7.10   Rewrite the function **compute( )** from section 4.5 using pointers.

7.11   Rewrite the function **printtable( )** from section 4.5 using pointers.

7.12   Rewrite the program **prog4_9.cpp** from section 4.5 so that it uses the pointer versions of the functions from exercises 7.9, 7.10, and 7.11.

7.13   Rewrite the function **savings( )** from section 4.5 using pointers.

7.14   Write a program to test the function **savings( )** from Exercise 7.13.

7.15   Write a function, using pointers, that will prompt the user to input an amount, an interest rate, and a final amount from the keyboard. These values are to be returned to the calling program.

7.16   Write a function that will use the data from Exercise 7.15 and will compute the number of months that it will take for the amount to earn enough interest so that we will end up with at least the final amount in an account. Assume that the interest is compounded monthly.

7.17   Write a program that will use the functions from Exercises 7.15 and 7.16 and will print a summary to the screen. The summary should be something like the following:

```
Amount = $xxxxx.xx
Final Amount = $yyyyy.yy
Interest Rate = z.z%
Years = dd
Months = mm
```

7.18   Write C++ statements that can be used to replace each of the following blocks of C statements.

a. int *intptr;
   intptr = (int *) malloc(sizeof(int));

b. float *fptr
   fptr = (float *)malloc(sizeof(float));

c. long int *lintptr;
   lintptr = (long int *)malloc(sizeof(long int));

d. double dptr;
   dptr = (double *)malloc(sizeof(double));

7.19 Write the C statements that can be used to replace each of the following blocks of C++ statements.

a. int *intptr;
   intptr = new int;

b. float *fptr;
   fptr = new float;

c. long int *lintptr;
   lintptr = new long int;

d. double *dptr;
    dptr = new double;

CHAPTER 8

Strings in C++

8.1 - Introduction

A **string** is simply a sequence of characters stored in memory. Strings can usually be manipulated using ordinary array processing techniques. Since strings occur often in programming, most languages have special functions that can be used to work with strings. The functions that are used to manipulate strings are, however, dependent of the language. Different programming languages have different functions that can be used. We will study how strings are stored in C++ and the functions that are available for input, for output, and for the manipulation of strings. We will write our own versions of some of these functions to illustrate programming techniques in C++. We will write the functions using arrays, then using arrays and pointers, and finally using only pointers. This will give us a review of the ideas that were discussed in Chapters 6 and 7.

After finishing this chapter, the reader should be able to understand

1.   how strings are stored in C and C++.

2.   how strings differ from arrays of characters.

3.   how to use the standard ANSII C string and character functions that are available in most implementations of C++.

4.   how to use the string and character functions that are available in the DOS versions of C++.

5.   which string functions are unique to the DOS versions of C++.

6.   how to write functions that work with strings, using arrays, using pointers and arrays, and finally using only pointers.

7.   how to use the string functions to sort arrays of strings.

8.2 - Strings in C++

A **string constant** is any sequence of characters enclosed in double quotes. For example, "Hello, World!" and "AbC12%@#" are string constants. Anytime that the C or C++ language uses a string constant, it uses a **null byte** to mark the end of a string. A null byte is byte that is numerically zero. This can be represented as 00H (hex), 0x00, or most often as **'\0'**. A string of characters terminated with a 00 byte is called an **ASCIIZ string**. The functions that are used to manipulate strings depend on this character (null byte) being stored at the end of any string. This is true whether the string is a string constant or when it is stored in a character array. Thus, when we store a string in an array with the statement

    char string[] = "Hello, World!";

we would have an array of characters in memory, 14 characters long, the 13 characters of the string plus the null byte. The double quotes are not stored as part of the string. The following figure illustrates how this string would be stored in memory. The second line is the ASCII code that shows the actual byte for each of the characters.

    H   e   l   l   o   ,   W   o   r   l   d   !   \0

    48 65 6C 6C 6F 2C 20 57 6F 72 6C 64 21 00

When a string is stored in an array, the individual characters can be manipulated like any other array using standard array handling techniques. The null character at the end of the string is used by the C++ library functions that perform operations with strings. We will need to make use of this fact when we write some of our own string functions.

Anytime that the C++ compiler sees a string (sequence of characters enclosed in double quotes "), it stores the sequence in memory and appends a terminating 00 byte, '\0', to the end of the sequence. For example, if it sees the statement

    cout << "Hello, world!\n";

it would store the following sequence of characters in memory.

    H   e   l   l   o   ,   W   o   r   l   d   ! '\n' '\0'

    48 65 6C 6C 6F 2C 20 57 6F 72 6C 64 21 0A   00

In C++, **'\n'** is the **new line** character. What is stored in memory depends on the operating system. In C++, under DOS, a line feed character, **0AH**, is stored. On the Macintosh, C++ stores a carriage return character, **0DH**, while under UNIX both a carriage return and a line feed are stored.

The compiler associates the string constant with the address of the memory location of the first character of the string.

As we have seen, the concept of a string is closely related to that of an array of characters. A string is like an array of characters, since the characters of the string are stored in consecutive memory locations. A string, however, must have a 00 byte, '\0', terminator while this is not the case for a character array.

Since a string is associated with the address of the memory location of the first character, once memory has been allocated for the pointer, a string can be assigned to a character pointer variable. For example, if we have a pointer defined with the statement:

    char *stptr;

then memory can be allocated with either of the statements

    stptr = (char*)malloc(20);

or

    stptr = new char[20];

We can then assign a string to this pointer variable as with the following statement:

    stptr = "Hello, world!\n";

The string can then be printed to the screen with either of the statements:

    cout << stptr;

or

    printf("%s", stptr);

As in the case of other arrays, C++ allows the use of string indexing to access the individual elements of a string that has been assigned to a string pointer. After the statements:

    char *stptr;

    stptr = new char[80];
    stptr = "Hello, world!\n";

we can use

stptr[0] to access the 'H'
stptr[1] to access the 'e'

...

stptr[13] to access the '\n'
stptr[14] to access the '\0'

Pointer arithmetic and dereferencing can also be used to access these individual elements.

*stptr   to access the 'H'
*(stptr + 1)   to access the 'e'

...

*(stptr + 14)   to access the '\0'

Try this: Given a string stored in memory, give the array notation and the pointer notation that can be used to reference the specified character.

char college[ ] = "Indiana State University";

	Array notation	Pointer Notation
'I'	_____	_____
'S'	_____	_____
'U'	_____	_____

When we use function, **printf( )** with the **%s** output format specifier for a string, or the object **cout**, each of these routines expect the corresponding parameter to be the address of the first character of a string. Both begin output with the byte found at that address, and proceed byte by byte until encountering the null byte.

In order to print the address of the string variable, we use either of the statements

printf("%x\n", stptr);

or

```
    cout << &stptr << endl;
```

The address printed is the address of the first character of the string. Consider the following program.

```cpp
// prog8_1.cpp - Program to illustrate string output.
#include <iostream.h>
int main()
{
  char *stptr;
  stptr = new char[20];
  stptr = "This is a string.";
  cout <<  stptr << endl;
  cout << &stptr << endl;
  ++stptr;
  cout << stptr << endl;
  cout << &stptr << endl;
  return 0;
}
```

A test run of the program produced the following output.

```
This is a string.
0x8f90ffe0
his is a string.
0x8f90ffe1
```

The second line is the address of the string, i.e. the address stored in **stptr**. The third line begins with the 'h' since the pointer was incremented to point to the second character of the string. The fourth line of output was the address of the second character of the string. We consider another example.

```cpp
//prog8_2.cpp - Program to illustrate character access.
#include <iostream.h>
int main()
{
  char *stptr;
  stptr = new char[20];
  stptr = "This is a string!\n";
  cout << stptr;

  *(stptr + 7) = '\n';          1)
  *(stptr + 8) = '\0';          2)
```

```
        cout << stptr;
        return 0;
}
```

The output from a test run of this program was the following.

```
This is a string!
This is
```

Statements 1) and 2) replace the 8th and 9th characters of the string, the ' ' and the 'a', with the characters '\n' and '\0'. Thus, when the string is printed, the '\0' byte is encountered and only the first 8 characters are printed to the screen. The 8th character is the newline character '\n'.

Try this: Given the string stored in memory, give the statements that would print out the 1st, 5th, and 10th characters, and the statements that would print out the addresses of the 1st, 5th, and 10th characters.

        char message[ ] = "Hello, World!";

Characters: _____   Addresses: _____
             _____   _____
             _____   _____

As we have seen, there are three ways that we can store a string in memory and assign the string address to a variable. We want to make sure that we understand the differences between these three ways.

1.   char string[ ] = "This is a string.";

2.   char *stptr = "This is a string.";

3.   a.   char *stptr;
      b.   stptr = new char[18];
      c.   sptr = "This is a string.";

The first statement defines an array of characters, stores the string in the array, and allocates 18 bytes of memory when the string is stored. The address assigned to the array is a constant and cannot be changed.

The second statement defines a pointer variable, stores the string in memory, and assigns the address of the first character of the string to the pointer variable. Memory has been allocated for this pointer variable and data has been stored. The pointer variable can be assigned a new address.

The third statement, 3a., defines a pointer variable, the fourth statement, 3b., allocates memory for this pointer variable to point to, and the address of this memory is assigned to the pointer. The fifth statement, 3c. stores a string at this location by assigning the address of the string to the pointer variable.

We illustrate these ideas with a program.

```
// prog8_3.cpp - Program to illustrate string assignment to
//                 pointers and arrays.
#include <iostream.h>
int main()
{
   char message[ ] = "This is string 1.";
   char *stptr1 = "This is string 2";
   char *stptr2;

   stptr2 = new char[17];
   stptr2 = "This is string 3";

   cout << "Address of message: " << &message << endl;
   cout << "Address of stptr1: " << &stptr1 << endl ;
   cout << "Address of stptr2: " << &stptr2 << endl;
   cout << "String stored at message = " << message << endl;
   cout << "String stored at stptr1 = " << stptr1 << endl;
   cout << "String stored at stptr2 = " << stptr2 << endl;

   stptr1 = "This is string 4";
   stptr2 = "This is string 5";

   cout << "Address of stptr1 = " << &stptr1 << endl;
   cout << "New string stored at stptr1 = " << stptr1 << endl;
   cout << "Address of stptr2 = " << &stptr2 << endl;
   cout << "New  string stored at stptr2 = " << stptr2 << endl;
   return 0;
}
```

Output from this program was the following:

```
Address of message = 0x8f90ffe0
Address of stptr1 = 0x8f90fff4
```

Address of stptr2 = 0x8f90fff2
String stored at message = This is string 1
String stored at stptr1 = This is string 2
String stored at stptr2 = This is string 3
Address of stptr1 = 0x8f90fff4
New string stored at stptr1 = This is string 4
Address of stptr2 = 0x8f90fff2
New string stored at stptr2 = This is string 5

The output from this program shows us that 2. and 3. do exactly the same thing. Both sets of statements allocate memory for a pointer variable, assign an address to the pointer, and store data in the allocated memory. When we use the array, we can not assign a new string to the array with the statement

message = "This is string 6";

The array, **message**, has been assigned a constant address and the address cannot be changed by assigning a new string.

In order to assign a new string to an array, we must use a different technique. As we stated above, when storage is created for the array an address is assigned to the array name and the address cannot be changed. We have to use one of the string library functions that has been written to handle this problem. The function is the function **strcpy()** and it's prototype is defined in the **string.h** header file. We illustrate this idea with the following program.

```
// prog8_4.cpp - Program to illustrate how to copy a string.
#include <iostream.h>
#include <string.h>
int main()
{
  static char message[] = "This is string 1";          1)
  cout << "The string: " <<  message;
  cout << "The address: " << &message << endl;
  strcpy(message, "This is string 2");                 2)
  cout << "The string: " << message;
  cout << "The address: " << &message << endl;
  return 0;
}
```

The output from this program was the following:

The string: This is string 1

The address: 0x08f90ffe0
The string: This is string 2
The address: 0x80f90ffe0

Note, that the address is the same for both strings. This is not a surprise since we copied the new string into the array with our library function **strcpy()**. We needed the **#include <string.h>** statement in our program in order to be able to use this string function. We discuss the string functions that are defined with this header file in section 8.5.

8.3 - String Input & Output Using ANSII C Functions

As we have seen, input and output of strings can be done using the standard C functions that are available in most versions of C++. These functions are defined in the header files, **stdio.h** and **conio.h**. The functions that we will discuss in this section are the following:

Table 8.1: ANSII String & Character I/O Functions

stdio.h	conio.h
gets( )	
puts( )	
getchar( )	getch( )
putchar( )	putch( )
	getche( )
	ungetch( )

The function for string input from the keyboard is

gets( )

This function accepts input from the keyboard, character by character, storing the characters in the designated buffer until the newline character is encountered. The newline character is generated when the <Enter> key is pressed. When the newline character, '\n', is encountered, a null - '\0', byte is stored in the buffer. For example, if we have a buffer, **message**, defined with the statement

char message[81];

the call to **gets( )** would be done with the statement

318

gets(message);

The function that is used for string output to the screen is the function

puts( )

This function prints the string, character by character, until the null byte, '\0', is encountered. The null byte is not printed. If the string is stored in the buffer, **message**, then the string is printed with the statement

puts(message);

When the string stored in message is printed to the screen, the null byte string terminator is replaced with the newline character, '\n'. On microcomputers under DOS and windows, the string is printed to the screen followed by a carriage return and a line feed. This prints the string and then moves the cursor to the beginning of the next line. We illustrate the use of these two functions with a program.

```
// prog8_5.cpp - Program to illustrate the use of gets() and puts().
#include <stdio.h>
int main()
{
  char message[81];

  printf("Enter a string: \n");
  gets(message);
  printf("The entered string is: \n");
  puts(message);
  return 0;
}
```

The output from a test run of this program is the following.

```
Enter a string:
Hello, World!<Enter>
The entered string is:
Hello, World!
```

As we saw in section 8.2, the output of a string can also be done using the all-purpose output function **printf( )**. The statement

printf("%s\n", message);

would give exactly the same result as the statement

    puts(message);

We use %s to let **printf( )** know that the data stored in **message** is a string. In addition, we must include newline character, **'\n'**, as part of the output format string in order to get the cursor to move to the beginning of a new line after the string has been printed. The **puts()** function is much more efficient than **printf()** for string output since it's only purpose is to output a string.

We also saw that when we try to use the general purpose input function, **scanf( )** for string input, we do not get the results that we expect. When we replace the statement

    gets(message);

with the statement

    scanf("%s", message);

in program **prog8_5.cpp**, we have the following output:

    Enter a string:
    Hello, World!<ret>
    The entered string is:
    Hello,

When we use **scanf( )** for string input, characters are accepted until either a new line character or a **blank** is encountered. Thus, this function is not nearly as useful for string input as **gets( )**. If we were writing a C program, we would almost always use **gets()** instead of **scanf( )** for string input since it is straight forward, easy to use, and gives us the entire string.

There is however, a problem. The function, **gets( )**, gets the string entered from the keyboard until it sees the <ret> regardless of the size of the buffer. Therefore, if we had a buffer defined with the statement

    char buffer[20];

executed the code

    printf("Input a string: ");
    gets(buffer);

320

and the user typed in an 80 character string of characters, then the 80 characters would be stored in memory overwriting whatever was stored. In section 10.7 we will discuss the function, **fgets( )**, that is used to take care of this problem. This function is designed to print a string to a file. The C++ language also contains a function, **getline( )**, that we can use to take care of this problem and we will discuss this function in section 8.4.

The ANSI C standard functions for character input and output are **getchar( )** and **putchar( )**. The prototypes for these two functions are also included in the **stdio.h** header file. The input function **getchar( )** returns a character with the statement

```
ch = getchar();
```

The function **putchar( )** outputs a character to the screen with the statement

```
putchar(ch);
```

We illustrate the use of **getchar()** by writing a function **get_st()** that will simulate the standard library function **gets()**. It will input a string from the keyboard and store it in a designated buffer, i.e. character array. The string will be stored, followed by a '\0', string terminator. Memory for the string is to be allocated in the calling program. The **stdio.h** header file will also be included in the main program.

```
void get_st(char buffer[])
{
  char ch;
  int I;
  I = 0;
  ch = getchar();
  while (ch != '\n') {
    buffer[i] = ch;
    I++;
    ch = getchar();
  } // end while
  buffer[i] = '\0';
  return;
}
```

Note that the while loop can be written in a more compact way as follows.

```
while (( ch = getchar() ) != '\n')
  buffer[i++] = ch;
```

In order to review some of the ideas from Chapter 7, we also write this function using pointers.

```cpp
void get_st(char *stptr)
{
    *stptr = getchar();
    while (*stptr != '\n' ) {
        stptr++;
        *stptr = getchar();
    } // end while
    *stptr = '\0';
    return;
}
```

The function **getchar()** does **buffered input** which means that **getchar()** gets characters from a special input buffer, rather than directly as they are entered from the keyboard. As a string is being entered, it is stored character by character in the input buffer until the <ret> key is pressed. The string is stored in the buffer, followed by the newline character. The function **getchar()** obtains the characters one at a time from the buffer, but not until the entire string has been stored in the input buffer. This is the reason that we have to type a <ret> following the character when we are inputting a single character from the keyboard. For example,

```cpp
printf("Press any key to continue: "):
ch = getchar( );
```

would execute as follows:

```
Press any key to continue: a<ret>
```

The pointer version of **get_st()** does the following. It first calls **getchar()** to get a character from the buffer and stores it in memory at the address stored at **stptr**. The pointer **stptr** is then incremented to point at the next memory location. The character just stored is then compared with the newline character, **'\n'**, and when this character is encountered, the loop is exited. Otherwise, another character is read and the process continues. When the program exits the while loop, the newline character, **'\n'**, is replaced with the null character, **'\0'**.

We can test the **get_st()** function with the following program.

```cpp
// prog8_6.cpp - Program to test the function get_st( ).
#include <iostream.h>
void get_st(char *stptr1);
```

```
int main()
{
    char *stptr;
    stptr = new char(20);
    cout << "Input your first name: ";
    get_st(stptr);
    cout << "Hello " << stptr << endl;
    return 0;
}
#include <a:\getst.cpp>
```

Output from this program was the following:

Input your first name: Linda <ret>
Hello Linda

There are other functions for character input and output that are unique to the DOS versions of C++. These functions are **getch( )**, **putch( )**, and **getche( )**. The prototypes for these functions are included in the header file, **conio.h**. The two functions **getch()** and **getche()** are a lot like **getchar()**, except that they are **not buffered**. This means that they do not use the special storage buffer in memory, but rather they get the characters as soon as they are entered at the keyboard. The function **getch()** does not echo the character typed to the screen while the function **getche()** does echo the character to the screen. This the reason for the **e** in **getche()**. There is also a standard function, **ungetch()**, that is used to push characters back into the keyboard buffer. The next program illustrates the use of two of these functions:

```
//prog8_7.cpp Program to illustrate the use of the functions
//              getch( ) and putch( ).
#include <conio.h>
#include <iostream.h>
int main( )
{
    char ch;
    cout << "Input a single character: "
    ch = getch( );
    cout << "You typed the character: ";
    putch(ch);
    putch('\n');
    return 0;
}
```

Output from this program was the following:

Input a single character: //<a> no <ret>
You typed the character: a

If we replace the statement

    ch = getch( );

with the statement

    ch = getche( );

then the output was the following:

Input a single character: <u>a</u>   // <a> no <ret>
You typed the character: a

The following is a description of each of the functions discussed above.

Table 8.2: ANSII C Character I/O Functions

===

getchar( )   int getchar(void);
                 Reads a single character from the keyboard buffer and echoes it to
                 the screen.
                 ANSI C standard.   stdio.h

putchar( )   int putchar(int ch);
                 Outputs a single character, ch, to the current text window. It returns
                 the character, ch, if successful and EOF if an error occurs.
                 ANSI C standard.   stdio.h

getch( )   int getch(void);
                 Reads a single character from the keyboard, without echoing it to the
                 screen. The input is not buffered.
                 Unique to DOS.   conio.h

putch( )   int putch(int ch);
                 Outputs the character, ch, to the current text window. Does not
                 translate '\n' into carriage-return/linefeed pairs. It returns the
                 character, ch, if successful and EOF if an error occurs.
                 Unique to DOS.   conio.h

324

getche( )   int getche(void);
Reads a single character from the keyboard and echoes it to the current text window, using direct video or BIOS. The input is not buffered.
Unique to DOS.   conio.h

ungetch( )   int ungetch(int ch);
Pushes the character, ch, back to the keyboard buffer, causing ch to be the next character read. Returns the integer ASCII value of the character, ch, if successful and EOF if an error occurs.
Available on most systems.   conio.h

==

8.4 String Input & Output Using C++

Using the stream class, **cout** from C++, a string stored in a buffer, **message**, can be printed with the statement

cout << message << endl;

The newline manipulator, **endl**, is printed to move the cursor to a new line. This would make the above statement equivalent to the statement

puts(message);

The newline could also be printed using the newline character with the statement

cout << message << '\n';

We will always use the newline manipulator, **endl**, since this will print a newline character and also flushes the output buffer. When we say that it **flushes the output buffer**, we mean that it causes everything in the output buffer to be printed, even if the buffer is not full. We can also flush the output buffer with the **flush** manipulator with the statement

cout << flush;

Printing the Address of a String

A string is of type **char *** and the operator, **<<**, has been overloaded to print data of type char *. As we have seen, we can print the address of the string with the statement

```
        cout << &message << endl;
```

using the address operator, **&**. In addition, we can cast the string pointer to a type of

void *

and print the address of a string using **cout**. This can be done with any pointer variable that we wish to print the output as an address. We illustrate this idea with the following program.

```
//prog8_9.cpp Program to illustrate the use of void *
//                   to print the address of a pointer variable.
#include <iostream.h>
int main( )
{
   char string[ ] = "Hello, World!";
   cout << "The string = "
        << string << endl;
   cout << "Address of the string = "
        << (void *)string << endl;
   return 0;
}
```

Output from this program was the following:

```
The string = Hello, World!
Address of the string = 0x8f90ffe0
```

   The **cout** stream also contains a member function for printing a single character. This function is **put( )**. The character 'A' can be printed with either of the statements

```
   cout.put('A');              or              cout.put(65);
```

Consecutive characters can be printed with consecutive calls to put( ). For example,

```
   cout.put('A').put('B');
```

would print

   AB

Character and String Input

The **cin**, stream contains member functions for character and string input. The member function, **getline( )**, can be used for string input and can be used in different forms. The second parameter of the function is the maximum number of characters that is to be read while the first parameter is the buffer to store the string. Thus, if we had a buffer defined to store a name with a maximum of 20 characters,

```
char name[21];
```

then the following statements would be used to input the name.

```
cout << "Input your name: ";
cin.getline(name, 21);
```

The statement

```
cin.getline(name, 21);
```

reads characters that are typed from the keyboard, stores them in the buffer, **name**, until it reads the <ret> or until 20 characters have been read. It then stores the null byte terminator in the buffer. We illustrate this version of **getline( )** with the following program.

```cpp
// prog8_10.cpp - Program to illustrate the cin.getline( ) function.
#include <iostream.h>
const int MAX = 21;
int main()
{
    char message[MAX];
    cout << "Enter a string: ";
    cin.getline(message, MAX);
    cout << "\nThe message = " << message << endl;
    return 0;
}
```

Output from this program was the following:

```
Enter a string: abcd1abcd2abcd3abcd4abcd5<ret>
The message = abcd1abcd2abcd3abcd4
```

The third version of **getline( )** has a third parameter, a delimiter character. The delimiter character is used any time that we want to terminate input with something other than the default. The default is the newline character, '\n'. The following example will use the '**$**' to indicate the end of input from the keyboard. Newline characters will simply be stored in the array. The statement

    getline(message, MAX, '$');

will terminate the input when MAX characters have been reached or a '$' is typed.

```cpp
// prog8_11.cpp - Program to illustrate the input of multiple lines
//                      from the keyboard.
#include <iostream.h>
const int MAX = 100;
int main()
{
  char message[MAX];
  cout << "Enter three short lines: " << endl
        << "Type a $ at the end of the last line: "
        << endl;
  cin.getline(message, MAX, '$');
  cout << "\nYou entered:\n" << message
        << endl;
  return 0;
}
```

Output from a run of this program was the following:

    Enter three short lines:
    Type a $ at the end of the last line:
    Now is the time<ret>
    for all good<ret>
    men.$

    You entered:
    Now is the time
    for all good
    men.

The C++ language also allows us to use the manipulator, **setw( )**, to limit the number of characters that **cin** will accept from the keyboard. This will also protect the program from array overflow. The use of **setw( )** for input is illustrated with the following program.

```
// prog8_10.cpp - Program to illustrate the use of setw() to
//                      protect the program from array overflow.
#include <iostream.h>
#include <iomanip.h>
int main()
{
  char string[11];
  cout << "Enter a string: ";
  cin >> setw(11) >> string;
  cout << "The string =  " << string << endl;
  return 0;
}
```

Output from this program was the following:

```
Enter a string: abcd1abcd2abcd3<ret>
The string = abcd1abcd2
```

The **cin** stream also includes the member function, **get( )**, that can be used for character input. This function has three versions, it can have a single argument, a character, that does buffered input and behaves just like the function **getchar( )**. We illustrate the use of this version of the function by rewriting the function **get_st( )** from section 8.3.

```
void get_st(char buffer[ ])
{
  char ch;
  int I;
  cin.get(ch);
  while (ch != '\n') {
    buffer[i] = ch;
    I++;
    cin.get(ch);
  } // end while
  buffer[i] = '\0';
  return;
}
```

We will ask the reader to write a program to test this function as one of the exercises.

When we use the member function, **get( )**, with a single argument, it returns one character from the input stream, including the blank. It returns EOF when end-of-file is encountered in the input stream. The IBM-PC uses <ctrl><z><ret> for end-of-file, while the

Macintosh use <ctrl><d><ret> and UNIX uses <ctrl><d>, with no <ret>. The next program illustrates this idea.

```cpp
//prog8_13.cpp Program to illustrate get( ) to
//                    detect end-of-file in the input stream.
#include <iostream.h>
int main( )
{
    int ch;
    cout << "Before input, cin.eof( ) is: "
         << cin.eof( ) << endl;
    cout << "Enter a short sentence " << endl
         << "followed by end-of-file: " << endl;
    while (ch = cin.get( ) != EOF)
        cout.put(ch);
    // end while
    cout << endl << "EOF on this system is: "
         << ch << endl;
    cout << "After input, cin.eof( ) is: "
         << ch << endl;
    return 0;
}
```

Output from this program was the following:

```
Before input, cin.eof( ) is: 0
Enter a short sentence
followed by end-of-file:
This is short^z<ret>
This is short
EOF on this system is: -1
After input, cin.eof( ) is: 1
```

The second version of **get( )** uses a buffer to store a string of characters and an integer specifying the maximum number of characters to store. This is just like using the member function **getline( )**.

```cpp
cin.get(buffer, size);
```

This statement reads characters from the input stream, stores them in the array, **buffer**, until it has read one less than specified by **size** or till it reads the newline character. The third version of the member function, **get( )**, has three arguments and also behaves just like the function **getline( )**.

330

cin.get(buffer, size, ch);

This statement reads characters from the input stream, stores them in the array, including the newline character, until it has read one less than **size** or until it reads the delimiter character, **ch**. We will illustrate the use of these two versions of the member function, **get()** by asking the reader to rewrite programs **prog8_10.cpp** and **prog8_11.cpp** as exercises.

8.5 - String Functions in C and in C++

In this section we will discuss the **ANSI C standard** string functions that are available in almost all versions of C++. We will also discuss some of the additional functions that are unique to C++ under DOS. We will describe each of the functions and illustrate how they are used in a program. The prototypes for all of these functions are defined in the header file **string.h**. We will include this header file in our programs.

===

strcat( )   char *strcat(char *dest, const char *src)

Appends a copy of the string pointed to by **src** to the end of the string pointed to by **dest**. The length of the resulting string is **strlen**(dest) + **strlen**(src). It returns a pointer to the concatenated strings.
ANSI C standard.

===

The following program illustrates how this function can be used. Two strings are entered from the keyboard and stored in the arrays using the function **gets()**. The strings are concatenated using the function **strcat()** and the new string is printed to the screen.

```
// prog8_14.cpp - Program to illustrate the use of the string function
//                        function strcat().
#include <stdio.h>
#include <string.h>
int main()
{
  char string1[40];
  char string2[40];
  char *stptr;

  printf("Enter a short string: ");
  gets(string1);
  printf("Enter a second short string: ");
```

```
      gets(string2);

      stptr = new char[80];
      stptr = strcat(string1, string2);
      printf("The sum of the strings =  %s\n",  stptr);
      return 0;
   }
```

A sample run of this program produced the following:

```
   Enter a short string: Hello,
   Enter a second short string: World!
   The sum of the strings = Hello,World!
```

==

strlen( )   unsigned int strlen(char *string);

                   Counts and returns the number of characters pointed to by
                   string, up to but not including the first null character, '\0'.
                   ANSI C compatible.

==

The following program illustrates how the function **strlen()** can be used in a program. It simply computes and prints the length of a string that is defined by the program.

```
   // prog8_15.cpp - Program to illustrate the use of the function strlen().
   #include <stdio.h>
   #include <string.h>
   int main()
   {
     char string[] = "This is a string!";

     printf("The length of the string: \n");
     puts(string);
     printf("is  %d\n", strlen(string));
     return 0;
   }
```

The output from this program was the following.

```
   The length of the string:
   This is a string!
   is 17
```

```
===================================================
strupr( )              char *strupr(char *string);

                       Converts all letters, 'a' -> 'z', in a string pointed to by string to
                       uppercase, 'A' -> 'Z'. No other characters are changed. It returns a
                       pointer to string.
                       ANSII C compatible.

strlwr( )              char *strlwr(char *string);

                       Converts all letters, 'A' -> 'Z', in a string pointed to by string to
                       lowercase, 'a' -> 'z'. No other characters are changed. It returns a
                       pointer to string.
                       ANSI C compatible.
===================================================
```

The following program illustrates the use of the function **strupr()** in a program. The program has a string entered from the keyboard, stores the string in the defined array, and calls the function **strupr()** to convert all lower case alphabetic characters to uppercase characters before it is displayed to the screen.

```cpp
// prog8_16.cpp - Program to illustrate the use of strupr() in a program.
#include <stdio.h>
#include <string.h>
int main()
{
  char string[80];

  printf("Input a string: \n");
  gets(string);
  printf("The string with all upper case: \n");
  printf("%s\n", strupr(string));
  return 0;
}
```

Output from this program was the following.

```
Input a string:
Now is the time!
The string with all upper case:
NOW IS THE TIME!
```

===

strcmp( )   int strcmp(const char *st1, const char *st2);

Performs an unsigned comparison of **st1** to **st2**, character by character until the corresponding characters differ or until the end of one of the strings is reached. This comparison is case sensitive. On most systems uppercase is less than lowercase. It returns a value
    < 0   if **st1** is less than **st2**.
    ==0   if **st1** is the same as **st2**.
    >0   if **st1** is greater than **st2**.
ANSI C compatible.

===

The following program illustrates the use of the function **strcmp()** in a program. The program compares two strings and prints the value that is returned by the function.

```
// prog8_17.cpp - Program to illustrate the use of strcmp().
#include <stdio.h>
#include <string.h>
int main()
{
  char st1[] = "AAA", st2[] = "aaa";
  int num;
  num = strcmp(st2, st1);
  if (num > 0)
    printf("st2 > st1"\n);
  else if (num == 0)
    printf("st2 = st1"\n);
  else if (num < 0)
    printf("st2 < st1"\n);
  // end if
  printf("Returned value = %d\n, num);
  return 0;
}
```

Output from this program was the following:

    st2 > st1
    Returned value = 32

We ran the program with other strings with the following results.

st2	st1	output	returned value
"A"	"aaa"	st2 > st1	32 = 'A' - 'a'
"BBB"	"aaa"	st2 > st1	31 = 'B' - 'a'
"B"	"aaa"	st2 > st1	31 = 'B' - 'a'
"bbb"	"aaa"	st2 < st1	-1 = 'b' - 'a'

From this output we can guess that in this implementation of C++, **strcmp( )** returns the difference between the first two characters that differ in the two strings.

===

strcpy( )   char *strcpy(char *dest, const *src);

Copies the string **src** to the memory pointed to by **dest**. It returns the address dest + strlen(src).
ANSI C compatible.

===

The following program illustrates how the function **strcpy()** can be used in a program.

```
// prog8_18.cpp - Program to illustrate the use of strcpy().
#include <stdio.h>
#include <string.h>
int main()
{
  char st1[80];
  char st2[] = "This is the string!";
  strcpy(st1, st2);
  printf("Original string: "\n);
  puts(st2);
  printf(\n"Copy of string: "\n);
  puts(st1);
  return 0;
}
```

The output from this program was the following:

```
Original string:
This is the string!
Copy of string:
This is the string!
```

==
strstr( )   char *strstr(const char *st1, const char *st2);

Scans the string st1 for the first occurrence of the substring st2.
Returns a pointer to the first element of the substring if found,
and returns NULL if the substring is not found.
ANSI C compatible.
==

The following program illustrates how this function can be used.

```cpp
// prog8.19.cpp - Program to illustrate the use of strstr().
#include <stdio.h>
#include <string.h>
int main()
{
  char *st1 = "abcdefghi", *st2 = "def";
  char *ptr;
  ptr = strstr(st1, st2);
  printf("This is the string:\n");
  puts(st1);
  printf("This is the search string:\n");
  puts(st2);
  printf("This is the resulting substring:\n");
  puts(ptr);
  return 0;
}
```

Output from this program was the following.

```
This is the string:
abcdefghi
This is the search string:
def
This is the resulting substring:
defghi
```

==
stricmp( )   int stricmp(const char *st1, const char *st2);

Performs an unsigned comparison of **st1** to **st2**, character by
character until the corresponding characters differ or until the end of
one of the strings is reached. This comparison is not case sensitive.

336

It returns a value

        < 0   if **st1** is less than **st2**.

        ==0   if **st1** is the same as **st2**.

        >0   if **st1** is greater than **st2**.

Unique to DOS.

===

The following program illustrates how the function **stricmp()** can be used in a program.

```cpp
// prog8_20.cpp - Program to illustrate the use of stricmp().
#include <stdio.h>
#include <string.h>
int main()
{
  char *st1 = "AAA", *st2 = "aaa";
  int num = stricmp(st1, st2);
  if (num > 0)
    printf("st1 > st2\n");
  else if (num == 0)
    printf("st1 = st2\n");
  else if (num < 0)
    printf("st1 < st2\n");
  // end if
  printf("Returned value = %d\n", num);
  return 0;
}
```

Output from this program was the following.

```
st1 > st2
Returned value = 32
```

===

strtok( )   char *strtok(char *st1, const char *st2);

Searches the string, st1, for tokens, which are separated by delimiters defined in the second string, st2. It considers, st1, to consist of a sequence of zero or more text tokens, separated by spans of one or more characters from the separator string, s2. The first call to **strtok** returns a pointer to the first character of the first token in **st1** and writes a null character into **s1** immediately following the returned token. Subsequent calls with NULL for the first argument will work through the string **st1** in this way, until no tokens remain. Returns a pointer to the token found in **st1**. A null pointer is returned when there are no more tokens.

ANSI C compatible.

==

The following program illustrates how the function **strtok()** can be used.

```cpp
// prog8_21.cpp - Program to illustrate the use of strtok().
#include <stdio.h>
#include <string.h>
int main()
{
  char *st1 = "abc,def.ghi", *st2 = ",.";
  char *ptr;
  ptr = strtok(st1, st2);
  printf("First search: \n");
  puts(st1);
  puts(ptr);
  ptr = strtok(NULL, st2);
  printf("Second search: \n");
  puts(st1);
  puts(ptr);
  ptr = strtok(NULL, st2);
  printf("Third search:\n");
  puts(ptr);
  return 0;
}
```

Output from this program was the following.

```
First search:
abc
abc
Second search:
abc
def
Third search:
gh
```

There are numerous string manipulator functions that have been written and

338

included in the newer versions of C++. Some of the more interesting ones are the following. We refer the reader to the manuals for a complete description of these functions and for examples of how these are used. The manuals will also describe the other string functions that are available.

Table 8.3: C++ String Manipulator Functions.

strchr( )	Scans a string for the first occurrence of a given character.
strdup( )	Copies a string into a newly created location.
strcspn( )	Scans a string for the initial segment not containing any subset of a given set of characters.
strncat( )	Appends a given number of characters of one string to another string. Similar to strcat().
strncpy( )	Copies a given number of bytes from one string into another, truncating or padding as necessary. Similar to strcpy().
strnset( )	Sets a given number of characters in a string to a specified character.
strrev( )	Reverses the characters in a string.
strset( )	Sets all characters in a given string to a specified character.
strncmp()	Compares a given number of bytes of one string with another string and returns a negative, zero or positive value. Similar to strcmp().

8.6 - Writing String Functions

In this section we will illustrate the relationship between arrays and pointers in C++ by writing our own versions of some of the standard string functions discussed in the previous section. We wrote our own version of **gets()** in section 8.2. We will write the functions using arrays, using pointers, and using pointers and pointer arithmetic. We omit the documentation in order to save space. Finally, we will also write a few useful string functions of our own.

The first example will be to write a function that will copy one string to an array. This would be our own version of **strcpy()**. We would have two parameters **string1[]** and **string2[]**.

string1 [ ]
string2 [ ]   string2 [ ]

```
void string_copy(char string2[], char string1[])
{
  int I = 0;

  while (string1[i] != '\0') {
   string2[i] = string1[i];
   I++;
  } // end while
  string2[i] = '\0';
  return;
}
```

If we write the function using pointers without pointer arithmetic, we would have the following.

```
void string_copy(char *sptr2, const char *sptr1)
{
  int I = 0;
  while ( *(sptr1 + I) != '\0' ) {
   *(sptr2 + I) = *(sptr1 + I);
   I++;
  } // end while
  *(sptr2 + I) = '\0';
  return;
}
```

Finally, we write the function using pointers and pointer arithmetic.

```
void string_copy(char *sptr2, const char *sptr1)
{
  while (*sptr1 != '\0') {
   *sptr2 = *sptr1;
   sptr2++;
   sptr1++;
  } // end while
  *sptr2 = '\0';
```

```
        return;
        }
```

We should study these examples carefully, since we will see C++ functions written in any and all of these notations. We can even further condense the code for the third version of the function.

```
        void string_copy(char *sptr2, *sptr1)
        {
          while (*sptr1 != '\0')
            *sptr2++ = sptr1++;
          // end while
          *sptr1 = '\0';
          return;
        }
```

In order to use this function in a program, we need to make sure that we have memory allocated for the copy of the string. When we use arrays we could do the following.

```
        // prog8_22.cpp - Program to illustrate the function string_copy().
        #include <stdio.h>
        int main()
        {
          void string_copy(char *pt2, const char *pt1);
          char st1[] = "Hello, world!";
          char st2[20];                           1)

          string_copy(st2, st1);
          printf("This is the string: %s\n", st1);
          printf("This is the copy: %s\n", st2);
          return 0;
        }
```

When we declare the second array in 1), we have set aside enough storage for the copy of the first string. When we use pointers in the main program we must also allocate storage for the copy.

```
        // prog8_23. cpp Program using pointers to illustrate the
        //                 function string_copy( ).
        #include <stdio.h>
        void string_copy(char *pt1, const char *pt2);
        int main()
        {
```

```
        char st1[] = "Hello, World!";
        char *st2;
        st2 = new char[20];              2)
        string_copy(st2, st1);
        printf("This is the string: %s\n", st1);
        printf("This is the copy: %s\n", st2);
        return 0;
    }
```

Statement 2) sets aside the same amount of memory for the string as statement 1) did in the first program when we used arrays.

The next example will be to write a function to compute and return the length of any string. This is our own version of the function **strlen( )**.

We will first write the function using array notation.

```
        int str_length(char string1[])
        {
          int I = 0;
          int length = 0;
          while (string1[i] != '\0') {
            length++;
            I++;
          } // end while
          return(length);
        }
```

Try this: Write the pointer version of the function str_length( ).

```
        int str_length(char *stptr)
        {
          int I = 0;
          int length = 0;
          while (_____) {

            _____

          } // end while
          return(length);
        }
```

The same function using a pointer and pointer arithmetic is can be written as follows:

342

```
int str_length(char *stptr)
{
  int length = 0;
  while (*stptr++ != '\0')
    length++;
  // end while
  return(length);
}
```

We can test this function with the following program.

```
// prog8_24.cpp - Program to test the function str_length()
#include <stdio.h>
int str_length(char *stptr);
int main()
{
  char message[80];
  printf("Input a string: ");
  gets(message);
  printf("The length of the string = %d\n", str_length(message));
  return 0;
}
#include <a:\strlen.cpp>
```

Output from a test run of this program was the following.

```
Input a string: This is a test string.<Ret>
The length of the string = 22
```

We will write some examples of string functions that are not included in the standard C++ libraries. The first example will be to write a function that will accept any string and any character and will remove any occurrence of that character from the string. We will have a string and a character as input parameters.

```
      string1[ ]                        string1[ ]
      ch1

void del_char(char *stptr1, char ch1)
{
  int I = 0, j = 0;
  while (stptr1[i] != '\0') {
```

343

```
        if (stptr1[i] != ch1) {
          stptr1[j] = stptr1[i];
          j++;
        } // end if
        I++;
      } // end while
      stptr1[j] = '\0';
      return;
    }
```

We can test this function with the following program.

```
    // prog8_25.cpp - Program to test del_char().
    #include <iodtrrs,.h>
    void del_char(char *stptr1, char ch1);
    int main()
    {
      char *stptr;
      stptr = new char[15];
      stptr = "111-22-3333";
      cout << "Original string: " << stptr << endl;
      del_char(stptr, '-');
      cout << "New string: " << stptr << endl;
      return 0;
    }
    #include <a:delchar.cpp>
```

The output from this program was the following.

```
    Original string: 111-22-3333
    New string: 111223333
```

Try this: Write the pointer version of the function **del_char( )**.

```
void del_char(_____)
{
    _____
    _____
    _____
    _____
    _____
    _____
    _____
    _____
    _____
    _____
    _____
}
```

As a final example, we will write a function that will accept a string and two characters **ch1** and **ch2**. It should replace every occurrence of the character **ch2** in the string with **ch1**. We would have a string and two characters as input parameters. The string would be an output parameter.

```
      string1[ ]                          string1[ ]
      ch1
      ch2
```

We will write the pointer version of the function first.

```
void char_replace(char *string1, char ch1, char ch2)
{
  while (*string1 != '\0') {
    if ( *string1 == ch2 )
      *string1 = ch1;
    // end if
    string++;
  } // end while
  return;
}
```

Try this: Write the array version of the function char_replace( )

```
void char_replace(char *string1, char ch1, char ch2)
{
    int I = 0;
    while (_____) {
        if (_____)

        _____
        // end if

        _____
    } // end while
    return;
}
```

We can test this function with the following program.

```
// prog8_26.cpp - Program to test the function char_replace().
#include <iostream.h>
void char_replace(char *string1, char ch1, char ch2);
int main()
{
    char *stptr;
    char ch1, ch2;
    stptr = new char[15];
    stptr = "111-22-3333";
    ch1 = '-';
    ch2 = '*';
    cout << "Original string = " << stptr << endl;
    char_replace(stptr, ch1, ch2);
    cout << "New string = " << stptr << endl;
    return 0;
}
#include <a:\charep.cpp>
```

Output from a test run of this program was the following.

```
Original string = 111-22-3333
New string = 111*22*3333
```

346

8.7- Arrays of Strings & Pointers

Suppose that we want to store a list of names in an array. Consider the following list of 10 names.

Smith, Blake
Grimshaw, Neil
Hood, Carol
Morgan, Glenna
Yardley, Nancy
Nowers, Morrell
Nelson, Phillip
Dalton, Fred
McQuarrie, Rhonda
Myers, Maureen

Arrays of 20 characters are large enough to hold the names, since the largest name has 18 characters, 17 plus the null terminator. Therefore, we can declare an array called names as an array of 10 arrays, each of 20 characters. Either of the following statements will define the array and initialize it with the above data.

```
static names[10][20] = {               static names[10][20] = {
    {"Smith, Blake"},                      "Smith, Blake",
    {"Grimshaw, Neil"},                    "Grimshaw, Neil",
    {"Hood, Carol"},                       "Hood, Carol",
    {"Morgan, Glenna"},                    "Morgan, Glenna",
    {"Yardley, Nancy"},                    "Yardley, Nancy",
    {"Nowers, Morrell"},                   "Nowers, Morrell",
    {"Nelson, Phillip"},                   "Nelson, Phillip",
    {"Dalton, Fred"},                      "Dalton, Fred",
    {"McQuarrie, Rhonda"},                 "McQuarrie, Rhonda",
    {"Myers, Maureen"} };                  "Myers, Maureen" };
```

The braces are not necessary around each array item when we are dealing with strings. However, the double quotes are necessary, we could <u>not</u> use

{Smith, Blake}

The following function will write the data contained in an array of strings with **size** elements to the screen, one per line. We would have the array and the size as input parameters.

```
      names1[ ][21]
      size1

      void prt_strings(char names1[][21], int size1)
      {
        int I;
        for (I = 0; I <= size1 - 1; I++)
          puts(names1[i]);                        1)
        return;
      }
```

Note, in 1), only the row index is used. Each **names1[i]** is associated with the address of the name and can be printed using **puts( )**.

When we define the array, **names[10][21]**, we set aside 10 arrays of 21 bytes each for a total of 210 bytes of storage. The names that we stored used a total of 138 bytes, including the null terminators. This is a waste of memory space that could be a problem if we were dealing large collections of data. The designers of C and C++ gave us a solution to this problem. Instead of storing the names in 21 character blocks, regardless of size, store them immediately adjacent to each other, separated by the null terminator. This is done by simply storing the beginning address of each name. We can do this by using an array of pointers that is defined with the following statement:

```
      char *names[10];
```

We can define the array and store the addresses with the statement:

```
      static char *names[] = {
              "Smith, Blake",
              "Grimshaw, Neil",
              "Hood, Carol",
              "Morgan, Glenna",
              "Yardley, Nancy",
              "Nowers, Morrell",
              "Nelson, Phillip",
              "Dalton, Fred",
              "McQuarrie, Rhonda",
              "Myers, Maureen" };
```

This would reduce the storage to 138 bytes for the names, plus 10 null bytes, plus 10*2 = 20 bytes for the array of addresses for a total of 168 bytes of storage.

After we have initialized the array, we can print out the data, one per line, with the

348

following block of code.

```
for (I = 0;, I <= 9; I++)
  puts(names[i]);
// end for
```

We can print the addresses, along with the names, with the following block of code.

```
for (I = 0; I <= 9; I++)
   cout << &names[i] <<  names[i] << endl;
// end for
```

The output from a program with the above code was the following.

```
424:  Smith, Blake
437:  Grimshaw, Neil
452:  Hood, Carol
464:  Morgan, Glenna
479:  Yardley, Nancy
494:  Nowers, Morrell
510:  Nelson, Phillip
526:  Dalton, Fred
539:  McQuarrie, Rhonda
557:  Myers, Maureen
```

Consider another example. Suppose that we want to input one line of text from the keyboard and store the collection of words so that we can process the line of text in some manner. The words will be strings of characters separated by one or more blanks. For example,

Now is the time for all good men to come to the aid of their country.

We will assume that one line will consist of no more than 256 characters and no more than 50 words. The idea is to first store the entire line in a buffer. After the line is stored we will parse the line and store the address of each word in an array of pointers. As we parse the line we will replace the first blank following each word with a null, '\0', terminator. We will need the following declarations.

```
char buffer[256];
char *word_ptr[50];
char *ch_ptr;
```

We would obtain one line of text with the statements

```
printf("Enter one line of text:\n");
gets(buffer);
```

We can parse the line, store the addresses, and insert the null terminators with the following block of code.

```
j = 0;
word_ptr[j] = buffer;
ch_ptr = buffer;
while (*ch_ptr != '\0') {            // parse the line
  while (*ch_ptr != ' ')            //  find first blank
    ch_ptr++;
  // end while
  j++;
  word_ptr[j] = ch_ptr;            // store word address
  *ch_ptr = '\0';                   // replace blank with null
  while (*ch_ptr == ' ')
    ch_ptr++;                       // find beginning of word
  // end while
} // end while
```

We can now write the above as a function and write a program to test it. The input parameters for this function would be the buffer containing the line, and the array of pointers to store the addresses of the words. The function would parse the line, store the addresses, and return the array of pointers to the words along with the count back to the calling program.

```
buffer1[]                  *word_ptr1[]
*word_ptr1[]               count1

void find_words(char *buffer1, char *word_ptr1[], int *count1)
{
  int j = 0;
  char *ch_ptr;
  word_ptr1[j] = buffer1;
  ch_ptr = buffer1;
  while (*ch_ptr != '\0') {            // parse the line
    while (*ch_ptr != ' ')            // find first blank
      ch_ptr++;
    // end while
    j++;
    word_ptr1[j] = ch_ptr;            // store word address
    *ch_ptr = '\0';                   // replace blank with null
```

350

```
      while (*ch_ptr == ' ')
        ch_ptr++;                          // find beginning of word
      // end while
    } // end while
    return;
  }
```

A program to test this function would be the following.

```
// prog8_27.cpp - Program to test the function find_words().
#include <stdio.h>
void find_words(char *buffer1, char *word_ptr1[], int count1);
int main()
{
  char buffer[80];
  char *word_ptr[50];
  int I, count;
  printf("Please type in a sentence:\n");
  gets(buffer);
  find_words(buffer, word_ptr, &count);
  printf(The list of words is the following:\n);
  for(I = 0; I < count - 1; I++)
    puts(word_ptr[i]);
  // end for
  return;
}
#include <a:\findwrds.cpp>
```

The reader should write this program and test it's output.

8.8 - Sorting String Data

In this section we will illustrate how we can use some of the special string handling functions that we discussed in section 8.5 to sort a collection of strings. These functions are defined in the header file **string.h**. We will use the sorting algorithm that we developed in section 6.9 and develop a function that can sort an array of strings in ascending order. For example, the phone book contains names that are sorted in alphabetical order and a dictionary contains a collection of words that are sorted in alphabetical order. As a first step, we will assume that alphabetical characters that the strings that we wish to sort contain are lowercase. The reason for this assumption is that the lowercase alphabetical characters appear after the uppercase characters in the ASCII code sequence of characters. Therefore, 'a' > 'A', 'b' > 'B', ... 'z' > 'Z' and "smith" > "Smith" > "SMITH". We will discuss strings that contain both upper and lower case alphabetic characters as a second example.

In order to write the version of the function **selsort( )** that will sort strings, we will make use of the string functions that we discussed in section 8.5. These two functions are

      strcmp( )   and   strcopy( )

We need to use these functions since we cannot assign one array to another and we cannot directly compare one string with another string. If you need to, review the discussion of these two functions in section 8.5. The function **strcmp( )** does a character by character comparison until the corresponding characters differ or until one of the strings or both reach the null, **'\0'** byte, string terminator. The function returns an integer value as follows:

strcmp(string1, string2)   > 0   string1 > string2
                            = 0   string1 = string2
                            < 0   string1 < string2

Some examples of string comparisons are given with the following:

strcmp("smith", "smith")   = 0
strcmp("Smith", "smith")   = -32   'S' < 's'
strcmp("weston", "easton")   = 18   'w' > 's'
strcmp("Smith", Smithson")   = 19   '\0' < 's'

The function **strcpy( )** copies a string to an array that is large enough to hold the string. If we have the following:

char string1[ ] = "Indiana State University";

352

```
char string1[ ] = "Indiana State University";
char buffer[80];
```

then the statements

```
strcopy(buffer, string1);
cout << "String1 = " << string1 << endl;
cout << "Buffer = " << buffer << endl;
```

will produce the following output:

```
String1 = Indiana State University
Buffer = Indiana State University
```

We can now write a version of the function **selsort( )** that will sort an array of strings in ascending order as long as the strings do not contain any uppercase alphabetic characters.

```
void sort1strings(char strings1[ ][31], int count1)
{
  char temp[31];
  for (int I = 0; I < count1 - 1; I++)
    for (int j = I + 1; j < count1; j++)
      if (strcmp(strings1[i], strings1[j]) > 0)  {
          strcopy(temp, strings1[i]);
          strcopy(strings1[i], strings1[j]);
          strcopy(strings1[j], temp);
        } // end if
    // end for j
  // end for I
  return;
}
```

We can test this function with the following program:

```
//prog8_26.cpp Program to test the function sort1strings( ).
#include <iostream.h>
#include <string.h>
void sort1strings(char strings1[ ][31], int count1);
void main( )
{
  char names[ ][31] = {"metz, shorty", "frye, jennie", "easton, linda",
                "bell, marty", "easton, richard", "bell, dave"};
```

```
      int count = 6;
      sort1strings(names, count);
      cout << "Sorted Strings" << endl << endl;
      for(int I = 0; I < count; I++)
        cout << names[i] << endl;
      // end for
      return 0;
    }
    #include <a:\sort1sts.cpp>
```

Output from this program was the following:

```
Sorted Strings

bell, david
bell, marty
easton, linda
easton, richard
frye, jennie
metz, shorty
```

If our names were written so that the first letter of the first and last names are uppercase and all other characters in the names are lowercase, then the function **sort1strings( )** will sort these strings in the desired order. For example,

```
char names[ ][31] = {"Metz, Shorty", "Frye, Jennie", "Easton, Linda",
            "Bell, Marty", "Easton, Richard", "Bell, David"};
```

we should be able to convince ourselves that the output would be the following:

```
Bell, David
Bell, Marty
Easton, Linda
Easton, Richard
Frye, Jennie
Metz, Shorty
```

We will ask the reader to rewrite program **prog8_26.cp**p so that it uses this data as one of the exercises.

When the strings contain both uppercase and lowercase alphabetic characters, we need to use a second function to compare strings that we discussed in section 8.5. This function is the function **stricmp( )**. This function works just like the function **strcmp( )** with

354

will ask the reader to write this version of the function and a program to test it as exercises. If we used the data

    char names[ ][31] = {"EASTON, Robert", "easton, ray", "eaStoN, NORMA",
                        "EASTon, Richard"};

the output from the program that uses this second function would be the following:

    Sorted Strings

    EASTON, Robert
    EASTon, Richard   // 'O' < 'o'
    eaSton, NORMA   // 'E' < 'e'
    easton, ray   // 'S' < 's'

8.9 - Summary.

In this chapter we have discussed how strings are handled in C++. We should understand the difference between, strings and array's of characters. We should understand how to output strings using the function **printf()** and the class **cout**. We should understand how to input strings from the keyboard using **gets( )** and **getline( )**. We should also understand the problems that we have when we try and use the function **scanf()** and the class **cin**. We would also understand how to use the manipulator, **setw()**, with **cin** to avoid array overflow, and how to use the function, **get()**, from the **cin** class in order to input blanks and multiple lines.

We should understand how pointers are used with strings and how and when we need to allocate memory before using a string with a pointer. We should be able to understand how to write functions that work with strings using either array or pointer notation.

We should understand how to use some of the library string functions that are included with the C++ language. We should be able to find out which of these functions are ANSI C standard and which are unique to our particular implementation.

We should also be able to define and use arrays of pointers to store arrays of strings in a program.

We illustrated how we can use the string functions that are defined in **string.h**, and in particular we used these functions to write a function that we can use to sort an array of strings.

8.10 - Questions

8.1 What is a string in C++?

8.2 What is the difference between a string and an array of characters?

8.3 How does C++ store the string "CS 256" in memory? Illustrate.

8.4 What is the ANSII C function used to input a string from the keyboard?

8.5 What is the C++ member function used to input a string from the keyboard?

8.6 Why don't we use **scanf( )** or **cin** for string input? Illustrate.

8.7 What header file do we need in our program in order to use the ANSII C string functions?

8.8 What is the ANSII C function to print a string?

8.9 What problems might we encounter when we use **gets( )** for string input?

8.10 What is the ANSII C function that is used to compute the length of a string? Illustrate how it is used.

8.11 What is the ANSII C function that is used to convert all lower case letters in a string to upper case? Illustrate how it is used.

8.12 What is the ANSII C function that is used to assign a string to an array? Illustrate how it is used.

8.13 What is the ANSII C function that is used to append one string onto the end of another string? Illustrate how it is used.

8.14 What is the ANSII C function that is used to compare two strings? Illustrate how it is used.

8.11 - Exercises

8.1 Give the statements that can be used using the function, **malloc( )**, to allocate memory for each of the following:

a. An array of 20 characters.
c. A location to store 10 reals.

b. A location to store 25 integers.
d. A location to store 25 doubles.

8.2 Give the statements that can be used, using the operator **new**, to allocate memory for each of the locations in 8.1.

8.3 Write a program to test the function **get_st1( )** from section 8.4.

8.4 Rewrite the **program 8_10** so that it uses the **get( )** member function rather than **getline( )**.

8.5 Rewrite the **program 8_11** so that it uses the **get( )** member function rather than **getline( )**.

8.6 Write a version of the function **get_st( )** from section 8.4 that will use two parameters, the buffer to store the string, and the maximum number of characters to be stored. The prototype for the function would be the following:
    void getstring(char buffer[ ], int size);

8.7 Write a program to test the function from 8.6.

8.8 Write the documentation for the function **string_copy( )** written in section 8.6.

8.9 Write the documentation for the function **str_length( )** written in section 8.6.

8.10 Write the documentation for the function **del_char( )** written in section 8.6.

8.11 Write the documentation for the function **char_replace( )** written in section 8.6.

8.12 Rewrite the program, **prog8_26**, so that it uses the second set of data. Run the program and check the output.

CHAPTER 9

Structures & Unions

9.1 Introduction

In section 6.1 we discussed arrays as one of the data structures available in C and C++. We recall that a **data structure** is a variable that can store more than one data item per variable name and that the **array** is a data structure where all of the data items have to be of the same data type. In this chapter we will study a second data structure where the data items can be of different data types. This data structure is simply called a **structure**. A structure in C++ corresponds to a record in Pascal. After completing this chapter the reader should be able to

1. define a structure variable for a collection of data.

2. define a structure data type that can be used to define structure variables of that type.

3. store data in a structure variable as it is defined.

4. store data in a structure variable as it is entered from the keyboard.

5. define and use nested structure variables.

6. print the data that is stored in a structure variable to the screen.

7. pass structure variables as parameters to functions.

8. define and use nested structures in programs.

9. define an array of structures to store a collection of data for use in a program.

10. define pointers to structures and use the structure-pointer notation to access the members of the structure.

11. understand how the structure data type is used when a program uses this type in functions that are external to the calling program.

12. define a union data type and union variables and understand how they are used in programs.

358

13. define and use nested unions, nested structures and unions, and nested unions and structures and understand how they are used in programs.

9.2 Structure Variables

A **structure** is defined and used in the same way as any other variable in C++. Since a structure is made up of different data types, the declaration must list these types along with the names that we will want to use for each of the different items. For example, we can define a structure to hold the data on one employee, a 20 character name, an 11 character social security number, an integer age, and a real pay rate. The declaration to define this structure variable called **oneemp** is the following:

```
struct {
    char name[21];
    char ssnum[12];
    int age;
    float pay rate;
} oneemp;
```

This definition reserves enough storage for each of the data items that are listed in the structure, and these data items are called **members** of the structure. The structure, **oneemp**, consists of the four members, **name**, **ssnum**, **age**, and **pay rate**. Each of the members of the structures is referenced by using both the name of the structure and the member name connected by a period. Thus, the four member variables of the structure, **oneemp**, are referenced with the variable names

```
oneemp.name
oneemp.ssnum
oneemp.age
oneemp.payrate
```

The member variables of a structure are used like any other variable of the same type, only the notation is different. Storing data in a structure variable is sometimes called **populating** the structure. The following block of code can be used to get data from the keyboard and store it in the structure **oneemp**.

```
cout << "Input a name: ";
cin.getline(oneemp.name, 21);
cout << "Input a social security number: ";
cin.getline(oneemp.ssnum, 12);
cout << "Input an age: ";
cin >> oneemp.age;
```

```
cout << "Input a pay rate: ";
cin >> oneemp.payrate;
```

The format that we used to define the structure, **oneemp**, listed the member variables on separate lines in order to make the statement easier to read. We could have used the statement:

```
struct  {char name[21]; char ssnum[12]; int age; float pay rate;} oneemp;
```

In addition we can define multiple variables with the one statement. For example, two variables emp1 and emp2 are defined as follows:

```
struct {
    char name[21];
    char ssnum[2];
    int age;
    float pay rate;
} emp1, emp2;
```

Try this: Define a single structure variable, **onestudent**, that will be able
to store a student name, an array of four real exam scores, a
real average, and a character grade.

```
struct {

    _____
    _____
    _____
    _____
} _____
```

Each structure that we define can have an associated **structure tag**. Structure tags are nothing more than **user defined data types** that can be used to define structure variables. This is done as follows:

```
struct empinfo {                        // structure tag
    char name[21];
    char ssnum[12];
    int age;
    float pay rate;
};
```

This statement assigns the structure a user defined type name **empinfo**. This type name is called a **structure tag** and can be used to define structure variables of this type. The structure variables of type **empinfo** are defined using this structure tag with either of the statements

     struct empinfo emp1, emp2;

or

     empinfo emp1, emp2;

The use of **struct** is optional. We prefer to define a structure tag, (user data type), and then use the data type to define the variables. We will have to do this when we study how we can pass structures as parameters to functions.

Try this: Define a structure tag, **studentdata**, for a structure that will hold the data for one student. Use this structure tag to define structure variables **student1** and **student2**.

     struct _____

        _____

        _____

        _____

        _____

     };

     _____

9.3 - Using Structures

     In this section we will see how we can use a structure variable to store data for use in a program. This is nothing more than being able to use the members of the structure as variables just as we have done with variables in previous sections. In addition we will see how we can print the data stored in a structure to the screen. Structure variables can also be assigned data as they are defined just as we did with array variables. The only difference is that the data stored in a structure variable can be of different data types. The first program defines a structure variable for one employee, allows data to be entered from the keyboard and stored in the structure, and finally prints a summary of the data that was entered to the screen.

```
//prog9_1.cpp - Program to illustrate data storage
//                using a structure.
#include <iostream.h>
#include <iomanip.h>
```

```cpp
int main( )
{
    struct empinfo {
        char name[21];
        char ssnum[12];
        int age;
        float pay rate;
    };
    struct empinfo  emp;
    // Get and store data
    cout << "Input a name: ";
    cin.getline(emp.name, 21);
    cout << "Input a social sec. number: ";
    cin.getline(emp.ssnum, 12);
    cout << "Input an age: ";
    cin >> emp.age;
    cout << "Input a pay rate: ";
    cin >> emp.payrate;
    //Print out the data
    cout << endl << endl;
    cout << "Name = " << emp.name << endl;
    cout << "Soc. sec. number = " << emp.ssnum << endl;
    cout << "Age = " << emp.age << endl;
    cout << "Pay rate = $" << setiosflags(ios::fixed | ios::showpoint)
         << setprecision(2) << setw(5) << emp.payrate << endl;
    return 0;
}
```

Output from this program was the following:

Input a name: Marti Bell
Input a Social sec. number: 111-22-3333
Input an age: 39
Input a pay rate: 34.25

Name = Marti Bell
Soc. sec. number = 111-22-3333
Age = 39
Pay rate = $34.25

As we did with arrays, the C++ programming language allows us to store data in a structure as it is defined. We call this **initializing the structure**. For example,

362

```
        struct empinfo {
          char name[21];
          char ssnum[12];
          int age;
          float pay rate;
        } emp = {"Dave Bell", "555-66-7777", 40, 30.25);
```

defines the structure variable, **emp**, of type **empinfo** and stores the indicated data in the member variables of the structure. This is illustrated with the following program.

```
//prog9_2.cpp - Program to illustrate structure
//                data storage as it is defined.
#include <iostream.h>
#include <iomanip.h>
int main( )
{
  struct empinfo {
    char name[21];
    char ssnum[12];
    int age;
    float pay rate;
  } emp = {"Bozell, Shirley", "222-22-5555", 39, 25.75};
  cout << "Name = " << emp.name << endl;
  cout << "Soc. sec. number = " << emp.ssnum << endl;
  cout << "Age = " << emp.age << endl;
  cout << "Pay rate = $" << setiosflags(ios::fixed | ios::showpoint)
       << setprecision(2) << setw(5) <<emp.payrate << endl;
  return 0;
}
```

Output from this program was the following:

```
Name = Bozell, Shirley
Soc. sec.number = 222-22-5555
Age = 39
Pay rate = $25.75
```

We cannot store data in the individual members of the structure as it is defined. We might be tempted to try the following:

```
        struct empinfo {
          char name[21] = "Morgie, Rogene";
          char ssnum[12] = "222-11-9999";
          int age = 39;
          float pay rate = 23.75;
```

```
        };
```

However, a little thought should tell us that this is illegal since we are simply defining a data type and not a variable of that type. Memory is not set aside for data storage until a variable is defined. We can define the data type and initialize the structure variable when it is defined as is illustrated with the following code.

```
        struct empinfo {
            char name[21];
            char ssnum[12];
            int age;
            float pay rate;
        };

        struct empinfo emp = {"Morgie, David", "999-88-7777", 40, 27.35};
```

We will ask the reader to rewrite program **prog9_2.cpp** to test this idea.

The next example illustrates the use of a structure variable of type **studentdata** in a program. This program will allow the user to input a name and four exam scores from the keyboard and this data will be stored in a structure variable. This data will then be used to compute an exam average and a final grade that will also be stored in the structure. The program will then print a summary of the results to the screen.

```
//prog9_3.cpp - Program to illustrate the use of a structure variable
//                   of type studentdata in a program.
#include <iostream.h>
#include <iomanip.h>
int main( )
{
  struct studentdata {
    char name[21];
    float exams[4];
    float average;
    char grade;
  };
  studentdata std1;
// Input the data
  cout << "Input a student name: ";
  cin.getline(std1.name, 21);
  cout << "Input exam #1: ";
  cin >> std1.exam[0];
  cout << "Input exam #2: ";
  cin >> std1.exam[1];
  cout << "Input exam #3: ";
```

```
      cin >> std1.exam[2];
      cout << "Input exam #4: ";
      cin >> std1.exam[3];
// Compute Exam Average
      std1.average = (std1.exam[0] + std1.exam[1] + std1.exam[2] + std1.exam[3]) / 4;
//Compute Grade
    if (std1.average >= 90.0) {
       std1.grade = 'A';
    } else if (std1.average >= 80) {
       std1.grade = 'B';
    } else if (std1.average >= 70) {
       std1.grade = 'C';
    ) else if (std1.average >= 60) {
       std1.grade = 'D';
    } else
       std1.grade = 'F';
    // end if
// Print out the summary
    cout << endl << endl;
    cout.setf(ios::fixed | ios::showpoint);
    cout.precision(1);
    cout << "Name = " << std1.name << endl;
    cout << "First exam = " << setw(4) << std1.exam[0] << endl;
    cout << "Second exam = " << setw(4) << std1.exam[1] << endl;
    cout << "Third exam = " << setw(4) << std1.exam[2] << endl;
    cout << "Fourth exam = " << setw(4) << std1.exam[3] << endl;
    cout.precision(2);
    cout << "Exam average = " << set(5) << std1.average << endl;
    cout << "Final grade = " << std1.grade << endl;
    return 0;
}
```

Output from this program was the following:

Input a student name: Clark Bozell
Input exam #1: 78.6
Input exam #2 89.5
Input exam #3 82.5
Input exam #4 73.8

Name = Clark Bozell
First exam = 78.6
Second exam = 89.5
Third exam = 82.5
Fourth exam = 73.8

Exam average = 81.10
Final grade = B

Structure Assignment

One of the more interesting features of structures is that the data stored in a structure <u>can</u> be copied to another structure variable of the same type with a simple assignment statement. In the original version of C, defined by Kernighan and Ritchie, this was not possible. This feature was added to the newer versions of C and is also available in most versions of C++.

Note: In C++, the data stored at one structure variable <u>can</u> be assigned directly to another structure variable of the same type.

We illustrate this idea with the following program:

```cpp
//prog9_4.cpp - Program to illustrate structure variable assignment.
#include <iostream.h>
#include <iomanip.h>
int main( )
{
   struct studentdata {
     char name[21];
     float exams[4];
     float average;
     char grade;
   };
   studentdata student1 = {"Mark J. Easton", 78.5, 82.4, 85.6, 74.3, 80.2, 'B'};
   studentdata student2;
// Structure assignment
   student2 = student1;
// Print the data
   cout << "Student 2 name = " << student2.name << endl;
   cout.setf(ios::fixed | ios::showpoint);
   cout.precision(1);
   cout << "Exam #1 = " << setw(4) << student2.exam[0] << endl;
   cout << "Exam #2 = " << setw(4) << student2.exam[1] << endl;
   cout << "Exam #3 = " << setw(4) << student2.exam[2] << endl;
   cout << "Exam #4 = " << setw(4) << student2.exam[3] << endl;
   cout << "Exam average = " << setprecision(2) << setw(5)
        << student2.average << endl;
   cout << "Final grade = " << student2.grade << endl;
```

```
    return 0;
}
```

Output from this program was the following:

```
Student 2 name = Mark J. Easton
Exam #1 = 78.5
Exam #2 = 82.4
Exam #3 = 85.6
Exam #4 = 74.3
Exam average = 80.20
Final grade = B
```

This type of assignment <u>cannot</u> be done with arrays; arrays must be copied by the assignment of each individual array element.

9.4 - Structures as Parameters to Functions

In this section we will discuss how we can pass a structure variable as a parameter to a function. Recall that we discussed the difference between passing data by value and passing data by reference. This is also the difference between input parameters and output parameters. For an input parameter, the function sets up a new storage location in memory and copies the data to that new location. For an output parameter the function simply passes the address of the variable in the calling program or function so that any data that is stored will be known by the calling function.

When we studied arrays in Chapter 6, we pointed out that C++ will not allow us to pass an array by value so that any time that we use an array for a parameter, it is automatically passed by reference. However, structures are not handled the same way, contrary to what we might expect. We must tell the function whether we want the structure variable to be passed by value or by reference, i.e. whether it is to be an input parameter or an output parameter. Once we understand this, structures variables are used as parameters just like any other variable. We illustrate this idea with some examples. The first example will be to write a function that will allow the user to input data for one employee and it will get the data, store it in a structure, and return this data in the structure to the calling program.

```
//getempdata( ) - Function to get a record of data for one employee
//                from the user, store it in the structure, and return it as
//                a parameter to the calling program or function.
void getempdata(struct empinfo &emp1)
{
    cout << "Input a name: ";
```

```
        cin.getline(emp1.name, 21);
        cout << "Input a social security number: ";
        cin.getline(emp1.ssnum, 12);
        cout << "Input an age: ";
        cin >> emp1.age;
        cout << "Input a pay rate: ";
        cin >> emp1.pay rate;
         return;
    }
```

Since the program uses the user defined data type, **empinfo**, this data type <u>must</u> be defined before it is ever used. Since the function prototype uses this data type, the data type <u>must</u> be defined right after the collection of include statements i.e. before the function prototype statement. We can now write a program to test the function.

```
//prog9_5.cpp - Program to test the function
//              getempdata( );
#include <iostream.h>
#include <iomanip.h>
struct empinfo {
   char name[21];
   char ssnum[12];
   int age;
   float pay rate;
};
void getempdata(struct empinfo &emp1);
int main( )
{
   empinfo emp;
   getempdata(emp);
   cout << "Name = " << emp.name << endl;
   cout << "Soc. sec. number = " << emp.ssnum << endl;
   cout << "Age = " << emp.age << endl;
   cout.setf(ios::fixed | ios::showpoint);
   cout.precision(2);
   cout << "Pay rate = $" << setw(5) << emp.payrate << endl;
   return 0;
}
#include <a:\getemp.cpp>
```

Try this: Write a function that will get the data for one student from the user, store it in a structure, and return this data to the calling program.

```
void getstudentdata(_____
{
  cout << _____
  _____
  cout << _____    //Exam # 1
  _____
  cout << _____
  _____
  cout << _____
  _____
  cout << _____
  _____
  return;
}
```

We now write a function that will accept the structure as a parameter and will compute and store the average of the four exam scores. It is important that we understand that since the data in the structure is to be changed, i.e. the average is to be computed and stored, that the structure must be an output parameter. We must pass the structure by reference.

```
void computeaverage(struct studentdata &std1)
{
  float sum = 0;
  for(int I = 0; I <= 3; I++)
    sum += std1.exam[i];
  // end for
  std1.average = sum / 4;
  return;
}
```

The function that will accept the data stored in the structure and compute the final grade assuming that the average of the exam scores has been computed is written as follows:

```
void computegrade(struct studentdata &std2)
{
  if(std2.average >= 90.0) {
    std2.grade = 'A';
  } else if(std2.average >= 80.0) {
    std2.grade = 'B';
```

```
    } else if(std2.average >= 70.0) {
      std2.grade = 'C';
    } else if(std2.average >= 60.0) {
      std2.grade = 'D';
    } else
      std2.grade = 'F';
    // end if
    return 0;
  }
```

Finally, we write a function that will print a summary of all of the data for one student stored in a structure variable to the screen. For this function, none of the data in the member variables is to be changed or computed, the data is simply to be printed to the screen. For this function, the structure is to be passed by value. It is an input parameter.

```
    void ptstudentdata(struct studentdata std3)
    {
      cout << "Name = " << std3.name << endl;
      cout << setiosflags(ios::fixed | ios::showpoint) << setprecision(1);
      cout << "Exam #1 = " << setw(4) << std3.exam[0] << endl;
      cout << "Exam #2 = " << setw(4) << std3.exam[1] << endl;
      cout << "Exam #3 = " << setw(4) << std3.exam[2] << endl;
      cout << "Exam #4 = " << setw(4) << std3.exam[3] << endl;
      cout << "Average = " << setprecision(2) << setw(5)
           << std3.average << endl;
      cout << "Final grade = " << std3.grade << endl;
      return;
    }
```

We can now use these functions and rewrite **prog9_3.cpp**. We will ask the reader to write programs to test each of the functions, **computeaverage( )**, **computegrade( )**, and **ptstudentdata( )** as exercises. Remember that the structure user defined data type must be defined before the collection of function prototype statements.

```
    //prog9_6.cpp - Program to get a student name and four exam scores
    //                from the user. The program will then compute the student
    //                average and final grade and print the summary of the data to
    //                the screen. This is a rewrite of prog9_3.cpp that uses functions
    #include <iostream.h>
    #include <iomanip.h>
    struct studentdata {
      char name[20];
      float exam[4];
      float average;
```

```
      char grade;
  };
  void getstudentdata(struct studentdata &std1);
  void computeaverage(struct studentdata &std2);
  void computegrade(struct studentdata &std3);
  void ptstudentdata(struct studentdata std4);
  int main( )
  {
     struct studentdata std;
     getstudentdata(std);
     computeaverage(std);
     computegrade(std);
     ptstudentdata(std);
     return 0;
  }
  #include <a:\getstud.cpp>
  #include <a:\compavg.cpp>
  #include <a:\compgrd.cpp>
  #include <a:\ptstudat.cpp>
```

Although most functions will use a parameter to return the data stored in a structure variable, it is also possible to return the data stored in a structure variable using the function name. This is done exactly as we did with any of the simple data types. The next function illustrates this idea.

```
  struct empinfo getemp( )
  {
     empinfo oneemp;
     cout << "Input a name: ";
     cin.getline(oneemp.name, 21);
     cout << "Input a social security number: ";
     cin.getline(oneemp.ssnum, 12);
     cout << "Input an age: ";
     cin >> oneemp.age;
     cout << "Input a pay rate: ";
     cin >> oneemp.payrate;
     return (oneemp);
  }
```

The program to test this function is the following and one more time we note that the definition of **empinfo** has to be done before the function prototype.

```
  //prog9_7.cpp - Program to test the function getemp( ) that illustrates
  //              returning data stored in a structure variable.
  #include <iostream.h>
```

```cpp
#include <iomanip.h>
struct empinfo {
  char name[21];
  char ssnum[12];
  int age;
  float pay rate;
};
struct empinfo getemp( void );
int main( )
{
  struct empinfo emp;
  emp = getemp( );
  cout << endl << endl;
  cout << "Name = " << emp.name << endl;
  cout << "Soc. Sec. Num. = " << emp.ssnum << endl;
  cout << " Age = " << emp.age << endl;
  cout << setiosflags(ios::fixed | ios::showpoint) << setprecision(2)
        << "Pay rate = $" << setw(5) << emp.payrate << endl;
  return 0;
}
#include <a:\getemp2.cpp>
```

9.5 Structures and External Functions

Using **structure tags** to define a structure data type is the first time that we have encountered a **user defined data type**. When this data type is defined in the **main( )** program and is used in other functions that are going to remain external to where the data type is defined, we have to let each external function know how this data type is defined. In order to do this we have to repeat the definition in each of the external functions that use this data type. We illustrate this idea by rewriting **prog9_5.cpp** so that the function **getempdata( )** will be called as an external function. The program is written as follows:

```cpp
//prog9_8.cpp - Program to illustrate user defined data types
//                    and external functions.
#include <iostream.h>
#include <iomanip.h>
struct empinfo {
  char name[21];
  char ssnum[12];
  int age;
  float pay rate;
};
extern void getempdata(struct empinfo &emp1);
```

```
int main( )
{
    struct empinfo emp;
    getempdata(emp);
    cout << "Name = " << emp.name << endl;
    cout << "Soc. Sec. Number = " << emp.ssnum << endl;
    cout << "Age = " << emp.age << endl;
    cout.setf(ios::fixed | ios::showpoint);
    cout.precision(2);
    cout << "Pay rate = " << setw(5) << emp.payrate << endl;
    return 0;
}
```

This program is saved in the file **a:\prog98.cpp**. The function **getempdata( )** is coded and saved in the file **a:\getemp2.cpp** and this code will <u>not</u> be included with the code for the program. Since the function will need to know how the structure data type **empinfo** is defined, the definition will have to be included with the function. We omit the documentation.

```
#include <iostream.h>
struct empinfo {
    char name[21];
    char ssnum[12];
    int age;
    float pay rate;
};
void getempdata(struct empinfo &emp1)
{
    cout << "Input a name:";
    cin.getline(emp1.name, 21);
    cout << "Input a Social Security Number: ";
    cin.getline(emp1.ssnum, 12);
    cout << "Input an age: ";
    cin >> emp1.age;
    cout << "Input a pay rate: ";
    cin >> emp1.pay rate;
    return;
}
```

The easy way to include the definition of the structure data type, **empinfo**, if it is to be used in several external functions is to create our own header file containing the definition. The file, **a:\empinfo.h**, would simply contain the code

```
struct empinfo {
    char name[21];
    char ssnum[12];
    int age;
    float pay rate;
};
```

The main program and each of the functions would include the code for the definition by simply using the compiler directive that we use to include any other header file. The only difference is that we have to tell the compiler that this header file is on our disk in drive A.

```
#include <a:\empinfo.h>
```

The above program and function would be written as follows:

```
#include <iostream.h>
#include <iomanip.h>
#include <a:\empinfo.h>
extern void getempdata(struct empinfo &emp1);
int main( )
{
    ...;
    ...;
    return 0;
}

#include <iostream.h>
#include <a:\empinfo.h>
void getempdata(struct empinfo &emp1)
{
    ...;
    ...;
    return;
}
```

We will ask the reader to write and test the program that uses the header file **a:\empinfo.h** as one of the exercises.

9.6 - Nested Structures

The members of a structure can be any other type of variable including another structure. We have used arrays as members of a structure. In this section we will discuss how we define and use structures where a member is also a structure. We call this using nested structures. The example that we will use is the structure **studentdata** that we have used to store a name, four exam scores, an exam average, and a grade. The four exam scores were stored in an array. The array was defined as follows:

```
float exam[4];
```

Anytime that we use an array, we can use a structure. The structure that is to be used in place of the array would be defined as follows:

```
struct examscores {
  float exam1;
  float exam2;
  float exam3;
  float exam4;
};

examscores exams;
```

The four exam scores would be stored in the following member variables for the structure, **exams**. These variables take the place of the indicated variables when we used the array.

Structure	Array
exams.exam1	exam[0]
exams.exam2	exam[1]
exams.exam3	exam[2]
exams.exam4	exam[3]

We can now define a different structure type to hold the data for one student. This data type will use nested structures.

```
struct student1data {
  char name[21];
  struct  examscores exams;
  float average;
  char grade;
};
```

The structure variable is defined with the statement

```
struct student1data std1;
```

The variables to store the data for one student would now be the following:

structure student1data	**structure studentdata**
std1.name	std1.name
std1.exams.exam1	std1.exam[0];
std1.exams.exam2	std1.exam[1];
std1.exams.exam3	std1.exam[2];
std1.exams.exam4	std1.exam[3]
std1.average	std1.average
std1.grade	std1.grade

We can now rewrite the function **getstudentdata( )** from **prog9_5.cpp**.

```
void getstudentdata(struct student1data &std1)
{
  cout << "Input a student name: ";
  cin.getline(std1.name, 21);
  cout << "Input exam #1: ";
  cin >> std1.exams.exam1;
  cout << "Input exam #2: ";
  cin >> std1.exams.exam2;
  cout << "Input exam #3: ";
  cin >> std1.exams.exam3;
  cout << "Input exam #4: ";
  cin >> std1.exams.exam4;
  return;
}
```

The new version of the function **computeaverage( )** would be the following:

```
void computeaverage(struct student1data &std2)
{
  std2.average = (std2.exams.exam1 + std2.exams.exam2 + std2.exams.exam3
              + std2.exams.exam4) / 4;
  return;
}
```

The function **computegrade( )** would not have to be changed while **ptstudentdata( )** will require some changes. The main program would be almost identical to **prog9_6.cpp** with the only change being the type of structure that is being used. We will ask the reader to write this program and the revision of **ptstudentdata( )** as exercises.

We illustrate the use of nested structures with one more example. A collection of data on a group of people includes a name, telephone number and birthday. The name will be stored as a 20 character string and the telephone number as a 12 character string while the birthday is to be stored as three integers, the month, the day, and the year. We can define a structure to hold the birthday as follows:

```
struct date {
    int month;
    int day;
    int year;
} ;
```

and the structure to hold the data on each person using nested structures as follows:

```
struct person {
    char name[21];
    char telephone[13];
    struct date birthday;
};
```

If we now define a structure variable **customer** of type **person** with the statement

```
struct person  customer;
```

then the member variables that will be used to store data for the customer are the following:

```
customer.name
customer.telephone
customer.birthday.month
customer.birthday.day
customer.birthday.year
```

9.7- Arrays of Structures

One of the most useful data structures is an **array of structures**. We can use an array of structures in place of a collection of parallel arrays that we discussed in section 6.10. In this section we will see how we can define an array of structures and how we can rewrite the examples from section 6.10 using this array. One of our examples was a program that used a collection of employee data that was stored in a collection of parallel arrays that were defined as follows:

```
const int MAX = 50;
char names[MAX][21];
char ssnums[MAX][12];
int ages[MAX];
float payrates[MAX];
```

In order to define an array of structures, we first must define a structure that will store the data on one employee. This is done with the following statements:

```
struct empinfo {
    char name[21];
    char ssnum[12];
    int age;
    float pay rate;
} ;
```

We next must define the array to hold at most **MAX** of these records of data and that is done with the following statement

```
struct empinfo emps[MAX];
```

This statement defines an array with **MAX** elements

```
emps[0], emps[1], emps[2], ... , emps[MAX - 1]
```

where each of these array elements are a structure variable of type **empinfo**. The record of data for the first employee would be stored in the structure variable, **emps[0]**, and the member variables for this structure variables are listed as follows:

```
emps[0].name
emps[0].ssnum
emps[0].age
emps[0].pay rate
```

We can now rewrite the function getempdata( ) from section 6.10 so that it gets the data from the keyboard, stores it in the array of structures and counts the number of records stored. The function would be written as follows:

```
void getempdata(struct empinfo emp1[ ], int &count1, int MAX1)
{
    char ans, ret;
// Print screen info
    gotoxy(4,3);
    cout << "Employee Name";
```

```
        gotoxy(40, 3);
        cout << "Social Security Number";
        gotoxy(4, 15);
        cout << "Age";
        gotoxy(40, 15);
        cout << "Pay rate"
    // Get and store data
        count1 = 0;
        do {
            gotoxy(4,4);
            cout << "xxxxxxxxxxxxxxxxxxxx";
            gotoxy(40, 4);
            cout << "xxx-xx-xxxx";
            gotoxy(4, 16);
            cout << "xx";
            gotoxy(40, 16);
            cout << "xx.xx";
            gotoxy(4, 4);
            cin.getline(emp1[count1].name, 21);
            gotoxy(40, 4);
            cin.getline(emp1[count1].ssnum, 12);
            gotoxy(4, 16);
            cin >> emp1[count1].age
            gotoxy(40, 16);
            cin >> emp1[count1].pay rate;
            count1++;
            gotoxy(5, 24);
            cout << "Input another? Y/N: ";
            cin >> ans;
            cin.get(ret);
        while (((ans == 'y') || (ans == 'Y')) && ( count1 < MAX1));
        return;
    }
```

In order to test the above function, we will have to be able to print out the data stored in the array. We will do this by writing another function.

```
    void ptempdata(struct empinfo emp2[ ], int count2)
    {
        cout <<setw(9) << "Names" << setw(35) << "Soc. Sec. Numbers"
            << setw(8) << "Ages" << setw(16) << "Payrates" << endl;
        for(int I = 0; I < count2; I++) {
        cout << setw(4) << " " << setiosflags(ios::left) << setw(20)
            << emps2[count2].name << setw(17) << emps2[count2].ssnum
            << setiosflags(ios::right) << setw(12) << emps2[count2].age
```

```
                << setw(14) << setprecision( 2) << emps2[count2].pay rate
                << endl;
        } // end for
        return;
    }
```

The program to test the functions **getempdata( )** and **ptempdata( )** would be the following:

```
//prog9_9.cpp - Program to test the functions getempdata( ) and
//                   ptempdata( ) that use an array of structures.
#include <iostream.h>
#include <iomanip.h>
#include <conio.h>
struct empinfo {
    char name[21];
    char ssnum[12];
    int age;
    float pay rate;
};
void getempdata(employee emp1[ ], int &count1, int MAX1);
void ptempdata(employee emp2[ ], int count2);
int main( )
{
    const int MAX = 50;
    employee emp[MAX];
    int count;
    clrscr( );
    getempdata(emp, count, MAX);
    ptempdata(emp, count);
    return 0;
}
#include <a:\getempar.cpp>
#include <a:\ptempar.cpp>
```

9.8 Pointers to Structures

When we study **dynamic data structures** we will need to be able to use pointers to structures. Pointers to structures are critical in the development of linked lists and trees. These two structures are examples of dynamic data structures. A **dynamic data structure** is a data structure whose size can be changed by the program using the structure. The array and the structure are not dynamic since their size is fixed once they have been defined.

A pointer to a structure variable is defined in the same way as a pointer to any other data type. If the structure is of type **empinfo**, where **empinfo** is defined as it was in the previous sections

```
struct empinfo {
    char name[21];
    char ssnum[12];
    int age;
    float pay rate;
};
```

then a pointer to the structure of type **empinfo** is defined with the statement

```
struct empinfo *stptr;
```

If we define a structure variable with the statement

```
struct empinfo emp;
```

then this allocates a block of memory for the structure variable, **emp**, and the structure pointer, **stptr**, can be assigned the address of that block of memory with the statement

```
stptr = &emp;
```

As we know, we now say that the pointer, **stptr**, points to the structure variable **emp**.

The member elements can now be referenced using either of the structure variables,

emp   and   *stptr

The member variables would be the following:

emp	***stptr**
emp.name	(*stptr).name
emp.ssnum	(*stptr).ssnum
emp.age	(*stptr).age
emp.payrate	(*stptr).pay rate

The parentheses are require since . has precedence over * as operators. The variable

```
*stptr.payrate
```

would be interpreted as

*(stptr.payrate)

which makes no sense. The use of these pointer variables is illustrated with the following program.

```
//prog9_10.cpp - Program to illustrate the use of pointers to structures
#include <iostream.h>
#include <iomanip.h>
int main( )
{
    struct empinfo {
        char name[21];
        char ssnum[12];
        int age;
        float pay rate;
    };
    Struct empinfo emp = {"Norma J. Easton", "777-88-5555", 90, 20.50};
    empinfo *stptr;

    stptr = &emp;
    cout << "Name = " << (*stptr).name << endl;
    cout << "Soc. Sec. Num. = " << (*stptr).ssnum << endl;
    cout << "Age = " << (*stptr).age << endl;
    cout << "Pay rate = $" << setiosflags(ios::fixed | ios::showpoint)
        << setprecision(2) << setw(5) << (*stptr).pay rate << endl;
    return 0;
}
```

The output from this program was the following:

```
Name = Norma J. Easton
Soc. Sec. Num. = 777-88-5555"
Age = 90
Pay rate = $20.50
```

Because pointers to structures were used so often in C and C++, another notation was created to access the member data of the structures without having to use the * operator. The new operator

                    ->   **(Minus sign)(Greater than sign)**

is used as follows:

382

Standard Pointer Notation	**New Structure Pointer Notation**
(*stptr).name	stptr->name
(*stptr).ssnum	stptr->ssnum
(*stptr).age	stptr->age
(*stptr).pay rate	stptr->pay rate

We will almost always use the new structure pointer notation rather that the standard pointer notation of the first column. The following program illustrates the use of this new notation.

```cpp
// prog9_11.cpp - Program to illustrate the use of the structure
//                 pointer notation.
#include <iostream.h>
#include <iomanip.h>
int main( )
{
  struct empinfo  {
    char name[21];
    char ssnum[12];
    int age;
    float pay rate;
  };
  struct empinfo emp = {"Robert R. Easton", "555-44-3333", 55, 29.50};
  struct empinfo *emptr;
  emptr = &emp;
  cout << "Name = " << emptr->name << endl;
  cout << "Soc. Sec. Nm. = " << emptr->ssnum << endl;
  cout << "Age = " << emptr->age << endl;
  cout << "Pay rate = $" << setiosflags(ios::fixed | ios::showpoint)
       << setprecision(2) << setw(5) << emptr->pay rate << endl;
  return 0
}
```

The output from this program was exactly the same as the output from **prog9_9.cpp**.

Try this: Use the **studentdata** structure data type defined in section 9.2 and define a structure variable **student** and a pointer variable **stdptr**. Assign the address of the structure to the pointer variable and write the structure-pointer variables that can be used to access the data stored in the member variables.

```
struct studentdata {
  char name[21];
  float exam[4];
  float average;
  char grade;
};
studentdata _____        // define structure
studentdata _____        // define pointer
_____            // assign address
```

```
student.name          _____
student.exam[0]       _____
student.exam[1]       _____
student.exam[2]       _____
student.exam[3]       _____
student.average       _____
student.grade         _____
```

9.9 - Unions

The C and C++ programming languages have another data type that we will discuss in this section because it resembles the structure. This data type is the **union** and a variable of that type is used to store a single data item; however the data item can be of different data types. The difference between a **union** and a **structure** is that a **union** reserves a block of memory large enough to accommodate the largest data item used by the **union** members. The **structure** variable reserves a block of memory large enough to hold all of the data items specified by the member variables of the structure. The **union** variable can only store data in one of the member variables while a **structure** variable can store data in all of it's member variables. A **union** variable is defined as follows:

```
union {
  float num1;
  int num2;
  char ch1;
} onevar;
```

384

This statement defines a union variable, **onevar**, that can store either a single real number, **num1**, a single integer, **num2**, or a single character, **ch1**. These data items would be stored in the member variables,

> onevar.num1
> onevar.num2
> onevar.ch1

The union variable, **onevar**, would have four bytes reserved since this is what is needed for the largest of these member variables. This is what is needed when the member variable, **onevar.num1** is assigned a data item. Only two of the bytes would contain data when the member variable, **onevar.num2** is used and only one of the bytes would contain data when the member variable, **onevar.ch1** is used. Only one of these member variables can contain data at any one time. This idea is illustrated with the following program:

```cpp
//prog9_12.cpp - Program to illustrate the use of a union variable
#include <iostream.h>
#include <iomanip.h>
int main( )
{
  union {
    float num1;
    int num2;
    char ch1;
  } onevar;
// Data assignment
  cout.setf(ios::fixed | ios::showpoint);
  cout.precision(2);
  onevar.num1 = 27.25;
  cout << "num1 = " << setw(5) << onevar.num1 << endl;
  cout << "num1 = " << onevar.num2 << endl;
  cout << "ch1 = " << onevar.ch1 << endl << endl;
  onevar.num2 = 125;
  cout << "num1 = " << setw(5) << onevar.num1 << endl;
  cout << "num2 = " << onevar.num2 << endl;
  cout << "ch1 = " << onevar.ch1 << endl << endl;
  onevar.ch1 = 'A';
  cout << "num1 = " << setw(5) << onevar.num1 << endl;
  cout << "num2 = " << onevar.num2 << endl;
  cout << "ch1 = " << onevar.ch1 << endl;
  return 0;
}
```

The output from this program was the following:

```
num1 = 27.25
num2 = 0
ch1 =

num1 = 27.25
num2 = 125
ch1 = }

num1 = 27.25
num2 = 65
ch1 = A
```

Just as we can use nested structures we can also use nested unions. In fact we can nest structures in unions and unions in structures. Here are some examples of these nested data structures.

```
union unex1 {
   float num1;
   int num2;
};

union nestunion {
   union unex1 unvar;
   char ch1;
};

nestunion  unvar1;
```

The member variables for the union variable, **unvar1**, would be the following:

```
unvar1.unvar.num1
unvar1.unvar.num2
unvar1.ch1
```

The amount of memory that is set aside for a union variable of type **unex1** is 4 since the largest data type is the float member variable **num1**. However the amount of memory set aside for a union variable of type **nestunion** is the size of it's largest member variable, which is also the float

```
unvar1.unvar.num1
```

We can justify these statements by using the **sizeof( )** operator in a statement

```
cout << "Size of the union unex1 = << sizeof(unex1) << endl
```

<< "Size of the union nestunion = << sizeof(nestunion) << endl;

We will ask the reader to write a program to execute this statement as one of the exercises.

An example of a union nested in a structure would be the following:

```
struct empdata {
    char name[21];
    union ssdata {
        char sstring[12];
        long int ssint;
    } ssnum;
};
```

This structure would allow the social security number to be stored either as a twelve character string if it is to include the dashes or as an integer if the dashes were not to be used. The member variables for the structure variable defined with the statement

    empdata emp;

would be

    emp.name   and   emp.ssnum.sstring
                                    emp.ssnum.ssint

where only one of the member variables, **emp.ssnum.sstring** and **emp.ssnum.ssint** can have data at one time.

The union data type is not widely used in C or in C++ programming, however, it is used in some library functions.

9.10 - Summary

In this Chapter we have studied the second data structure that can be used to store data in a program. Recall that a data structure is a variable that can store more than one data item using one variable name. The array was the first data structure that we studied in Chapter 6 and when we use an array all of the data items must be of the same data type. The **structure** is a data structure where the data items may be of different data types. The **structure** corresponds to the **record** in Pascal.

We discussed how we can define a **structure** data type and how we can use this data type to define structure variables. We discussed how we can pass structure variables as parameters to functions and what we must do if the functions that use a structure variable are to remain external to the calling function or program.

We discussed how we can define and use nested structures and how we can define an array of structures. We illustrated the use of an array of structures in place of using a collection of parallel arrays. We discussed pointers to structures and the special pointer notation that is used to access the members of a structure that is pointed to by a pointer variable.

We discussed the **union** data type and how we can define union variables and understand how they can be used in programs. We discussed nested unions, nested structures and unions, and nested unions and structures.

9.11 - Questions

9.1 What is a data structure?

9.2 What are the two data structures that we have studied so far?

9.3 How do arrays and structures differ as data structures?

9.4 What is a record? How does it relate to a structure?

9.5 What is a field? How does it relate to a member?

9.6 Why are the array and structure called static data structures?

9.7 What is a structure tag?

9.8 What is different about copying data stored in a structure and copying data stored in an array?

9.9 What is the difference between using a structure as a parameter to a function and using an array as a parameter to a function?

9.10 When we use an array of structures to store data in a program, what might we be replacing?

9.11 How does a union variable differ from a structure variable?

9.12 - Exercises

9.1 A program is to use a the following data for a collection of books:

Title	25 characters
Author	20 characters
Year	integer
Price	real

Define a structure data type, **bookdata**, and a structure variable, **book**, to store the data for one book in a program.

9.2 A program is to use the following data for a collection of movies:

Title	25 character	
Year	integer	
Rating	6 characters	***½
Actor1	20 characters	
Actor2	20 characters	

Define a structure data type, **moviedata**, and a structure variable, **movie**, to store the data for one movie in a program.

9.3 Write a function, **getbookdata( )**, that will get one record of data from the keyboard, store it in the structure variable, and return it to the calling program.

9.4 Write a program to test the function, **getbookdata( )**.

9.5 Write a function, **getmoviedata( )**, that will get one record of data from the keyboard, store it in a stucture variable, and return it to the calling program.

9.6 Write a program to test the function **getmoviedata( )**.

9.7 Rewrite the program, **prog9_2.cpp**, so that it tests the structure initialization

    struct employee emp = {"Morgie, David", "999-88-7777", 40, 27.35};

9.8 Write a program to test the function, **getstudentdata( )**, from section 9.4.

9.9 Write a program to test the function, **computeaverage( )**, from section 9.4.

9.10 Write a program to test the function, **computegrade( )**, from section 9.4.

9.11 Write a program to test the function, **ptstudentdata( )**, from section 9.4.

9.12 Rewrite the function, **getbookdata( )**, from exercise 9.1 so that it returns the data in the structure using the function name.

9.13 Write a program to test the function from exercise 9.12.

9.14 Rewrite the function, **getmoviedata( )**, from exercise 9.2 so that it returns the data in the structure using the function name.

9.15 Write a program to test the function from exercise 9.14.

9.16 Write a program to compute the size of the union variables of type, **unex1** and **nestunion**, and print these sizes to the screen.

9.17 Write the documentation for the function **computeaverage( )** from section 9.4.

9.18 Write the documentation for the function **computegrade( )** from section 9.4.

9.19 Rewrite the function **ptstudentdata( )** from section 9.6 so that it uses the structure **student1data** that uses nested structures.

9.20 Rewrite the main program discussed in section 9.6 that would use the structure **student1data**.

CHAPTER 10

File Processing

10.1 Introduction

Most computer programs, i.e. computer applications, need to store data so that it is saved after the computer is turned off. This is done using files that are saved on the hard disk of the computer and on your floppy disk in one of the disk drives. The DOS operating system allows us to use file names that can have 1 to 8 characters in the name and 0 to 3 characters in the extension. Windows 95 allows filenames of up to 255 characters. A DOS filename is of the form

name.ext

The filename can also include the path that specifies the drive and directory where the file is located. The extension should indicate the type of file. For example, **cpp** is used for a C++ program, **pas** for a Pascal program, **dat** for a data file, etc.

    path\filename
    a:\cpp\progs\prog21.cpp

The name of the file on the disk is called the **physical file name**.

Every programming language has the ability to save data in a file and read data from a file to use in a program. Different programming languages identify the physical filename with a name, number, file pointer, or whatever is used in the program. For example, BASIC uses a number and the identification is done with a BASIC statement of the form

    OPEN "A:\BASIC\DATA1.DAT" FOR INPUT AS #1

Pascal uses a name and identifies this **logical file name** with the **physical file name** using statements of the form

    assign(infile, "a:\pascal\data1.dat");
    reset(infile);

The C and C++ programming languages use file pointers and these ideas will be explained in the next few sections.

There are two different ways to access data in a file, sequential access and random access. **Sequential access** means that you have to start at the beginning and read every data item to get to the one that you want to access. In order to read the 100th item from a file we would have to first read the items 1 through 99. Thus, we would have to do 100 reads. **Random access** means that we can simply move to the data item that we want to access and then read that data item. In order to access the 100th data item, we simply move to that item and then read it. This takes 1 move and one read. Sequential access files are a lot like songs on a cassette tape. If we want to play the 4th song on the tape we have to fast-forward through the first 3 songs to get to the 4th song. Random access files are a lot like songs on a compact disk. When we want to play the 4th song, we simply move to the 4th song and then play it. Sequential files are limiting but take less programming to use. They are used in a number of programming applications. We will study sequential access files in sections 10.2 and 10.3. Random access files are much more flexible but require more programming to use. We will study random access files in sections 10.6 and 10.7.

After completing this chapter, the reader will be able to

1.   use the C statements to open and close a file.

2.   use C statements to read characters from and write characters to a file.

3.   use the C++ statements to open and close a file.

4.   use C++ statements to read characters from and write characters to a file.

5.   understand what is meant be a sequential file.

6.   understand how to send data to a printer.

7.   use the C and also the C++ statements to write strings to a file and read strings from a file.

8.   understand what is meant by a random access file.

9.   use files as parameters to functions.

10.   use command line parameters in programs.

11.   understand how to convert file access programs that have been written in C to programs written in C++.

392

10.2 Sequential Files Using C

The C and C++ programming languages view each file as a sequential stream of bytes. Each file ends with an end-of-file marker or at a specific byte number that is maintained by the operating system. In order to be able to use a data file in any program language, the file has to be opened. After the program is through using the file, then the file must be closed. The C and C++ programming languages themselves have no input/output facilities but instead rely on libraries of input and output functions. In this section we will discuss the library of functions that are used in the C programming language and are also available in C++.

In order to use the standard C input/output functions for files, we must include the header file, **stdio.h**. Files in C are accessed by means of a file pointer that is defined using the built-in file pointer type, **FILE**. The file pointer would be defined using the statement

FILE *fptr;

The functions that are used to open and close a file are the two functions, **fopen( )** and **fclose( )**. The function, **fopen( )**, expects two parameters, the first one being the file name and the second the file mode. The statement to open the file would be the following

fopen("filename", "mode");

There are only three operations that we can use with sequential files. These are

1. Create a file.
2. Read from a file.
3. Add data to a file.

The filename can include the drive and the path as we might expect. The various mode are given in the following table.

Table 10.1: File Access Modes in C

Mode	Meaning	File does not exist
"r"	Open the file for reading	Error
"w"	Open the file for writing	Creates a new file
"a"	Open the file for adding data to the end of the file	Creates a new file
"r+"	Opens the file for reading and writing.	Error
"w+"	Opens the file for reading and writing	Creates a new file

| "a+" | Opens the file for reading and writing at the end of the file | Creates a new file |

==

> **Note:** If we open an existing file with either of the modes, "w" or "w+", then the contents of the file will be lost.

The statement that will open the file, **prog20.cpp** on our disk in drive A for reading is the following:

    fptr = fopen("a:\prog20.cpp", "r");

If a file is successfully opened, then **fopen( )** returns a pointer to the file pointer, **fptr**. If the file cannot be successfully opened, then **fopen( )** returns the defined constant **NULL**. In addition, only **FOPEN_MAX** files can be open at any time in a C program. The constants **NULL** and **FOPEN_MAX** are defined in the header file, **stdio.h**

When a file is opened, a file position marker is set to some location of the file. When the modes, "r", "w", "r+", and "w+" are used then the position marker is set to the first element of the file. When the modes, "a" and "a+" are used, then the position marker is set to the end of the file. Every time that we read from or write to a file the file position marker is moved to the next position of the file.

The functions, **fseek( )** and **rewind( )** can be used to explicitly set the file position marker. The function, **rewind( )**, moves the position marker to the first element of the file, while the function, **fseek( )**, can be given a specific position. We will discuss these functions in section 10.5. The function **fclose( )** is used to close a file and the statement to close the file that has been opened with file pointer, **fptr**, is the following.

    fclose(fptr);

> **Note:** We must remember to close every file that we have open in a program before we exit. The closing of the file writes all of the data remaining in the file buffer to the file. It also writes the end of file marker to the file. Failure to close a file can result in some of the data being lost.

The statements that we can use to open a file and then see whether or not it has been successfully opened, are either of the following:

394

```
fptr = fopen("filename", "mode");
if (fptr == NULL)
        printf("Cannot open file: %s\n", filename);
else {

        // Code to read from or write to the file

} // end else
```

or

```
if (fptr = fopen("filename", "mode")) == NULL) {
        printf("Cannot open file: %s\n", filename);
        exit(0);
} // end if

        // Code to read from or write to the file
```

This second block of code is a nice example of how we can use the function, **exit()**, to exit from a function or program. The **exit( )** function allows us to exit from a program before we reach the final statement **return 0;**. Among other things the **exit( )** function makes sure that all files that have been opened in the program are closed. Returning the value of zero, **exit(0)**, indicates that the program terminated normally; any other value indicates that the program terminated due to an error. The value returned is used by the calling environment, (normally the operating system), to respond appropriately to the error. Some programmers choose to return the value of 0 in the above code while others choose to return 1. We choose to return 0 considering this type of program termination to be normal.

Note: In order to use the **exit( )** function we can include either of the header files **stdlib.h** or **process.h**

Try this: Write the statements to define a file pointer and open the file, data1.dat, on a disk in drive A for reading.

_____

_____

_____

Write the block of code to check and see if the file was successfully opened and if not exit normally from the program.

_____

_____

_____

_____

10.3 Character Input and Output Using C

The functions that are used to read data from a file or from the keyboard and to write data to a file or to the screen are the following functions. The functions are used as indicated and are defined in the header file **stdio.h**. We need the following declarations:

```
FILE *fptr;
char ch;
```

Table 10.2: Character Input / Output Functions in C

===

Reading characters.

===

fget( )	ch = fget(fptr);	Reads one character from the file and returns EOF when end-of-file is reached.
getc( )	ch = getc(fptr);	Written as a macro using fget( ).
getchar( )	ch = getchar( );	Standard input, keyboard.

===

Writing characters.

===

fputc( )	fputc(ch, fptr);	Writes one character to the file.
putc( )	putc(ch, fptr);	Writes one character to the file. Written as a macro using fputc( ).
putchar( )	putchar(ch);	Standard screen output.

===

The following program would print the contents of the file **prog20.cpp** to the screen.

```
// prog10_1.cpp  Program to display the contents of the file
//                prog20.cpp from our disk in drive A, to the screen.
#include <stdio.h>
#include <stdlib.h>
```

```
int main( )
{
  FILE *fptr;
  char ch;
// Open the file
  fptr = fopen("a:\prog20.cpp", "r");
  if (fptr == NULL) {
    printf("Error! ** Cannot open the file a:\prog20.cpp\n");
    exit(0);
  } // end if
// Print the contents
  while ( (ch = fgetc(fptr) ) != EOF)
    putchar(ch);
  // end while
// Close file
  fclose(fptr);
  return 0;
}
```

We can make this program into a program that we can find more useful by allowing the user to input the name of the file that is to be displayed at the screen. We would modify the program by adding the following statements:

```
char filename[80];

printf("Input the name of the file: ");
gets(filename);
fptr = fopen(filename, "r");
```

We will ask the reader to write a version of **prog10_1.cpp** using this code as one of the exercises.

10.4 - Sequential Files Using C++

In order to use the C++ streams to read data from and write data to files, we must include the header file, **fstream.h**. Files are accessed using file pointers and file pointers are defined with three file streams. The stream **ifstream** is used for file input, **ofstream** for file output, and **fstream** for files that will be used for both input and output. The definitions for these three stream classes are contained in the header file **fstream.h**. A file pointer is defined for output with the statement

```
ofstream  fptr1;
```

and for input with the statement

ifstream fptr2;

Once a file pointer has been defined, we can use it's member functions, **open( )**, to open a file, and **close( )**, to close a file. The statement that is used to open a file is the statement

fptr.open("filename", mode);

The statement to open the file assigns the **file pointer** to the file specified by the **physical filename**. The various modes are given in the following table.

Table 10.3: File Access Modes in C++

Mode	Meaning	Use
in	Open the file for reading	ios::in
out	Open the file for writing	ios::out
app	Open for appending	ios::app
ate	Open and seek end-of-file	ios::ate
binary	Open the file in binary mode	ios::binary
trunc	Discard file contents if the file exists	ios::trunc
nocreate	If the file does not exist, then do not create	ios::nocreate
noreplace	If file exists, do not open unless appending or seeking end-of-file.	ios::noreplace

The following statement would be used to open the file, **prog20.cpp**, for reading on a disk in drive A.

fptr.open("a:\prog20.cpp", ios::in);

The statement returns an integer value, 0 = false, if the file cannot be opened. We can then check to see if the file has been opened with the code

fptr.open(filename, ios::in);   or   fptr.open(filename, ios::in);
if(fptr ==0) {   if(!fptr) {

} // end if   } // end if

The statement to open the file can be combined with the code to check so that we can also use the following code in our programs:

```
if (fptr.open("filename", ios::in) == 0) {
    cout << "Error! *** File << filename
        << " cannot be opened " << endl;
    exit(0);
} // end if
```

The statement to close the file that has been opened and assigned to the file pointer, **fptr**, is

```
fptr.close( );
```

The two statements

```
fstream fptr1;
fptr1.open("filename, ios::in);
```

can be written as the single statement

```
fstream fptr1.open(filename, ios::in);
```

We will continue to use two statements rather than combining them into one.

Try this: Write the C++ statements to define a file pointer and open the file, data1.dat, on a disk in drive A for reading.

_____
_____
_____

Write the block of code to check and see if the file was successfully opened and if not, exit normally from the program.

_____
_____
_____
_____

10.5 - Character Input and Output Using C++

The most commonly used member functions for reading from and writing to files using the C++ file streams are described in the following table. We would need the following declarations:

```
ifstream infptr;
ofstream outfptr;
char ch;
```

Table 10.4: Character Member File Input / Output Functions in C++

```
==========================================================
        get( )       infptr.get(ch);      Read one character from the
                                          file pointed to by infptr.
        put( )       outfptr.put(ch);     Write one character to the
                                          file pointed to by outfptr.

==========================================================
```

The functions, **get( )** and **put( )** are used for characters. The statement to read one character from the file that has been opened successfully and assigned the file pointer, **fptr**, is the following

```
    fptr.get(ch);
```

This statement returns the value, 0 , when end of file has been read. We can now write the program to print the contents of a file to the screen using the C++ file streams. This is a rewrite of the second version of **prog10_1.cpp** from section 10.3.

```
//prog10_2.cpp - Program to print the contents of a text file to the screen
//               using the C++ file streams. The filename is to be entered
//               by the user from the keyboard.
#include <fstream.h>
#include <process.h>
int main( )
{
  ifstream infptr;
  char ch;
  char filename[80];
  cout << "Input the name of the file: ";
  cin >> filename;
  infptr.open(filename, ios::in);
  if(!infptr) {
    cout << "Error! *** File " << filename
        << " cannot be opened. " << endl;
    exit(0);
  } // end if
  while(infptr.get(ch) != 0)
    cout << ch;
  // end while
```

```
      infptr.close( );
      return 0;
}
```

The next program is a program to copy the contents of one file to another file. It is similar to the **copy** program from MS-DOS.

```
//prog10_3.cpp - Program to copy one file to another file. The filenames are
//                 to be input by the user from the keyboard.
#include <fstream.h>
#include <conio.h>
#include <process.h>
int main( )
{
   char infile[80];
   char outfile[80];
   char ch;
   ifstream infptr;
   ofstream outfptr;
   clrscr( );
   gotoxy(5,5);
   cout << "Input the name of the source file: ";
   cin >> infile;
   gotoxy(5, 10);
   cout << "Input the name of the new file: ";
   cin >> outfile;
   infptr.open(infile, ios::in);
   if(!infptr) {
     clrscr( );
     gotoxy(20, 13);
     cout << "Error! *** " << infile
           << " cannot be opened.";
     exit(0);
   } // end if
   outfptr.open(outfile, ios::out);
   if(!outfptr) {
     clrscr( );
     gotoxy(20, 13);
     cout << "Error!*** " << outfile
           << " cannot be opened.";
     exit(0);
   } // end if
   clrscr( );
   gotoxy(30, 13);
   cout << "COPYING FILE - Please wait";
```

```
      while(infptr.get(ch) != 0)
        outfptr.put(ch);
      // end while
      gotoxy(30, 15);
      cout << "File copied.";
      infptr.close( );
      outfptr.close( );
      return 0;
  }
```

In addition, reading and writing with an open file can be done almost identically as using **cin** to read data input from the keyboard and **cout** to write data to the screen. We illustrate these ideas with the following programs.

```
//prog10_4.cpp Program to illustrate stream output to a file.
#include <fstream.h>
#include <iomanip.h>
#include <process.h>
int main( )
{
    char names[ ][21] = {"Easton, Linda", "Frye, Jennie", "Metz, Shorty"};
    char ssnums[ ][12] = {"111-11-1111", "222-22-2222", "333-33-3333"};
    float payrates[ ] = {25.50, 23.75, 24.25};
    fstream outptr;
    outptr.open("a:\employee.dat", ios::out);
    if(!outptr) {
      cout << "Error! *** - a:\employee.dat not opened successfully." << endl;
      exit(0);
    } // end if
    outptr.setf(ios::fixed | ios::showpoint);
    outptr.precision(2);
    for(int I = 0; I < 3; I++)
      outptr << setiosflags(ios::left) << ' ' << names[i] << ' '
              << ssnums[i] << ' ' << setprecision(2) << setw(5)
              << payrates[i] << endl;
    } // end for
    outptr.close( );
    return 0;
}
```

When we display the contents of the file **employee.dat** we have the following:

```
Easton, Linda_____ 111-11-1111 25.50
Frye, Jennie_____ 222-22-2222 23.75
Metz, Shorty_____ 333-33-3333 24.25
```

The program to read data from the file **employee.dat** and store it in parallel arrays is not simple as it might first appear. When we read the name with stream input with the statement

```
infptr >> names[i];
```

this only reads to the first blank so that we have read only the last name and the comma. When we attempt to use the member function, **getline( )**, to read the first 20 characters and then read the social security number and the pay rate with the statements

```
infptr.getline(names[i], 21);
infptr >> ssnums[i] >> payrates[i];
```

then this works fine for the first line, but fails with the second line because the last data item that we read on the line was numeric. This causes the next **getline( )** to read the end-of-line so that it reads a null string. This is similar to what we encountered in Chapter 6 when we were entering data from the keyboard. We would have to replace the above block of code with the following:

```
infptr.getline(names[i], 21);
infptr.getline(ssnums[i], 12);
infptr >> payrates[i];
infptr.get(cr);
infptr.get(lf);
```

Since DOS stores both a carriage return and a linefeed at the end of a line, we must use the member function **get( )** twice. The complete program would be the following:

```
//prog10_5.cpp Program to illustrate data input from a file.
#include <fstream.h>
#include <iomanip.h>
#include <process.h>
int main( )
{
    char names[3][21];
    char ssnums[3][12];
    float payrates[3];
    char cr, lf;
    ifstream infptr;
    infptr.open("a:\employee.dat", ios::in);
    if(!infptr) {
        cout << "Error! - a:\employee.dat cannot be opened." << endl;
        exit(0);
    } // end if
```

```
    for(int I = 0; I < 3; I++) {
       infptr.getline(names[i], 21);
       infptr.getline(ssnums[i], 12);
       infptr >> payrates[i];
       infptr.get(cr);
       infptr.get(lf);
    } // end for
    infptr.close( );
    cout.setf(ios::fixed | ios::showpoint);
    cout.precision(2);
    for (I = 0; I < 3; I++)
       cout << names[i] << ssnums[i] << ' '
             << payrates[i] << endl;
    // end for
    return 0;
}
```

Another method that is often used, is to read all data as character data. Since this would mean that we would be reading the pay rate as a string, we will need to store this string in a buffer, convert the string to numeric, and then store the numeric value in the array, **payrates[ ]**. The function that is used to convert the string to floating point is the function

atof( )

This function is defined in the header file **math.h**. The program to illustrate this method is the following:

```
//prog10_6.cpp Program to illustrate stream input from a file.
#include <fstream.h>
#include <iostream.h>
#include <math.h>
#include <process.h>
int main( )
{
   char names[3][21];
   char ssnums[3][12];
   char paybuff[8];
   float payrates[3];
   ifstream inptr;
   inptr.open("a:\employee.dat", ios::in);
   if(!inptr) {
      cout << "Error! *** - a:\employee.dat could not be opened."
            << endl;
```

```
        exit(0);
    } // end if
    for(int I = 0; I < 3; I++) {
        inptr.getline(names[i], 21);
        inptr.getline(ssnums[i],12);
        inptr.getline(paybuff, 8);              // 'b'xx.xxcrlf = 8 characters
        payrates[i] = atof(paybuff);
    } // end for
    cout.setf(ios::fixed | ios::showpoint);
    cout.precision(2);
    for(I = 0; I < 3; I++)
        cout << names[i] << ' ' << ssnums[i] << ' '
            << payrates[i] << endl;
    // end for
    inptr.close( );
    return 0;
}
```

Note that we made the last **getline( )** read 8 characters in order to get past end-of-line. Output from this program was the following:

```
Easton, Linda_____ 111-11-1111 25.50
Frye, Jennie_____ 222-22-2222 23.25
Metz, Shorty_____ 333-33-3333 24.75
```

In order to do only stream input, we would have to read the last name and first name as separate data items since the stream input uses a blank as a data separator. We can define arrays to store the data as follows:

```
char lnames[3][11];
char fnames[3][11];
char ssnums[3][12];
float payrates[3];
```

In addition, the data file would have to have data stored in a different format, the last name in the first 10 places and the first name in the second 10 places. The file would look like the following:

```
Easton____Linda_____111-11-1111_25.50
Frye_____Jennie_____222-22-2222_23.25
Metz_____Shorty_____333-33-3333_24.75
```

The program to read and store the data would be the following:

```cpp
//prog10_7.cpp Program to read data from a file containing
//                      multiple data items on a line, using stream
//                      input.
#include <fstream.h>
#include <iostream.h>
#include <iomanip.h>
#include <process.h>
int main( )
{
   char lnames[3][11];
   char fnames[3][11];
   char ssnums[3][12];
   float payrates[3];
   char cr, lf;
   ifstream infptr;
   infptr.open("a:\empb.dat", ios::in);
   if(!infptr) {
      cout << "Error! *** - cannot open a:\empb.dat. ";
      exit(0);
   } // end if
   for(int I = 0; I < 3; I++) {
      infptr >> lnames[i] >> fnames[i]
              >> ssnums[i] >> payrates[i];
      infptr.get(cr);
      infptr.get(lf);
   } // end for
   cout.setf(ios::left | ios::fixed | ios::showpoint);
   cout.precision(2);
   for(I = 0; I < 3; I++)
      cout << setw(10) << lnames[i] << setw(10) << fnames[i]
           << ssnums[i] << ' ' << setw(5) << payrates[i] << endl;
   // end for
   infptr.close( );
   return 0;
}
```

We will ask the reader to create the data file and run this program as one of the exercises.

We can also rewrite the program using stream input so that it will read an unknown number of records of data, store them in the parallel arrays, and count the number. It will read at most **MAX** records. This program uses the **peek( )** member function to look ahead for end-of-file.

```cpp
//prog10_8.cpp Program to illustrate reading and checking for
//              end-of-file
#include <fstream.h>
#include <iostream.h>
#include <math.h>
#include <process.h>
int main( )
{
  const int MAX = 25;
  char lnames[MAX][11];
  char rnames[MAX][11];
  char ssnums[MAX][11];
  float payrates[MAX];
  int ch, count;
  char cr, lf;
  fstream infptr;
  infptr.open("a:\empb.dat", ios::in);
  if(!infptr) {
    cout << "Error! *** - a:\empb.dat cannot be opened. "
         << endl;
    exit(0);
  } // end if
  count = 0;
  while (((ch = infptr.peek( )) != EOF)) && (count < MAX) {
    infptr >> lnames[count] >> fnames[count] >> ssnums[count]
           >> payrates[count];
    infptr.get(cr);
    infptr.get(lf);
    count ++
  } // end while
  count--;                    // Count one too many
  infptr.close( );
  return 0;
}
```

Another method that we could use, is to check for end-of-file by using the member function **eof( )**. This is illustrated with the following block of code. We will ask the reader to write the complete program as one of the exercises.

```cpp
count = 0;
while (1) {                              // Always true
  infptr.getline(names[count], 21);
  infptr.getline(ssnums[count], 12);
  infptr.getline(paybuff, 8);
  payrates[count] = atof(paybuff);
```

```
        count++;
        if((infptr.eof( )) || (count == MAX))
          break;
        // end if
    } // end while
```

10.6 - Output to a Printer

The functions that we have discussed in the previous section, such as **open( )**, can be used with any device, as well as with files. If we want our program to write to the printer, then we can treat the printer as if it were a file. Recall, that the stream name for the printer hooked to our computer is known as either, **LPT1** or **PRN**. These are the names that the operating system uses for the first parallel printer port.

The pointer to be used with the printer is defined with the statement

```
        ofstream prtout;
```

and the stream to the printer attached to LPT1 is opened with the statement.

```
        prtout.open("LPT1", ios::out);
```

After the stream, **prtout**, to the printer has been defined with the above two statements, then the statement

```
        prtout << "This line goes to the printer.\n");
```

would send the message to the printer. We use

```
        prtout <<
```

anytime that we want to send output to the printer.

We will rewrite the function from Chapter 4, **printtable( )**, so that we have a version that will print the table. We will then show how we can rewrite the Savings Account Program, **prog4_10.cpp**, so that the user can choose to send the output either to the printer or to the screen.

```
    // prttable( ) - Function to print the table at the printer.
    #include <fstream.h>
    void prttable(float &amount5, int mths5, float mrate5)
    {
        float intearned;
```

```
prtout.setf(ios::fixed);
prtout.setf(ios::showpoint);
prtout.precision(2);
for(int I = 1; I <= mths5; I++) {
    intearned = amount5 * mrate5;
    amount5 += intearned;
    prtout << setw(13) << I
            << setw(23) << "$"
            << setw(5) << intearned
            << setw(24) <<  "$"
            << setw(8) << amount5 << endl;
} // end for
return;
}
```

Try this: Write the program to test prttable( ).

```
#include _____
#include _____
void prttable(_____
int main( )
{
    int _____
    float _____

    _____

    prtout.open(_____
    if (_____

        _____

        _____
    } // end if
    prttable(_____
    cout << _____
        << _____
    return 0;
}
```

We will ask the reader to write the printer versions of the functions, **ptheadings( )** and **summary( )**, and programs to test these functions as exercises. The main program would be modified as follows:

```
// prog10_9.cpp - Revision of prog4_10.cpp so that the user can choose
//                 to send the output either to the screen or to the
//                 printer.
```

```cpp
#include <fstream.h>
#include <stdlib.h>
extern void printheadings( );
extern void prtheadings( );
extern compute(int years1, float rate1, int &months1, float &mrate1);
extern getdata(float &amount2, float &rate2, int &years2);
extern printtable(float &amount3, int months3, float mrate3);
extern prttable(float &amount5, int months5, float mrate5);
extern summary(float amount4, float oldamount4, float rate4, int years4);
extern ptsummary(float amount6, float oldamount6, float rate6, int years6);
int main( )
{
    float amount, oldamount, intrate, mrate;
    int years, months;
    ofstream prtout;
    getdata(amount, intrate, years);
    compute(years, intrate, months, mrate);
    cout << "Do you want the output at the printer?"
    cin >> ans;
    if ((ans == 'Y') || (ans == 'y')) {
        prtout.open("LPT1", ios::out);
        if (!prtout) {
            cout << "Error! *** Printer not activated!!! "
                    << endl;
            exit(0);
        } // end if
        prtheadings( );
        oldamount = amount;
        prttable(amount, months, mrate);
        prtsummary(amount, oldamount, intrate, years);
        prtout.close( );
    } else {
        printheadings( );
        oldamount = amount;
        printtable(amount, months, mrate);
        summary(amount, oldamount, intrate, years);
    } end if
    return 0;
}
```

10.7 - String Input & Output With Files Using C

The C and C++ programming languages allow us to input and output data items other than simply characters. One of these data items is the string. The C functions that are used to read strings from and write strings to files are the functions

fgets( )   and   fputs( )

The function, **fgets( )**, expects three arguments, the array to store the string, the maximum number of characters to read and store, and the file pointer. If we had an array and a file pointer defined with the statements

char name[21];
FILE fptr;

then the following statement would be used to read one string of characters from the file pointed to by, **fptr**, into the array, **name**. A maximum of 21 characters would be read from the file.

fgets(name, 21, fptr);

This statement reads characters into the array until 20 characters are read or until the newline character is reached. If the newline character is read, it is stored in the array and then the null terminator is added to the end of the array. When 20 characters are read, then the null terminator is added to the end of the array. If no characters are read and stored, then **fgets( )** returns **NULL**.

Suppose that we have a file called **employee.dat** on our disk in drive A: that contains data in the following format:

Columns 1   --> 20 Name
Columns 21 --> 32 Social Security Number
Columns 34--> 38 Pay Rate

A line of data might look like the following:

Easton, Holly A.____111-11-1111 25.75<ret>   // <ret> = <cr><lf>

The following program uses string functions and will display the data in the file at the screen.

```
//prog10_10.cpp Program to illustrate the string input file functions,
//               fgets( ) and fputs( ), in C.
#include <stdio.h>
```

```
#include <stdlib.h>
#define SIZE 40
int main( )
{
  FILE *fptr;
  char record[SIZE + 1];
  fptr = fopen("a:\employee.dat", "r");
  if (fptr == NULL) {
    printf("\n\Cannot open a:\employee.dat\n");
    exit(0);
  } // end if
  while (fgets(record, SIZE + 1, fptr) != NULL)
    fputs(record, stdout);                          // or puts(record)
  // end while
  fclose(fptr);
  return 0;
}
```

Note: In November of 1988, Robert Morris Jr., unleashed a self producing program (worm) throughout Internet. No data was destroyed, however some 6000 computers were rendered useless when they were shut down or were unable to function normally because they were overrun by the "worm" program. Among other things, Morris took advantage of the fact that much of the code was written using **gets( )**. The "worm" program provided input to **gets( )** that exceeded the array used and in this way was able to fill some storage beyond the array with offending code. Because of this virus, the code for the Internet program has been rewritten so that the function **gets( )** is replaced with **fgets( )**.

The following table describes the string input and output functions that are included in the C programming language and therefore are also available in C++.

Table 10.5: String Input / Output Functions in C.
==

gets( )	fgets( )
Uses only one argument, the array. Reads from stdin, standard input. Maximum number of characters to read in not specified. Stops when it reads the "newline" or "eof".	Uses 3 arguments, the array, the maximum number of characters to read, and the file pointer. Reads from the file specified by the file pointer.

Discards the "newline", does not store it in the array.
Adds a null terminator, '\0', at the end of the array.
Returns NULL when "eof" is read.

Stops when it reads the "newline", "eof", or the specified number of characters.
If the "newline" character is read, then it is stored in the array.
A null terminator is added to the end of each string.
Returns NULL when "eof" is read.

puts( )
Uses one argument, the array.
Writes the string in the array to standard output.
Does not write the '\0' to stdout
Does write a "newline".

fputs( )
Uses two arguments, the array and the file pointer.
Writes the string to the file specified by the file pointer.
Does not write the '\0' to the file.
Does not <u>add</u> a "newline" to the end of the string written to the file.

===

There are two additional functions that are available in C that are more specialized than **fgets( )** and **fputs( )**. These are the functions **fread( )** and **fwrite( )**. The function **fread( )** expects four arguments, the additional argument is the number of strings to be read. The following statement is used.

```
fread(array, size, count, pointer);
```

The array, however, must be large enough to hold **count** strings of length **size**. If a data file, **inventry.dat**, contains at most 500 inventory codes of the form

```
abc1234
```

with 5 codes per line, with exactly one blank between each code

```
abc1234 def2222 ghi7777 aaa3456 deh7654
```

then each line of codes would contain 40 characters counting the newline. The following program will read and display the codes from the file, one per line.

```cpp
//prog10_11.cpp Program to illustrate the use of the function
//                fread( ).
#include <stdio.h>
#include <stdlib.h>
int main( )
}
```

```
        FILE *fptr;
        char buffer[40];
        fptr = fopen("a:\inventry.dat", "r");
        if (!fptr) {
          printf("Error! *** - a:\inventry.dat cannot be opened!\n");
          exit(0);
        } // end if
        while (fread(buffer, 8, 5, fptr) != NULL) {
          for(int I = 0; I < 5; I++ )
            fwrite(buffer + I, 8, 1, stdout);
          // end for
        } // end while
        fclose(fptr);
        return 0;
      }
```

There are two other functions, **fscanf( )** and **fprintf( )** that are used in C for reading formatted data from and writing formatted data to files. These functions are used exactly like **scanf( )** and **printf( )**. The following program illustrates how to write a list of names, social security numbers, and payrates to a file.

```
      //prog10_12.cpp Program to illustrate the use of fprintf( ).
      #include <stdio.h>
      #include <stdlib.h>
      int main( )
      {
        FILE *fopen( ), *fptr;
        char *names[ ] = {"Easton, Holly", "Frye, Jennie", "Bozell, Clark"};
        char ssnums[] = {"111-11-1111", "222-22-2222", "333-33-3333"};
        float payrates[ ] = {25.50, 20.25, 23.75};
        fptr = fopen("a:\employee.dat", "w");
        if (!fptr) {
          printf("Error! *** - cannot open a:\employee.dat\n");
          exit(0);
        } // end if
        for(int I = 0; I < 3; I++)
          fprintf(fptr, "%-20s %11s %5.2f\n", names[i], ssnums[i], paryates[i]);
        // end for
        fclose(fptr);
        return 0;
      }
```

When we display the contents of the file **employee.dat** with the DOS command we have the following:

C:\>TYPE A:\EMPLOYEE.DAT<ret>
Easton, Holly_____111-11-1111 25.20
Frye, Jennie_____222-22-2222 20.25
Bozell, Clark_____333-33-3333 23.75
C:\>

10.8 - String Input & Output With Files Using C++

   In section 8.4 we discussed string input and output using the stream classes **cin** and **cout**. The member functions that were discussed were **get( )** and **getline( )** for string input and **put( )** for string output. These member functions can also be used with file streams. We illustrate how they are used by writing a program to read and display the data in the file **employee.dat** by reading one line at a time. The first program uses the member function **getline( )**.

```
//prog10_13.cpp Program to illustrate string input from a file using the
//                    stream member function getline( ).
#include <fstream.h>
#include <iostream.h>
#include <process.h>
int main( )
{
   char buffer[40];
   ifstream infptr;
   infptr.open("a:\employee.dat", ios::in);
   if(!infptr) {
     cout << "Error! *** - cannot open a:\employee.dat "
          << endl;
     exit(0);
   } // end if
   while (infptr.getline(buffer, 40) != EOF)
     cout << buffer << endl;
   // end while
   return 0;
}
```

If we want to use the member function **get( )** we would use the following block of code.

```
while (infptr.get(buffer, 40) != EOF)
   cout << buffer;
// end while
```

We would also want to define our buffer so that it can store one more character

```
          char buffer[41];
```

The reason for the difference is that when the functions encounter the newline character to terminate the input, the function **getline( )** discards the newline character and stores the null byte string terminator. The member function **get( )** stores the newline character followed by the null byte string terminator. This is the only difference between these two functions. We will ask the reader to write the version of **prog10_11.cpp** that uses the function **get( )** as one of the exercises.

We illustrate the use of the function **put( )** to write string data to a file by writing a program that will make a copy the file **a:\employee.dat**. The new file will be called **a:\emp2.dat**.

```cpp
//prog10_14.cpp Program to illustrate the use of the function
//              put( ) for file stream output.
#include <fstream.h>
#include <process.h>
int main( )
{
  char buffer[41];
  ifstream infptr;
  ofstream outfptr;
  infptr.open("a:\employee.dat", ios::in);
  if(!infptr) {
    cout << "Error! *** - cannot open a:\employee.dat "
         << endl;
    exit(0);
  } // end if
  outfptr.open(a:\emp2.dat", ios::out);
  if(!outfptr) {
    cout << Error! *** - cannot open a:\emp2.dat"
         << endl;
    exit(0)
  } // end if
  while(infptr.get(buffer, 40) != EOF)
    ourfptr.put(buffer);
  // end while
  infptr.close( );
  outfptr.close( );
  return 0;
}
```

10.9 Files as Parameters to Functions

In this section we will illustrate how files can be passed as parameters to functions. This is straight forward and simply requires that we declare the file parameter as a reference parameter to **ifstream** for input, **ofstream** for output, or **fstream** for either. The first function will be a function to print the contents of a text file to the screen. The file will be opened in the calling program. The function is written as follows:

```
//ptfile( ) Function to print the contents of a text file
//          to the screen.
void ptfile(ifstream &infptr1)
{
  char ch;
  while(infptr1) {
    infptr1.get(ch);
    cout << ch;
  } // end while
}
```

Note that the file pointer has to be passed by reference. The program to test this program would be the following:

```
//prog10_15.cpp Program to test the function ptfile( ).
#include <fstream.h>
#include <process.h>
void ptfile(ifstream &infptr1);
{
  ifstream infptr;
  infptr.open("a:\test.dat", ios::in);
  if (!infptr) {
    cout << "Error! *** - a:\test.dat cannot be opened."
         << endl;
    exit(0);
  } // end if
  ptfile(infptr);
  infptr.close( );
  return 0;
}
```

Output from this program was the following:

```
Now is the time
for all good men
and women to
```

come to the aid
of their country.

Try this: Write the function statement for a function that will copy file1
to file2. The function is called copyfile( ) and the files will be
opened in the calling function.

_____copyfile(_____

Try this: Declare two file pointers to be used in the calling program to test
the function copyfile( ).

_____stream _____;
_____stream _____;

The function **copyfile( )** that will make a copy of an existing text file can be written
as follows:

```
void copyfile(ifstream &infptr1, ofstream &outfptr)
{
  char ch;
  while (infptr) {
    infptr.get(ch);
    outfptr.put(ch);
  } // end while
  return;
}
```

The program to test the function **copyfile( )** would be the following. We will also use
the above function **ptfile( )** in order to see that the file was copied exactly.

```
//prog10_16.cpp Program to test the function copyfile( ).
#include <fstream.h>
#include <process.h>
void copyfile(ifstream &infptr1, ofstream &outfptr1);
void ptfile(ifstream &infptr2);
int main( )
{
  ifstream infptr;
  ofstream outfptr;
  infptr.open("a:\test.dat", ios::in);
  if (!infptr) {
    cout << "Error! *** - a:\test.dat cannot be opened."
         << endl;
```

418

```
      exit(0);
   } // end if
   ptfile(infptr);
   infptr.close( );
   infptr.open("a:\test.dat", ios::in);
   outfptr.open("a:\test2.dat", ios::out);
   if (!outfptr) {
      cout << "Error! *** - a:\test2.dat cannot be opened."
         << endl;
      exit(0);
   } // end if
   copyfile(infptr, outfptr);
   infptr.close( );
   outfptr.close( );
   infptr.open("a:\test2.dat", ios::in);
   if (!infptr) {
      cout << "Error! *** - a:\test2.dat cannot be opened."
         << endl;
      exit(0);
   } // end if
   ptfile(infptr);
   infptr.close( );
   return 0;
}
```

Output from this program was the following:

> Now is the time
> for all good men
> and women to
> come to the aid
> of their country.
>
> -----------------------------------
>
> Now is the time
> for all good men
> and women to
> come to the aid
> of their country.

> **Note:** When we pass files as parameters to functions, the file pointers must be passed by reference. The address of the file pointer is passed using:
>
> | | |
> |---|---|
> | ofstream &ofptr; | // output |
> | ifstream &ifptr; | // input |
> | fstream &fptr | // input and output |

10.10 - Command Line Parameters

Parameters can be used with any function in a program, including the **main( )** function. In this section we will describe how we can pass data to **main( )** which will allow us to write programs that use command line parameters. We have seen programs that use command line parameters. The programs from DOS, **type**, **copy**, and **rename** all use command line parameters. For example

    C:\>type a:\prog10_1.cpp

displays the contents of the file to the screen. The filename including the path is the only command line parameter. The statement

    C:\>copy a:\prog10_1.cpp c:\tcplus\prog101.cpp

copies the file from our disk in drive A to our hard drive and renames the file. This command uses two command line parameters. After we have finished this section, we will be able to write programs that can be executed in the same way.

Using parameters with **main( )** is not difficult, it is done exactly as we have described above by typing the data that is to be passed following the program name on the command line used to begin program execution. The program **main( )** has to be modified as follows:

    int main(int argc, char *argv[ ])

The first argument, **argc**, returns the number of command line parameters including the program name. The second argument, **argv[ ]**, returns an array of pointers to the list of command line parameters. These are the addresses of where these parameters are stored as strings. The next program illustrates how we use these command line parameters that are passed to **main( )** by simply displaying them at the screen.

> **Note**: The parameter names argc and argv[ ] are reserved words and cannot be changed by the programmer.

```
// prog10_17.cpp - Program to display the command line
//                     arguments.
#include <iostream.h>
int main(int argc, char *argv[ ])
{
   cout << "Number of arguments = "
        << argc << endl;
   for(int I = 0; I < argc; I++)
     cout << "Argument " << I
          << " = " << argv[i]
          << endl;
   // end for
   return 0;
}
```

The following is an example of output from this program.

```
C:>prog10_14 one two three<ret>
Number of arguments = 4
Argument 0 = prog10_14
Argument 1 = one
Argument 2 = two
Argument 3 = three
```

The next program prints the contents of a file to the screen. It is a revision of **prog10_1.cpp** and is executed exactly like the MS-DOS program **type**. The program is called **dispfile** and would be used with the following statement.

```
C:\>dispfile a:\prog10_15.cpp<ret>
```

```
//prog10_18.cpp The executable file is called dispfile.exe.
//                Program to display the contents of a text file at
//                the screen using command line parameters.
#include <fstream.h>
#include <process.h>
int main(int argc, char *argv[ ] )
{
   ifstream infile;
   char ch;
   if (argc != 2) {
     cout << "Error! format C:\>dispfile filename<ret> "
          << endl;
     exit(0);
   } // end if
```

```
        infile.open(argv[1], ios::in);
        if (!infile) {
          cout << "Error - Cannot open "
                << argv[1] << endl;
          exit(0);
        } // end if
        while (infile.get(ch) != 0)
          cout << ch;
        // end while
        fclose(infile);
        return 0;
      }
```

It is easy to modify the above program so that it sends the contents of the file to the printer. We would replace the appropriate code with the following:

```
        ofstream outfile;
        outfile.open("LPT1", ios::in);
        while(infile.get(ch) != 0)
          outfile.put(ch);
        // end while
```

We will ask the reader to write this program as one of the exercises.

10.11 - Random Access Files Using C

Sequential access files are inappropriate for so-called "instant access" applications in which a particular record of information must be located immediately. Airline reservation systems, student record systems, banking systems, etc. are examples of such applications. In order to get this kind of access we use random access files. These files are usually files of records where each record can be accessed directly without having to search through other records in order to get to it. Creating a **random access file** allows us to read or write any piece of data without having to access all of the data that precedes it as we did with a sequential access file. We can instruct a program to move directly to a specific data item. Each data item in a random access file is usually a **record** which is analogous to a **structure** in C and C++. A record is a collection of one or more data items that are referred to as **fields**. The fields of a record correspond to the members of a structure. Generally, we create a structure in a program that corresponds to the record of data in the file. We can then store data in the structure and write it to the file or read one record of data from the file and store it in the structure.

A variety of techniques can be used to create a random access file, however the

422

simplest technique is to require that all records in the file be of the same size. Using records of a fixed size makes it easy for a program to calculate the exact location of any record using the record number, **key**, and the record size. The following figure illustrates how C++ views a random access file of records where each record is 100 bytes long.

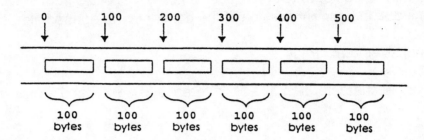

Another way of viewing a random access file is to think on it as a large array of records on the disk. In an array we can access any particular item without having to start at the beginning. We can view a random access file in the same way, accessing any particular record in the file.

As with sequential files, we must open a file for random access before we can read any data from or write any data to the file. We can use the access modes that we discussed in section 10.2, "r+", "w+", and "a+". The "+" on each of these modes indicates that we can both read from and write to the file after it has been opened successfully. The modes, "w+" and "a+" both create a new file if the specified file does not exist, while the mode "r+" returns an error. The statement to open an existing file for random access would be the following:

        fptr = fopen("filename", "r+");

Try this: Write the statements to define a file pointer and open the
        file empdata.dat on our disk in drive A for random access.

        _____

        _____

The functions that we use for reading from and writing to a random access file are the functions **fread( )** and **fwrite( )**. The functions are used as follows:

        fread(buffer, size, number, fptr);   fwrite(buffer, size, number, fptr);

where

        buffer   ~   Address of the storage area for the data read.
        size   ~   Number of bytes of each record of data to be read.

number	~	Number of records of data to be read.
fptr	~	File pointer.

These functions do not expect any particular type of data nor do they do any conversions. They simply attempt to read or write the requested number of bytes from the file referenced by, **fptr**, beginning at the current position of the pointer in the opened file. For example,

    fread(&ch, sizeof(ch), 1, fptr);

would read a single character from the file referenced by **fptr**, and stores it at **ch**. The statement

    fwrite(&num, sizeof(int), 1, fptr);

would write the two bytes, (size of one integer), stored at **num**, to the file referenced by **fptr**.

Try this: Write the block of code to read 80 characters from the file referenced by **fptr** and store it in the array, **buffer**, defined with the statement
char buffer[80];

_____

_____

When a file is opened for use in a program, the C programming language keeps track of where the program is reading from or writing to by use of what is also called a file pointer. This is a different file pointer than the one that we use to reference the file in the program. When the file is opened for reading, **"r"** and **"r+"**, or writing, **"w"** and **"w+"**, the file pointer points to the first byte of the file. When the file is opened for appending, **"a"** and **"a+"**, the file pointer points to the end of the file. For random access we need to be able to move to a particular byte of a file and this is done with the function **fseek( )**. The statement to use this function is the following:

    fseek(fptr, offset, start);

where

fptr	~	File pointer.
offset	~	Long integer specifying the number of bytes to move the file pointer. Positive means forward and negative means backwards.

424

start ~ Position in the file to move offset bytes.
　　　　　　　0 = Beginning of the file.
　　　　　　　1 = Current Position.
　　　　　　　2 = End of the file.

In ANSII C there are constants defined in **stdio.h** for each of these starting positions.

> **SEEK_SET** = 0 = Beginning of the file.
> **SEEK_CUR** = 1 = Current position.
> **SEEK_END** = 2 = End of the file.

The statements

> fseek(fptr, (long) 0, 0);　　or　　fseek(fptr, (long) 0, SEEK_SET);

positions the file pointer at the first byte of the file referenced by fptr. The statements

> fseek(fptr, (long) 0, 2);　　or　　fseek(fptr, (long) 0, SEEK_END);

positions the file pointer at the end of the file. This is not the same as the last byte of data in the file. In order to position the file pointer at the last byte of data in the file we would use the statement

> fseek(fptr, (long) -1, SEEK_END);

A useful function is the function **ftell( )** that returns the current byte position of the file pointer from the beginning of the file as a **long int**. The statement

> position = ftell(fptr);

stores the current number of the byte in the file that is being pointed to by the file pointer.

Try this: Write the statements to position the file pointer at the end of the file and then compute the size of the file using ftell( ).

> long int size;
>
> _____
>
> _____

The following block of code can also be used to count the number of characters in a file.

```
count = 0;
fseek(fptr, (long) 0, SEEK_SET);
while(ch = fget(ftr))
```

```
        count++;
    // end while
```

This next block of code would print the last 100 characters of a file, backwards, to the screen.

```
    fseek(fptr, (long) -1, SEEK_END);
    for(int I = 1; I <= 100; I++) {
        ch = fget(fptr);
        putchar(ch);
        fseek(fptr, (long)-2, SEEK_CUR);
    } // end for
```

Try this: Use the code from the previous Try this: and write the block of code
that will print the entire contents of a file backwards to the screen.
int size;
char ch;

_____

_____

_____

_____

_____

_____

_____

_____

        Most applications use records of data that are stored in a random access file. These records are made up of fields that contain the different types of data that are to be stored in each record. In C and C++, records of data correspond to structures and the fields of the record correspond to the members of the structure. Consider the structure that we used in Chapter 9 for a collection of employee data. We used the following structure definition:

```
struct empinfo {
        char name[21];
        char ssnum[12];
        int age;
        float pay rate;
};

struct empinfo emp1;
```

If we have data stored in the structure, **emp1**, then the following statement would write that record to the end of file that has been opened for random access.

426

```
fseek(fptr, (long) 0, SEEK_END);
fwrite(&emp1, sizeof(empinfo), 1, fptr);
```

The next block of code would read the 5th record from the file and store it in the structure, emp1.

```
fseek(fptr, (long) 4, SEEK_SET);          // File pointer at beginning of 5th record
fread(&emp1, sizeof(empinfo), 1, fptr);
```

We will discuss these ideas in more detail in section 10.11 when we discuss random access files using C++. Note that the address of the structure is expected as the first parameter of **fread( )**.

10.12 Random Access Files Using C++

In this section we will study how we use random access files in C++. We will discuss the same ideas that we did in section 10.10 using C. In addition we will show how we can create a file of records and write functions that will allow us to work with the file of records that has been created.

Using C++, we can use any of the read access modes that we used for sequential files, such as (**ios::in**), if all that we want to do is read the data in the file. However, if we want to modify any of the data in the file, then we have to use additional modes. The following table contains the file access modes in C++.

Table 10.6: File Access Modes in C++

Mode	Description
app	Open file for appending
ate	Open file and seek the end of the file
in	Open file for reading
out	Open file for writing
binary	Open file in binary mode
trunc	Discard contents, if file exists
nocreate	If file doesn't exist, do not create
noreplace	If file exists, open fails unless we are appending or seeking end of file

If we want to write a program to create a file, the only thing that we want to do is write records to the file. We would use the following open statement.

fptr.open("filename", ios::out);

If we want to create a file and then be able to write records to the file and in addition read a record from the file, change the data, and then write the record back to the file, then we would need to use two of the access modes. We would use this statement to open the file.

fptr.open("filename", ios::in | ios::out);

The operator, |, is called the **bitwise OR operator.** We have used this operator before with the **cout** member function, **setf( )** and with the stream manipulator **setiosflags()**. We use this operator anytime that we want to open a file for two or more access modes. If we have a binary file that we want to open so that we can both read data from the file and write data to the file, then we would use the statement.

fptr.open("filename", ios::in | ios::out | ios::binary);

Moving to a Particular Record

When a file is opened for use in a program, C++ also keeps track of where the program is reading from or writing to by use of a file pointer. When the file is opened for reading or writing, the file pointer points to the first byte of the file. When the file is opened for appending, the file pointer points to the end of the file. In C++ we use the function

seekg( )

to move the file pointer to a particular byte of a random access file. The format for using the function, **seekg( )**, is

fptr.seekg(longnum, position);

where

longnum	Number of bytes to be skipped, must be a long integer.
position	Any one of three positions

ios::beg	Beginning of file
ios::cur	Current file position
ios::end	End of file

This member function, **seekg( )**, is defined in **fstream.h**. The following statement can be

428

used to position the file pointer at the beginning of the file.

```
fptr.seekg(0L, ios::beg);
```

We must use 0L rather than 0 so that we match the prototype for **seekg( )**. We discussed using the L suffix on numeric constants in section 2.6.

Try this: Write the statement to position the file pointer at
the end of the file.

```
fptr.seekg(_____
```

If we want to position the file pointer at the 100th byte of the file, then we would use the following statement

```
fptr.seekg(100L, ios::beg);
```

We will illustrate the use of the above ideas by writing a program to print the contents of a file first to the screen and then to the printer by reading the file twice.

```
//prog10_19.cpp Program to print the contents of a file to the
//                screen and then to the printer by reading the
//                contents of the file twice.
#include <fstream.h>
#include <stdio.h>
#include <process.h>
int main( )
{
    ifstream inptr;              // file pointer
    ofstream scrptr;             // screen pointer
    ofstream prtptr;             // printer pointer
    char ch;
    inptr.open("a:\prog10_4.cpp", ios::in);
    if (!inptr) {
        cout << "Error! Can't open a:\prog10_4.cpp" << endl;
        exit(0);
    } // end if
    scrptr.open("CON", ios::out);
    while (inptr.get(ch)
        scrptr << ch;
    // end while
    scrptr.close( );
    inptr.seekg(0L, ios::beg);
    prtptr.open("LPT1", ios::out);
    while(inptr.get(ch))
```

429

```
        prtptr << ch;
      // end while
      prtptr.close( );
      inptr.close( );
      return 0;
    }
```

We could have used standard output to print the file to the screen rather than using a file pointer.

```
      while(inptr.get(ch))
        cout << ch;
      // end while
```

However, we wanted to emphasize the use of file pointers. In addition, we could have closed the file after we had printed the contents to the screen and then opened it again before we sent the contents to the printer.

```
      inptr.close( );
      inptr.open("a:\prog10_4.cpp", ios::in);
```

Using **seekg( )** to position the file pointer at the beginning of the file is more efficient.

If our file consists of records where each record is a structure of type **empinfo**, then we would need to do additional calculations to move the file pointer to a particular record. If we want to move the file pointer to the 100th record of the file, then we can use the **sizeof( )** function to compute the number of bytes in each record. We can then multiply this number of bytes by 99L to calculate the total number of bytes that we have to move the file pointer. In order to get to the 100th record, we have to move past the first 99. Thus, we would use the statement

```
      fptr.seekg((99L * sizeof(struct empinfo)), ios::beg);
```

If we use the statement

```
      fptr.seekg(0L, ios::end);
```

to position the file pointer at the end of the file, then this is not the last character in the file. In order to move the file pointer to the last character in the file, we would have to use the statement

```
      fptr.seekg(-1L, ios::end);
```

The statement

```
        fptr.seekg(-1L, ios::cur);
```

moves the file pointer back one position.

Suppose that we want to move backwards through a file one character at a time. We would first have to position the file pointer at the last character of the file with the statement:

```
        fptr.seekg(-1L, ios::end);
```

Now since each read of one character moves the file pointer ahead one position, in order to move backwards through a file, we would have to follow each read with the statement to move the file pointer back two characters.

```
        fptr.seekg(-2L, ios::cur);
```

The following block of code would print the last 100 characters of a file to the screen backwards:

```
        fptr.seekg(0L, ios::end);              // pointer at end of file
        for(int I = 1; I <= 100; I++) {
          fptr.seekg(-1L, ios::cur);           // move file pointer back one character
          fptr.get(ch);                        // read character and move to next char.
          cout << ch;                          // print character
          fptr.seekg(-1L, ios::cur);           // move file pointer back to printed char.
        } // end for
```

This can be simplified

```
        fptr.seekg(-1L, ios::end);
        for(int I = 1; I <= 100; I++) {
          fptr >> ch;
          cout << ch;
          fptr.seekg(-2L, ios::cur);
        } // end for
```

> **Note:** The member function, **seekp( )**, is defined in the header file,. **ostream.h**, and can be used to perform the same operation as the function **seekg( )**.

The C++ language also contains two member functions that can be used to return the current position of file pointer. These member functions are

tellg( )   and   tellp( )

The following statement returns the position of the file pointer and assigns it to the long integer variable, **position**.

```
position = fptr.tellg( );
```

The following block of code would count the number of characters in the file.

```
fptr.seekg(0L, ios::end);
size = fptr.tellg( );
```

We will ask the reader to write a function to compute the size of any file as one of the exercises.

Try this: Write the code that will count the number of characters in a text file pointed to by fptr and then print the file backwards to the screen.

```
fptr.seekg(_____
count = _____
size = _____
fptr.seekg(_____
for(_____

      _____
      _____
   _____
} // end for
```


Creating a file of records.

If we want to create a file of records, we can either read the data from a text file that we have created with an editor, or we can enter the data from the keyboard. The following block of code can be used to create a file containing 5 records of employee data.

```
struct empinfo {
       char name[21];
       char ssnum[12];
       int age;
       float pay rate;
};
struct empinfo emp1;
char ret;
```

432

```
fstream fptr;
fptr.open("a:\employee.dat", ios::out);
if(!fptr) {
   cout << "Error! *** Cannot open a:\employee.dat" << endl;
   exit(0);
} // end if
for(int I = 1; I <= 5; I++) {
   cout << "Enter a name: "
   cin.getline(emp1.name, 20);
   cout << "Enter a social security number: ";
   cin.getline(emp1.ssnum, 11);
   cout << "Enter an age: ";
   cin >> emp1.age;
   cout << "Enter a pay rate: "
   cin >> emp1.pay rate;
   cin.get(ret);
   fptr.write((char *)&emp1, sizeof(empinfo));
} // end for
fptr.close( );
```

Now that we have a file of records, the following block of code would read the third record from the file and store it in the structure **emp1**.

```
fptr.seekg(2L*sizeof(empinfo), ios::beg);
fptr.read((char *)&emp1, sizeof(empinfo);
```

We use

```
2L*sizeof(empinfo)
```

since we must move past the first two records in order to point to the third record and the **L** is used to cast the integer as a long integer so that the types will match.

The following function will read the **count** employee record from the file referenced by the specified file pointer and store in the indicated structure.

```
void reademp(fstream &fptr1, long int count1, struct empinfo emp1)
{
   fptr1.seekg((count1 - 1) * sizeof(empinfo), ios:: beg);
   fptr1.read((char *) &emp1, sizeof(empinfo));
   return;
}
```

Try this: Write the companion function, **writeemp( )**, that will write the data stored in the indicated structure to the count record of the file referenced by the given file pointer.

```
void writeemp(_____
{
        _____
        _____
      _____
}
```

We will ask the reader to write programs to test these two functions as exercises.

10.13 Other File I/0 C++ Functions

The C++ language contains other disk I/O functions that we might find useful in some of our programming applications. We include a discussion of these functions in this section for completeness. The function

    read(array, count)

reads the count number of bytes from the specified file and stores them in the array. This function is a buffered I/O function. This function enables us to read as much data as we wish to store in an array with a single function call. For example, if we have five records of employee data stored in the file, **empdata.dat**, on our disk in drive A, then the following block of code would read all five records and store them in an array in our program.

```
struct empinfo {
        char name[21];
        char ssnum[12];
        int age;
        float pay rate;
} ;
struct empinfo emps[5];
fstream fptr;
fptr.open("a:\empdata.dat", ios::in | ios::out);
if(!fptr) {
   cout << "Error! *** a:\empdata.dat - cannot be opened." << endl;
   exit(0);
} // end if
fptr.read(emps, 5L * sizeof(empinfo));
```

This is a very powerful function. If we have 500 employee records in a file on our disk, then the **read( )** function can be used to read all 500 records from the file and store it in an array for use in a program with a single statement.

The function, **write( )**, is the mirror image of the function, **read( )**. It is used to write an array of records, (structures), to a file. The statement

        fptr.write(fptr, 5L * sizeof(empinfo));

would write the five records to the file that had been opened and is referenced by the file pointer, **fptr**.

Try this: Write the block of code that will open a file, and add the
        five records of data stored in emps[ ] to the end of the file.

        _____
        _____
        _____

The following function would read count records of data from the file and store them in and array in the calling program or function.

        void readrecs(fstream &fptr1, struct empinfo emps1[ ], int count1)
        {
          fptr1.read(emps1, count1(L) * sizeof(empinfo));
          return;
        }

Try this: Write the corresponding function, writerecs( ), that will write
        count records stored in an array at the end of a file.

        void writerecs(_____
        {
          fptr2.seekg(_____
          _____
          _____
        }

The two member functions, **read( )** and **write( )**, are defined in the header file, **fstream.h**. We will ask the reader to write programs to test the two functions, **readrecs()** and **writerecs()** as exercises.

The next function, **remove( )**, erases the specified file from a disk and returns the value 0, if it was erased successfully or -1 if an error occurred. This function is defined in the header file, **stdio.h**. The following statement would be used to erase the file, **prog10_4.bak**, from our disk in drive A.

```
remove("a:\prog10_4.bak");
```

The following block of code would request the name of a file from the user and erase the file from the specified disk. It will print a message indicating whether or not the file was successfully deleted.

```
char filename[12];
int okay;
cout <<"Input the name of the file: "
cin >> filename;
okay = remove(filename);
if (okay == 0) {
   cout << "The file " << filename
        << " was deleted. " << endl;
} else {
   cout << "Error! *** " << filename
        << " was not deleted. " << endl;
} // end if
```

We will ask the reader to use this block of code and write a function that will delete the specified file. This will be done as one of the exercises. We will also ask the reader to write a program to test this function as one of the exercises.

10.14 - Converting C to C++

In this section we will review what we have discussed in the previous sections in this Chapter by discussing how we can convert programs that use file access and have been written in C, to programs written in C++. Recall that the following block of code is used to declare a file pointer in C:

```
#include <stdio.h>

FILE *fptr;
```

The block of code to open the file, **filename.ext**, check to see if it has been opened, and if not exit the program is the following:

```
fptr = fopen("filename.ext", "r");
if(fptr == NULL)  {
  printf("Cannot open file: filename.ext\n");
  exit(0);
}  // end if
```

The function, **exit( )**, is defined in the header file, **stdlib.h**. The block of code to read from the file, until end-of-file, is the following:

```
while((ch = fgetc(fptr)) != EOF) {
  ...;
  ...;

} // end while
```

The file is closed with the statement:

```
fclose(fptr);
```

Using C++, we need to include the header files:

```
#include <fstream.h>
#include <process.h>
```

The file pointer is defined with the statement

```
ifstream  fptr1;
```

for input, and

```
ofstream  fptr2;
```

for output. We can open the file, **filename.ext**, for input, check to see if it has been opened, and if not exit the program with the code:

```
fptr1.open("filename.ext", ios::in);
if(!fptr1) {
  cout << "Error! *** filename.ext cannot be opened" << endl;
  exit(0);
} // end if
```

We can read from the file, until end-of-file, with the code:

```
        while(fptr1.get(ch) != 0)  {
            ...;
            ...;

        } // end while
```

and we can close the file with the statement:

```
        fptr1.close( );
```

Try this: The following program, written in C, displays the contents of a file to the screen. The filename is input by the user from the keyboard. Write the C++ version of this program.

```
#include <stdio.h>
#include <stdlib.h>
int main( )
{
    FILE  *fptr;
    char filename[30];
    char ch;
    printf("Input the filename: ");
    gets(filename);
    fptr = fopen("filename", "r");
    if(fptr == NULL) {
        printf("Error! *** Cannot open %s\n", filename);
        exit(0);
    } /* end if */
    while(( ch = fgetc(fptr)) != EOF)
        putchar(ch);
    /*end while */
    fclose(fptr);
    return 0;
}
```

_____
_____
_____
_____
_____
_____
_____
_____
_____
_____
_____
_____
_____
_____
_____
_____
_____
_____
_____
_____
_____

10.15 - Summary

In this Chapter we discussed how files are handled in both C and C++. We discussed how we can open a file, check to see if the file has been opened and if not exit the program, read data from or write data to a file, and close the file before ending the program. We studied how we can read characters from and write characters to a file in C and also in C++. We discussed what is meant by a **sequential file**. We illustrated how we can treat the printer as a file so that we can send data to the printer. We discussed how we can read and write strings from and to a file using either C or C++. We discussed what is meant by a **random access file** and how we can read a particular record from a file or write data to a particular record of a file using either C or C++.

We discussed how we can use files as parameters to functions and how we can write programs that use command line parameters to furnish the file names to a program. The C and C++ programming languages are probably the easiest languages to use to write programs that make use of command line parameters.

Finally, we illustrated how we can convert programs that use file access and that are written in C to programs that are written in C++.

10.16 - Questions

10.1 What are the two kinds of disk file access?

10.2 How do sequential access files differ from random access files?

10.3 What are the three file operations that we can perform on sequential access files?

10.4 What do we need to do before we can access any file?

10.5 What should we do after we have finished with a file?

10.6 What does it mean to append data to a file?

10.7 What is the file pointer used for?

10.8 Explain the difference between the mode "r" and the mode "r+".

10.9 Explain the difference between the mode "w" and the mode "w+".

10.10 Explain the difference between the mode "a" and the mode "a+".

10.11 Explain the difference between the mode "a" and the mode "ab".

10.12 How can we tell whether a file has been opened properly?

10.13 What happens if we open a file for reading and the file does not exist?

10.14 What happens if we open a file for writing and the file does exist?

10.15 What happens if we open a file for appending data and the file does not exist?

10.16 How can we tell when we have reached the end of the file reading data?

10.17 Why do we want to use files in a program?

10.18 How might we use arg[0] in a program?

10.19 What is the difference between a record and a structure?

10.20 What do we mean by a field and what do we mean by a member when we are discussing records and structures?

10.21 What function do we use in C to position the file pointer at a specified byte? Where is this function defined?

10.22 What functions can we use in C++ to position the file pointer at a specified byte? Where are these functions defined?

10.23 What function do we use in C to return the position of the file pointer? Where is this function defined? How do we use this function?

10.24 What functions can we use in C++ to return the position of the file pointer? Where are these functions defined? How do we use these functions?

10.17 - Exercises

10.1 What is the error in the following:

```
FILE fileptr;
fptr = fopen("a:test.dat", "a+");
```

10.2 What is the error in the following:

```
FILE *fptr;
fptr = fopen("a:sometestdata.dat", "r");
fclose(*fptr);
```

10.3 What is the error in the following:

```
FILE *fptr;
int c;
fptr = fopen("out.dat", "r");
while ((c = getchar( ) ) != EOF)
   fputc(fptr, c);
// end while
fclose("out.dat");
```

10.4 Fill in the blank to check correctly for end-of-file.

```
while(fgets(record, 50, fptr) != _____)
```

10.5 What is the maximum number of bytes read by **fgets()** in exercise 10.4?

10.6 What is wrong with the following:

```
fptr.open(filename, ios::in);
if (!fptr) {
   cout << "\n\n*** The file does not exist ***\n";
   exit(0);
} // end if
while (fptr.get(ch)) {
   cout >> ch;
} // end while
fptr.close( );
```

10.7 What is printed if the command line is

```
C:\>prog20 one two three four<ret>
```

when we execute

```
cout << argc << endl
     << argv[4] << end
     << argv[2] << endl;
```

10.8 Write the version of **prog10.1** to allow the user to input the filename from the keyboard.

10.9 Write the program to test the function reademp( ) from section 10.11.

10.10 Write the program to test the function writeemp( ) from section 10.11.

10.11 Write the program to test the function readrecs( ) from section 10.12.

10.12 Write the program to test the function writerecs( ) from section 10.12.

10.13 Write a function to read the characters from a file and change all of uppercase characters to lowercase. The filename should be a parameter.

10.14 Write a program to test the function from exercise 10.13.

10.15 Write a function to count the number of non alphabetic characters in a file. The file should be a parameter to the function.

10.16 Write a function to test the function from exercise 10.15.

10.17 Write a program to use the function **getempdata( )** from section 9.4. to create a file containing as many records of data as the user wishes to input from the keyboard. Use a do - while programming structure.

10.18 Write a function **erasefile( )** that will remove a file from a disk. The code was discussed in section 10.13

10.19 Write a program to test the function **erasefile( )** from exercise 10.18.

10.20 Write a program that will use the function **erasefile( )** and remove the file from the disk that is specified on the command line.

CHAPTER 11

Introduction to Object Oriented Programming

11.1 Introduction

C++ has added many new capabilities to traditional C compilers. However, the most important addition in C++ is the ability to do what is called *object oriented programming.* OOP (object oriented programming) has in recent years become one of the most important aspects of modern programming. To the traditional programmer object oriented programming may at first seem rather strange, but it is a very powerful approach to programming. In this chapter we will use examples to lead to an understanding of this very important and modern approach to programming.

After completing this chapter, the programmer should be able to:

1, Understand encapsulation and data privacy.

2. Develop basic class declarations.

3. Write class functions.

4. Write class constructors.

5. Use derived classes and inheritance.

6. Develop overloaded constructors.

7. Develop overloaded operators.

8. Use pointers to objects.

9. Understand abstraction.

11.2 What is Object Oriented Programming?

In traditional programming we tend to think of the data as being separate from the functions which operate on the data. Too often, we concentrate so heavily on writing the functions that we tend to ignore the extreme importance of the data. In object oriented programming we not only emphasize the importance of the data but we actually unite the data together with the functions which operate on that data. That is, we treat the data and the operations on the data as a unified *object.* This binding together of data and the operations on that data is called *encapsulation.*

For example, an inventory object could consist of the inventory data together with the operations we would normally perform on that data. These operations could include the addition of a new record, the modification of a record, the deletion of a record, etc. Another example of an object could be a terminal together with the operations on the terminal. These operations could include clearing the screen, positioning the cursor, writing data to the screen, etc.

Now that we have a general idea of what OOP means, let us see how we can implement it in C++. As a very simple example, suppose our data consists only of a name. For operations, assume that we would like to be able to input the name from a keyboard and also to be able to display the name on the screen. In C++, we can declare an object type as a *class,* or a *structure,* or a *union.* The class declaration is the most general, and we will use it in our example. (We will discuss structure and union declarations a little later.)

We will declare a class called **OneNameClass**.

```
// Header file -- ONENAME.H
class OneNameClass
{
  private:
    char name[60];
  public:
    void getname(void);
    void displayname(void);
};
```

In this class declaration, we have declared **name** to be an array of characters. We have also declared the two functions, **getname()**, and **displayname()**. Thus, our new class type includes both the data and also the functions which can operate on that data. It is very important to note that the above is just like a structure or type declaration. That is, we have described the structure of a class called **OneNameClass**, but we have not as yet allocated any memory for a specific object of this data type. We could do this with the following:

OneNameClass myname;

This declares **myname** to be an *instance* of **OneNameClass** and allocates memory for it. The word **public** which precedes the two functions is used to make the two functions public to the main program and other functions. However, the word **private** preceding the declaration for the **name** array indicates that **name** cannot be accessed by other functions. This means that no other function can directly access the **name** array. Thus, the only way to affect the **name** array is by calling either the **getname()** or the **displayname()** function. Why would we want to declare **name** in this way? Well, by making **name** private, it is completely protected except for access by the designated functions in **OneNameClass** (or as we will discuss later, a **friendly** function). Let us save the above declaration in the header file, **ONENAME.H**.

So far we have declared the two functions, **getname()** and **displayname()**, but as yet we have not written the actual code for the functions. Thus, for our next step, we will write the actual code for the two functions and save in a file called **ONENAME.CPP**.

```
// Coding for the functions in onenameclass -- In file ONENAME.CPP
#include <stdio.h>
#include "onename.h"


//******************************************************************
// getname - Function in class OneNameClass to allow the user to
//           input a name from the keyboard.
//******************************************************************
void OneNameClass::getname(void)
{
  printf("Enter the name: ");
  gets(name);
}
//******************************************************************
// displayname - Function in class OneNameClass to display the
//               name on the console.
//******************************************************************
void OneNameClass::displayname(void)
{
  printf("The name is %s\n",name);
}
```

Notice that in each function definition, the name of the function is preceded by

OneNameClass::

The :: operator is called a *scope resolution operator.* Since there can be other functions in other classes with the same name, then **OneNameClass::** tells the compiler that we are defining the function which was declared in **OneNameClass**.

Now that we have written the code for the two functions, let us now turn our attention to writing a very simple test program to try out our new class.

```
// Test program for class OneNameClass -- File TSTCL1A.CPP
#include "onename.h"
int main(void)
{
  OneNameClass myname;
  myname.getname();
  myname.displayname();
  return(0);
}
```

Notice that we declared the return type for **main** as **int**. This is how it is prototyped in C++. Then at the end of the program, we returned a value of 0 to indicate a good return. The **void** in the parentheses after the function name means there are no parameters for function **main**. The use of the word **void** is optional in C++; that is, empty parentheses in C++ declares that there are no parameters for the function just as **void** does.

We have defined **myname** to be an instance (or object) of type **OneNameClass**. Then,

```
        myname.getname();
```

calls the function **getname()** in object **myname** to allow the user to input Name. Then,

```
        myname.displayname();
```

calls the function **displayname()** in object **myname** to display **name**. Notice that each function is called by preceding the function name with the object name. Thus, we specify which object and which function we are calling. Also, notice that we do <u>not</u> directly reference the private variable **name** at all.

To test the program, we can create and compile a project file consisting of **TSTCL1A.CPP** and **ONENAME.CPP**.

In this example, we have used more than one file. However, if so desired we could have written everything in one file as follows:

446

```
// File TSTCL1B.CPP
#include <stdio.h>
class OneNameClass
{
  private:
    char name[60];
  public:
    void getname(void);
    void displayname(void);
};
int main(void)
{
  OneNameClass myname;
  myname.getname();
  myname.displayname();
  return(0);
}
//*****************************************************************
// getname - Function in class OneNameClass to allow the user to
//           input a name from the keyboard.
//*****************************************************************
void OneNameClass::getname(void)
{
  printf("Enter the name: ";
  gets(name);
}
//*****************************************************************
// displayname - Function in class OneNameClass to display the
//               name on the console.
//*****************************************************************
void OneNameClass::displayname(void)
{
  printf("The name is %s\n",name);
}
```

However, in larger programs the use of separate files provides us with several advantages. Smaller separate files are certainly easier to edit. Also, if we use a project file in Turbo C++, then recompilations need only be done on changed files. In addition, the use of separate files emphasizes one of the advantages of object oriented programming. This advantage is the reusability of code. Once we have developed a class, it is normally possible to use it in a wide variety of applications.

As mentioned previously, by declaring the variable **name** to be private, we are protecting it from being changed by other parts of the program. Another important advantage of object oriented programming is this ability to protect or hide data from other functions and operations throughout the rest of the program.   In our example, the only functions which have access to the variable, **name**, are **getname()** and **displayname()** which are declared as part of the class. Thus, the only way we can access **name** is by using either one of the functions.

However, if so desired, it is possible to declare the variable, **name**, to be public as follows:

```cpp
//  File TSTCL1C.CPP
#include <stdio.h>
class OneNameClass
{
  public:
    char name[60];
  public:
    void getname(void);
    void displayname(void);
};
int main(void)
{
  OneNameClass myname;
  myname.getname();
  myname.displayname();
  printf("The value of name is %s\n",myname.name);
  return(0);
}
//*****************************************************************
// getname - Function in class OneNameClass to allow the user to
//           input a Name from the keyboard.
//*****************************************************************
void OneNameClass::getname(void)
{
  printf("Enter the name: ";
  gets(name);
}
//*****************************************************************
// displayname - Function in class OneNameClass to display the
//               name on the console.
//*****************************************************************
void OneNameClass::displayname(void)
{
  printf("The name is %s\n",name);
}
```

Notice that in function **main**, we can now directly access **name** with

        myname.name

However, making variable, **name**, public now allows it to be accessed and changed throughout the program just like a normal global variable. Thus, we have lost one of the advantages of OOP.

Now suppose that instead of just a single name, we decide that we want our object to contain an array of names. To accomplish this, we will declare a class type called **NamesArrayClass** as follows:

```
// Header file -- NAMES1.H
class NamesArrayClass
{
  private:
    char namesarray[50][60];
    int counter;
  public:
    void initcounter(void);
    void getname(void);
    void displayallnames(void);
};
```

We have declared the variable, **namesarray**, to consist of a two-dimensional array of **char** elements. We interpret the declaration to mean 50 strings of 60 characters each. We have also declared an **int** variable called **counter**. The variable, **counter**, will be used to store the exact number of names entered into the array.

Also, we have declared three functions, **initcounter()**, **getname()**, and **displayallnames()**. The **initcounter()** function will initialize variable, **counter**, to 0. The function **getname()** will allow the user to input one name from the keyboard into the array, **namesarray**. It will also increment the value for variable, **counter**. The **displayallnames()** function will display all names which have been entered into the array.

```
// Coding for the functions in NamesArrayClass -- In file NAMES1.CPP
#include "names1.h"
#include <stdio.h>
//*************************************************************
// initcounter - Function in class NamesArrayClass to
//               initialize variable, counter, to 0.
//*************************************************************
```

```
void NamesArrayClass::initcounter(void)
{
  counter = 0;
}
//**************************************************************
// getname - Function in class NamesArrayClass to allow the user
//           to enter one name from the keyboard into array,
//           namesarray.
//**************************************************************
void NamesArrayClass::getname(void)
{
  printf("Enter a name: ");
  gets(namesarray[counter]);
  counter++;
}
//**************************************************************
// displayallnames - Function in class NamesArrayClass to
//                   display all names in array, namesarray.
//**************************************************************
void NamesArrayClass::displayallnames(void)
{
  for(int j = 0; j < counter; j++)
  printf("%s\n",namesarray[j]);
}
```

Now, let us write a small test program.

```
//  Test program for NamesArrayClass - File TESTCL2.CPP
#include "names1.h"
int main(void)
{
  NamesArrayClass mynames;
  mynames.initcounter();
  for(int I = 0; I <= 3; I++)
    mynames.getname();
  mynames.displayallnames();
  return (0);
}
```

We have defined **mynames** to be an instance (object) of **NamesArrayClass**. Then, we call **initcounter()** which initializes counter to 0. The **for** loop is used to call **GetName()** four times. Each time **getname()** is called, the user will type in one name. Also, the name will be inserted into the array, and **counter** will be incremented. Finally, we call **displayallnames()** which will display all four of the names which were input by the user.

It is possible to make a few changes in our declaration of the class and in the way we wrote the definitions of the functions. One nice change would be to use what is called a *constructor* rather than using function **initcounter()**. To do this we would replace the declaration

```
void initcounter(void);
```

with the complete declaration and definition as follows:

```
NamesArrayClass(void)
{
   counter = 0;
}
```

Thus, the class declaration for **NamesArrayClass** would now become the following:

```
// Header file -- NAMES2.H
class NamesArrayClass
{
  private:
    char namesarray[50][60];
    int counter;
  public:
    NamesArrayClass(void)
    {
      counter = 0;
    }
    void getname(void);
    void displayallnames(void);
};
```

Notice that the function name, **NamesArrayClass()**, is the same as the **class** name. Thus, the function becomes what is called a *constructor.* When a class declaration includes such a constructor, then every time we define an instance of the class, the constructor will be executed immediately after the allocation of memory. Thus, the constructor provides an automatic initialization for every defined instance of the class. A constructor cannot return a value. Thus, no return type precedes a constructor.

Notice also that we wrote the actual code (the function definition) at the same time that we declared the function. This is called an *inside* definition as opposed to defining the function *outside* of the class declaration. An inside definition for a function is normally only done when the actual code for the definition is quite simple and short. In fact, there are some restrictions with regard to the types of statements that can be made in inside definitions. Since the definition for the constructor, **NamesArrayClass()**, was quite short we did an inside definition. If we had decided to write an outside definition, then the declaration (made inside of the declaration for **NamesArrayClass()**) would have been

```
NamesArrayClass(void);
```

Then, the outside definition would become the following:

```
NamesArrayClass::NamesArrayClass(void)
{
  counter = 0;
}
```

In addition to this change, we could change the definitions of the other two functions (**getname()** and **displaynames()**) by using **cin** and **cout** rather than to use **printf** and **gets**.

```
// Coding for the functions in NamesArrayClass -- In file NAMES2.CPP
#include <iostream.h>
include "names2.h"
void NamesArrayClass::getname(void)
{
  char ch;
  cout << "Enter a name: ";
  cin.get(namesarray[counter],59);
  cin.get(ch);
  counter++;
}
void NamesArrayClass::displayallnames(void)
{
  int j = 0;
  while(j < counter)
  cout << namesarray[j++] << '\n';
}
```

Notice that we used **cin.get(namesarray[counter],59);** to input each name. If we would have just used

```
cin >> name
```

then we would have had problems with spaces. For example, if the user would type

John J. Smith

then **cin** would have sent only the first word, **John**, to variable, **name**. Thus, we would have lost the trailing words, **J. Smith**. Another reason for using **cin.gets** is that the second parameter specifies the maximum number of characters that will be accepted. Thus, we will only accept a maximum of 59 characters. (We must allow for the terminating 0 byte.) Since **cin.get(namesarray[counter],59)** will stop getting characters when the newline character (carriage return) is encountered, we need to clear the newline character out of the buffer. Thus, we use **cin.get(ch)** to get this character, and then we are ready for the next input line.

One other change that could be made is the use of the keyword **struct** instead of **class** in the class declaration for **NamesClass**. Thus, we could have written the declaration for **NamesClass** as follows:

```
struct NamesArrayClass
{
  private:
    char namesarray[50][60];
    int counter;
  public:
    NamesArrayClass(void)
    {
      counter = 0;
    }
    void getname(void);
    void displayallnames(void);
};
```

In this case we are required to type in the keyword **private** since the default in a **struct** declaration is **public.** When using the keyword **class** to declare a class, the default is **private**. Thus, when using the keyword **class** it is not necessary to specify **private**. Either keyword, **struct** or **class**, can be used to declare a class; the only difference is that in a **struct** declaration the default is **public** and in a **class** declaration the default is **private.** It is also possible to use the keyword **union** instead of **class** or **struct**. If **union** is used, then just as with **struct** the default for data and member functions is **public.**

We will continue our discussion of object oriented programming using C++ in the next section.

11.3 Derived Classes and Inheritance

A very important capability in object oriented programming is *inheritance*. This means that we can allow a class to inherit all aspects of another class. Then, the new class can add new data and functions of its own. Thus, this very powerful capability allows us to acquire all aspects of a previously developed **base** class and then add new capabilities that were not in the base class.

As an example, suppose we develop a base class called **BaseEmpClass** as follows:

```
// Declarations for class, BaseEmpClass -- In file BASEEMP1.H
class BaseEmpClass
{
  protected:
    char name[26];
    char addr[36];
    char phone[13];
  public:
    void getname(void);
    void getaddr(void);
    void getphone(void);
    void getbaseinfo(void);
    void displaybaseinfo(void);
};
```

Notice that we have preceded the data declarations with the keyword **protected** rather than **private**. Remember that **private** means the data cannot be accessed outside of the class. Thus, since we are planning to inherit this data into other classes, we will specify **protected** rather than **private**. Although, this seems to be a very minor change, it is very important. The keyword **protected** means that all derived classes may have access. Thus, we are allowing all derived classes to have access to the variables, **name, phone,** and **addr**. However, access by anything other than derived classes is still denied. We will say more about this a little later.

We have declared three data items, **name, addr,** and **phone**. Each of these is a character array. We have also declared five functions, **getname(), getaddr(), getphone(), getbaseinfo()**, and **displaybaseinfo()**. Following is the code for these five functions:

```
// Coding for functions in class, BaseEmpClass -- In file BASEEMP1.CPP
#include "baseemp1.h"
#include <stdio.h>
//*************************************************************
// getname -   Function in class, BaseEmpClass, to allow the user
//                  to input name from the keyboard.
//*************************************************************
void BaseEmpClass::getname(void)
{
  printf("\nInput the name (max. of 25 chars): ");
  gets(name);
```

454

```
}
//*************************************************************
// getphone -  Function in class, BaseEmpClass, to allow the
//                 user to input a phone number from the keyboard.
//*************************************************************
void BaseEmpClass::getphone(void)
{
  printf("\nInput the phone number (ex. 111-222-3333): ");
  gets(phone);
}
//*************************************************************
// getaddr -  Function in class, BaseEmpClass, to allow the user to
//                 input an address from the keyboard.
//*************************************************************
void BaseEmpClass::getaddr(void)
{
  printf("\nInput the address (max. of 35 chars): ");
  gets(addr);
}
//*************************************************************
// getbaseinfo -  Function in class, BaseEmpClass, to allow the user
//                   to input all three data items, the name, phone,
//                   and address.
//*************************************************************
void BaseEmpClass::getbaseinfo(void)
{
  getname();
  getphone();
  getaddr();
}
//*************************************************************
// displaybaseinfo -  Function in class, BaseEmpClass, to display
//                       the name, phone, and address.
//*************************************************************
void BaseEmpClass::displaybaseinfo(void)
{
  printf("\nThe name is %s",name);
  printf("\nThe phone is %s",phone);
  printf("\nThe address is %s",addr);
}
```

The function **getbaseinfo()** can be called to get all three data items, or we can call the individual functions, **getname()**, **getaddr()**, or **getphone()** to get one data item at a time. Now, let us write a simple test program.

```
// Simple test program for class, BaseEmpClass -- File TSTBASE1.CPP
#include "baseemp1.h"
int main(void)
{
  BaseEmpClass oneemp;
  oneemp.getbaseinfo();
  oneemp.displaybaseinfo();
  return(0);
}
```

This little test program just declares **oneemp** to be an instance of class, **BaseEmpClass**. Then, we call function **getbaseinfo()** to allow the user to input a name, phone, and address. Finally, we call **displaybaseinfo()** to display the name, phone, and address that were input.

In this example, we are assuming that the class, **BaseEmpClass**, contains very general information which is normally kept for all employees. Now to extend our example, suppose we want to derive a new class called **HourlyEmpClass** for those workers who are paid by the hour. For these workers, we will add two new data items, **hourlyrate** and **hours** (the number of hours worked).

```
// Header file -- In file HRLYEMP1.H
#include "baseemp1.h"
class HourlyEmpClass : public BaseEmpClass
{
  private:
    float hourlyrate;
    float hours;
  public:
    void gethourlyrate(void);
    void gethours(void);
    void displayhourlyrate(void);
    void displayhours(void);
};
```

In the above, the line

```
class HourlyEmpClass : public BaseEmpClass
```

not only declares the new class, **HourlyEmpClass**, but also indicates that this new class is derived from the base class, **BaseEmpClass**. The new class will inherit everything from the base class which was declared as either **protected** or **public** in the base class. Thus, the new class will inherit the data items, **name**, **phone**, and **addr**. Also, the new class inherits the functions declared in the base class.

Hourlyrate and **hours** were declared as **private** in the new class. Thus, only the functions in class, **HourlyEmpClass**, can access these two data items. Now, let us write the code for the new functions in **HourlyEmpClass**.

```cpp
// Coding for functions in class, HourlyEmpClass -- In file HRLYEMP1.CPP
#include "hrlyemp1.h"
#include <iostream.h>
#include <iomanip.h>
//************************************************************
// gethourlyrate -  Function in class, HourlyEmpClass, to allow
//                   the user to input the value for hourlyrate.
//************************************************************
void HourlyEmpClass::gethourlyrate(void)
{
  cout << "Input the hourly rate (a real number): ";
  cin >> hourlyrate;
}
//************************************************************
// gethours -   Function in class, HourlyEmpClass, to allow the
//                   user to input the value for hours (the number
//                   of hours worked).
//************************************************************
void HourlyEmpClass::gethours(void)
{
  cout << "\nInput the number of hours worked (a real number): ";
  cin >> hours;
}
//************************************************************
// displayhourlyrate -        Function in class, HourlyEmpClass, to
//                   display the value for hourlyrate.
//************************************************************
void HourlyEmpClass::displayhourlyrate(void)
{
  cout << "\nThe hourly rate is " << setprecision(2) << hourlyrate;
}
//************************************************************
// displayhours -   Function in class, HourlyEmpClass, to display
//                   the value for hours.
//************************************************************
void HourlyEmpClass::displayhours(void)
{
  cout << "\nThe number of hours is " << setprecision(2) << hours;
}
```

Now let us write a test program for class, **HourlyEmpClass**:

```
// Test program for class, HourlyEmpClass -- In file TSTHRLY1.CPP
#include "hrlyemp1.h"
int main(void)
{
  HourlyEmpClass onehrlyemp;
  onehrlyemp.getbaseinfo();
  onehrlyemp.gethourlyrate();
  onehrlyemp.gethours();
  onehrlyemp.displaybaseinfo();
  onehrlyemp.displayhourlyrate();
  onehrlyemp.displayhours();
  return(0);
}
```

In the test program we first declare **onehrlyemp** to be an instance of class, **HourlyEmpClass**. Since the class, **HourlyEmpClass**, was derived from **BaseEmpClass**, then the object, **onehrlyemp**, will contain all of the data and functions declared in both classes. Thus, it will include the data items, **name**, **phone**, and **addr**, as well as **hourlyrate** and **hours**. During execution, the user will be asked to input a name, phone number, address, hourly rate, and number of hours. Then all of this data will be displayed.

Note that for this example to be fully implemented in a real world type of application, we would probably wish to add other data items and other functions to both the base class, **BaseEmpClass**, and the derived class, **HourlyEmpClass**. Also, we have declared the special class, **HourlyEmpClass**, for those workers who are paid by the hour. In a real world situation we could also declare a class for those workers who are salaried.

In the next section, we will investigate multiple inheritance.

11.4 Multiple inheritance

It is possible for a class to be derived from more than one base class. For example in the following:

```
class Base1
{
};
class Base2
{
}:
```

```
class New : public Base1, public Base2
{
};
```

class **New** is derived from both of the base classes, **Base1** and **Base2**.

How might we use this concept with our employee example? Suppose we develop another base class called **FamilyInfoClass**.

```
// Header file -- FAMINF1.H
class FamilyInfoClass
{
  private:
    int numchildren;
  public:
    void getnumchildren(void);
    void displaynumchildren(void);
};
```

The only data item included is **numchildren** which represents the number of children. However, it would certainly be possible to include several family related data items. Now, let us write the code for the two functions.

```
//Coding for the functions in FamilyInfoClass -- In file FAMINF1.CPP
#include <iostream.h>
#include "faminf1.h"
//***********************************************************
// getnumchildren -  Function in class, FamilyInfoClass, to
//                   allow the user to input the number
//                   of children.
//***********************************************************
void FamilyInfoClass::getnumchildren(void)
{
  cout << "\nInput the number of children (integer): ";
  cin >> numchildren;
}
//***********************************************************
// displaynumchildren -     Function in class, FamilyInfoClass to
//                    display the number of children.
//***********************************************************
void FamilyInfoClass::displaynumchildren(void)
{
  cout << "\nThe number of children is " << numchildren;
}
```

We will now rewrite the declaration for class, **HourlyEmpClass**, so that it is derived from both the base class, **BaseEmpClass**, and the base class, **FamilyInfoClass**.

```
// Header file - HRLYEMP2.H
#include "baseemp1.h"
#include "faminf1.h"
class HourlyEmpClass : public BaseEmpClass, public FamilyInfoClass
{
  private:
    float hourlyrate;
    float hours;
  public:
    void gethourlyrate(void);
    void gethours(void);
    void displayhourlyrate(void);
    void displayhours(void);
};
```

The line

```
class HourlyEmpClass : public BaseEmpClass, public FamilyInfoClass
```

indicates that class, **HourlyEmpClass**, is derived from both of the classes, **BaseEmpClass** and **FamilyInfoClass**.

We will now rewrite the test program for class, **HourlyEmpClass**.

```
// Test program #2 for class, HourlyEmpClass -- In file TSTHRLY2.CPP
#include "hrlyemp2.h"
int main(void)
{
  HourlyEmpClass onehrlyemp;
  onehrlyemp.getbaseinfo();
  onehrlyemp.gethourlyrate();
  onehrlyemp.gethours();
  onehrlyemp.getnumchildren();
  onehrlyemp.displaybaseinfo();
  onehrlyemp.displayhourlyrate();
  onehrlyemp.displayhours();
  onehrlyemp.displaynumchildren();
  return(0);
}
```

Notice that the object, **onehrlyemp**, now includes all data in the base classes,

BaseEmpClass and **FamilyInfoClass**, as well as the data in **HourlyEmpClass**. Thus, by calling the appropriate functions, we can now access all of the data.

11.5 Constructor Overloading and Object Arguments

In this section we will develop a class which represents a length. The two data items will be **numfeet** and **numinches**.

```
// Header file -- LEN1.H
class LengthClass
{
  private:
    int numfeet;
    float numinches;
  public:
    void getlength(void);
    void displaylength(void);
    void addlengths(LengthClass,LengthClass);
};
```

Notice that the class, **LengthClass**, contains three functions, **getlength()**, **displaylength()**, and **addlengths()**. **Getlength()** will allow the user to type in the values for **numfeet** and **numinches**. **Displaylength()** will display the values for **numfeet** and **numinches**. The third function is different in that it has two arguments, each of which is of type **LengthClass**.

```
// Coding for functions in class, LengthClass -- In file LEN1.CPP
#include "len1.h"
#include <iostream.h>
//*************************************************************
// getlength -  Function in class, LengthClass, to allow
//              the user to input the values for numfeet
//              and numinches.
//*************************************************************
void LengthClass::getlength(void)
{
  cout << "\nInput the number of feet (integer): ";
  cin >> numfeet;
  cout << "\Input the number of inches (real): ";
  cin >> numinches;
}
//*************************************************************
// displaylength -  Function in class, LengthClass, to display
```

```
//              the values for numfeet and numinches.
//***********************************************************
void LengthClass::displaylength(void)
{
  cout << "\nThe length is " << numfeet << "\' " << numinches << "\""
}
//***********************************************************
// addlengths -  Function in class, LengthClass, to add the
//               lengths of two objects and assign the result
//               as the length for the object.
//***********************************************************
void LengthClass::addlengths(LengthClass length1,
                             LengthClass length2)
{
  numfeet = length1.numfeet + length2.numfeet;
  numinches = length1.numinches + length2.numinches;
  if (numinches >= 12.0)
  {
    ++numfeet;
    numinches -= 12.0;
  }
}
```

The **addlengths()** function sets the values for **numfeet** and **numinches** for the present object to the sums for the two argument objects. The function also checks to see if the calculated value for **numinches** is greater than or equal to 12.0. If so, we increment the variable, **numfeet**, by one and subtract 12.0 from the value for **numinches**. Now, let us write a small test program.

```
// Test program #1 for class, LengthClass -- In file TSTLEN1.CPP
#include "len1.h"
int main(void)
{
  LengthClass len1,len2,len3;
  len1.getlength();
  len2.getlength();
  len3.addlengths(len1,len2);
  len3.displaylength();
  return (0);
}
```

When run, the program will allow the user to input the values for **numfeet** and **numinches** for object **len1**; it will let the user input the values for **numfeet** and **numinches** for object **len2**; and it will call function **addlengths** for object **len3**. This will set the values for **numfeet** and **numinches** for object **len3** to the sums for objects **len1** and **len2**. Finally, the program will display the values for **numfeet** and **numinches** for object **len3**.

There are some changes we could make to class, **LengthClass**. First of all, it would be nice to include at least one constructor. By doing this, we could initialize the values for **numfeet** and **numinches** automatically when we create a new object. In fact, let us see how we can include two different constructors. One will be when no parameters are given when the new object is created. A second will be when we provide two parameters when the new object is created.

```cpp
// Header file -- LEN2.H
class LengthClass
{
  private:
    int numfeet;
    float numinches;
  public:
    LengthClass(void)   // First constructor when no parameters given
    {
      numfeet = 0;
      numinches = 0.0;
    }
    LengthClass(int ft, float in)  // Second constructor when two
                                   // parameters
    {
      numfeet = ft;
      numinches = in;
    }
    void getlength(void);
    void displaylength(void);
    void addlengths(LengthClass,LengthClass);
};
```

Notice that we have used the same name for both forms of the constructor. Thus, we have overloaded the constructor. However, there should be no confusion in selecting the appropriate one since the number of parameters (0 or 2) will dictate which constructor should be used. Let us take a look at a new test program to see how this will work.

```cpp
// Test program #2 for class, LengthClass -- In file TSTLEN2.CPP
#include  "len2.h"
int main(void)
{
  LengthClass len1(6,10.5);
  LengthClass len2(5,6.5);
```

```
        LengthClass len3;

        len3.addlengths(len1,len2);
        len3.displaylength();
        return(0);
    }
```

When the test program executes, the second constructor will be used when objects, **len1** and **len2**, are created. Thus, when **len1** is created, the second constructor will set the value for **numfeet** to 6 and the value for **numinches** to 10.5. Similarly, when **len2** is created, the second constructor will set the value of **numfeet** to 5 and the value for **numinches** to 6.5. However, since no parameters are used when **len3** is created, then the first constructor will be called. Thus, **numfeet** and **numinches** for **len3** will be initialized to 0. **Addlengths**() for object **len3** is then called to set **numfeet** and **numinches** for **len3** to the sums for **len1** and **len2**. Finally, the values of **numfeet** and **numinches** for **len3** will be displayed.

11.6 Overloading of Operations

In our example with the class, **LengthClass**, one of our functions was **addlengths**(). We called this function with the following:

```
        len3.addlengths(len1,len2);
```

The syntax for this would be much nicer and simpler if we could replace it with the following:

```
        len3 = len1 + len2;
```

In order to do this, we will have to define what the operator **+** means for objects of class, **LengthClass**. In other words, we must overload the **+** operator to mean what we want it to mean. First of all, we must modify the class declaration.

```
    // Header file -- LEN3.H
    class LengthClass
    {
      private:
        int numfeet;
        float numinches;
      public:
        LengthClass(void)   // First constructor when no parameters given
        {
          numfeet = 0;
```

```
          numinches = 0.0;
        }
        LengthClass(int ft, float in)  // Second constructor when two
                                       //   parameters
        {
          numfeet = ft;
          numinches = in;
        }
        void getlength(void);
        void displaylength(void);
        LengthClass operator + (LengthClass);
    };
```

To declare the operator **+**, we included the line

```
        LengthClass  operator + (LengthClass);
```

The **LengthClass** at the beginning is the return type. Thus, the result of the operation will be of type, **LengthClass**.   Next, the keyword, **operator**, is inserted followed by the operator we are going to overload (the **+**). Finally, we include the argument list. However, why did we include only one argument?   It would seem that we should have two arguments. That is, in

```
        len3 = len1 + len2;
```

it would appear that we should have an argument for **len1** and an argument for **len2**. However, we actually only need to list the argument type for **len2**. The reason for this is that when the right hand side of the assignment statement is parsed, **len1** is found first, and then the **+** is found. It is assumed that the **+** is a member of object **len1** since it occurred immediately after **len1**. Thus, the first operand for the **+** operation is assumed to be **len1**. Therefore, all we need to specify in the parameter list is the argument type for the second operand (**len2**). We can now write the code for the overloading of the + operation.

```
        // Coding for the functions in class, LengthClass -- In file LEN3.CPP
        #include "len3.h"
        #include <iostream.h>

        //*************************************************************
        // getlength -  Function in class, LengthClass, to allow
        //              the user to input the values for numfeet
        //              and numinches.
        //*************************************************************
        void LengthClass::getlength(void)
```

```
{
  cout << "\nInput the number of feet (integer): ";
  cin >> numfeet;
  cout << "\Input the number of inches (real): ";
  cin >> numinches;
}
//*********************************************************
// displaylength -  Function in class, LengthClass, to display
//                     the values for numfeet and numinches.
//*********************************************************
void LengthClass::displaylength(void)
{
  cout << "\nThe length is " << numfeet << "\' " << numinches << '\"'
}
//*********************************************************
// operator + -   The overloading of operator+ in class,
//                   LengthClass.
//*********************************************************
LengthClass LengthClass::operator + (LengthClass x2)
{
  int feet;
  float inches;
  feet = numfeet + x2.numfeet;
  inches = numinches + x2.numinches;
  if (inches >= 12.0)
  {
    inches -= 12.0;
    ++feet;
  }
  return LengthClass(feet,inches);
}
```

Notice in the coding that

        feet = numfeet + x2.numfeet;

adds **numfeet** for the object we are in (in our case **len1**) to **numfeet** for the second operand (in our case, **len2**), and assigns the sum to a local variable, **feet**. Similarly,

        inches = numinches + x2.numinches;

adds **numinches** for **len1** to **numinches** for **len2**, and assigns the result to the local variable **inches**. Then if **inches** is >= 12.0, we subtract 12.0 from **inches** and increment **feet** by one. Finally, we initialize and return an unnamed object of class, **LengthClass**, with the values of **feet** and **inches**. Then in,

> len3 = len1 + len2;

the returned unnamed object is assigned to object **len3**. Let us now write a small test program.

```
// Test program #3 for class, LengthClass -- In file TSTLEN2.CPP
#include  "len3.h"
int main(void)
{
  LengthClass len1(6,10.5);
  LengthClass len2(5,6.5);
  LengthClass len3;
  len3 = len1 + len2;
  len3.displaylength();
  return(0);
}
```

This program will first create and initialize the objects, **len1**, **len2**, and **len3**. It will then use the + operator to add the lengths for **len1** and **len2** and assign the sum to object **len3**. Finally, the function, **displaylength()** will display the length that was just determined for object **len3**.

11.7 Pointers to Objects

Let us now take a look at how we might set up a pointer to an object. Recall our little test program for class, **OneNameClass**, that we wrote in section 15.2:

```
// Test program for class OneNameClass -- File TSTCL1A.CPP
#include "onename.h"
int main(void)
{
  OneNameClass myname;
  myname.getname();
  myname.displayname();
  return(0);
}
```

In this test program, the line

> OneNameClass myname;

created myname as an instance (object) of type **OneNameClass**. Let us modify this line to be the following:

> OneNameClass *mynameptr = new OneNameClass;

First of all, this declares **mynameptr** to be a pointer to class type **OneNameClass**. Then, **new** is used to create a new instance of type **OneNameClass**. Finally, the value of the new pointer is assigned to **mynameptr**. Let us now rewrite the little test program.

```
// Test program for class OneNameClass -- File TSTCL1D.CPP
#include "onename.h"
int main(void)
{
  OneNameClass *mynameptr = new OneNameClass;
  mynameptr->getname();
  mynameptr->displayname();
  return(0);
}
```

Notice that since **mynameptr** is a pointer, we use the -> operator to access members of the object.

If desired we could have written the two lines

> OneNameClass *mynameptr;
> mynameptr = new OneNameClass;

instead of the one line

> OneNameClass *mynameptr = new OneNameClass;

11.8 Virtual Pointers

It is possible for different classes to use functions having the same name. This overloading will cause no problems as long as it is possible to determine which of the functions is to be called. However, suppose it is not possible to determine which function should be used, or suppose we would like to be able to call the same named function in different classes with the same identical call.

For example, suppose in two or more classes we have the function, **displayclass()**, which displays the name of the class. We will assume there are no arguments for the function. Let us also assume that we would like to execute the simple statement

```
            classptr->displayclass();
```

in a program and have it call the appropriate **displayclass()** function depending on which class object is being pointed to by **classptr**.

Let us begin by considering an example that will **not** do what we want.

```
// Header file -- VIRTUAL1.H
class A
{
  public:
    void displayclass(void);
}
class B1 : public A
{
  public:
    void displayclass(void);
}
class B2 : public A
{
  public:
    void displayclass(void);
}
```

In the above class declarations, class **B1** and class **B2** are both derived from base class, **A**. Also, notice that the same function, **displayclass()**, is declared in each class. We will now write the declarations for the three **displayclass()** functions.

```
// Function definitions -- File VIRTUAL1.CPP
#include <iostream.h>
void A::displayclass(void)
{
  cout << "This is base class A\n";
}
void B1::displayclass(void)
{
  cout << "This is derived class B1\n";
}
void B2::displayclass(void)
{
  cout << "This is derived class B2\n";
}
```

The **displayclass()** functions are identical except that they display a different class name. Now, let us write a small test program:

```
// Test program -- TSTVIR1.CPP
#include "VIRTUAL1.H"

int main(void)
{
  A *classptr;
  B1 b1obj;
  B2 b2obj;
  for (int j = 0; j < 2; j++)
  {
    if (j == 0)
      classptr = &b1obj;
    else
      classptr = &b2obj;
    classptr->displayclass();
  }
}
```

In this test program, we declare **classptr** as a pointer to class **A**. We then create **b1obj** as an object of class **B1** and also create **b2obj** as an object of class **B2**. We then set up a for loop which will execute twice, once with a **j** value of 0 and again with a **j** value of 1. In the loop, if **j** is equal to 0, we assign the address of **b1obj** to classptr; otherwise, we assign the address of **b2obj** to **classptr**. Finally, each time through the loop we call

```
        classptr->displayclass();
```

to display the class. You might well suspect the following output:

```
        This is derived class B1
        This is derived class B2
```

However, this is **not** what we see. What we actually do see is the following:

```
        This is base class A
        This is base class A
```

Why do we get this rather than what we would have suspected? The reason is that the compiler will select which **displayclass()** function to use based on the type of the pointer rather than the value of the pointer. Thus, since **classptr** was declared to be a pointer to class **A**, then the compiler will always select the **displayclass()** function from class **A**. Also, you might have wondered why the compiler would allow either

```
                 classptr = &b1obj;
                          or
                 classptr = &b2obj;
```

in the first place, since it would appear that we are trying to assign different types of pointers. However, the C++ compiler does consider a pointer to a derived class to be compatible with a pointer to the base class.

To solve the above problem and get what we expect, we merely need to make one small change in our declaration for class **A**:

```
// Header file -- VIRTUAL2.H
class A
{
  public:
    virtual displayclass(void);
}
class B1 : public A
{
  public:
    void displayclass(void);
}
class B2 : public A
{
  public:
    void displayclass(void);
}
```

Notice that the only change was to declare the return type for **displayclass()** in class A to be of type **virtual** rather than **void**. We also need to make the same change in the coding for the function:

```
// Function definitions -- File VIRTUAL2.CPP
#include <iostream.h>
virtual A::displayclass(void)
{
  cout << "This is base class A\n";
}
void B1::displayclass(void)
{
  cout << "This is derived class B1\n";
}
```

Now, if we run the same test program, **TSTVIR1.CPP**, we get what we want:

This is derived class B1
This is derived class B2

Thus, in order to accomplish what we wanted to do, the base class must contain the desired function and, also, it must declare the return type for the function to be **virtual**. When this is done, the compiler will now look at the value which has been assigned to **classptr** instead of just the type. Thus,

classptr = &b1obj;

will assign the address of **b1obj** to **classptr**. Then,

classptr->displayclass();

will call the function **displayclass()** for object **b1obj** (of class **B1**), and the result will be

This is class B1

All of this illustrates another example of **polymorphism** in which something (in this case, a function) does different things. Recall that polymorphism is one of the strengths of C++ and object oriented programming.

11.9 Abstraction

When we design a C or C++ program and write functions to perform major functions of the program, then we are using a form of abstraction, which is commonly called *procedural abstraction*. When we call one of these functions, we just consider its major purpose. We assume that the function will take care of all of the details necessary to perform its purpose.

When we attempt to do the same kind of abstraction with data, then it is called *data abstraction*. That is, when we think of a data object, we should not have to worry about the fine details of exactly how it is implemented. With what we have been discussing in this chapter, it should be rather obvious that we can easily attain data abstraction by using object oriented programming techniques. The declaration of a **class** allows us to hide the details of our data. Assuming that we declare the data within the class as **private** or **protected**, then the only way to access this data is with the functions declared as part of the class or within a derived class. Thus, we are not only abstracting what the data actually is, but we are also protecting the data from unwanted access. Object oriented programming not only allows data abstraction, it promotes it in a very simple and natural way.

However, in object oriented programming, the term **abstract** is also used in connection with the declaration of a particular type of class. If a class is created only to serve as a base class for other classes, and no objects of this type are actually created, then the class can be referred to as an **abstract class**. Thus, the main purpose of an abstract class is just to serve as a base for other derived classes.

11.10 Summary

In this chapter we have investigated some of the powerful capabilities of object oriented programming. We have seen that this relatively new approach to programming emphasizes the importance of the data as well as the operations on that data. In order to accomplish this objective, the data in an object is united with the operations which are performed on that data.

Object oriented programming incorporates several very important capabilities and concepts: **encapsulation; data hiding, abstraction,** and **protection**; **inheritance**; and **polymorphism**. **Encapsulation** is the process of uniting the data with the operations on that data.

Data hiding, abstraction, and **protection** can be accomplished by declaring the data in one or more classes as either **private** or **protected**. In this way we can control exactly what has access to the data. These classes can be declared in one or more separate header files.

Inheritance allows the programmer to develop new classes which are derived from already created classes. In this way, the programmer can build on already developed and debugged classes, rather than having to reinvent the wheel.

Polymorphism refers to the use of the same thing for different purposes. Polymorphism is involved in object oriented programming in several ways. One way is the overloading of operators. That is, we may use the same operator to do different operations for different types of data. Another is the overloading of functions, in which different functions can have the same name, but do different things depending on their use and their argument lists. Also, as we saw in section 15.8, we can extend this polymorphism to the use of virtual functions.

At first, object oriented programming may seem quite strange and complicated. However, it is an extremely powerful and logical approach to programming. This power has led to its rapid increase in popularity. At this point in time, every programmer should be aware of the power of object oriented programming and know how to use it.

11.11 Questions

11.1   What do the letters OOP stand for?

11.2   What does encapsulation mean?

11.3   If **SpecialClass** is a class name, then what does the following statement do?
SpecialClass myobject;

11.4   What is the difference between **private** and **public?**

11.5   What is the difference between **private** and **protected?**

11.6   What is the difference between **protected** and **public?**

11.7   What does it mean to say that one class inherits another?

11.8   What is a **constructor** function?

11.9   What is one major advantage of using a **constructor** function?

11.10 What does **multiple inheritance** mean?

11.11 a.)   What does **constructor overloading** mean?

b.)   Give an example.

11.12 a.)   What does **overloading of operators** mean?

b.)   Give an example.

11.13 a.)   What is a **virtual pointer?**

b.)   Give an example where we could use a **virtual pointer.**

11.14 How does OOP allow us to use what is called **data abstraction?**

11.15 What is **polymorphism?**

11.12 Exercises

11.1   Write the code for a simple class called **OneTestScore** which will include an integer variable called **score** and two functions **void gettestscore(void)** and **void displaytestscore(void).** Enter the code in a file called **onescore.h.**

11.2   In a second file called **onescore.cpp** write the code for the two functions. The **gettestscore()** function will ask the user to input the score, and the function, **displaytestscore()** will display the score that was input.

11.3   Create a third file called **testsc1.cpp** to test the creation of an object called **mytestscore** of the class **OneTestScore** and then call the two functions to input the score and then display it. Run the project and test it.

11.4   Combine the files from excercises 11.1, 11.2, and 11.3 into one file. Then, run and test it.

11.5   Create a new class called **TestScoresArrayClass** which will declare a data array for 50 integers called **testscoresarray** and a float variable called **average..** Declare four functions in the class: **void initcounter(void), void getonetestscore(void), void displayalltestscores(void)** and **void displaytestavg(void).** Store in a header file.

11.6   In another file, write the code for the four functions needed for exercise 11.5.

11.7   In another file, write a test program to test the **TestScoresArrayClass** and its functions. Run the project and test it.

11.8   Combine the files in exercises 11.5, 11.6, and 11.7 into one file. Then, run and test it.

11.9   Modify the class **TestScoresArrayClass** so that it includes a constructor function. Then rewrite any necessary code and rerun the program.

11.10   Refer to section 11.3. Write a new class, **SalariedEmpClass** which inherits the base class, **BaseEmpClass.** Decide what could be included in the new class.

11.11   Continue exercise 11.10 by writing the code for functions in the new class, **SalariedEmpClass.**

11.12   Write a test program to test the new class, **SalariedEmpClass** and its new functions (from exercises 11.10 and 11.11).

11.13 In section 11.6 we overloaded the '+' operator. What would be necessary to overload the '-' operator? Write the code to do this.

11.14 Write a test program to test your overloaded '-' operator (from exercise 11.13).

11.15 Refer to section 11.7 on pointers to objects. Then rewrite exercises 11.1, 11.2, and 11.3 so that we use a pointer to the class **OneTestClass.**

APPENDIX A

Number Systems

A.1 Bits, Bytes, Words and Number Systems

All data storage within a computer is provided by a collection of electronic switches that are either on or off. The computer stores data by setting a particular collection of these switches to the correct on or off position. Because each switch has only two states, it is convenient to code a number using only two digits, rather than the ten digits that we are used to. The two digits are the digits 0 and 1. Each of these digits is referred to as a **bit**. Memory on a IBM microcomputer uses a collection of 8-bits as a basic unit of storage. Each of these units has it's own address. Therefore, a collection of 8-bits is called a **byte**. A byte is also defined as the number of bits to code one character. There were computers, built by Control Data Corporation and called Cyber computers, that used 6 bits to code one character. Most computer systems, however, use 8-bits. Since the basic storage size for an integer is two bytes, this two bytes size is called a **word**. We also use the terms, **double word**, for two words or four bytes, **quad word**, for four words or eight bytes, and **nibble** or **nybble** for a collection of 4-bits, the high or low four bits of a byte. We summarize the above as follows:

Bit - A 0 or a 1.

Nibble - Four bits.

Byte - Number of bits needed to code one character.
On a microcomputer this is 8 bits

Word - Two bytes

Double word - Two words or four bytes.

Quad word - Four words or 8 bytes.

In order to be able to program in assembler language and understand how assembly language instructions are coded in machine code, it is critical that we are able to count and perform arithmetic in binary just as we are able to in decimal. We illustrate the counting as follows:

Binary	Decimal
0	0
1	1
10	2
11	3
100	4
101	5
110	6
111	7
1000	8
1001	9
1010	10
1011	11
1100	12
1101	13
1110	14
1111	15

When we count in decimal, we first use the ten digits

$$0, 1, 2, 3, 4, 5, 6, 7, 8, 9$$

and then when we run out move to a new position and repeat the process.

$$10, 11, 12, 13, 14, 15, 16, 17, 18, 19$$

The 1 represents the number of 10's and the second digit represents the number of one's. Thus

$$14 = 1*10 + 4$$

The number 123 in decimal would represent

$$123 = 1*10*10 + 2*10 + 3$$

Each time that we add a new position, the position represents a new power of 10. The exact same process is taking place in binary, we simply run out of digits faster.

$$0, 1, 10, 11, 100, 101, 110, 111, ...$$

Each digit represents a power of 2 since we are using only two digits. Thus the number

$$11 = 1*2 + 1$$

and

$$1101 = 1*2*2*2 + 1*2*2 + 0*2 + 1$$

The other thing that we need to point out from the above table is that when we use four binary digits, we can represent 16 numbers, decimal 0 through 15. Because of this and the fact that it gets very tedious to keep writing binary digits, we introduce another number system that uses a different symbol for each of these 16 numbers. This number system is called the **hexadecimal**, base 16, number system. It uses the 16 symbols

$$0, 1, 2, 3, 4, 5, 6, 7, 8, 9, A, B, C, D, E, F$$

Counting in hexadecimal, base 16, works exactly the same as it did in the other two number systems. When we run out of symbols we move to another position and it represents another power of the base, in this case base 16. Thus, the number

$$9D = 9*16 + D = 9*16 + 13$$

in decimal and the number

$$A7B = A*16*16 + 7*16 + B = 10*16*16 + 7*16 + 11$$

When we have the number

$$1011$$

it is not clear what this number represents since it could be binary, decimal, or even hexadecimal. Thus, we use a symbol following to represent the base.

$$1011B \qquad 1011D \qquad 1011H$$

would represent binary, decimal, and hexadecimal respectively. We also use subscripts following the number. Therefore, we will see

$$1011_2 \qquad 1011_{10} \qquad 1011_{16}$$

We could use any number system that we want with this same process. The only ones that we are interested in are the ones we have described above. We will need to know how to count and perform arithmetic in each of these number systems. We will also need to know how to convert from one number system to another. We will discuss how this is done in the next section. One important thing to remember is that the number is the same no matter which number system is used to represent the number. Each of these representations gives the same number.

$$01100111_2 \qquad 67_{16} \qquad 103_{10}$$

A.2 Conversion, Decimal <--> Binary

In this section we will discuss how we can convert from the decimal representation of a number to the binary representation and conversely from the binary representation to the decimal representation. The conversion from decimal to binary can be done either using division or repeated subtraction. Unless we specify otherwise, we will be working with one byte. We begin with the conversion of 97 to binary using one byte. The powers of 2 for one byte are the following:

$$\overline{128} \quad \overline{64} \quad \overline{32} \quad \overline{16} \quad \overline{8} \quad \overline{4} \quad \overline{2} \quad \overline{1}$$

Considering 97 we have no 128's, 1 - 64, 1 - 32, and a 1.

$$97 = 64 + 33$$
$$= 64 + 32 + 1$$

Thus, the binary representation of 97 is the following:

$$= 01100001$$

Convert 107 to binary. Again we look at the powers of 2 for one byte and compute the binary representation using repeated subtraction.

$$\overline{128} \quad \overline{64} \quad \overline{32} \quad \overline{16} \quad \overline{8} \quad \overline{4} \quad \overline{2} \quad \overline{1}$$

$$107 = 64 + 43$$
$$= 64 + 32 + 11$$
$$= 64 + 32 + 8 + 3$$
$$= 64 + 32 + 8 + 2 + 1$$

Thus, the binary representation of 107 is the following:

$$= 01101011$$

Using division we would divide by 2, keeping track of the remainders, and stopping when the quotient becomes zero. We illustrate this process with the above examples.

```
            0
      2     1     1
      2     3     1
      2     6     0
      2     12    0
      2     24    0
      2     48    0
      2     97    1
```

The remainders that make up the binary digits of the representation are then taken in the reverse order.

1100001

We fill in the necessary high bits with zeros to complete the byte.

01100001

We repeat the process for 107.

```
            0
      2     1     1
      2     3     1
      2     6     0
      2     13    1
      2     26    0
      2     53    1
      2     107   1
```

The binary representation of 107 filling in the high bit with 0 is the following:

01101011

We prefer the method of repeated subtraction but which method you prefer to use does not make a difference.

Binary to Decimal

The process of converting binary to decimal is simply to add up the respective powers of 2. We illustrate with some examples.

Convert 01011101 to decimal.

01011101 = 1*64 + 1*16 + 1*8 + 1*4 + 1
       = 93

Convert 01110110 to decimal.

01110110 = 1*64 + 1*32 + 1*16 + 1*4 + 1*2
       = 116

A.3 Conversion, Decimal <--> Hex

    In this section we will see how we convert from decimal to hexadecimal and back. In order to convert from decimal to hexadecimal, we simply need to find the number of 16's by division. This is the case since a byte in hex is of the form

$$ABH = A*16 + B$$

We convert 97 decimal to hex by dividing by 16.

```
              6
         16 97
            96
             1
```

Thus

$$97 = 61H$$

Convert 107 to hex. As before, we divide by 16.

```
              6
         16  107
             96
             11
```

Thus

$$107 = 6BH$$

    In order to convert from hexadecimal to decimal, we simply compute the sum of the multiples of the powers of 16.

Convert 7D to decimal.

$$7D = 7*16 + D$$
$$= 7*16 + 13$$
$$= 112 + 13$$
$$= 125$$

Convert A9 to decimal.

$$A9 = A*16 + 9$$
$$= 10*16 + 9$$
$$= 160 + 9$$
$$= 169$$

A.4 Conversion, Binary <--> Hex

In this section we will discuss how to convert back and forth between binary and hexadecimal. As before we will consider one byte. If we consider the number

$$ABH = A*16 + B$$

each of the symbols A and B is a hex digit representing a decimal number from 0 to 15. As we saw in section 1.2, each of these decimal numbers can be represented with four binary digits, 0000 --> 1111. Thus,

$$A*16 + B = xxxx*16 + yyyy$$
$$= xxxxyyyy$$

binary. In order to convert from binary to hex, we simply convert each nibble to the corresponding hex digit.

Convert 10110011 to hex.

Since

$$1011 = 11_{10}$$
$$= B$$

and

$$0011 = 3$$

we have

$$1011011 = B3H$$

Convert 01111011 to hex.

We have

$$01111100 = 0111\ \ 1100$$
$$= 7\ \ 12_{10}$$
$$= 7\ \ C$$
$$= 7CH$$

In order to convert from hexadecimal to binary, we simply reverse the process.

Convert 10011101 to hex.

$$10011101 = 1001\ \ 1101$$
$$= 9\ \ 13_{10}$$
$$= 9DH$$

A.5 Negative Numbers

In this section we want to discuss how negative integers are stored in binary. In order to do this we ask the question, what is the binary representation of -11?

Since 11 is

        0 0 0 0 1 0 1 1

we need to find

        x x x x x x x x

so that the sum is

        0 0 0 0 0 0 0 0

If we consider the number

        1 1 1 1 1 1 1 1

and add 1

        1 1 1 1 1 1 1 1
                      1
        ----
    1   0 0 0 0 0 0 0 0

    carry

we get the 0-byte. Thus, the first step is to find the number to add to 11 to get all 1's. This is called the **1's complement**. The 1's complement of 11 is found as follows:

$$11 = 00001011$$

The 1's complement is obtained by simply changing all of the 0's to 1's and all of the 1's to zeros.

$$0\ 0\ 0\ 0\ 1\ 0\ 1\ 1$$

The 1's complement is

$$1\ 1\ 1\ 1\ 0\ 1\ 0\ 0$$

When we add the 1's complement to the original number, then we get all 1's.

Add

```
0 0 0 0 1 0 1 1
1 1 1 1 0 1 0 0
--------------------
1 1 1 1 1 1 1 1
```

Now when we add 1, we get all 0's.

adding 1

```
        1 1 1 1 1 1 1 1
                      1
     --------------------
  1     0 0 0 0 0 0 0 0
carry
```

Adding 1 to the 1's complement gives us the **2's complement** which is the binary representation of -11 since it gives us zero when we add it to the binary representation of 11. We consider another example. The binary representation of -11 is

$$-11 = 1\ 1\ 1\ 1\ 0\ 1\ 0\ 1$$

Find the binary representation of -113. We begin by finding the binary representation of 113.

$$113 \quad = 64 + 32 + 16 + 1$$
$$= 01110001$$

We now find the 1's complement.

$$1\text{'s comp} \quad = 10001110$$

We now find the 2's complement

$$10001110$$
$$+1$$
$$\text{---------------}$$
$$10001111$$

Thus,

$$-113 \quad = 10001111$$

A.6 Character Codes

The following table is a list of the 256 IBM extended ASCII characters.

DECIMAL VALUE → / HEXADECIMAL VALUE ↓	0 / 0	16 / 1	32 / 2	48 / 3	64 / 4	80 / 5	96 / 6	112 / 7
0 / 0	BLANK (NULL)	►	BLANK (SPACE)	0	@	P	`	p
1 / 1	☺	◄	!	1	A	Q	a	q
2 / 2	☻	↕	"	2	B	R	b	r
3 / 3	♥	‼	#	3	C	S	c	s
4 / 4	♦	¶	$	4	D	T	d	t
5 / 5	♣	§	%	5	E	U	e	u
6 / 6	♠	▬	&	6	F	V	f	v
7 / 7	•	↨	'	7	G	W	g	w
8 / 8	◘	↑	(	8	H	X	h	x
9 / 9	○	↓	)	9	I	Y	i	y
10 / A	◙	→	*	:	J	Z	j	z
11 / B	♂	←	+	;	K	[	k	{
12 / C	♀	∟	,	<	L	\	l	¦
13 / D	♪	↔	−	=	M	]	m	}
14 / E	♫	▲	.	>	N	^	n	~
15 / F	☼	▼	/	?	O	_	o	∆

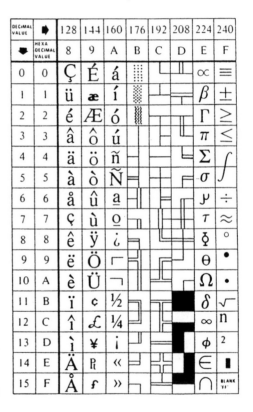

DECIMAL VALUE → / HEXADECIMAL VALUE ↓	128 / 8	144 / 9	160 / A	176 / B	192 / C	208 / D	224 / E	240 / F
0 / 0	Ç	É	á	░	└	╨	∝	≡
1 / 1	ü	æ	í	▒	┴	╤	β	±
2 / 2	é	Æ	ó	▓	┬	╥	Γ	≥
3 / 3	â	ô	ú	│	├	╙	π	≤
4 / 4	ä	ö	ñ			└	Σ	⌠
5 / 5	à	ò	Ñ			┌	σ	⌡
6 / 6	å	û	ª		╟	╪	µ	÷
7 / 7	ç	ù	º		╚	╫	τ	≈
8 / 8	ê	ÿ	¿				Φ	°
9 / 9	ë	Ö	⌐		┌	┘	Θ	•
10 / A	è	Ü	¬			┌	Ω	•
11 / B	ï	¢	½		╦	█	δ	√
12 / C	î	£	¼		╠	█	∞	ⁿ
13 / D	ì	¥	¡	┘		▌	φ	²
14 / E	Ä	₧	«	╛	╬	█	∈	■
15 / F	Å	ƒ	»			█	∩	BLANK

486